# Revolutionary America 1763–1815

"Cogliano and Phimister's outstanding collection of primary sources on the eras of the American Revolution and Early Republic will be a tremendous asset for students of American history. The sources they have included in this collection are not only important, but also, in many cases, quite unexpected—shedding new light on an important subject."

—Richard R. Beeman, Professor of History, University of Pennsylvania

"This sourcebook narrates American nation-building from many perspectives, relaying all the drama and uncertainty of a revolutionary age. Readers confront the fraught relationship of personal liberty and governmental authority, a tension that remains at the heart of American civic culture."

—Seth Rockman, Professor of History, Brown University

*Revolutionary America 1763–1815: A Sourcebook* is a collection of dynamic primary sources intended to accompany the second edition of *Revolutionary America 1763–1815: A Political History*. While the structure of this collection parallels the textbook, it can be used independently as well to bring a more personal perspective to the revolutionary period of American history.

Each chapter begins with a brief introduction and contains excerpts of original documents from the Revolutionary period, including government documents, letters, and diary entries, as well as numerous images. A companion website holds a wealth of primary source document resources, including many of the documents from within this book, as well as links to other valuable online resources. This collection helps give students a sense of the human experience of that turbulent time, bringing life to the struggle to found the United States.

For additional information and classroom resources for both the text and the sourcebook please visit the *Revolutionary America* companion website at www.routledge.com/textbooks/revolutionaryamerica.

**Francis D. Cogliano** is Professor of American History at the University of Edinburgh where he specializes in the history of revolutionary and early national America. He is the author of *Revolutionary America 1763–1815: A Political History*.

**Kirsten E. Phimister** holds a Ph.D. in American history from the University of Edinburgh.

# Revolutionary America 1763–1815

## A Sourcebook

Edited by
**Francis D. Cogliano**
**Kirsten E. Phimister**

Routledge
Taylor & Francis Group

NEW YORK AND LONDON

First published 2011
by Routledge
270 Madison Avenue, New York, NY 10016

Simultaneously published in the UK
by Routledge
2 Park Square, Milton Park, Abingdon, Oxon OX14 4RN

*Routledge is an imprint of the Taylor & Francis Group, an informa business*

© 2011 Taylor & Francis

Typeset in Minion by EvS Communication Networx, Inc.
Printed and bound in the United States of America on acid-free paper by Sheridan Books, Inc.

*Library of Congress Cataloging in Publication Data*
Revolutionary America 1763–1815 : a sourcebook / edited by Francis D. Cogliano and Kirsten E. Phimister.
p. cm.
Companion to: Revolutionary America 1763–1815 : a political history / Francis D. Cogliano.
Includes index.
1. United States—Politics and government—1775–1783—Sources. 2. United States—Politics and government—To 1775—Sources. 3. United States—Politics and government—1783–1865—Sources.
I. Cogliano, Francis D. II. Phimister, Kirsten E. III. Cogliano, Francis D. Revolutionary America.
E210.R485 2010
973.3—dc22
2009043886

ISBN 10: 0-415-99711-9 (hbk)
ISBN 10: 0-415-99712-7 (pbk)
ISBN 10: 0-203-85290-7 (ebk)

ISBN 13: 978-0-415-99711-9 (hbk)
ISBN 13: 978-0-415-99712-6 (pbk)
ISBN 13: 978-0-203-85290-3 (ebk)

*To My Parents*

*—KEP*

# Contents

# Figures

# Acknowledgments

We are enormously grateful to Kimberly Guinta and Matthew Kopel at Routledge for their patience and perseverance with the preparation of this volume. They have been an unfailing source of support and advice throughout the duration of this project. We would also like to thank Lynn Goeller and her team for their careful copyediting, typesetting, proofreading, and indexing of the manuscript. A special thanks must also go to Nora Allavoine Duncan, for transcribing and translating French material, and to Bo Clarke, for his assistance with preliminary proofreading. Finally, we would like to thank family and friends for providing support, encouragement, and light relief in the compilation of this volume.

# Introduction

There is no better or more enjoyable way to study the era of the American Revolution than through the eyes and thoughts of those who experienced it. Students of the Revolution are blessed with an astounding amount of primary source material which is readily accessible in print and on the Internet.[1] These sources are a crucial starting point for any serious study of the Revolution. This volume intends to provide students with samples of this material so that they can experience, first-hand, the raw materials which historians use to interpret the past. The eleven chapters in this volume parallel those in its companion, Francis D. Cogliano, *Revolutionary America 1763–1815: A Political History*, 2nd edition. While each of the books may be read independently, interested readers may read the chapters together. The main text provides an overview and interpretation of key events while the sourcebook allows readers to consider the sources upon which those interpretations rest and to render judgments of their own.

This volume begins with a set of documents which consider the experience of Native Americans during the half-century from 1763 to 1815. This period was decisive in Native American history as it witnessed the final military defeat of Native Americans east of the Mississippi and the beginnings of the policy of their displacement which culminated in the removal policy of the Jacksonian era. The documents in chapter 1 recount this sorrowful story. It also demonstrates one of the main challenges of Indian history—the relative dearth of sources from the Native American perspective. Historians are compelled to reconstruct Native American history by reading between the lines of sources produced by their European and American allies and adversaries such as Thomas Jefferson's account of Logan's Lament or missionary Samuel Kirkland's response to Burgoyne's defeat on behalf of the Oneidas and the Onondagas.

In 1763 British North Americans reveled in their Britishness and celebrated Britain's victory over France in the Seven Years' War. The documents in chapter

1

2 set the scene for the coming upheaval in British North America. Benjamin Franklin's *Observations on the Increase of Mankind* notes the steady growth of the population of British America, widely regarded as a measure of power in the eighteenth century. This growth suggests that the American colonies, a source of wealth and power, *might* also become a problem for the British government. In 1763 most colonial Americans considered themselves to be loyal British subjects and the inheritors of the legacy and language of the rights to which all Britons were entitled, as articulated in the 1689 Bill of Rights. Political coordination among the colonies seemed unlikely given the failure of the Albany Plan of Union—which Franklin proposed for the common defense of the colonies at the outset of the Seven Years' War in 1754. Nonetheless, when the colonists felt that their rights, as stipulated in the Bill of Rights, had been traduced they banded together to protest. The documents in chapter 3 trace the deteriorating relationship between the colonies and Britain between the adoption of the Stamp Act in 1765 and the imposition of martial law in Massachusetts in 1774. Included among these documents is Benjamin Franklin's testimony before Parliament in 1766 when the Pennsylvanian testified to the strength and mutual benefits of the transatlantic relationship which had been endangered by the Stamp Act. We see the first attempts by the colonies to overcome their differences and to cooperate in the resolutions of the Stamp Act Congress and can measure how far the colonial position had evolved nearly a decade later with the First Continental Congress's 1774 Declaration of Rights and Grievances.

In 1774 colonists opposed to British taxation and other parliamentary acts found themselves pulled in two directions. On one hand they asserted that the colonies should be free to govern themselves and should not be subject to interference from a Parliament in which they were not represented. On the other hand they also declared themselves loyal, and subservient, to King George III. The events of 1775 and 1776, covered by the documents in chapter 4, allowed rebellious Americans to resolve this Janus-like dilemma. During these two crucial years open warfare broke out between British forces and rebels in America (by no means all of the colonists, it must be remembered). Although Congress appealed to George III for assistance to resolve the crisis, it also took on the attributes of a national government and waged war against Britain—which explains why the king rejected their petition and declared the colonists to be in rebellion. Faced with war and formally cast as rebels by their monarch, the colonists undertook a debate about their relationship with Britain—the question first raised by the Stamp Act a decade before. Perhaps the most important contribution to the debate was Thomas Paine's pamphlet, *Common Sense*, published in January 1776, which made a powerful case for independence. In June 1776 Congress began to debate independence and appointed a committee to prepare a draft Declaration of Independence. Thomas Jefferson prepared the draft. After voting on independence, Congress adopted Jefferson's draft after making significant amendments to the text—both documents are included here. With its adoption the United States was created.

Declaring independence and winning it were different matters altogether. Chapter 5 presents a series of documents which illustrate the lengthy military struggle which the Declaration of Independence necessitated. William Campbell, the last royal governor of South Carolina, reminds us that the War of Independence was a brutal civil war as he describes the lynching of a free African American and the tarring and feathering of a suspected Loyalist by Patriots. The letters and diaries of William Russell, a rebel imprisoned by the British, and Samuel Curwen, a Loyalist who went into exile, reveal the human cost of the war.

The creation of the American republic on the declared premise that "all men are created equal" raised crucial ethical and political questions in a society in which one-fifth of the population were enslaved Africans. The documents in chapter 6 examine the experience of African Americans during the age of the American and French revolutions. A 1777 petition by Massachusetts slaves demonstrates that some slaves were conversant with the Whig ideology at the heart of the American resistance movement and sought to highlight the contradiction between the American protests in favor of liberty and chattel slavery. Dunmore's Proclamation shows that in many cases, especially in the South, it was the British, not the rebels who offered the best chance for freedom to American slaves. Slavery exposed a sectional rift in the revolutionary movement as suggested by the debates in the Constitutional Convention and the subsequent compromises made over the issue in the resulting Constitution. Although each of the northern states abolished slavery during the Revolution and the early years of the new republic, slavery survived in the South, sowing the seeds for persistent sectional conflict and eventually war in the nineteenth century. The inability of the revolutionaries to adequately address the contradiction between their stated principals and slavery is probably their greatest failure, a failure which had disastrous consequences for millions of Americans.

One of the significant achievements of the American revolutionaries was the establishment of enduring republican governments. The creation of these governments—through the drafting of written constitutions—is the major theme of chapters 7 and 8. Independence required each of the new states to draft a new constitution, and they experimented with different forms. At the same time that they were creating new state constitutions, American republicans also struggled to forge a national government. Received wisdom suggested that it was impossible to have a geographically extensive republic and Americans strove to create a lasting government that could govern a large country. The first national constitution, the Articles of Confederation, created a loose pact among the sovereign states. The 1780s were characterized by a degree of economic and political instability which some conservative republicans blamed on the democratic excesses in the states and the apparent weakness of the national government under the Articles of Confederation. They set about replacing the Articles of Confederation with a new national government. The documents that follow relate to the drafting of the Constitution at the Constitutional Convention and the intense debate over its ratification in the states.

Women were largely excluded from the revolutionary constitutional settlement. As chapter 9 shows, this exclusion arose despite the myriad contributions of women to the Revolution. Newspaper accounts and the letters of Deborah Franklin attest to the vital role played by women in the pre-war movement against British taxation. The letters of Abigail Adams, as well as those of Baron Ottendorf, present accounts of how the War of Independence affected women. After the war, republicans, particularly males, struggled to conceptualize the place of women in the new American polity. The extract from Benjamin Rush's address, *Thoughts upon Female Education,* illustrates the redefinition of women's place in American life as Republican Mothers, responsible for inculcating republican values through the promotion of virtue. This was a concept which could benefit women through the improvement of female education, but also largely rendered female political participation to the household. For exceptions see the extracts from the New Jersey constitutions of 1776 and 1844 which chronicle early female voting in America. The Revolution did provide women with the language and principles to assert a claim to greater equality as evidenced by the 1848 Declaration of Sentiments with which the chapter concludes.

The documents in chapters 10 and 11 trace the early years of the United States under the new constitution. Chapter 10 begins with Alexander Hamilton's policy papers, his reports on credit and manufactures which laid the foundation of Federalist political economy. Eventually opposition to Hamilton's fiscal and political program coalesced around Thomas Jefferson and James Madison. Included is an extract from Jefferson's *Notes on the State of Virginia,* which outlined a vision of the social, economic, and political development for the United States which was very different from that of Hamilton and the Federalists. In his valedictory Farewell Address, Washington called on Americans to eschew foreign entanglements. The wars of the French Revolution made this impossible. After the conclusion of the Jay Treaty and the election of John Adams, war with France appeared to be inevitable and the Federalist-dominated Congress adopted the Alien and Sedition Acts in anticipation of the conflict. These restricted civil liberties and prompted Madison and Jefferson to draft the Virginia and Kentucky Resolutions which asserted the right of states to nullify federal legislation which they deemed unconstitutional.

Jefferson, elected president in the controversial election of 1800, adopted a more liberal view of presidential power after he assumed office. He was committed to the westward expansion of the United States. As early as the Ordinance of 1784, he sketched a plan for the orderly expansion of the republic and the addition of new states to the union. As president he was able to realize this ambition through the Louisiana Purchase and the Lewis and Clark expedition which are illustrated in several of Jefferson's letters. Notwithstanding his diplomatic triumph in Louisiana, Jefferson's second administration was marred by constant international tensions as France and Britain interfered with American trade. In response, Jefferson induced Congress to adopt a trade embargo in 1807 which proved disastrous for the American economy and politically unpopular as evidenced by the "Ograbme" cartoon in the chapter. Jefferson was unable to solve the foreign policy challenges facing the United States, and his successor, James Madison, asked Congress to declare war on Britain in June of 1812. Notwithstanding its difficulties on the battlefield, the United States experienced a surge in nationalism during the war as illustrated by contemporary cartoons and poetry. The war also prompted a political crisis within the Federalist opposition which flirted with secession at the Hartford Convention, the journal of which is reproduced here. The war ended with the resounding American victory at New Orleans—news of which was spread by broadsides such as the one in this chapter. The victory at New Orleans, a triumph over Britain of course, seemed a vindication of the United States and the republican experiment launched in 1776.

We have endeavored to provide documents in their entirety or in lengthy extracts. We feel this is vital to give students a sense for the era of the American Revolution through its documents. This means that they will encounter the sometimes irregular usage and spelling of the eighteenth and early nineteenth centuries which often strike modern readers as idiosyncratic. We have retained these to give students a feel for the language of the period. Owing to space constraints it has not always been possible to provide complete documents. In such cases we have often provided links to the full texts of key documents at this volume's companion website (http://www.routledge.com/textbooks/revolutionaryamerica/). At the website interested readers will find links to additional documents as well as study questions to guide their reading.

We have endeavored to reproduce the documents faithfully. In the interests of clarity, however, we have introduced modern and consistent capitalization.

## Note

1. For an overview of the primary sources relating to the revolutionary era see Francis D. Cogliano, *Revolutionary America 1763–1815: A Political History*, 2nd edition (New York: Routledge, 2009), 287–291.

# CHAPTER 1

# Native Americans and
# the American Revolution

## Introduction

At the end of the Seven Years' War native power in eastern North America, as measured by population and land, was still substantial. James Glen's 1761 account (document 1) of South Carolina's relations with Indian tribes in the southeast, particularly the Choctaws, Creeks, Chickasaws, and Cherokees is testimony to the strength and autonomy of those tribes. Glen's report, nonetheless, presages future challenges confronting Native Americans. These challenges became acute at the end of the Seven Years' War as numerous British American settlers pushed westward, encroaching on Indian lands. The grievances of the Paxton Boys (document 2) arising, in part, from anti-Indian animus resulted in violent conflict which the British found difficult to contain. When racial conflict occurred it was difficult to distinguish friend from foe—the Paxton Boys massacred peaceful Christian Indians who had been taken into protective custody. Similarly when Dunmore's War (1774–75) broke out in the Ohio-Pennsylvania-Virginia borderland, settlers slaughtered the family of the Mingo war chief Tachnedorus (known to whites as Logan) despite the fact that Logan had been friendly to settlers (document 3).

Tensions between European settlers and Native Americans were subsumed by the subsequent conflict between the British and their North American colonists. When the War of Independence began, Native Americans found themselves in a position of relative (and temporary) power as both the British and the American rebels sought to cultivate their support (documents 4, 5, and 7). Mediators and leaders like Joseph Brant (documents 5 and 6) emerged as important players in the complex dynamic of power relations between and among Native Americans, the rebels, and the British. Although many tribes sympathized with the British, concluding that a British victory would be less threatening to them than a rebel triumph, many were compelled by necessity to conclude agreements with the United States (documents 7 and 8). With the rebel victory in the war, Native Americans were confronted by a new, more dangerous situation. The United States, which had secured capacious boundaries at the Peace of Paris, and, possessed of a growing and population determined to settle western lands, posed a mortal threat to the Native Americans, who could no longer count on the support of Britain (document 9). The United States government compelled tribes to make land and trade concessions. Native Americans resisted these encroachments by force in the 1790s and through religious and cultural revival movements in the first decade of the nineteenth century. Western Indians attempted to unite under Tecumseh and Tenskwatawa and to offer military resistance (with British backing) during the War of 1812 (document 10). At the war's end, the United States used this resistance to justify and force still more land concessions (document 11). By 1815 the power and autonomy of Native Americans east of the Mississippi, described by James Glen in 1761, had vanished. Within a generation many thousands would be forcibly removed from their land and forced to move west.

## 1.   Southern Indians during the Seven Years' War[1]

*James Glen (1701–1777) served as governor of South Carolina from 1743 to 1756. Based on his lengthy service, he wrote a lengthy descriptive analysis of the colony which includes his observations of Native American tribes in the region. Glen emphasizes the political, economic, and diplomatic significance of Native Americans to the government of the colony during the Seven Years' War.*

The concerns of this country are so closely connected and interwoven with *Indian* affairs, and not only a great Branch of our Trade, but even the Safety of this Province, do so much depend upon our continuing in Friendship with the *Indians*, that I thought it highly necessary to gain all the Knowledge I could of them; and I hope that the Accounts which I have from Time to Time transmitted of *Indian* Affairs will shew, that I am pretty well acquainted with the Subject.

However, I think it expedient upon the present Occasion to give a general Account of the several Tribes and Nations of *Indians* with whom the Inhabitants of this Province are or may be connected in Interest; which is the more necessary, as all we have to apprehend from the French in this Part of the World, will much more depend upon the *Indians* than upon any Strength of their own; for that is so inconsiderable in itself, and so far distant from us, that without *Indian* Assistance, it cannot, if exerted, do us much Harm.

There are among our Settlements several small Tribes of *Indians*, consisting only of some few Families each; but those Tribes of *Indians* which we, on Account of their being numerous and having Lands of their own, call Nations, are all of them situated on the western Side of this Province, and at various Distances, as I have already mentioned.

The *Catawbaw* Nations of *Indians* hath about Three Hundred fighting Men; brave Fellows as any on the Continent of *America*, and our firm Friends; their Country is about Two Hundred Miles from *Charles-Town*.

The *Cherokees* live at the Distance of about Three Hundred Miles from *Charles-Town*, though indeed their hunting Grounds stretch much nearer to us; they have about Three Thousand Gun-Men, and are in Alliance with this Government.

I lately made a considerable Purchase from that *Indian* Nation, of some of those hunting Grounds, which are now become the Property of the *British* Crown, at the Charge of this Province; I had the Deeds of Conveyance formally executed in their own Country, by their head Men, in the Name of the whole People, and with their universal Approbation and good Will.

They inhabit a Tract of Country about Two Hundred Miles in Extent, and form a good Barrier, which is naturally strengthened by a Country hilly and mountainous; but said to be interspersed with pleasant and fruitful Vallies, and watered by many limpid and wholesome Brooks and Rivulets, which run among the Hills, and give those real Pleasures which we in the lower lands have only in Imagination.

The *Creek Indians* are situated about Five Hundred Miles from *Charles-Town*; their Number of fighting Men is about Two Thousand Five Hundred, and they are in Friendship with us.

The *Chickesaws* live at the Distance of near Eight Hundred Miles from *Charles-Town*; they have bravely stood their Ground against the repeated Attacks of the *French* and their *Indians*; but are now reduced to Two or Three Hundred Men.

The *Chactaw* Nation of Indians is situated at a somewhat greater Distance from us, and have till within this Year or Two been in the Interest of the *French*; by whom they were reckoned to be the most numerous of any Nation of *Indians* in *America*, and said to consist of many Thousand Men.

The People of most Experience in the Affairs of this Country, have always dreaded a *French* War, from an Apprehension that an *Indian* War would be the Consequence of it, for which Reasons I have, ever since the first breaking out of War with *France*, redoubled my Attention to *Indian* Affairs; and, I hope, not without Success.

For notwithstanding all the Intrigues of the *French*, they have not been able to get the least Footing among our Nations of *Indians*; as very plainly appears by those Nations still continuing to give fresh Proofs of their Attachment to us; and I have had the Happiness to bring over and fix the Friendship of the *Chactaw* Nation of *Indians* in the *British* Interest.

This powerful Engine, which the *French*, for many years past, played against us and our *Indians*, even in Times of Peace, is now happily turned against themselves, and I believe they feel the Force of it…

I shall be particularly cautious of doing any Thing inconsistent with the Peace so lately concluded; but I think it incumbent on me to say, that it will be impossible to retain those *Indians*, or any other, in His Majesty's Interest, unless we continue to trade with them.

And since War and Hunting are the Business of their Lives, both Arms and Ammunition, as well as Cloaths and other Necessaries, are the Goods for which there is the greatest Demand among them; I therefore hope to receive Instructions in this particular, as a Rule for my Conduct.

There are a pretty many *Indians* among the *Kays*, about the Cape of *Florida*, who might be easily secured to the *British* Interest; but as they have little Communication with any others on the main Land, and have nor any Goods to trade for, they could not be of any Advantage either in Peace of War: There are also a few *Yamasees*, about Twenty Men, near *St. Augustine*; and these are all the *Indians* in this Part of the World that are in the Interest of the Crown of *Spain*.

The *French* have the Friendship of some few of the *Creek Indians*, such as inhabit near the *Holbama* Fort; and some of the *Chactaw Indians* have not as yet declared against them; They have also some Tribes upon *Mississippi* River and *Ouabash*, and in other Parts; but most of these, and all other *Indians* whatsoever, inhabit above a Thousand Miles from *Charles-Town*; and yet it may be proper to give Attention even to what happens among those who are so far from us; for to an *Indian*, a Thousand Miles is as One Mile, their Provisions being in the Woods, and they are never out of the Way; they are slow, saying *the Sun will rise again to morrow*, but they are steddy...

If ever the *French* Settlements on the *Mississippi* grow great, they may have pernicious Effects upon *South Carolina*, because they produced the same Sorts of Commodities as are produced there, *viz. Rice and Indigo*; but hitherto, the only Inconvenience that I know of, is, their attempting to withdraw our *Indians* from us, and attacking those who are most attached to our Interest.

I beg Leave to assure you, that I shall never do any thing inconsistent with that good Faith which is the Basis of all His Majesty's Measures; but it is easy for me at present to divert the *French* in their own Way, and to find them Business for double the Number of Men they have in that Country.

However, this, and even the Tranquillity of *South Carolina*, will depend upon preserving our Interest with the *Indians*, which it will be very difficult to do, unless the Presents are continued to them, and those Forts built which I have formerly proposed, or at least, one of them, and that to be in the Country of the *Cherokees*.

## 2.  Petition from the Paxton Boys, 1764[2]

*At the end of the Seven Years' War tensions increased along the frontier. Native Americans took up arms in Pontiac's Rebellion to resist encroachment on their lands by white settlers whose numbers increased steadily following the British victory in the war. In December 1763 a group of Scots-Irish vigilantes from Paxton Township,*

*Pennsylvania, murdered six peaceful Conestoga Indians whom they suspected of supporting the hostile tribes. The so-called Paxton Boys then marched on Philadelphia to demand greater protection from Indians. This petition from two of the Paxton Boys to the government of Pennsylvania enumerates their grievances and reveals the depth and virulence of anti-Indian sentiment among some settlers as well as their hostility toward the government.*

…During the late and present *Indian* Wars, the Frontiers of this Province have been repeatedly attacked and ravaged by Skulking parties of the Indians, who have with the most savage Cruelty, murdered Men, Women and Children, without distinction; and have reduced near a Thousand Families to the most extream Distress. It grieves us to the very Heart, to see such of our Frontier Inhabitants as have escaped from savage Fury, with the loss of their Parents, their Children, their Husbands, Wives, or Relatives, left destitute by the Public, and exposed to the most cruel Poverty and Wretchedness; while upwards of One Hundred and Twenty of the Savages, who are with great Reason suspected of being guilty of these horrid Barbarities under the Mask of Friendship, have procured themselves to be taken under the Protection of the Government, with a view to elude the Fury of the brave Relatives of the Murdered; and are now maintained at the public Expence: Some of these Indians now in the Barracks of *Philadelphia* are confessedly a part of the *Wyalusing Indians*, which Tribe is now at War with us; and the others are the *Moravian Indians*, who living among us under the Cloak of Friendship, carried on a Correspondence with our known Enemies on the *Great-Island.* We cannot but observe with Sorrow and Indignation, that some Persons in this Province are at pains to extenuate the barbarous Cruelties practiced by these savages on our Murdered Brethern and Relatives, which are shocking to human Nature, and must pierce every Heart but those of the hardened Perpetrators or their Abettors. Nor is it less Distressing to hear others pleading, that altho' the *Wyalusing* Tribe is at War with us; yet that part of it which is under the Protection of the Government may be friendly to the *English*, and Innocent. In what Nation under the Sun was it ever the Custom, that when a neighbouring Nation took up Arms, not an individual of the Nation should be touched, but only the Persons that offered Hostilities? Who ever proclaimed war with a part of a Nation, and not with the Whole? Had these Indians disapproved of the Perfidy of their Tribe, and been willing to cultivate and preserve Friendship with us, why did they not give Notice of the War before it happened, as it is known to be the Result of long Deliberations, and a preconcerted Combination amongst them? Why did they not leave their Tribe immediately, and come amongst us before there was ground to suspect them, or War was actually waged with the Tribe? No, they stayed amongst them, were privy to their Murders and Ravages, untill we had destroyed their Provisions, and when they could no longer subsist at Home, they came, not as Deserters, but as Friends, to be maintained thro' the Winter, that they may be able to scalp and butcher us in the Spring…

We humbly conceive that it is contrary to the Maxims of good Policy and ex-treamly dangerous to our Frontiers, to suffer any *Indians* of what Tribe soever, to live within the inhabited Parts of this Province, while we are engaged in an *Indian* War; as Experience has taught us that they are all Persidious, and their Claim to Freedom and Independency puts it in their Power to act as Spies, to entertain and give Intelligence to our Enemies, and to furnish them with Provisions and warlike Stores. To this fatal Intercourse between our pretended Friends and open Enemies we must ascribe the greatest Part of the Ravages and Murders that have been committed in the Course of this and the last *Indian* War...

### 3.   Logan's Lament, 1775[3]

*During the summer of 1774 a conflict, known as Dunmore's War, arose between settlers and Indians in western Pennsylvania and Ohio. The war began when Vir-ginians massacred the family of a Mingo war chief, Tachnedorus, known to whites as John Logan at Yellow Creek on April 30, 1774. At the end of the war Logan is said to have delivered this speech, reflecting on his loss. Thomas Jefferson included Logan's Lament, which appeared in newspapers in 1782 in* The Notes on the State of Virginia *as an example of Native American oratory. When the speech appeared some commentators queried its authenticity and historians have continued to dispute whether Logan delivered it.*

I appeal to any white man to say if he ever entered Logan's cabin hungry, and he gave him not meat; if he ever came cold and naked and he clothed him not. During the course of the last long and bloody war, Logan remained idle in his cabin, an advocate for peace.

Such was my love for the whites, that my countrymen pointed as I passed, and said, "Logan is a friend of the white man." I have even thought to live with you but for the injuries of one man, Colonel Cresap, who last spring in cold blood and unprovoked murdered the relatives of Logan, not even sparing his wife and children.

There runs not a drop of my blood in the veins of any living creature. This has called on me for revenge. I have sought it; I have killed many; I have fully glutted my vengeance. For my country, I rejoice in the beams of peace.

But do not harbor a thought that mine is the joy of fear. Logan never felt fear. He will not turn on his heel to save his life. Who is there to mourn for Logan? Not one.

### 4.   Congress Appeals to the Six Nations, July 13, 1775[4]

*At the outset of the War of Independence, both the British and the rebels realized that Native American support would be vital to the war effort. Relatively small num-bers of Native Americans could cause either of the belligerents to divert substantial resources away from the main theater of conflict along the eastern seaboard. For their part Native Americans viewed the conflict as an opportunity to stop or reverse the encroachment of white settlers onto their lands. Many tribes viewed the British as the best potential allies because they were less likely to threaten native lands and they could provide Indians with a steady supply of arms and other trade goods. The rebels sought to cultivate alliances with Native Americans or, at least, to secure Indian neutrality in the conflict. This is a message which Congress delivered to the Iroquois Six Nations, probably the most powerful Indian Confederacy in eastern North America, attempting to discourage their intervention in the war.*

*A Speech to the Six Confederate Nations, Mohawks, Oneidas, Tuscaroras, Onondagas, Cayugas, Senekas, from the Twelve United Colonies, convened in Council at Philadelphia.*

Brothers, Sachems, and Warriors,
...in our consultation we have judged it proper and necessary to send you this talk, as we are upon the same island, that you may be informed of the reasons of this great council, the situation of our civil constitution, and our disposition towards you our Indian brothers of the Six Nations and their allies.
(*Three Strings, or a small Belt.*)

...Brothers, Listen!
Notwithstanding all our entreaties, we have but little hope the king will send us any more good talks, by reason of his evil counsellors; they have persuaded him to send an army of soldiers and many ships of war, to rob and destroy us. They have shut up many of our harbours, seized and taken into possession many of our vessels: the soldiers have struck the blow, killed some of our people, the blood now runs of the American children: They have also burned our houses and towns, and taken much of our goods.

Brothers! We are now necessitated to rise, and forced to fight, or give up our civil constitution, run away and leave our farms and houses behind us. This must not be. Since the king's wicked counsellors will not open their ears, and consider our just complaints, and the cause of our weeping, and hath given the blow, we are determined to drive away the king's soldiers, and to kill and destroy all those wicked men we find in arms against the peace of the twelve United Colonies upon this island. We think our cause is just; therefore hope God will be on our side. We do not take up the hatchet and struggle for honor and conquest; but to maintain our civil constitution and religious privileges, the very same for which our forefathers left their native land and came to this country.

Brothers and Friends!
We desire you will hear and receive what we have now told you, and that you will open a good ear and listen to what we are now going to say. This is a family

quarrel between us and Old England. You Indians are not concerned in it. We don't wish you to take up the hatchet against the king's troops. We desire you to remain at home, and not join on either side, but keep the hatchet buried deep. In the name and in behalf of all our people, we ask and desire you to love peace and maintain it, and to love and sympathise with us in our troubles; that the path may be kept open with all our people and yours, to pass and repass, without molestation.

Brothers! we live upon the same ground with you. The same island is our common birth-place. We desire to sit down under the same tree of peace with you: let us water its roots and cherish its growth, till the large leaves and flourishing branches shall extend to the setting sun, and reach the skies.

Brothers, Observe Well!
What is it we have asked of you? Nothing but peace, notwithstanding our present disturbed situation—and if application should be made to you by any of the king's unwise and wicked ministers to join on their side, we only advise you to deliberate, with great caution, and in your wisdom look forward to the consequences of a compliance. For, if the king's troops take away our property, and destroy us who are of the same blood with themselves, what can you, who are Indians, expect from them afterwards?

Therefore, we say, brothers, take care—hold fast to your covenant chain. You now know our disposition towards you, the Six Nations of Indians, and your allies. Let this our good talk remain at Onondaga, your central council house. We depend upon you to send and acquaint your allies to the northward, the seven tribes on the river St. Lawrence, that you have this talk of ours at the great council fire of the Six Nations. And when they return, we invite your great men to come and converse farther with us at Albany, where we intend to re-kindle the council fire, which your and our ancestors sat round in great friendship.

Brothers and Friends!
We greet you all farewell.
(*The large belt of intelligence and declaration.*)

Brothers!
We have said we wish you Indians may continue in peace with one another, and with us the white people. Let us both be cautious in our behaviour towards each other at this critical state of affairs. This island now trembles, the wind whistles from almost every quarter—let us fortify our minds and shut our ears against false rumors—let us be cautious what we receive for truth, unless spoken by wise and good men. If any thing disagreeable should ever fall out between us, the twelve United Colonies, and you, the Six Nations, to wound our peace, let us immediately seek measures for healing the breach. From the present situation of our affairs, we judge it wise and expedient to kindle up a small council fire

at Albany, where we may hear each other's voice, and disclose our minds more fully to each other.
(*A small belt.*)

*Ordered*, That a similar talk be prepared for the other Indian nations, preserving the tenor of the above, and altering it so as to suit the Indians in the several departments.

## 5.   Joseph Brant Speaks to Lord George Germain, March 14, 1776[5]

*Like other Americans, the members of the Iroquois Confederacy were divided by the War of Independence. Some of the Confederacy allied with the British, others remained neutral, and others supported the rebels. This may have been a deliberate strategy by the diplomatically adroit Iroquois to maintain their authority regardless of the outcome of the war. One of the most important leaders of the faction which supported the British was the Mohawk war chief, Thayendanegea or Joseph Brant (c. 1743–1807). In late 1775 Brant travelled with a delegation to London to negotiate with the British government over Iroquois entry into the war. This is a speech which Brant delivered to Lord George Germain (1716–1785), the American Secretary. Brant returned to America in July 1776 and fought with the British army in the campaigns around New York City. He was subsequently commissioned as an officer and led Mohawk warriors against the rebels. Brant was probably the most famous Native American participant in the War of Independence.*

Brother Gorah,
We have cross'd the great Lake and come to this kingdom with our Superintendent, Col. Johnson, from our Confederacy the Six Nations and their allies, that we might see our Father, the Great King, and joyn in informing him, his Councillors and wise men, of the good intentions of the Indians our brethren, and of their attachment to His Majesty and his Government.

Brother. The Disturbances in America give great trouble to all our Nations, as many strange stories have been told to us by the people of that country. The Six Nations who always loved the king, sent a number of their Chiefs and Warriors with their Superintendent to Canada last summer, where they engaged their allies to joyn with them in the defense of that country, and when it was invaded by the New England people they alone defeated them.

Brother. In that engagement we had several of our best Warriors killed and wounded, and the Indians think it very hard they should have been so deceived by the White people in that country, the enemy returning in great numbers, and no White people supporting the Indians, they were obliged to return to their villages and sit still. We now Brother hope to see these bad children chastised, and that we may be enabled to tell the Indians who have always been faithfull and ready to assist the King, what his Majesty intends.

Brother. The Mohocks our particular nation, have on all occasions shewn their zeal and loyalty to the Great King; yet they have been very badly treated by the people in that country, the City of Albany laying an unjust claim to the lands on which our Lower Castle is built, as one Klock, and others do to those of Conijoharrie our Upper Village. We have often been assured by our late great friend Sr William Johnson who never deceived us, and we know he was told so that the King and wise men here would do us justice; but this notwithstanding all our applications has never been done, and it makes us very uneasie. We also feel for the distress in which our Brethren on the Susquehanna are likely to be involved by a mistake made in the Boundary we setled in 1768. This also our Superintendent has laid before the King, and we beg it may be remembered. And also concerning Religion and the want of Ministers of the Church of England, he knows the designs of those bad people and informs us he has laid the same before the King. We have only therefore to request that his Majesty will attend to this matter: it troubles our Nation & they cannot sleep easie in their beds. Indeed it is very hard when we have let the Kings subjects have so much land for so little value, they should want to cheat us in this manner of the small spots we have left for our women and children to live on. We are tired out in making complaints & getting no redress. We therefore hope that the Assurances now given us by the Superintendent may take place, and that he may have it in his power to procure us justice.

Brother. We shall truly report all that we hear from you, to the Six Nations on our return. We are well informed there have been many Indians in this Country who came without any authority, from their own, and gave us much trouble. We desire Brother to tell you this is not our case. We are warriors known to all the Nations, and are now here by approbation of many of them, whose sentiments we speak.

Brother. We hope these things will be considered and that the King or his great men will give us such an answer as will make our hearts light and glad before we go, and strengthen our hands, so that we may joyn our Superintendent, Col. Johnson in giving satisfaction to all our Nations, when we report to them on our return, on our return; for which purpose we hope soon to be accommodated with a passage.

Dictated by the Indians and taken down by

Jo. Chew. Secretary

## 6. Joseph Brant, 1786[6]

*This portrait of Brant was painted in London after the War of Independence by Gilbert Stuart (1755–1828). Brant had returned to England to seek British diplomatic support as well as financial compensation for the losses sustained by the Mohawks in the war.*

**Figure 1.1** Joseph Brant, 1786, by Gilbert Stuart.

### 7.   A Missionary Speaks on Behalf of the Oneidas and Onondagas, 1777[7]

*Although Brant and the Mohawks fought for the British, others among the Iroquois Confederacy opted for neutrality or supported the rebels. This letter from Samuel Kirkland (1741–1808), a Presbyterian missionary, expresses qualified support for the rebels on behalf of the Oneidas and Onondagas in the wake of Burgoyne's surrender in October 1777. It is evidence of the delicate diplomacy that Native Americans conducted during the War of Independence.*

I delivered your Message to the *Oneida* Sachems, informing them of the Capture of Gen. *Burgoyne*, and his whole Army; and I presented the Warriors your Request, that a Number of their best Men (not exceeding thirty or forty) should immediately repair *to Albany*, where they would receive further Directions. I also sent their Head Warriors with the Belt of Information to the *Onondagoes* four days ago: To each of the above you have the following Replies…

*Brother* Arahocktea,
We have heard your Voice—Your Belt has come in good Time, and brings great News.—*Brother*, We congratulate you upon the extraordinary Success of your

Army. Your Enemy, once very strong in that Quarter, are now subdued—This is Matter of great Rejoicing. Indeed we have long expected it would be his Fate, as he talked very proudly amongst all the *Indians*, and told what he would do to the *Americans*—He despised them. The Army he sent against Fort *Schuyler*, spake very insolently—quite too proud—'That they would trample all down before them, and at first Sight of them the Fort would vanish'—but now the Proud are brought low! this is right.

Brother, We send your Belt of Intelligence forward to the *Cayugas* and *Senecas*—We hope its influence will be very extensive—we expect it will soon reach *Niagara*.

Brother, The great God has brought about this happy Revolution, as you observed in your Speech to us. We must all ascribe the Honour, the Wisdom and Victory to him.

Brother, We wish you a Continuation of Success. Farewell.

Tehorgweahten

## 8. Treaty with the Delawares, 1778[8]

*Although many tribes allied with the British during the War of Independence, others did so with the rebels. This 1778 treaty between the Delawares and the United States addresses concerns which were present throughout the war such as fair trade and the right of rebel forces to cross Indian territory.*

*Articles of agreement and confederation, made and entered into by Andrew and Thomas Lewis, Esquires, Commissioners for, and in Behalf of the United States of North-America of the one Part, and Capt. White Eyes, Capt. John Kill Buck, Junior, and Capt. Pipe, Deputies and Chief Men of the Delaware Nation of the other Part.*

Article I
That all offences or acts of hostilities by one, or either of the contracting parties against the other, be mutually forgiven, and buried in the depth of oblivion, never more to be had in remembrance.

Article II
That a perpetual peace and friendship shall from henceforth take place, and subsist between the contracting parties aforesaid, through all succeeding generations: and if either of the parties are engaged in a just and necessary war with any other nation or nations, that then each shall assist the other in due proportion to their abilities, till their enemies are brought to reasonable terms of accommodation: and that if either of them shall discover any hostile designs forming against the other, they shall give the earliest notice thereof, that timeous measures may be taken to prevent their ill effect.

Article III
And whereas the United States are engaged in a just and necessary war, in defence and support of life, liberty and independence, against the King of England and his adherents, and as said King is yet possessed of several posts and forts on the lakes and other places, the reduction of which is of great importance to the peace and security of the contracting parties, and as the most practicable way for the troops of the United States to some of the posts and forts is by passing through the country of the Delaware nation, the aforesaid deputies, on behalf of themselves and their nation, do hereby stipulate and agree to give a free passage through their country to the troops aforesaid, and the same to conduct by the nearest and best ways to the posts, forts or towns of the enemies of the United States, affording to said troops such supplies of corn, meat, horses, or whatever may be in their power for the accommodation of such troops, on the commanding officer's, &c. paying, or engageing to pay, the full value of whatever they can supply them with. And the said deputies, on the behalf of their nation, engage to join the troops of the United States aforesaid, with such a number of their best and most expert warriors as they can spare, consistent with their own safety, and act in concert with them; and for the better security of the old men, women and children of the aforesaid nation, whilst their warriors are engaged against the common enemy, it is agreed on the part of the United States, that a fort of sufficient strength and capacity be built at the expense of the said States, with such assistance as it may be in the power of the said Delaware Nation to give, in the most convenient place, and advantageous situation, as shall be agreed on by the commanding officer of the troops aforesaid, with the advice and concurrence of the deputies of the aforesaid Delaware Nation, which fort shall be garrisoned by such a number of the troops of the United States, as the commanding officer can spare for the present, and hereafter by such numbers, as the wise men of the United States in council, shall think most conducive to the common good.

Article IV
For the better security of the peace and friendship now entered into by the contracting parties, against all infractions of the same by the citizens of either party, to the prejudice of the other, neither party shall proceed to the infliction of punishments on the citizens of the other, otherwise than by securing the offender or offenders by imprisonment, or any other competent means, till a fair and impartial trial can be had by judges or juries of both parties, as near as can be to the laws, customs and usages of the contracting parties and natural justice: The mode of such trials to be hereafter fixed by the wise men of the United States in Congress assembled, with the assistance of such deputies of the Delaware nation, as may be appointed to act in concert with them in adjusting this matter to their mutual liking. And it is further agreed between the parties aforesaid, that neither shall entertain or give countenance to the enemies of the other, or protect in their respective states, criminal fugitives, servants or slaves, but the

same to apprehend, and secure and deliver to the State or States, to which such enemies, criminals, servants or slaves respectively belong.

Article V
Whereas the confederation entered into by the Delaware nation and the United States, renders the first dependent on the latter for all the articles of clothing, utensils and implements of war, and it is judged not only reasonable, but indispensably necessary, that the aforesaid Nation be supplied with such articles from time to time, as far as the United States may have it in their power, by a well-regulated trade, under the conduct of an intelligent, candid agent, with an adequate salary, one more influenced by the love of his country, and a constant attention to the duties of his department by promoting the common interest, than the sinister purposes of converting and binding all the duties of his office to his private emolument: Convinced of the necessity of such measures, the Commissioners of the United States, at the earnest solicitation of the deputies aforesaid, have engaged in behalf of the United States, that such a trade shall be afforded said nation conducted on such principles of mutual interest as the wisdom of the United States in Congress assembled shall think most conducive to adopt for their mutual convenience.

Article VI
Whereas the enemies of the United States have endeavored, by every artifice in their power, to possess the Indians in general with an opinion, that it is the design of the States aforesaid, to extirpate the Indians and take possession of their country to obviate such false suggestion, the United States do engage to guarantee to the aforesaid nation of Delawares, and their heirs, all their territorial rights in the fullest and most ample manner, as it hath been bounded by former treaties, as long as they the said Delaware nation shall abide by, and hold fast the chain of friendship now entered into. And it is further agreed on between the contracting parties should it for the future be found conducive for the mutual interest of both parties to invite any other tribes who have been friends to the interest of the United States, to join the present confederation, and to form a state whereof the Delaware nation shall be the head, and have a representation in Congress: Provided, nothing contained in this article to be considered as conclusive until it meets with the approbation of Congress. And it is also the intent and meaning of this article, that no protection or countenance shall be afforded to any who are at present our enemies, by which they might escape the punishment they deserve.

## 9. Chickasaw Chiefs Appeal to Congress, 1783[9]

*With the rebel victory in the War of Independence, Native Americans lost a crucial ally in Britain and were confronted by a burgeoning population desirous of western land. This petition from chiefs of the Chickasaw nation describes the deleterious impact the war had on their people and their ongoing difficulties in its aftermath—notably access to trade goods and threats to their land. The relative weakness of the United States government during the Confederation period meant that Congress could do little to address these problems even if it were inclined to do so.*

Friend & Brother,
This is the first talk we ever sent you—we hope it will not be the last. We desire you to open your Ears to hear, and your heart to understand us, as we shall always be ready to do to your talks, which we expect will be good, as you are a great and wise man.

Brother,
When our great father the King of England called away his warriors, he told us to take your People by the hand as friends and brothers. Our hearts were always inclined to do so & as far as our circumstances permitted us, we evinced our good intentions as Brothers the Virginians can testify—It makes our hearts rejoice to find that our great father, and his children the Americans have at length made peace, which we wish may continue as long as the Sun and Moon, And to find that our Brothers the Americans are inclined to take us by the hand, and Smoke with us at the great Fire, which we hope will never be extinguished.

Brother,
Notwithstanding the Satisfaction all these things give us we are yet in confusion & uncertainty. The Spaniards are sending talks amongst us, and inviting our young Men to trade with them. We also receive talks from the Governor of Georgia to the same effect—We have had Speeches from the Illinois inviting us to a Trade and Intercourse with them—Our Brothers, the Virginians Call upon us to a Treaty, and want part of our land, and we expect our Neighbors who live on Cumberland River, will in a Little time Demand, if not forcibly take part of it from us, also as we are informed they have been marking Lines through our hunting grounds: we are daily receiving Talks from one Place or other, and from People we Know nothing about. We Know not who to mind or who to neglect. We are told that the Americans have 13 Councils Compos'd of Chiefs and Warriors. We Know not which of them we are to Listen to, or if we are to hear some, and Reject others, we are at a loss to Distinguish those we are to hear. We are told that you are the head Chief of the Grand Council, which is above these 13 Councils: if so why have we not had Talks from you,—We are head men and Chiefs and Warriors also: and have always been accustomed to speak with great Chiefs & warriors—We are Likewise told that you and the Great men of your Council are Very Wise—we are glad to hear it, being assured that you will not do us any Wrong, and therefore we wish to Speak with you and your Council, or if you Do not approve of our so Doing, as you are wise, you will tell us who shall

speak with us, in behalf of all our Brothers the Americans, and from where and whom we are to be supplyed with necessarries in the manner our great father supplied us—we hope you will also put a stop to any encroachments on our lands, without our consent, and silence all those People who sends us Such Talks as inflame & exasperate our Young Men, as it is our earnest desire to remain in peace and friendship with our Br: the Americans for ever.

Brother,
The King our Common father always left one of his beloved Men among us, to whom we told anything we had to say, and he soon obtained an answer—and by him our great Father, his Chiefs & headmen spoke to us.

Our great father always gave him goods to cover the nakedness of our old men who could not hunt, our women and our children, and he was as one mouth, and one tongue between us, and was beloved of us all. Such a man living among us particularly at this time, would rescue us from the darkness and confusion we are in. By directing us to whom we should speak, and putting us in the right Path that we should not go wrong.

We have desired our Br. Mr. Donne, who brought talks from General Clark, and has been some time among us, to deliver this talk to you, and speak it in our behalf to your Grand Council, that you may know our want, and as you are wise, that you may direct us what to do for the best. He has Promised, at our desire to take it to your great council fire & to bring as your answer, that you may be no more in the dark—believe what he tells you from us; we have told him all that is in our hearts.

Brothers, we are very poor for necessaries, for Amunition particularly. We can supply ourselves from the Spaniards but we are averse to hold any intercourse with them, as our hearts are always with our Brothers the Americans. We have advised our young men to wait with patience for the answer to this talk, when we rest assured of having supplies, and every thing so regulated that no further confusion may ensue. We wish that this land may never again be stained with the blood of either white or Red men, that peace may last forever and that both our women and children may sit down in safety under their own shade to enjoy without fear or apprehension the Blessing which the good Spirit enriches them with. Brother, we again desire you and your chiefs to Listen to what we say that we shall not have to Repeat it again, and as you are all Wise, you will know what to do.

## 10.   The Eve of War, 1811[10]

*In the decades after the War of Independence, Native Americans in the Ohio and Mississippi River valleys faced increasing pressure as American settlers encroached on their land. Despite a brief period of successful military resistance in the early 1790s, Indians could do little to check American expansion. During the first de-*

*cade of the nineteenth century, a pan-Indian revival movement took root in the northwest under the leadership of two Shawnee brothers, Tecumseh (1768–1813) and Tenskwatawa (1775–1836). Tenskwatawa, known as the Prophet, preached a message of cultural renewal while Tecumseh organized Indians to provide armed resistance to the United States. Their confederacy posed the most potent Native American threat to the United States since the War of Independence. In this letter William Eustis (1753–1825), the United States Secretary of War, attempts to conciliate Indians prior to the outbreak of the War of 1812 and warns the tribes against the Prophet.*

My Children. Your Great Father, the President, takes you by the hand, and commands me to say to you, —

My Children. Your Father opens his ears to your complaints. You say the animals of the forrest are leaving you and that your hunting fails. It was once so with his white Children. They killed and drove away the game from their fields. But they planted corn and have had plenty ever since. Do you the same, plant corn and you will have abundance for your wives and children thro' the long winters. Your Great Father will give you a plough and a horse to enable you to cultivate the earth.

My Children. You say your Great Father has stopped the white men's goods which used to come among you. It is true that no British goods can come within the U. States this year. The white people as well as the red suffer by this. But it cannot be helped. It is the law of the Great Council and must be obeyed.

My Children. Your Great Father has sent to Michilimacinac many goods; many more have been sent this year. From these he hopes you will be able to get sufficient supplies. If you cannot get everything you want, you must learn to do as the white people have, to do without as well as you can.

My Children. You complain that you do not receive your proportion of the supplies which are sent out every year to your nation.

My Children. Your Great Father sends to you all the goods and money stipulated in the Treaty. You must call meeting of all the chiefs of the nation, at which the Governor will be present, and you must agree among yourselves on the proportion of goods and money which each part of the tribe ought to receive. The Governor will report to your Great Father and then you will receive accordingly.

My Children. You say you have shut your ears to the bad birds sent by the Pattawomie who calls himself a prophet. Beware of the man. He is not good. He has already caused the destruction of many young men belonging to you and other tribes. All who go to him with arms will be destroyed.

My Children. Your Great Father takes you again by the hand he bids you farewell; and he commands me to give you clothing some gun-powder and other things in token of his good will towards you and your nation. He is pleased with your conduct since you have been here, and trusts that by such behaviour through the country and in the great towns where he will send you, you will merit the regard of his white children.

## 11.   Aftermath of the War of 1812[11]

*During the War of 1812 the United States decisively defeated the Indians in the northwest and consolidated its hegemony over the region. In so doing it completed the conquest which the British began during the Seven Years' War two generations before. Writing from the British post on Drummond Island in Lake Huron, between Michigan and Upper Canada (Ontario), Lieutenant Colonel Robert McDonall expresses concern about the impact of the war and the Treaty of Ghent on Native Americans, and apprehension over the treatment the Indians are likely to receive from the United States.*

I am induced to…investigate certain charges prefered by the American Government against Lieut. Cadotte of the Indian Department and also against the Govt. Generally, that its agents had instigated the Indians to hostilities since the Peace…

His Excellency directed me to a full and complete investigation of the circumstances complained of, I was fortunate, in still having at this remote Post, so many of the necessary evidences. Solemnly convinced in my own mind that the charges in themselves were a base calumny & utterly without foundation. I felt myself peculiarly interested in their refutation, conscious that their chief object was to shut out eyes to the manifest infringement of the Treaty of Ghent, & to the horrible tragedy which they meditate against the Indians of the Mississippi. Unfortunate men! forced by us into the War, assured by us again and again, of our faithful adherence to their cause, and if our constant protection, & now, 'abandoned at their utmost need,' to the merciless vengeance of a relentless Enemy. Their pretext is, that they continue the war: It is false, not an act of hostility has been committed (we have every reason to believe) since the 24 May and it is clearly proved that the Indians then knew nothing of the Peace. It is clearly proved by Capt. Andersons evidence, that when it became known, they not only assented thereto, but were anxious to observe it, upon the real terms on which it was made…These too well ascertained facts, strips the American Government of every pretext for their meditated hostilities, and reduces them to the bold alternative of cutting of the Indians by a glaring violation of a recent treaty, and rendering themselves liable to the usual consequences.

One observation I conceive it my duty to suggest, and to recommend its being fully explained to our Minister at Washington, that a series of vague surmises, undefined conjectures, reports of Indians Agents on the frontier, founded on no evidence & perhaps purposely vamped up to answer some purpose of the Govt. in General too, the absurd information of some ignorant Indian Chief; that charges of this nature, so flimsy, so totally unsupported, and involving such serious consequences, should in future be wholly inadmissible, & instantly rejected. If it suited the purpose of the American Government not a week would elapse but they could with the utmost facility obtain from their Indian Agents, accusations much more voluminous, when their own *assertion* or *opinion* is only necessary—proof of the fact alledged being altogether unnecessary.

A decided protest should also be made against the principle assumed by them, that every petty reconoutre (very often provoked by themselves) which takes place between them & the various Indian nations on their vast frontier, is to be ascribed to British influence & agency; I trust the proceedings of the Court will sufficiently evince the absurdity of such a supposition. If there appears that unusual pains had been taken, almost unprecedented exertions used, to restrain the Indians from hostilities, even when threats were made use of, and much provocation given by themselves, and also a disposition evinced by the American Government in no respect compatible with the Treaty of Ghent. When conduct like this, originating in the most anxious desire that the Indians should observe the Peace, has only tended to provoke the most odious calumneys, what chance is there, that they will desist from future accusations, or there ever being an end to the altercation…

A collection of Indian Speeches, which I have enclosed for His Excellency's perusal at his leisure, will throw some light upon the subject. They are in some measure interesting, as exhibiting correct specimens of Indian Eloquence, and in some instances of judgment & penetration which could scarcely be expected; I have been struck with that of La Feuille so deeply evincing bitterness of his sorrow at having parted with those *marks of destinction* which his Father Wabasha had recd from the English, and on his death bed enjoined him never to part with. The note which follows this speech is worth attention at the present moment…

## Notes

1. James Glen, *A Description of South Carolina; Containing Many curious and interesting Particulars relating to the Civil, Natural and Commercial History of that Colony…* (London: R. and J. Dodsley, 1761), 59–65. This document has been edited for length.
2. *A Declaration and Remonstrance Of the distressed and bleeding Frontier Inhabitants Of the Province of Pennsylvania, Presented by them to the Honourable the Governor and Assembly of the Province, Shewing the Causes Of their late Discontent and Uneasiness and the Grievances under which they have laboured, and which they humbly pray to have redress'd* (Philadelphia, 1764), 12–16. This document has been edited for length. The full version can be found at the book's website (http://www.routledge.com/textbooks/revolutionaryamerica/).
3. Thomas Jefferson, *Notes on the State of Virginia* (Philadelphia: Prichard and Hall, 1788), 67–68.
4. *Journals of the Continental Congress*, Vol. 2, 177, 181–183. This document has been edited for length. The full version can be found at the book's website.
5. "Speech of Captain Brant to Lord George Germain," in E. B. O'Callaghan (ed.), *Documents Relative to the Colonial History of the State of New-York; Procured in Holland, England and France, by John Romeyn Brodhead, Esq.*, Vol. 8 (Albany, NY: Weed, Parsons and Company, 1857), 670–671.
6. Gilbert Stuart (1775–1828), Joseph Brant, 1786, Oil on canvas. The Northumberland Estates, Alnwick Castle, Collection of the Duke of Northumberland at the Metropolitan Museum of Art, New York.
7. Copy of a Letter from the Rev. Samuel Kirkland, Missionary and Interpreter for the Six Nations:

Together with a Message from the Six Nations Chiefs, to Major General Gates, commanding the Army of the United States, in the Northern Department, dated at Oneida, October 31, 1777 (Yorktown, PA: Hall and Sellers, 1777). This document has been edited for length. The full version can be found at the book's website (http://www.routledge.com/textbooks/revolutionaryamerica/).

8. "Treaty with the Delawares, 1778," in Charles J. Kappler (ed.), *Indian Affairs: Laws and Treaties*, Vol. 2: Treaties (Washington, DC: Government Printing Office, 1904), 3–5.

9. "To His Excellency the President of the Honorable Congress of the United American States," in William P. Palmer (ed.), *Calendar of Virginia State Papers and Other Manuscripts, Preserved in the Capitol at Richmond*, Vol 3: From January 1, 1782, to December 31, 1784 (Richmond, VA: James E. Goode, 1883), 515–517.

10. "William Eustis to the Indians, October 8, 1811," *Michigan Pioneer and Historical Collections*, 8 (1886), 601.

11. "Robert McDonall to Major Foster, October 10, 1815," *Mississippi Pioneer and Historical Collections*, 16 (1890), 325–327. This document has been edited for length. The full version can be found at the book's website (http://www.routledge.com/textbooks/revolutionaryamerica/).

# CHAPTER 2

# British North America in 1763

## Introduction

During the eighteenth century it was a commonplace belief that there was a close relationship between power and population. Benjamin Franklin assessed the consequences of the burgeoning population of British North America, which doubled every generation, in his 1751 essay, "Observations Concerning the Increase of Mankind" (document 2). The American population grew through natural increase and migration. Some people emigrated to British North America of their own volition, but many were compelled to do so either as slaves from Africa or as indentured servants from Europe. These involuntary migrants, whose labor was essential to the success of the colonies, were a restive element of the population, as evidenced by Robert Berverley's description of servants and slaves in Virginia (document 3) and the advertisements for runaway servants and slaves (document 4) that were a constant feature of American newspapers during the colonial period.

Despite a common history and culture, the various colonies that constituted British North America found it difficult to cooperate on matters of common interest such as defense. In 1754 Benjamin Franklin drafted the Albany Plan of Union which was intended to promote military and political collaboration among the colonies on the eve of the Seven Years' War. The plan failed despite Franklin's propaganda efforts (documents 5 and 6). Notwithstanding the failure of the colonies to unite for their common defense, the British triumphed in the Seven Years' War. The 1763 Peace of Paris (document 7) ended the Seven Years' War and decisively altered the balance of power in North America. Under the terms of the treaty the British now controlled all of North America east of the Mississippi River (document 8). Most British North Americans lived in the thirteen colonies along the eastern seaboard. They delighted in Britain's victory in the late war and gloried in their identity as Britons. Many Americans believed that they had the rights of free-born Englishmen as laid down in the 1689 Bill of Rights (document 1), and that these liberties were as relevant in North America as they were in Britain. Americans also believed they possessed the right to settle in newly acquired territories in the west. As a result, conflicts between settlers and Native Americans were endemic after the Seven Years' War. In an effort to contain the problem, and to implement a system to govern the new territory, King George III issued a proclamation on October 7, 1763, which prohibited settlers from settling on lands west of the Appalachian Mountains and established three additional North American colonies: Quebec, East Florida, and West Florida (document 8). That these difficulties arose so quickly after the Peace of Paris presaged future difficulties between Britain and its main colonies in North America.

## 1.   Bill of Rights, 1689[1]

*When Parliament invited William and Mary to become joint sovereigns of England in 1688, it presented them with a Declaration of Rights which was formally adopted by Parliament and endorsed by the monarchs in 1689. As a consequence, the status of the English, latterly British, state as a constitutional monarchy was confirmed. The Bill of Rights acknowledges the rights of British subjects including the right to petition the monarch, trial by jury, freedom of speech, the right to bear arms and the constitutional limits on the monarch, including the requirement to seek the consent of the people through Parliament on legislation. British North Americans believed these rights applied to the colonies and took these as the point of departure when they sought to assert their rights in response to Parliament's efforts to tax them after the Seven Years' War.*

*...The Subject's Rights.*
And thereupon the said Lords Spirituall and Temporall and Commons pursuant to their respective Letters and Elections being now assembled in a full and free Representative of this Nation takeing into their most serious Consideration the best meanes for attaining the Ends aforesaid Doe in the first place (as their Auncestors in like Case have usually done) for the Vindicating and Asserting their auntient Rights and Liberties, Declare

*Dispensing Power.*
That the pretended Power of Suspending of Laws or the Execution of Laws by Regall Authority without Consent of Parlyament is illegall.

*Late dispensing Power.*
That the pretended Power of Dispersing with Laws or the Execution of Laws by Regall Authoritie as it hath beene assumed and exercised of late is illegall.

*Ecclesiastical Courts illegal.*
That the Commission for erecting the late Court of Commissioners for Ecclesiasticall Causes and all other Commissions and Courts of like nature are Illegall and Pernicious.

*Levying Money.*
That levying Money for or to the Use of the Crowne by pretence of Prerogative without Grant of Parlyament for longer time or in other manner then the same is or shall be granted is Illegall.

*Right to petition.*
That it is the Right of the Subjects to Petition the King and all Commitments and Prosecutions for such Petitioning are Illegall.

*Standing Army.*
That the raising or keeping a standing Army within the Kingdome in time of Peace unlesse it be with Consent of Parlyament is against Law.

*Subjects' Arms.*
That the Subjects which are Protestants may have Arms for their Defence suitable to their Conditions and as allowed by Law.

*Freedom of Election.*
That Election of Members of Parlyament ought to be free.

*Freedom of Speech.*
That the Freedome of Speech and Debates or Proceedings in Parlyament ought not to be impeached or questioned in any Court or Place out of Parlyament.

*Excessive Bail.*
That excessive Baile ought not to be required nor excessive Fines imposed nor cruell and unusuall Punishments inflicted.

*Juries.*
That Jurors ought to be duely impannelled and returned and Jurors which passe upon Men in Trialls for High Treason ought to be Freeholders.

*Grants of Forfeitures.*
That all Grants and Promises of Fines and Forfeitures of particular persons before Conviction are illegall and void.

*Frequent Parliaments.*
And that for Redresse of all Grievances and for the amending strengthening and preserveing of the Lawes Parlyaments ought to be held frequently...

## 2.  Benjamin Franklin, Observations Concerning the Increase of Mankind, Peopling of Countries, 1751[2]

*Franklin (1706–1790) was a successful Philadelphia printer, businessman, and scientist when he published this essay in 1751. In this essay Franklin reflects on the causes and consequences of American population growth during the eighteenth century. He compares the growth of the American population to that of Europe, particularly Britain. While population growth was seen as a measure of power and wealth, Franklin expresses concerns about the cultural impact of the growth of the German and African populations in Pennsylvania.*

...5. *Europe* is generally full settled with Husbandmen, Manufacturers, &c. and therefore cannot now much increase in People: *America* is chiefly occupied by Indians, who subsist mostly by Hunting. But as the Hunter, of all Men, requires the greatest Quantity of Land from whence to draw his Subsistence, (the Husbandman subsisting on much less, the Gardner on still less, and the Manufacturer requiring least of all), The *Europeans* found *America* as fully settled as it well could be by Hunters; yet these having large Tracks, were easily prevail'd on to part with Portions of Territory to the new Comers, who did not much interfere with the Natives in Hunting, and furnish'd them with many Things they wanted.

6. Land being thus plenty in *America*, and so cheap as that a labouring Man, that understands Husbandry, can in a short Time save Money enough to purchase a Piece of new Land sufficient for a Plantation, whereon he may subsist a Family; such are not afraid to marry; for if they even look far enough forward to consider how their Children when grown up are to be provided for, they see that more Land is to be had at Rates equally easy, all Circumstances considered.

7. Hence Marriages in *America* are more general, and more generally early, than in *Europe*. And if it is reckoned there, that there is but one Marriage per Annum among 100 Persons, perhaps we may here reckon two; and if in *Europe* they have but 4 Births to a Marriage (many of their Marriages being late) we may here reckon 8, of which if one half grow up, and our Marriages are made, reckoning one with another at 20 Years of Age, our People must at least be doubled every 20 Years.

8. But notwithstanding this Increase, so vast is the Territory of *North-America*, that it will require many Ages to settle it fully; and till it is fully settled, Labour will never be cheap here, where no Man continues long a Labourer for others, but gets a Plantation of his own, no Man continues long a Journeyman to a Trade, but goes among those new Settlers, and sets up for himself, &c. Hence Labour is no cheaper now, in *Pennsylvania*, than it was 30 Years ago, tho' so many Thousand labouring People have been imported.

9. The Danger therefore of these Colonies interfering with their Mother Country in Trades that depend on Labour, Manufactures, &c. is too remote to require the Attention of *Great-Britain*.

10. But in Proportion to the Increase of the Colonies, a vast Demand is growing for British Manufactures, a glorious Market wholly in the Power of *Britain*, in which Foreigners cannot interfere, which will increase in a short Time even beyond her Power of supplying, tho' her whole Trade should be to her Colonies: Therefore *Britain* should not too much restrain Manufactures in her Colonies....

12. 'Tis an ill-grounded Opinion that by the Labour of Slaves, *America* may possibly vie in Cheapness of Manufactures with *Britain*. The Labour of Slaves can never be so cheap here as the Labour of working Men is in *Britain*. Any one may compute it. Interest of Money is in the Colonies from 6 to 10 per Cent. Slaves one with another cost 30£ Sterling per Head. Reckon then the Interest of the first Purchase of a Slave, the Insurance or Risque on his Life, his Cloathing and Diet, Expences in his Sickness and Loss of Time, Loss by his Neglect of Business (Neglect is natural to the Man who is not to be benefited by his own Care or Diligence), Expence of a Driver to keep him at Work, and his Pilfering from Time to Time, almost every Slave being *by Nature* a Thief, and compare the whole Amount with the Wages of a Manufacturer of Iron or Wool in *England*, you will see that Labour is much cheaper there than it ever can be by Negroes here. Why then will *Americans* purchase Slaves? Because Slaves may be kept as long as a Man pleases, or has Occasion for their Labour; while hired Men are continually leaving their Master (often in the midst of his Business), and setting up for themselves.

13. As the Increase of People depends on the Encouragement of Marriages, the following Things must diminish a Nation, *viz*. 1. The being conquered; for the Conquerors will engross as many Offices, and exact as much Tribute or Profit on the Labour of the conquered, as will maintain them in their new Establishment, and this diminishing the Subsistence of the Natives discourages their Marriages, and so gradually diminishes them, while the Foreigners increase. 2. Loss of Territory. Thus the *Britons* being driven into *Wales*, and crowded together in a barren Country insufficient to support such great Numbers, diminished 'till the People bore a Proportion to the Produce, while the *Saxons* increas'd on their abandoned Lands; 'till the Island became full of *English*. And were the *English* now driven into *Wales* by some foreign Nation, there would in a few Years be no more Englishmen in *Britain*, than there are now People in *Wales*. 3. Loss of Trade. Manufactures exported, draw Subsistence from Foreign Countries for Numbers; who are thereby enabled to marry and raise Families. If the Nation be deprived of any Branch of Trade, and no new Employment is found for the People occupy'd in that Branch, it will also be soon deprived of so many People. 4. Loss of Food. Suppose a Nation has a Fishery, which not only employs great Numbers, but makes the Food and Subsistence of the People cheaper: If another Nation becomes Master of the Seas, and prevents the Fishery, the People will diminish in Proportion as the Loss of Employ, and Dearness of Provision, makes it more difficult to subsist a Family. 5. Bad Government and insecure Property. People not only leave such a Country, and settling Abroad incorporate with other Nations, lose their native Language,

and become Foreigners; but the Industry of those that remain being discourag'd, the Quantity of Subsistence in the Country is lessen'd, and the Support of a Family becomes more difficult. So heavy Taxes tend to diminish a People. 6. The Introduction of Slaves. The Negroes brought into the *English* Sugar *Islands*, have greatly diminish'd the Whites there; the Poor are by this Means depriv'd of Employment, while a few Families acquire vast Estates; which they spend on Foreign Luxuries, and educating their Children in the Habit of those Luxuries; the same Income is needed for the Support of one that might have maintain'd 100. The Whites who have Slaves, not labouring, are enfeebled, and therefore not so generally prolific; the Slaves being work'd too hard, and ill fed, their Constitutions are broken, and the Deaths among them are more than the Births; so that a continual Supply is needed from *Africa*. The Northern Colonies having few Slaves increase in Whites. Slaves also pejorate the Families that use them; the white Children become proud, disgusted with Labour, and being educated in Idleness, are rendered unfit to get a Living by Industry...

19. The great Increase of Offspring in particular Families, is not always owing to greater Fecundity of Nature, but sometimes to Examples of Industry in the Heads, and industrious Education; by which the Children are enabled to provide better for themselves, and their marrying early, is encouraged from the Prospect of good Subsistence.

20. If there be a Sect therefore, in our Nation, that regard Frugality and Industry as religious Duties, and educate their Children therein, more than others commonly do; such Sect must consequently increase more by natural Generation, than any other Sect in *Britain*...

22. There is in short, no Bound to the prolific Nature of Plants or Animals, but what is made by their crowding and interfering with each others Means of Subsistence. Was the Face of the Earth vacant of other Plants, it might be gradually sowed and overspread with one Kind only; as, for Instance, with Fennel; and were it empty of other Inhabitants, it might in a few Ages be replenish'd from one Nation only; as, for Instance, with *Englishmen*. Thus there are suppos'd to be now upwards of One Million *English* Souls in *North-America*, (tho' 'tis thought scarce 80,000 have been brought over Sea) and yet perhaps there is not one the fewer in *Britain*, but rather many more, on Account of the Employment the Colonies afford to Manufacturers at Home. This Million doubling, suppose but once in 25 Years, will in another Century be more than the People of *England*, and the greatest Number of *Englishmen* will be on this Side the Water. What an Accession of Power to the *British* Empire by Sea as well as Land! What Increase of Trade and Navigation! What Numbers of Ships and Seamen! We have been here but little more than 100 Years, and yet the Force of our Privateers in the late War, united, was greater, both in Men and Guns, than that of the whole *British* Navy in Queen *Elizabeth*'s Time. How important an Affair then to *Britain*, is the present Treaty for settling the Bounds between her Colonies and the *French*, and

how careful should she be to secure Room enough, since on the Room depends so much the Increase of her People?

23. In fine, A Nation well regulated is like a Polypus; take away a Limb, its Place is soon supply'd; cut it in two, and each deficient Part shall speedily grow out of the Part remaining. Thus if you have Room and Subsistence enough, as you may by dividing, make ten Polypes out of one, you may of one make ten Nations, equally populous and powerful; or rather, increase a Nation ten fold in Numbers and Strength.

And since Detachments of *English* from *Britain* sent to *America*, will have their Places at Home so soon supply'd and increase so largely here; why should the *Palatine Boors* be suffered to swarm into our Settlements, and by herding together establish their Language and Manners to the Exclusion of ours? Why should *Pennsylvania*, founded by the *English*, become a Colony of *Aliens*, who will shortly be so numerous as to Germanize us instead of our Anglifying them, and will never adopt our Language or Customs, any more than they can acquire our Complexion.

24. Which leads me to add one Remark: That the Number of purely white People in the World is proportionably very small. All *Africa* is black or tawny. *Asia* chiefly tawny. *America* (exclusive of the new Comers) wholly so. And in *Europe*, the *Spaniards, Italians, French, Russians* and *Swedes*, are generally of what we call a swarthy Complexion; as are the *Germans* also, the *Saxons* only excepted, who with the *English*, make the principal Body of White People on the Face of the Earth. I could wish their Numbers were increased. And while we are, as I may call it, *Scouring* our Planet, by clearing *America* of Woods, and so making this Side of our Globe reflect a brighter Light to the Eyes of Inhabitants in *Mars* or *Venus*, why should we in the Sight of Superior Beings, darken its People? why increase the Sons of *Africa*, by Planting them in *America*, where we have so fair an Opportunity, by excluding all Blacks and Tawneys, of increasing the lovely White and Red? But perhaps I am partial to the Complexion of my Country, for such Kind of Partiality is natural to Mankind.

### 3.   Servants and Slaves in Virginia, 1722[3]

*In this extract from his* History of Virginia, *Robert Beverley (1673–1722), a planter and historian, presents an early description of life in the colony. In this extract Beverley compares the labor and status of indentured servants and slaves in Virginia. Sensitive to British criticism, he argues that servants and slaves are well treated but makes a distinction between the work required of female white servants and female African slaves. According to Beverley, the latter were required to work in the fields while the former were excused from this, although it is unlikely that this distinction was observed in practice. Servants, unlike slaves, had legal rights which Beverley is careful to enumerate.*

50. Their Servants their distinguish by the Names of Slaves for Life, and Servants for a time.

Slaves are the Negroes, and their Posterity, following the Condition of the Mother, according to the Maxim, *partus sequitur ventrem*. They are call'd Slaves, in Respect of the Time of their Servitude, because it is for Life.

Servants, are those which serve only for a few Years, according to the time of their Indenture, or the Custom of the Country. The Custom of the Country takes place upon such as have no Indentures. The Law in this Case, is, that if such Servants be under nineteen Years of Age, they must be brought into Court, to have their Age adjudged; and from the Age they are jud'd to be of, they must serve until they reach four and twenty: But if they be adjudged upwards of nineteen, they are then only to be Servants for the Term of five Years.

51. The Male-Servants, and Slaves of both Sexes, are imployed together in tilling and manuring the Ground, in sowing and planting Tobacco, Corn, &c. Some Distinction indeed is made between them in their Cloaths, and Food; but the Work of both is no other than what the Overseers, the Freemen, and the Planters themselves do.

Sufficient Distinction is also made between the Female-Servants, and Slaves; for a white Woman is rarely or never put to work in the Ground, if she be good for any thing else; And to discourage all Planters from using any Woman so, their Law makes Female-Servants working in the Ground Tithables, while it suffers all other white Women to be absolutely exempted: Whereas on the other hand, it is a common thing to work a Woman Slave out of Doors; nor does the Law make any Distinction in her Taxes, whether her Work be Abroad, or at Home.

52. Because I have heard how strangely cruel, and severe, the Service of this Country is represented in some Parts of *England*; I can't forbear affirming, that the Work of their Servants and Slaves is no other than what every common Freeman does. Neither is any Servant requir'd to do more in a Day, than his Overseer. And I can assure you with great Truth, that generally their Slaves are not worked so hard, nor so many Hours in a Day, as the Husbandmen, and Day-labourers in *England*. An Overseer is a Man, that having served his time, has acquired the Skill and Character of an experienced Planter, and is therefore intrusted with the Direction of the Servants and Slaves.

But to complete this Account of Servants, I shall give you a short Relation of the Care their Laws take, that they be used as tenderly as possible.

*By the Laws of their Country.*
1. All Servants whatsoever have their Complaints heard without Fee, or Reward; but if the Master be found faulty, the Charge of the Complaint is cast upon him, otherwise the Business is done *ex Officio*.
2. Any Justice of the Peace may receive the Complaint of a Servant, and order every thing relating thereto, till the next County-Court, where it will be finally determin'd.

3. All Masters are under the Correction and Censure of the County-Courts, to provide for their Servants good and wholsome Diet, Clothing and Lodging.

4. They are always to appear upon the first notice given of the Complaint of their Servants, otherwise to forfeit the Service of them, until they do appear.

5. All Servants Complaints are to be receiv'd at any time in Court, without Process; and shall not be delay'd for want of Form; but the Merits of the Complaint must be immediately inquir'd into by the Justices; and if the Master cause any delay therein, the Court may remove such Servants, if they see Cause, until the Master will come to Trial.

6. If a Master shall at any time disobey an Order of Court made upon any Complaint of a Servant; the Court is impower'd to remove such Servant forthwith to another Master, who will be kinder; giving to the former Master the Produce only, (after Fees deducted) of what such Servants shall be sold for by publick Outcry.

7. If a Master should be so cruel, as to use his Servant ill, that is faln sick, or lame in his Service, and thereby render'd unfit for Labour, he must be remov'd by the Church-Wardens out of the way of such Cruelty, and boarded in some good Planter's House, till the time of his Freedom, the Charge of which must be laid before the next Country-Court, which has Power to levy the same from time to time; upon the Goods and Chattels of the Master; after which, the Charge of such Boarding is to come upon the Parish in general.

8. All hired Servants are intituled to these Privileges.

9. No Master of a Servant can make a new Bargain for Service, or other Matter with his Servant, without the Privity and Consent of the Country-Court, to prevent the Masters over-reaching, or scaring such Servant into an unreasonable Compliance.

10. The Property of all Money and Goods sent over thither to Servants, or carry'd in with them, is reserv'd to themselves, and remains intirely at their Disposal.

11. Each Servant at his Freedom received of his Master ten Bushels of Corn, (which is sufficient for almost a Year) two new Suits of Cloaths, both Linen and Woollen, and a Gun 20s. value, and then becomes as free in all Respects, and as much entituled to the Liberties and Privileges of the Country, as any other of the Inhabitants or Natives are, if such Servants were not Aliens.

12. Each Servant has then also a Right to take up fifty Acres of Land, where he can find any unpatented.

This is what the Laws prescribe in Favour of Servants, by which you may find, that the Cruelties and Severities imputed to that Country, are an unjust Reflection. For no People more abhor the thoughts of such Usage, than the *Virginians*, nor take more Precaution to prevent it now, whatever it was in former Days.

### 4. Advertisements for Runaways, 1752, 1766[4]

*Although Robert Beverley was keen to assert that servants and slaves were well treated, many sought refuge through flight. Advertisements for runaways were common in colonial newspapers. These two advertisements from the* Virginia Gazette *are typical. They provide a wealth of descriptive detail on people, often at the margins of historical records but whose labor was essential in eighteenth-century America.*

RAN away from the Subscriber in *Lancaster* County, a Convict Servant, named *Sarah Knox*, of middle Size, a swarthy Complexion and has a short Nose, talks broad, and says she was born in *Yorkshire*, had been in the Army for several Years, with the Camp in *Flanders*, and at the Battle of *Culloden*, where she lost her Husband; she had on when she went away, a Woman's black Hat, an old red Silk Handkerchief round her Neck, and old dirty blue Stuff Gown, with check Linen Cuffs, old Stays, a black and white strip'd Country Cloth Petticoat, an old blue quilted ditto, a check Linen Apron, and a brown Linen Shift. She may go by the Name of *Sarah Howard, Wilson*, or something else, pretend to be a dancing Mistress, will make a great many Courtesies, and is a very deceitful insinuating Woman, and a great Lyar. Whoever apprehends and conveys her to me shall have a Pistole Reward besides what the Law allows, or if any Person find her qualified to teach Dancing, or to serve in any other Way he may purchase between 5 and 6 Years Service of her at fifteen Pounds Currency, from David Currie.

RUN away from the subscriber, on or about the 10th of *February* last, a *Virginia* born Negro man named GEORGE AMERICA, about 5 feet 8 or 9 inches high, about 30 years old, of a yellow complexion, is a tolerable good shoemaker, and can do something of the house carpenters work, walks quick and upright, and has a scar on the back of his left hand; had on a cotton waistcoat and breeches, osnaburgs shirt, and yarn stockings. As the said slave is outlawed, I do hereby offer a reward of 5l. to any person that will kill and destroy him, and 40s. if taken alive. THOMAS WATKINS.

### 5. Albany Plan of Union, 1754[5]

*In June 1754—less than a month before Virginia militia under George Washington skirmished with French and Indian troops in Pennsylvania, triggering the Seven Years' War—delegates from the northern colonies met with representatives of the Six Nations of the Iroquois Confederacy to discuss diplomacy and common defence. The colonial delegates endorsed a "Plan of Union" drafted by Benjamin Franklin which called for each colony to elect representatives to a continental assembly to be presided over by a royal governor for the purpose of common defense. Franklin anticipates many of the difficulties which would beset the Continental Congress during the War of Independence and the framers of the Constitution in 1787. The plan ultimately failed because neither the British government nor the individual colonies were prepared to cede their authority to the proposed continental assembly.*

…That humble Application be made for an Act of the Parliament of Great Britain, by Virtue of which, one General Government may beformed in America, including all the said Colonies, within and under which Government, each Colony may retain its present Constitution, except in the Particulars wherein a Change may be directed by the said Act, as hereafter follows.

1.  That the said General Government be administered by a President General, To be appointed and Supported by the Crown, and a Grand Council, to be Chosen by the Representatives of the People of the Several Colonies, met in their respective Assemblies.
2.  That within    Months after the passing of such Act, The House of Representatives in the Several Assemblies, that happen to be Sitting within that time, or that shall be Specially for that purpose Convened, may and Shall Choose Members for the Grand Council, in the following Proportions, that is to say.

| | |
|---|---|
| Massachusetts Bay | 7 |
| New Hampshire | 2 |
| Connecticut | 5 |
| Rhode Island | 2 |
| New York | 4 |
| New Jersey | 3 |
| Pensilvania | 6 |
| Maryland | 4 |
| Virginia | 7 |
| North Carolina | 4 |
| South Carolina | 4 |
| | 48 |

3.  Who shall meet for the first time at the City of Philadelphia, in Pensilvania, being called by the President General as soon as conveniently may be, after his Appointment.
4.  That there shall be a New Election of Members for the Grand Council every three years; And, on the Death or Resignation of any Member his Place should be Supplyed by a New Choice at the next Sitting of the Assembly of the Colony he represented.
5.  That after the first three years, when the Proportion of Money arising out of each Colony to the General Treasury can be known, The Number of Members to be Chosen, for each Colony shall from time to time in all ensuing Elections be regulated by that proportion (yet so as that the Number to be Chosen by any one Province be not more than Seven, nor less than Two).

6.  That the Grand Council shall meet once in every Year, and oftener if Occasion require, at such Time and place as they shall adjourn to at the last preceding meeting, or as they shall be called to meet at by the President General, on any Emergency, he having first obtained in Writing the Consent of seven of the Members to such call, and sent due and timely Notice to the whole.

7.  That the Grand Council have power to chuse their speaker, and shall neither be Dissolved, prorogued, nor Continue Sitting longer than Six Weeks at one Time without their own consent or the Special Command of the Crown.

8.  That the Members of the Grand Council shall be Allowed for their Service ten shillings Sterling per Diem, during their Sessions or Journey to and from the Place of Meeting; Twenty miles to be reckoned a days journey.

9.  That the Assent of the President General be requisite, to all Acts of the Grand Council, and that it be His Office, and Duty to cause them to be carried into Execution.

10. That the President General with the Advice of the Grand Council, hold or Direct all Indian Treaties in which the General Interest or Welfare of the Colony's may be concerned; And make Peace or Declare War with Indian Nations.

11. That they make such Laws as they Judge Necessary for regulating all Indian trade.

12. That they make all Purchases from Indians for the Crown, of Lands not not within the Bounds of Particular Colonies, or that shall not be within their Bounds when some of them are reduced to more Convenient Dimensions.

13. That they make New Settlements on such Purchases, by Granting Lands in the Kings name, reserving a Quit Rent to the Crown, for the use of the General Treasury.

14. That they make Laws for regulating and Governing such new Settlements, till the Crown shall think fit to form them into Particular Governments.

15. That they raise and pay Soldiers, and build Forts for the Defence of any of the Colonies, and equip Vessels of Force to Guard the Coasts and Protect the Trade on the Ocean, Lakes, or Great Rivers; but they shall not Impress Men in any Colonies, without the Consent of its Legislature.

16. That for these purposes they have Power to make Laws And lay and Levy such General Duties, Imposts, or Taxes, as to them shall appear most equal and Just, Considering the Ability and other Circumstances of the Inhabitants in the Several Colonies, and such as may be Collected with the least Inconvenience to the People, rather discouraging Luxury, than Loading Industry with unnecessary Burthens.

17. That they may Appoint a General Treasurer and Particular Treasurer in each Government, when Necessary, And, from Time to Time may Order

the Sums in the Treasuries of each Government, into the General Treasury, or draw on them for Special payments, as they find most Convenient.

18. Yet no money to Issue, but by joint Orders of the President General and Grand Council Except where Sums have been Appropriated to particular Purposes, And the President General is previously empowered by an Act to draw such Sums.

19. That the General Accounts shall be yearly Settled and Reported to the Several Assembly's.

20. That a Quorum of the Grand Council impower'd to act with the President General, do consist of Twenty-five Members, among whom there shall be one, or more from a Majority of the Colonies.

21. That the Laws made by them for the Purposes aforesaid, shall not be repugnant but as near as may be agreeable to the Laws of England, and Shall be transmitted to the King in Council for Approbation, as Soon as may be after their Passing and if not disapproved within Three years after Presentation, to remain in Force.

22. That, in case of the Death of the President General The Speaker of the Grand Council for the Time Being shall Succeed, and be Vested with the Same Powers, and Authority, to Continue till the King's Pleasure be known.

23. That all Military Commission Officers Whether for Land or Sea Service, to Act under this General Constitution, shall be Nominated by the President General But the Approbation of the Grand Council is to be Obtained before they receive their Commissions, And all Civil Officers are to be Nominated, by the Grand Council, and to receive the President General's Approbation, before they Officiate.

24. But in Case of Vacancy by Death or removal of any Officer Civil or Military under this Constitution, The Governor of the Province in which such Vacancy happens, may Appoint, till the pleasure of the President General and Grand Council can be known.

25. That the Particular Military as well as Civil Establishments in each Colony remain in their present State, General Constitution Notwithstanding. And that on Sudden Emergencies any Colony may Defend itself, and lay the Accounts of Expence thence Arisen before the President General and Grand Council, who may allow and order payment of the same As far as they Judge such Accounts Just and reasonable.

## 6. Join, or Die, 1754[6]

*In order to promote support for a common colonial defense policy such as the Albany Plan, Franklin published this image of the colonies as represented by a dismembered rattlesnake. Together the snake is able to defend itself but broken into its constituent parts—the individual colonies—it is powerless. This image of*

**Figure 2.1** Join, or Die, 1754.

*America would recur throughout the revolutionary period. That rattlesnake appealed as a symbol for America because it was indigenous and, though lethal, it attacked only when it was threatened or attacked first.*

## 7. Treaty of Paris, 1763[7]

*This treaty, signed on February 10, 1763, ended the Seven Years' War. In order to retain the lucrative West Indian colony of Guadeloupe, France ceded Quebec and all of its claims to territory east of the Mississippi River to Britain. Spain ceded East and West Florida to Britain but eventually received New Orleans and Louisiana as compensation. The treaty marked the high-water mark of the British Empire in North America.*

Article I. There shall be a Christian, universal, and perpetual peace, as well by sea as by land, and a sincere and constant friendship shall be re-established between their Britannick, most Christian, Catholick and most Faithful Majesties, and between their heirs and successors, kingdoms, dominions, provinces, countries, subjects, and vassals, of what quality or condition soever they be, without exception of places or of persons…

IV. His most Christian Majesty renounces all pretensions, which he has heretofore formed, or might form, to Nova-Scotia or Acadia, in all its parts, and guaranties the whole of it, and with all its dependencies, to the King of Great Britain: Moreover, his Most Christian Majesty cedes, and guaranties to his said Britannick Majesty, in full right, Canada, with all its dependencies, as well as the island of Cape Breton, and all the other islands, and coasts, in the gulph and river St. Lawrence…His Britannick Majesty, on his side, agrees to grant the liberty of the Catholick religion to the inhabitants of Canada. He will, consequently, give the most precise and most effectual orders, that his new Roman Catholic subjects may profess the worship of their religion, according to the rites of the Romish church, as far as the laws of Great-Britain permit. His Britannick Majesty farther agrees, that the French inhabitants, or others who had been subjects of the Most Christian King in Canada, may retire, with all safety and freedom, wherever they shall think proper, and may sell their estates, provided it be to subjects of his Britannick Majesty, and bring away their effects, as well as their persons, without being restrained in their emigration, under any pretence whatsoever, except that of debts, or of criminal prosecutions: The term, limited for this emigration, shall be fixed to the space of eighteen months, to be computed from the day of the exchange of the ratification of the present treaty.

V. The subjects of France shall have the liberty of fishing and drying on a part of the coasts of the island of Newfoundland, such as it is specified in the XIIIth article of the treaty of Utrecht; which article is renewed and confirmed by the present treaty, (except what relates to the island of Cape Breton, as well as to the other islands and coasts in the mouth and in the gulph of St. Lawrence:) And his Britannick Majesty consents to leave to the subjects of the most Christian King the liberty of fishing in the gulph St. Lawrence, on condition that the subjects of France do not exercise the said fishery, but at the distance of three leagues from all the coasts belonging to Great Britain, as well those of the continent, as those of the islands situated in the said gulph St. Lawrence. And as to what relates to the fishery on the coasts of the island of Cape Breton out of the said gulph, the subjects of the most Christian King shall not be permitted to exercise the said fishery, but at the distance of fifteen leagues from the coasts of the island of Cape Breton; and the fishery on the coasts of Nova-Scotia or Acadia, and every where else out of the said gulph, shall remain on the foot of former treaties.

VI. The King of Great Britain cedes the islands of St. Pierre and Mcquelon, in full right, to his most Christian Majesty, to serve as a shelter to the French fishermen; And his said most Christian Majesty engages not to fortify the said islands; to erect no buildings upon them but merely for the convenience of the fishery; and to keep upon them a guard of fifty men only for the police.

VII. In order to re-establish peace on solid and durable foundations, and to remove for ever all subject of dispute with regard to the limits of the British and French territories on the continent of America; it is agreed, that for the future, the confines between the dominions of his Britannick Majesty, and those of his most Christian Majesty, in that part of the world, shall be fixed irrevocably by a line drawn along the middle of the River Mississippi, from its source to the river Iberville, and from thence, by a line drawn along the middle of this river, and the lakes Maurepas and Pontchartrain to the sea; and for this purpose, the most Christian King cedes in full right, and guaranties to his Britannick Majesty the river and port of the Mobile, and every thing which he possesses, or ought to possess, on the left side of the river Mississippi, except the town of New-Orleans, and the island in which it is situated, which shall remain to France; provided that the navigation of the river Mississippi shall be equally free, as well to the subjects of Great-Britain, as to those of France, in its whole breadth and length, from its source to the sea, and expressly that part which is between the said island of New-Orleans and the right bank of that river, as well as the passage both in and out of its mouth: It is farther stipulated, that the vessels belonging to the subjects of either nation shall not be stopped, visited or subjected to the payment of any duty whatsoever. The stipulations inserted in the IVth article, in favour of the inhabitants of Canada, shall also take place, with regard to the inhabitants of the countries ceded by this article.

VIII. The King of Great Britain shall restore to France the islands of Guadeloupe, of Mariegalante, of Desirade, of Martinico, and of Belleisle; and the fortresses of these islands shall be restored in the same condition they were in, when they were conquered by the British arms; provided that his Britannick Majesty's subjects, who shall have settled in the said islands, or those who shall have any commercial affairs to settle there, or in the other places restored to France by the present treaty, shall have liberty to sell their lands and their estates, to settle their affairs, to recover their debts, and to bring away their effects, as well as their persons, on board vessels, which they shall be permitted to send to the said islands, and other places restored as above, and which shall serve for this use only, without being restrained on account of their religion, or under any other pretence whatsoever, except that of debts or of criminal prosecutions…

IX. The most Christian King cedes and guaranties to his Britannick Majesty, in full right, the islands of Grenada, and the Grenadines, with the same stipulations in favour of the inhabitants of this colony, inserted in the IVth article for those of Canada: And the partition of the islands called neutral, is agreed and fixed, so that those of St. Vincent, Dominico, and Tobago, shall remain in full right to Great Britain, and that of St. Lucia shall be delivered to France, to enjoy the same likewise in full right; and the high contracting parties guaranty the partition so stipulated…

XVIII. His Catholick Majesty desists, as well for himself as for his successors, from all pretension, which he may have formed, in favour of the Guipuscoans, and other his subjects, to the right of fishing in the neighbourhood of the island of Newfoundland.

XIX. The King of Great Britain shall restore to Spain all the territory which he has conquered in the island of Cuba, with the fortress of the Havana, and this fortress, as well as all the other fortresses of the said island, shall be restored in the same condition they were in when conquered by his Britannick Majesty's arms; provided that his Britannick Majesty's subjects, who shall have settled in the said island, restored to Spain by the present treaty, or those who shall have any commercial affairs to settle there, shall have liberty to sell their lands and their estates, to settle their affairs, recover their debts, and to bring away their effects, as well as their persons, on board vessels which they shall be permitted to send to the said island restored as above, and which shall serve for that use only, without being restrained on account of their religion, or under any other pretence whatsoever, except that of debts or of criminal prosecutions…

XX. In consequence of the restitution stipulated in the preceding article, his Catholick Majesty cedes and guaranties, in full right, to his Britannick Majesty, Florida, with the Fort St. Augustine, and the Bay of Pensacola, as well as all that Spain possesses on the continent of North-America, to the east, or to the south-east of the river Mississippi: and in general, every thing that depends on the said countries and lands, with the sovereignty, property, possession, and all rights, acquired by treaties or otherwise, which the Catholick King and the crown of Spain have had, till now, over the said countries, lands, places, and their inhabitants; so that the Catholick King cedes and makes over the whole to the said King and to the crown of Great Britain, and that in the most ample manner, and form. His Britannick Majesty agrees, on his side, to grant to the inhabitants of the countries, above ceded, the liberty of the Catholick religion: He will consequently give the most express and the most effectual orders, that his new Roman Catholic subjects may profess the worship of their religion according to the rites of the Romish church, as far as the laws of Great-Britain permit: His Britannick Majesty further agrees, that the Spanish inhabitants, or others who had been subjects of the Catholick King in the said countries, may retire with all safety and freedom, wherever they think proper; and may sell their estates, provided it be to his Britannick Majesty's subjects, and bring away their effects, as well as their persons without being restrained in their emigration, under any pretence whatsoever, except that of debts, or of criminal prosecutions…

## 8. Governing a New World[8]

*As a consequence of the 1763 Treaty of Paris, King George III found himself with a vastly expanded empire in North America and numerous new subjects—including former French subjects in Canada and the Mississippi Valley, former Spanish subjects in the Floridas, and Native Americans throughout eastern North America. These new subjects, especially Indians, quickly found themselves at odds with the Anglo-American colonists of the long-established British settlements along the eastern seaboard. In order to manage this vast, heterogeneous domain, George III issued a Royal Proclamation on October 7, 1763. This proclamation can be read as a sequel to the Peace of Paris. It called for the creation of new British colonies in Quebec, the Floridas, and Grenada and forbade Anglo-Americans from encroaching on Indian lands west of the Appalachian Mountains.*

Whereas we have taken into our royal consideration the extensive and valuable acquisitions in America, secured to our crown by the late definitive treaty of peace, concluded at Paris the 10th day of February last; and being desirous that all our loving subjects, as well of our Kingdom as of our colonies in America, may avail themselves, with all convenient speed, of the great benefits and advantages which must accrue therefrom to their commerce, manufactures, and navigation; we have thought fit, with the advice of our privy council, to issue this our royal proclamation, hereby to publish and declare to all our loving subjects, that we have, with the advice of our said privy council, granted our letters patent, under our great seal of Great Britain, to erect within the countries and islands, ceded and confirmed to us by the said treaty, four distinct and separate governments, stiled and called by the names of Quebec, East Florida, West Florida and Grenada...

And whereas we are desirous, upon all occasions, to testify our royal sense and approbation of the conduct and bravery of the officers and soldiers of our armies, and to reward the same, we do hereby command and impower our governors of our said three new colonies, and other our governors of our several provinces on the continent of North America, to grant, without fee or reward, to such reduced officers as have served in North America during the late war, and are actually residing there, and shall personally apply for the same, the following quantities of land, subject, at the expiration of ten years, to the same quit-rents as other lands are subject to in the province within which they are granted, as also subject to the same conditions of cultivation and improvement; viz.

> To every person having the rank of a field officer, 5000 acres.
> To every captain, 3000 acres.
> To every subaltern or staff officer, 2000 acres.
> To every non-commission officer, 200 acres.
> To every private man, 50 acres...

And whereas it is just and reasonable, and essential to our interest, and the security of our colonies, that the several nations or tribes of Indians, with whom we are connected, and who live under our protection, should not be molested or disturbed in the possession of such parts of our dominions and territories as, not having been ceded to, or purchased by us, are reserved to them, or any of them, as their hunting grounds; we do therefore, with the advice of our privy council, declare it to be our royal will and pleasure, that no governor or commander in chief, in any of our colonies of Quebec, East Florida, or West Florida, do presume, upon any pretence whatever, to grant warrants of survey, or pass any patents for lands beyond the bounds of their respective governments, as described in their commissions; as also that no governor or commander in chief of any of our other colonies or plantations in America, do presume for the present, and until our further pleasure be known, to grant warrant of survey, or pass patents for any lands beyond the heads or sources of any of the rivers which fall into the Atlantic Ocean from the west and north west; or upon any lands whatever, which not having been ceded to, or purchased by us, as aforesaid, are reserved to the said Indians, or any of them...

[A]nd we do hereby strictly forbid, on pain of our displeasure, all our loving subjects from making any purchases or settlements whatever, or taking possession of any of the lands above reserved. without our especial leave and licence for that purpose first obtained.

And we do further strictly enjoin and require all persons whatever, who have either wilfully or inadvertently seated themselves upon any lands within the countries above described, or upon any other lands, which not having been ceded to, or purchased by us, are still reserved to the said Indians as aforesaid, forthwith to remove themselves from such settlements.

And whereas great frauds and abuses have been committed in the purchasing lands of the Indians, to the great prejudice of our interests, and to the great dissatisfaction of the said Indians: in order therefore to prevent such irregularities for the future, and to the end that the Indians may be convinced of our justice and determined resolution to remove all reasonable cause of discontent, we do, with the advice of our privy council, strictly enjoin and require, that no private person do presume to make any purchase from the said Indians of any lands reserved to the said Indians within those parts of our colonies where we have thought proper to allow settlement; but that if at any time any of the said Indians should be inclined to dispose of the said lands, the same shall be purchased only for us, in our name, at some public meeting or assembly of the said Indians, to be held for that purpose by the governor or commander in chief of our colony respectively within which they shall lie: and in case they shall lie within the limits of any proprietaries, conformable to such directions and instructions as we or they shall think proper to give for that purpose: and we do, by the advice of our privy council, declare and enjoin, that the trade with the said Indians shall be free and open to all our subjects whatever, provided that every person who may incline to trade with the said Indians, do take out a licence for carrying on such trade, from the governor or commander in chief of any of our colonies respectively, where such person shall reside, and also give security to observe such regulations as we shall at any time think fit, by ourselves or by our commissaries, to be appointed for this purpose, to direct and appoint for the benefit of the said trade…

## Notes

1. "William and Mary, 1688: An Act declareing the Rights and Liberties of the Subject and Setleing the Succession of the Crowne. [Chapter II. Rot. Parl. pt. 3. nu. 1.]," *Statutes of the Realm: Volume 6: 1685–94* (1819), 142–145. This document has been edited for length. The full version can be found at the book's website (http://www.routledge.com/textbooks/revolutionaryamerica/).
2. Benjamin Franklin, *Observations On the late and present Conduct of the French, with Regard to their Encroachments upon the British Colonies in North America....To which is added, wrote by another Hand; Observations concerning the Increase of Mankind, Peopling of Countries, &c* (Boston: S. Kneeland, 1755), 2–8, 10–15. This document has been edited for length. The full version can be found at the book's website (http://www.routledge.com/textbooks/revolutionaryamerica/).
3. Robert Beverley, *The history of the Present State of Virginia, in four parts by a Native and Inhabitant of the Place*, 2nd edition (London: F. Fayram, J. Clarke and T. Bickerton, 1722), 235–239, originally published by R. Parker in London in 1705.
4. *Virginia Gazette*, Williamsburg, July 3, 1752; *Virginia Gazette*, Williamsburg, April 11, 1766.

5. Benjamin Franklin, "Plan of a proposed Union of the several Colonies of Massachusett's Bay, New Hampshire, Connecticut, Rhode Island, New York, New Jersey, Pennsylvania, Maryland, Virginia, North Carolina, and South Carolina for their mutual Defence and Security, and for extending the British Settlements in North America," in Leonard W. Labaree and Whitfield J. Bell, Jr. (eds.), *The Papers of Benjamin Franklin*, Vol. 5 (New Haven, CT: Yale University Press, 1962), 387–392.
6. Benjamin Franklin, "Join or Die," *The Pennsylvania Gazette*, May 9, 1754. Available from Library of Congress, Prints and Photographs Division, Washington, DC.
7. *The Definitive Treaty of Peace and Friendship between his Britannick Majesty, the Most Christian King, and the King of Spain. Concluded at Paris, the 10th Day of February 1763* (Charleston, SC: Robert Wells, 1763), 3–7. This document has been edited for length. The full version can be found at the book's website (http://www.routledge.com/textbooks/revolutionaryamerica/).
8. "By the King. A Proclamation, October 7, 1763," in *The Annual Register, or a View of the History, Politics and Literature, For the Year 1763* (London: R. & J. Dodsley, 1764), 208–213. This document has been edited for length. The full version can be found at the book's website (http://www.routledge.com/textbooks/revolutionaryamerica/).

# CHAPTER 3

# The Imperial Crisis

## Introduction

In the decade between the adoption of the Stamp Act on March 22, 1765, and the outbreak of the War of Independence on April 19, 1775, relations between Parliament and Britain's North American colonies underwent a profound change. Faced with mounting debts and a desire to compel Americans to contribute to their own defense, successive British governments sought an effective and acceptable means to tax Americans. In so doing they inadvertently called into question the political and constitutional relationship between the colonies and Britain. The dispute began with the Stamp Act (document 1), the first effort by Parliament to levy a direct internal tax on its overseas colonies. The act encouraged the American colonists to question their constitutional relationship with Britain both as individual colonies (document 2) and collectively (document 3). The act was unpopular in America and engendered popular protests, boycotts, and riots (documents 4 and 5). The protests were so widespread and effective that it was impossible to enforce the Stamp Tax. In early 1766 Parliament considered how to address the impasse—Parliament had adopted a tax and its colonists refused to pay it. Faced with colonial intransigence (document 6), Parliament repealed the act (document 7). It sought to preserve its right to tax the colonies in the future by adopting the Declaratory Act (document 8) which asserted its right to legislate for the colonies.

The Stamp Act crisis and its aftermath was perhaps *the* crucial moment in the imperial crisis. Notwithstanding the Declaratory Act, Parliament had ceded its authority in the face of the colonial resistance. For much of the next decade, as British-American relations deteriorated, Parliament sought to reassert and re-establish its authority in the face of increased colonial resistance. The disputes between the two sides became increasingly violent, as in the "Boston

Massacre" of March 5, 1770 (documents 9 and 10). With each phase of the crisis the Americans sought to define their constitutional relationship with Britain. The Declaration of Rights and Grievances (document 11) adopted by the First Continental Congress on October 14, 1774, asserted that Parliament had no authority over the colonies except in the case of trade legislation, and this was subject to colonial consent and could only be used to regulate trade, not to raise revenue. Americans would govern themselves with the approval of the King. That this was considered a compromise position in 1774 reveals how far the colonists had come in their thinking since 1765—compare the Declaration of Rights and Grievances with the resolutions of the Stamp Act Congress (document 4). Having identified their grievances and articulated what they believed to be their constitutional position, the colonists were not, yet, prepared for armed resistance or independence. They sought redress of their grievances and to redefine their relationship *within* the British Empire. In 1774 they believed that this could be achieved through economic coercion and sought to achieve this through non-importation agreements (document 12).

## 1.   The Stamp Act, March 22, 1765[1]

*Prime Minister George Grenville proposed the Stamp Act—which levied a tax on a wide range of items: including wills, deeds, diplomas, almanacs, bills, bonds, newspapers, and playing cards—with the intention of raising revenue in the American colonies and asserting parliamentary authority over the colonies. The Act, which levied an internal tax on overseas colonies for the first time, passed by a wide margin in March 1765. Under its terms, the Act, which would be implemented by specially appointed tax officers, would take effect from November 1, 1765.*

An Act for granting and applying certain Stamp Duties, and other Duties, in the *British* Colonies and Plantations in *America*, towards further defraying the Expences of defending, protecting, and securing the same; and for amending such Parts of the several Acts of Parliament relating to the Trade and Revenues of the said Colonies and Plantations, as direct the Manner of determining and recovering the Penalties and Forfeitures therein mentioned.

WHEREAS by an Act made in the last Session of Parliament, several Duties were granted, continued, and appropriated, towards defraying the Expences of defending, protecting, and securing, the *British* colonies and *plantations* in America: And whereas it is just and necessary, that Provision be made for raising a further Revenue within Your Majesty's Dominions in *America*, towards defraying the said Expences: We, Your Majesty's most dutiful and loyal Subjects, the commons of *Great Britain* in Parliament assembled, have therefore resolved to give and grant unto Your Majesty the several Rates and Duties herein after mentioned; and do most humbly beseech Your Majesty that it may be enacted, and be it enacted by the King's most Excellent Majesty, by and with the Advice and Consent of the Lords Spiritual and Temporal, and Commons, in this present Parliament assembled, and by the Authority of the same, That from and after the first Day of November, One thousand seven hundred and sixty five, there shall be raised, levied, collected, and paid unto His Majesty, His Heirs, and Successors, throughout the Colonies and Plantations in America which now are, or hereafter may be, under the Dominion of His Majesty, His Heirs and Successors,

For every Skin or Piece of Vellum or Parchment, or Sheet or Piece of Paper, on which shall be ingrossed, written or printed, any Declaration, Plea, Replication, Rejoinder, Demurrer, or other Pleading, or any Copy thereof, in any Court of Law within the British Colonies and Plantations in America, a Stamp Duty of Three Pence...

VIII. Provided always, That nothing in this act contained shall extend to charge with any Duty, any Deed, or other Instrument, which shall be made between any Indian Nation and the Governor, Proprietor of any Colony, Lieutenant Governor, or Commander in Chief, alone, or in Conjunction with any other Person or Persons, or with any Council, or any Council and Assembly of any of the said Colonies or Plantations, for or relating to the granting, surrendering, or conveying, any Lands belonging to such Nation, to, for, or on Behalf of His Majesty, or any such Proprietor, or to any Colony or Plantation.

IX. Provided always, That this Act shall not extend to charge any Proclamation, Forms of Prayer and Thanksgiving, or any printed Votes of any House of Assembly in any of the said Colonies and Plantations, with any of the said Duties on Pamphlets or News Papers; or to charge any Books commonly used in any of the Schools within the said Colonies and Plantations, or any Books containing only Matters of Devotion or Piety; or to charge any single Advertisement printed by itself, or the daily Accounts or Bills of Goods imported and exported, so as such Accounts or Bills do contain no other Matters than what have been usually comprized therein; any thing herein contained to the contrary notwithstanding...

XII. And be it further enacted by the Authority aforesaid, That the Commissioners for managing the said Duties, for the time being, shall and may appoint a fit Person or Persons to attend in every court of Publick Office within the said Colonies and Plantations, to take Notice of the Vellum, Parchment, or Paper, upon which any of the Matters or Things hereby charged with a Duty shall be ingrossed, written, or printed, and of the Stamps or Marks thereupon, and of all other Matters and Things tending to secure the said Duties; and that the Judges in the several Courts, and all other Persons to whom it may appertain, shall, at the Request of any such Officer, make such Orders, and do such other Matters and Things, for the better securing of the said Duties, as shall be lawfully or reasonably desired in that Behalf: And every Commissioner and other Officer, before he proceeds to the Execution of any Part of this Act, shall take an Oath in the Words, or to the Effect following (that is to say)

I *A. B.* do swear, That I will faithfully execute the Trust reposed in me, pursuant to an Act of Parliament made in the Fifth Year of the Reign of His Majesty King *George* the Third, for granting certain Stamp Duties, and other Duties, in the *British* Colonies and Plantations in *America*, without Fraud or Concealment; and will from time to time true Account make of my Doing therein, and deliver the same to such Person or Persons as His Majesty, His Heirs, or Successors, shall appoint to receive such Account; and will take no Fee, Reward, or Profit, for the Execution or Performance of the said Trust, or the Business relating thereto, from any Person or Persons, other than such as shall be allowed by His Majesty, His Heirs, and Successors, or by some other Person or Persons under Him or Them to that Purpose authorized.

Or if any such Officer shall be of the people commonly called Quakers, he shall take a solemn Affirmation to the Effect of the said Oath; which Oath or Affirmation shall and may be administered to any such Commissioner or Commissioners by any two or more of the same Commissioners, whether they have or have not previously taken the same: And any of the said Commissioners, or any Justice of the Peace, within the kingdom of Great Britain, or any Governor, Lieutenant Governor, Judge, or other Magistrate, within the said Colonies or Plantations, shall and may administer such Oath or affirmation to any subordinate Officer.

## 2.   Virginia Resolves, May 29, 1765[2]

*The Stamp Act caused some Americans to question the nature of their relationship with Parliament. On May 29, 1786, Patrick Henry (1736–1799) proposed a series of seven resolutions to the Virginia House of Burgesses in response to the Stamp Act. Ultimately, the Burgesses only adopted the most mild of the resolutions (the first four). Many newspapers such as the Maryland Gazette published all of the resolutions including those which suggested that Virginians were not obliged to obey laws adopted without their consent. As a consequence the Virginia Resolves energized and radicalized the opposition to the Stamp Act.*

*We have had several* MS *Copies of some late* Resolves *of the House of Burgesses in* Virginia, *just before their Dissolution, desiring a Place for them in this Paper. The following are received from a Gentleman in that Colony; and, if any Error in them, the Fault lies not here.*

RESOLVES of the House of Burgesses in VIRGINIA, *June* 1765.

That the first Adventurers and Settlers of this his Majesty's Colony and Dominion of *Virginia*, brought with them, and transmitted to their Posterity, and all other his Majesty's Subjects since inhabiting in this his Majesty's Colony, all the Liberties, Privileges, Franchises, and Immunities, that at any Time have been held, enjoyed, and possessed, by the people of *Great Britain*.

That by Two Royal Charters, granted by King *James* the First, the Colonies

aforesaid are Declared Entitled, to all Liberties, Privileges and ]
Denizens and Natural Subjects (to all Intents and Purposes) as if
Abiding and Born within the Realm of *England*.

That the Taxation of the People by Themselves, or by Pers
Themselves to Represent them, who can only know what Taxes th
able to bear, or the easiest Method of Raising them, and must themselves be
affected by every Tax laid on the People, is the only Security against a Burthensome Taxation; and the Distinguishing Characteristic of *British* FREEDOM;
and, without which, the ancient Constitution cannot exist.

That his Majesty's Liege People of this his most Ancient and Loyal Colony,
have, without Interruption, the inestimable Right of being Governed by such
Laws, respecting their internal Polity and Taxation, as are derived from their own
Consent, with the Approbation of their Sovereign, or his Substitute; which Right
hath never been Forfeited, or Yielded up, but hath been constantly recognized
by the Kings and People of *Great Britain*.

*Resolved therefore*, That the General Assembly of this Colony, with the Consent
of his Majesty, or his Substitute, HAVE the Sole Right and Authority to lay Taxes
and Impositions upon It's Inhabitants: And, That every Attempt to vest such
Authority in any other Person or Persons whatsoever, has a Manifest Tendency
to Destroy AMERICAN FREEDOM.

That His Majesty's Liege People, Inhabitants of this Colony, are not bound
to yield Obedience to any Law or Ordinance whatsoever, designed to impose
any Taxation upon them, other than the Laws or Ordinances of the General
Assembly aforesaid.

That any Person who shall, by Speaking, or Writing, assert or maintain, That
any Person or Persons, other than the General Assembly of this Colony, with
such Consent as aforesaid, have any Right or Authority to lay or impose any Tax
whatever on the Inhabitants thereof, shall be Deemed AN ENEMY TO THIS
HIS MAJESTY'S COLONY.

### 3. The Stamp Act Congress Asserts American Rights and Grievances, October 19, 1765[3]

*The Stamp Act Congress, consisting of twenty-seven delegates from nine colonies
met in New York City during the first half of October 1765. The delegates drafted a
set of fourteen resolutions as a colonial response to the Stamp Act and the constitutional relationship between the colonies and Parliament. The Congress advanced
ideological and economic arguments in opposition to the Stamp Act, asserting that
Parliament did not have the authority to tax the colonies in such a manner and that
it did not make economic sense for either the colonies or Britain. At the heart of the
resolutions was a contradiction, as the Congress asserted that the colonists were loyal
British subjects who owed allegiance to the King and to Parliament, yet it denied
that Parliament had the right to exercise practical authority over the colonies.*

The Members of this Congress, sincerely devoted, with the warmest Sentiments of Affection and Duty to his Majesty's Person and Government, inviolably attached to the present happy Establishment of the Protestant Succession, and with Minds deeply impressed by a Sense of the present and impending Misfortunes of the *British* Colonies on this Continent; having considered as maturely as Time will permit, the Circumstances of the said Colonies, esteem it our indispensable Duty, to make the following Declarations of our humble Opinion, respecting the most Essential Rights and Liberties of the Colonists, and of the Grievances under which they labour, by Reason of several late Acts of Parliament.

I. That his Majesty's Subjects in these Colonies, owe the same Allegiance to the Crown of *Great-Britain*, that is owing from his Subjects born within the Realm, and all due Subordination to that August Body the Parliament of *Great-Britain*.

II. That his Majesty's Liege Subjects in these Colonies, are entitled to all the inherent Rights and Liberties of his Natural born Subjects, within the Kingdom of *Great-Britain*.

III. That it is inseparably essential to the Freedom of a People, and the undoubted Right of *Englishmen*, that no Taxes be imposed on them, but with their own Consent, given personally, or by their Representatives.

IV. That the People of these Colonies are not, and from their local Circumstances cannot be, Represented in the House of Commons in *Great-Britain*.

V. That the only Representatives of the People of these Colonies, are Persons chosen therein by themselves, and that no Taxes ever have been, or can be Constitutionally imposed on them, but by their respective Legislature.

VI. That all Supplies to the Crown, being free Gifts of the People, it is unreasonable and inconsistent with the Principles and Spirit of the *British* Constitution, for the People of *Great-Britain*, to grant to his Majesty the Property of the Colonists.

VII. That Trial by Jury, is the inherent and invaluable Right of every *British* Subject in these Colonies.

VIII. That the late Act of Parliament, entitled, *An Act for granting and applying certain Stamp Duties, and other Duties, in the* British *Colonies and Plantations in* America, &c. by imposing Taxes on the Inhabitants of these Colonies, and the said Act, and several other Acts, by extending the Jurisdiction of the Courts of Admiralty beyond its ancient Limits, have a manifest Tendency to subvert the Rights and Liberties of the Colonists.

IX. That the Duties imposed by several late Acts of Parliament, from the peculiar Circumstances of these Colonies, will be extremely Burthensome and Grievous; and from the scarcity of Specie, the Payment of them absolutely impracticable.

X. That as the Profits of the Trade of these Colonies ultimately center in *Great-Britain*, to pay for the Manufactures which they are obliged to take from thence, they eventually contribute very largely to all Supplies granted there to the Crown.

XI. That the Restrictions imposed by several late Acts of Parliament, on the Trade of these Colonies, will render them unable to purchase the Manufactures of *Great-Britain*.

XII. That the Increase, Prosperity, and Happiness of these Colonies, depend on the full and free Enjoyment of their Rights and Liberties, and an Intercourse with *Great-Britain* mutually Affectionate and Advantageous.

XIII. That it is the Right of the *British* Subjects in these Colonies, to Petition the King, or either House of Parliament.

*Lastly*, That it is the indispensable Duty of these Colonies, to the best of Sovereigns, to the Mother Country, and to themselves, to endeavour by a loyal and dutiful Address to his Majesty, and humble Applications to both Houses of Parliament, to procure the Repeal of the Act for granting and applying certain Stamp Duties, of all Clauses of any other Acts of Parliament, whereby the Jurisdiction of the Admiralty is extended as aforesaid, and of the other late Acts for the Restriction of *American* Commerce.

## 4. The Death of Liberty, October 31, 1765[4]

*Despite American resolutions and street protests, it seemed that the Stamp Act would take effect on November 1, 1765. In anticipation of the Act coming into force, William Bradford, the publisher of the* Pennsylvania Journal, *announced the suspension of the publication of his paper on October 31. He made the announce-*

**Figure 3.1** The Stamp Act, 1765. Courtesy of the Granger Collection, New York.

*ment in the form of a death announcement which heralded the death of liberty
in the colonies. The Stamp Act did not take effect in a meaningful way and the
suspension of the* Pennsylvania Journal *proved to be temporary.*

## 5.   New York Stamp Act Riot[5]

*Popular protests throughout the colonies rendered the Stamp Act a dead letter.
This account from the* Pennsylvania Gazette *describes a demonstration that took
place in New York City on November 1, 1765—the day the Stamp Act should have
come into effect. A crowd attacked the home of Lieutenant Governor Cadwallader
Colden who was meant to be New York's stamp distributor. The second, brief, note
reports that Boston printers intended to publish their newspapers in defiance of
the Stamp Act.*

The late extraordinary and unprecedented preparations in Fort George, and the
securing of the stamped paper in that garrison, having greatly alarmed and dis-
pleased the inhabitants of this city, a vast number of them assembled last Friday
evening in the commons, from whence they marched down the Fly (preceded
by a number of lights) and having stopped a few minutes at the Coffee-house,
proceeded to the Fort walls, where they broke open the stable of the L--------t
G-------r, took out his coach, and after carrying the same through the principal
streets of the city, in triumph marched to the commons, where a gallows was
erected; on one end of which was suspended the effigy of the person whose property the coach was; in his right hand he held a stamped bill of lading, and on his
breast was affixed a paper with the following inscription, *The rebel drummer in
the year* 1715: At his back was fixed a drum, the badge of his profession; at the
other end of the gallows hung the figure of the devil, a proper companion for the
other, as 'tis supposed it was intirely at his instigation he acted: After they had
hung there a considerable time, they carried the effigies, with the gallows intire,
being preceded by the coach, in a grand procession to the gate of the Fort, where
it remained for some time, from whence it was removed to the Bowling green,
under the muzzles of the Fort guns, where a bon-fire was immediately made,
and the drummer, devil, coach, &c. were consumed amidst the acclamations of
some thousand spectators, and we make no doubt, but the L--------t G-------r,
and his friends, had the mortification of viewing the whole proceeding from the
ramparts of the Fort: But the business of the night not being yet concluded, the
whole body proceeded with the greatest decency and good order to Vaux-Hall,
the House of M-----r J----s, who, it was reported, was a friend to the stamp act,
and had been over officious in his duty, from whence they took every individual
article, to a very considerable amount; and having made another bon-fire, the
whole was consumed in the flames, to the great satisfaction of every person present; after which they dispersed, and every man went to his respective habitation.
The whole affair was conducted with such decorum, that not the least accident

happened. The next evening another very considerable body assembled at the same place, having been informed that the L- ---t G------r had qualified himself for the distribution of the stamped paper, were determined to march to the Fort, in order to insist upon his delivering it into their hands, or to declare that he would not undertake to distribute the same; but before this resolution could be executed, the minds of the people were eased by the L---t G---r's sending the following declaration from the Fort, viz.

THE Lieutenant Governor declares he will do nothing in relation to the stamps, but leave it to Sir Henry Moore, to do as he pleases on his arrival.

...

We have certain information from Boston, that the printers there intend to continue their papers, and to risk the penalties—and that if any of them were to stop on account of the stamp act, their offices would be in danger from the enraged people.

### 6. Examination of Benjamin Franklin Before the House of Commons, 1766[6]

*In January and February of 1766 Parliament considered its response to the wide-spread American opposition to the Stamp Act. In February, Benjamin Franklin (1706–1790), who represented the interests of several colonies in London, was invited to testify before the House of Commons on the American response to the Stamp Act. Franklin went to great lengths to present the Americans as loyal subjects whose response to a pernicious and dangerous tax was reasonable.*

Q. What is your name, and place of abode?

A. Franklin, of Philadelphia.

Q. Do the Americans pay any considerable taxes among themselves?

A. Certainly many, and very heavy taxes.

Q. What are the present taxes in Pennsylvania, laid by the laws of the colony?

A. There are taxes on all estates real and personal, a poll tax, a tax on all offices, professions, trades and businesses, according to their profits; an excise on all wine, rum, and other spirits; and a duty of Ten Pounds per head on all Negroes imported, with some other duties.

Q. For what purposes are those taxes laid?

A. For the support of the civil and military establishments of the country, and to discharge the heavy debt contracted in the last war...

Q. Are not the Colonies, from their circumstances, very able to pay the stamp duty?

A. In my opinion, there is not gold and silver enough in the Colonies to pay the stamp duty for one year.

Q. Don't you know that the money arising from the stamps was all to be laid out in America?

A. I know it is appropriated by the act to the American service; but it will be spent in the conquered Colonies, where the soldiers are, not in the Colonies that pay it.

Q. Is there not a ballance of trade due from the Colonies where the troops are posted, that will bring back the money to the old colonies?

A. I think not. I believe very little would come back. I know of no trade likely to bring it back. I think it would come from the Colonies where it was spent directly to England; for I have always observed, that in every Colony the more plenty the means of remittance to England, the more goods are sent for, and the more trade with England carried on…

Q. Do you think it right that America should be protected by this country, and pay no part of the expence?

A. That is not the case. The Colonies raised, cloathed and paid, during the last war, near 25000 men, and spent many millions.

Q. Were you not reimbursed by parliament?

A. We were only reimbursed what, in your opinion, we had advanced beyond our proportion, or beyond what might reasonably be expected from us; and it was a very small part of what we spent. Pennsylvania, in particular, disbursed about 500,000 Pounds, and the reimbursements, in the whole, did not exceed 60,000 Pounds…

Q. Do not you think the people of America would submit to pay the stamp duty, if it was moderated?

A. No, never, unless compelled by force of arms…

Q. What was the temper of America towards Great-Britain before the year 1763?

A. The best in the world. They submitted willingly to the government of the Crown, and paid, in all their courts, obedience to acts of parliament. Numerous as the people are in the several old provinces, they cost you nothing in forts, citadels, garrisons or armies, to keep them in subjection. They were governed by this country at the expence only of a little pen, ink and paper. They were led by a thread. They had not only a respect, but an affection, for Great-Britain, for its laws, its customs and manners, and even a fondness for its fashions, that greatly increased the commerce. Natives of Britain were always treated with particular regard; to be an Old England-man was, of itself, a character of some respect, and gave a kind of rank among us.

Q. And what is their temper now?

A. O, very much altered.

Q. Did you ever hear the authority of parliament to make laws for America questioned till lately?

A. The authority of parliament was allowed to be valid in all laws, except such as should lay internal taxes. It was never disputed in laying duties to regulate commerce…

Q. In what light did the people of America use to consider the parliament of Great-Britain?

A. They considered the parliament as the great bulwark and security of their liberties and privileges, and always spoke of it with the utmost respect and veneration. Arbitrary ministers, they thought, might possibly, at times, attempt to oppress them; but they relied on it, that the parliament, on application, would always give redress…

Q. And have they not still the same respect for parliament?

A. No; it is greatly lessened.

Q. To what causes is that owing?

A. To a concurrence of causes; the restraints lately laid on their trade, by which the bringing of foreign gold and silver into the Colonies was prevented; the prohibition of making paper money among themselves; and then demanding a new and heavy tax by stamps; taking away, at the same time, trials by juries, and refusing to receive and hear their humble petitions.

Q. Don't you think they would submit to the stamp-act, if it was modified, the obnoxious parts taken out, and the duty reduced to some particulars, of small moment?

A. No; they will never submit to it…

Q. You say the Colonies have always submitted to external taxes, and object to the right of parliament only in laying internal taxes; now can you shew that there is any kind of difference between the two taxes to the Colony on which they may be laid?

A. I think the difference is very great. An external tax is a duty laid on commodities imported; that duty is added to the first cost, and other charges on the commodity, and when it is offered to sale, makes a part of the price. If the people do not like it at that price, they refuse it; they are not obliged to pay it. But an internal tax is forced from the people without their consent, if not laid by their own representatives. The stamp-act says, we shall have no commerce, make no exchange of property with each other, neither purchase nor grant, nor recover debts; we shall neither marry, nor make our wills, unless we pay such and such sums, and thus it is intended to extort our money from us, or ruin us by the consequences of refusing to pay it…

Q. Can any thing less than a military force carry the stamp-act into execution?

A. I do not see how a military force can be applied to that purpose.

Q. Why may it not?

A. Suppose a military force sent into America, they will find nobody in arms; what are they then to do? They cannot force a man to take stamps who chooses to do without them. They will not find a rebellion; they may indeed make one.

Q. If the act is not repealed, what do you think will be the consequences?

A. A total loss of the respect and affection the people of America bear to this country, and of all the commerce that depends on that respect and affection.

Q. How can the commerce be affected?

A. You will find, that if the act is not repealed, they will take very little of your manufactures in a short time.

Q. Is it in their power to do without them?

A. I think they may very well do without them.

Q. Is it their interest not to take them?

A. The goods they take from Britain are either necessaries, mere conveniences, or superfluities. The first, as cloth, &c. with a little industry they can make at home; the second they can do without, till they are able to provide them among themselves; and the last, which are much the greatest part, they will strike off immediately. They are mere articles of fashion, purchased and consumed, because the fashion in a respected country, but will now be detested and rejected. The people have already struck off, by general agreement, the use of all goods fashionable in mournings, and many thousand pounds worth are sent back as unsaleable.

Q. Is it their interest to make cloth at home?

A. I think they may at present get it cheaper from Britain, I mean of the same fineness and neatness of workmanship; but when one considers other circumstances, the restraints on their trade, and the difficulty of making remittances, it is their interest to make every thing.

Q. Suppose an act of internal regulations, connected with a tax, how would they receive it?

A. I think it would be objected to.

Q. Then no regulation with a tax would be submitted to?

A. Their opinion is, that when aids to the Crown are wanted, they are to be asked of the several assemblies, according to the old established usage, who will, as they always have done, grant them freely. And that their money ought not to be given away without their consent, by persons at a distance, unacquainted with their circumstances and abilities. The granting aids to the Crown, is the only means they have of recommending themselves to their sovereign, and they think it extremely hard and unjust, that a body of men, in which they have no representatives, should make a merit to itself of giving and granting what is not its own, but theirs, and deprive them of a right they esteem of the utmost value and importance, as it is the security of all their other rights...

Q. You say they do not object to the right of parliament in laying duties on goods to be paid on their importation; now, is there any kind of difference between a duty on the importation of goods, and an excise on their consumption?

A. Yes; a very material one; an excise, for the reasons I have just mentioned, they think you can have no right to lay within their country. But the sea is yours; you maintain, by your fleets, the safety of navigation in it; and keep it clear of pirates; you may have therefore a natural and equitable right to some toll or duty on merchandizes carried through that part of your dominions, towards defraying the expence you are at in ships to maintain the safety of that carriage...

Q.  If the act should be repealed, and the legislature should shew its resentment to the opposers of the stamp-act, would the Colonies acquiesce in the authority of the legislature? What is your opinion they would do?

A.  I don't doubt at all, that if the legislature repeal the stamp-act, the Colonies will acquiesce in the authority.

Q.  But if the legislature should think fit to ascertain its right to lay taxes, by any act laying a small tax, contrary to their opinion, would they submit to pay the tax?

A.  The proceedings of the people in America have been considered too much together. The proceedings of the assemblies have been very different from those of the mobs, and should be distinguished, as having no connection with each other. The assemblies have only peaceably resolved what they take to be their rights; they have taken no measures for opposition by force; they have not built a fort, raised a man, or provided a grain of ammunition, in order to such opposition. The ringleaders of riots they think ought to be punished; they would punish them themselves, if they could. Every sober sensible man would wish to see rioters punished; as otherwise peaceable people have no security of person or estate. But as to any internal tax, how small soever, laid by the legislature here on the people there, while they have no representatives in this legislature, I think it will never be submitted to. They will oppose it to the last. They do not consider it as at all necessary for you to raise money on them by your taxes, because they are, and always have been, ready to raise money by taxes among themselves, and to grant large sums, equal to their abilities, upon requisition from the Crown. They have not only granted equal to their abilities, but, during all the last war, they granted far beyond their abilities, and beyond their proportion with this country, you yourselves being judges, to the amount of many hundred thousand pounds, and this they did freely and readily, only on a sort of promise from the secretary of state, that it should be recommended to parliament to make them compensation. It was accordingly recommended to parliament, in the most honourable manner, for them. America has been greatly misrepresented and abused here, in papers, and pamphlets, and speeches, as ungrateful, and unreasonable, and unjust, in having put this nation to immense expence for their defence, and refusing to bear any part of that expence. The Colonies raised, paid and clothed, near 25000 men during the last war, a number equal to those sent from Britain, and far beyond their proportion; they went deeply into debt in doing this, and all their taxes and estates are mortgaged, for many years to come, for discharging that debt. Government here was at that time very sensible of this. The Colonies were recommended to parliament. Every year the King sent down to the house a written message to this purpose, That his

Majesty, being highly sensible of the zeal and vigour with which his faithful subjects in North-America had exerted themselves, in defence of his Majesty's just rights and possessions, recommended it to the house to take the same into consideration, and enable him to give them a proper compensation. You will find those messages on your own journals every year of the war to the very last, and you did accordingly give 200,000 Pounds annually to the Crown, to be distributed in such compensation to the Colonies. This is the strongest of all proofs that the Colonies, far from being unwilling to bear a share of the burthen, did exceed their proportion; for if they had done less, or had only equalled their proportion, there would have been no room or reason for compensation. Indeed the sums reimbursed them, were by no means adequate to the expence they incurred beyond their proportion; but they never murmured at that; they esteemed their Sovereign's approbation of their zeal and fidelity, and the approbation of this house, far beyond any other kind of compensation; therefore there was no occasion for this act, to force money from a willing people; they had not refused giving money for the purposes of the act; no requisition had been made; they were always willing and ready to do what could reasonably be expected from them, and in this light they wish to be considered.

Q. But suppose Great-Britain should be engaged in a war in Europe, would North-America contribute to the support of it?

A. I do think they would, as far as their circumstances would permit. They consider themselves as a part of the British empire, and as having one common interest with it; they may be looked on here as foreigners, but they do not consider themselves as such. They are zealous for the honour and prosperity of this nation, and, while they are well used, will always be ready to support it, as far as their little power goes…The trade with the Indians, though carried on in America, is not an American interest. The people of America are chiefly farmers and planters; scarce any thing that they raise or produce is an article of commerce with the Indians. The Indian trade is a British interest; it is carried on with British manufactures, for the profit of British merchants and manufacturers; therefore the war, as it commenced for the defence of territories of the Crown, the property of no American, and for the defence of a trade purely British, was really a British war—and yet the people of America made no scruple of contributing their utmost towards carrying it on, and bringing it to a happy conclusion.

Q. Do you think then that the taking possession of the King's territorial rights, and strengthening the frontiers, is not an American interest?

A. Not particularly, but conjointly a British and an American interest…

Q. Is it not necessary to send troops to America, to defend the Americans against the Indians?

A. No, by no means; it never was necessary. They defended themselves when they were but an handful, and the Indians much more numerous. They continually gained ground, and have driven the Indians over the mountains, without any troops sent to their assistance from this country. And can it be thought necessary now to send troops for their defence from those diminished Indian tribes, when the Colonies are become so populous, and so strong? There is not the least occasion for it; they are very able to defend themselves…

Q. What used to be the pride of the Americans?
A. To indulge in the fashions and manufactures of Great-Britain.
Q. What is now their pride?
A. To wear their old cloaths over again, till they can make new ones.

## 7.  Parliament Repeals the Stamp Act, March 18, 1766[7]

*As a revenue-raising measure the Stamp Act had been a disaster. In March 1766 Parliament recognized the inevitable and voted to repeal the act.*

WHEREAS an Act was passed in the last session of Parliament intitailed, *An Act for granting and applying certain Stamp Duties, and other Duties in the* British *Colonies and Plantations in* America, *towards further defraying the Expenses of defending, protecting, and securing the same; and for amending such Parts of the several Acts of Parliament relating to the Trade and Revenues of the said Colonies and Plantations, as direct the Manner of determining and recovering the Penalties and Forfeitures therein mentioned*: And whereas the Continuance of the said Act would be attended with many Inconveniencies, and may be productive of Consequences greatly detrimental to the Commercial Interests of these Kingdoms; May it therefore please Your most Excellent Majesty, that it may be enacted; and be it enacted by the King's most Excellent Majesty, by and with the Advice and Consent of the Lords Spiritual and Temporal, and Commons, in this present Parliament assembled, and by the Authority of the same, That from and after the first Day of May, One thousand seven hundred and sixty-six, the above-mentioned Act, and the several Matters and Things therein contained, shall be, and is and are hereby repealed and made void to all intents and Purposes whatsoever.

## 8.  Parliament Declares Its Authority, March 18, 1766[8]

*The Stamp Act was more than a revenue-raising tax. The measure was meant to assert Parliamentary control over the colonies. With its repeal in the face of sustained, and often illegal, colonial resistance, Parliament was eager to assert its authority even as it repealed the tax. As a consequence it adopted the Declaratory Act which asserted that the colonies were subordinate to the Parliament.*

An Act for the better securing the Dependency of His Majesty's Dominions in *America* upon the Crown and Parliament of *Great Britain*.

WHEREAS several of the Houses of Representatives in His Majesty's Colonies and Plantations in *America*, have of late, against Law, claimed to themselves, or to the General Assemblies of the same, the sole and exclusive Right of imposing Duties and Taxes upon His Majesty's Subjects in the said Colonies and Plantations; and have, in pursuance of such Claim, passed certain Votes, Resolutions, and Orders, derogatory to the Legislative Authority of Parliament;, and inconsistent with the Dependency Of the said Colonies and Plantations upon the Crown of *Great Britain*: May it therefore please Your most Excellent Majesty, that it may be declared; and be it declared by the King's most Excellent Majesty, by and with the Advice and Consent of the Lords Spiritual and Temporal, and Commons, in this present Parliament assembled, and by the Authority of the same, That the said Colonies and Plantations in America have been, are, and of Right ought to be, subordinate unto, and dependent upon, the Imperial Crown and Parliament of Great Britain; and that the King's Majesty, by and with the Advice and Consent of the Lords Spiritual and Temporal, and Commons of Great Britain, in Parliament assembled, had, hath, and of Right ought to have, full Power and Authority to make Laws and Statutes of sufficient Force and Validity to bind the Colonies and People of America, Subjects of the Crown of Great Britain, in all Cases whatsoever,

II. And be it further declared and enacted by the Authority aforesaid, That all Resolutions, Votes, Orders, and Proceedings, in any of the said Colonies or Plantations, whereby the Power and Authority of the Parliament of Great Britain, to make Laws and Statutes as aforesaid, is denied, or drawn into Question, arc, and are hereby declared to be, utterly null and void to all Intents and Purposes whatsoever.

## 9. The Boston Massacre[9]

*On March 5, 1770, a confrontation took place in Boston between a group of civilians, mainly young men, and British soldiers who had been sent to the city to protect customs officials after the adoption of the Townshend Duties. Tensions between Bostonians and British soldiers were persistent and resulted in a number of conflicts. In the incident described here the soldiers, goaded by the civilians, fired into the crowd killing five. This incident was a turning point in British-American relations as it confirmed the belief of Patriots that the British Army was in America to take away their liberties.*

A few minutes after nine o'clock, four youths, named Edward Archbald, William Merchant, Francis Archbald, and John Leech, jun. came down Cornhill together, and separating at Doctor Loring's corner, the two former were passing the narrow alley leading to Murray's barrack, in which was a soldier brandishing a broad sword of an uncommon size against the walls, out of which he struck fire plentifully. A person of mean countenance armed with a large cudgel bore him company. Edward Archbald admonished Mr. Merchant to take care of the sword, on which the soldier turned round and struck Archbald on the arm, then pushed at Merchant and pierced thro' his cloaths inside the arm close to the arm-pit and grazed the skin. Merchant then struck the soldier with a short stick he had, & the other Person ran to the barrack & bro't with him two soldiers, one armed with a pair of tongs the other with a shovel: he with the tongs pursued Archbald back thro' the alley, collar'd and laid him over the head with the tongs. The noise bro't people together and John Hicks, a young lad, coming up, knock'd the soldier down, but let him get back up again; and more lads gathering, drove them back to the barrack, where the boys stood some time as it were to keep them in. In less than a minute 10 or 12 of them came out with drawn cutlasses, clubs and bayonets, and set upon the unarmed boys and young folks, who stood them a little while, but finding the inequality of their equipment dispersed,—On hearing the noise, one Samuel Atwood, came up to see what was the matter, and entering the alley from the dock-square, heard the latter part of the combat, and when the boys had dispersed he met the 10 or 12 soldiers aforesaid rushing down the alley towards the square, and asked them if they intended to murder people? They answered Yes, by G-d, root and branch! With that one of them struck Mr. Atwood with a club, which was repeated by another, and being unarmed he turned to go off and received a wound on the left shoulder which reached the bone and gave him much pain. Retreating a few steps, Mr. Atwood met the two officers and said, Gentlemen, what is the matter? They answered, you'll see by and by. Immediately after, those heroes appeared in the square, asking where were the boogers? where were the cowards? But notwithstanding their fierceness to naked men, one of them advanced towards a youth who had a split of a raw stave in his hand, and said damn them here is one of them; but the young man seeing a person near him with a drawn sword and good cane ready to support him, held up his stave in defiance, and they quietly passed by him up the alley by Mr. Silsby's to Kingstreet, where they attacked single and unarmed persons till they raised much clamor, and then turned down Cornhill street, insulting all they met in like manner, and pursuing some to their very doors. Thirty or forty persons, mostly lads, being by this means gathered in Kingstreet, Capt. Preston, with a party of men with charged bayonets, came from the main guard to the Commissioners house, the soldiers pushing their bayonets, crying, Make way! They took place by the Custom-house, and continuing to push to drive the people off, pricked some in several places; on which they were clamorous, and, it is said, threw snow-balls. On this, the Captain commanded them to fire, and more snow-balls coming, he again said, Damn you, Fire, be the consequence what it will! One soldier then fired, and a townsman with a cudgel struck him over the hands with such force that he dropt his firelock; and rushing forward aimed a blow at the Captain's head, which graz'd his hat and fell pretty heavy upon his arm: However, the soldiers continued the fire, successively, till 7 or 8, or as some say 11 guns were discharged.

By this fatal manœuvre, three men were laid dead on the spot, and two more struggling for life; but what shewed a degree of cruelty unknown to British troops, at least since the house of Hanover has directed their operations, was an attempt to fire upon or push with their bayonets the persons who undertook to remove the slain and wounded!

Mr. Benjamin Leigh, now undertaker in the Delph Manufactory, came up, and held some conversation with Capt. Preston, relative to his conduct in this affair, advised him to draw off his men, with which he complied.

The dead are Mr. Samuel Grey, killed on the spot, the ball entering his head and beating off a large portion of his skull.

A mulatto man, named Crispus Attucks, who was born in Framingham, but lately belonged to New-Providence and was here in order to go for North-Carolina, also killed instantly; two balls entering his breast, one of them in special goring the right lobe of the lungs, and a great part of the liver most horribly.

Mr. James Caldwell, mate of Capt. Morton's vessel, in like manner killed by two balls entering his back.

Mr. Samuel Maverick, a promising youth of 17 years of age, son of the widow Maverick, and an apprentice to Mr. Greenwood, Ivory-Turner, mortally wounded, a ball went through his belly, & was cut out at his back: He died the next morning.

A lad named Christopher Monk, about 17 years of age, an apprentice to Mr. Walker, Shipwright; wounded, a ball entered his back about 4 inches above the left kidney, near the spine, and was cut out of the breast on the same side; apprehended he will die.

A lad named David Parker, an apprentice to Mr. Eddy, the Wheelwright, wounded, a ball entered in his thigh.

## 10.   Paul Revere's Engraving of the Boston Massacre[10]

*Although most of the British soldiers involved in the shootings on March 5, 1770, were acquitted when tried for the killings, the incident was a propaganda triumph for the Sons of Liberty who labeled it "the Boston Massacre"—the name by which it is usually known. Crucial in fostering the image of the incident as a massacre was this image, produced by the prominent Boston silversmith and Patriot, Paul Revere (1734–1818). This image, which portrayed the British firing deliberately at unarmed Americans, was widely distributed and became the fixed interpretation of the incident.*

The BLOODY MASSACRE perpetrated in King— Street BOSTON on March 5th 1770 by a party of the 29th REGT

Engrav'd Printed & Sold by PAUL REVERE BOSTON

Unhappy Boston! see thy Sons deplore,
Thy hallow'd Walks besmear'd with guiltless Gore,
While faithless P—n. and his savage Bands,
With murd'rous Rancour stretch their bloody Hands;
Like fierce Barbarians grinning o'er their Prey,
Approve the Carnage, and enjoy the Day.

If scalding drops from Rage from Anguish Wrung
If speechless Sorrows lab'ring for a Tongue,
Or if a weeping World can ought appease
The plaintive Ghosts of Victims such as these;
The Patriot's copious Tears for each are shed,
A glorious Tribute which embalms the Dead.

But know Fate summons to that awful Goal,
Where Justice strips the Murd'rer of his Soul:
Should venal C—ts the scandal of the Land,
Snatch the relentless Villain from her Hand,
Keen Execrations on this Plate inscrib'd,
Shall reach a Judge who never can be brib'd.

The unhappy Sufferers were Messrs. Samᴸ Gray, Samᴸ Maverick, Jamˢ Caldwell, Crispus Attucks & Patᴸ Carr
Killed. Six wounded; two of them (Christʳ Monk & John Clark) Mortally

**Figure 3.2**  The Boston Massacre, 1770. Courtesy of the Granger Collection, New York.

## 11.   First Continental Congress, Declaration of Rights and Grievances, October 14, 1774[11]

*The First Continental Congress met in Philadelphia in September and October of 1774. On October 14 the Congress adopted this Declaration of Rights and Grievances which intended to enumerate colonial grievances, to propose a plan for the redress of those grievances, and to define the constitutional relationship between Parliament and the colonies. This declaration represented a compromise position in 1774 but is testimony to how radical the colonial position had become since 1765.*

Whereas, since the close of the last war, the British Parliament, claiming a right to bind the people of America, by statute in all cases whatsoever, hath in some acts expressly imposed taxes on them, and in others, under various pretences, but in fact for the purpose of raising a revenue, hath imposed rates and duties payable in these colonies, established a board of commissioners, with unconstitutional powers, and extended the jurisdiction of courts of Admiralty, not only for collecting the said duties, but for the trial of causes merely arising within the body of a country.

And whereas, in consequence of other statutes, judges, who before held only estates at will in their offices, have been made dependant on the Crown alone for their salaries, and standing armies kept in times of peace:

And it has lately been resolved in Parliament, that by force of a statute, made in the thirty-fifth year of the reign of king Henry the eighth, colonists may be transported to England, and tried there upon accusations for treasons, and misprisions, or concealments of treasons committed in the colonies; and by a late statute, such trials have been directed in cases therein mentioned.

And whereas, in the last session of parliament, three statutes were made; one, intituled "An act to discontinue, in such manner, and for such time as are therein mentioned, the landing and discharging, lading, or shipping of goods, wares & merchandise, at the town, and within the harbour of Boston, in the province of Massachusetts-bay, in North-America;" another, intituled "An act for the better regulating the government of the province of the Massachusetts-bay in New England;" and another, intituled "An act for the impartial administration of justice, in the cases of persons questioned for any act done by them in the execution of the law, or for the suppression of riots and tumults, in the province of the Massachusetts-bay, in New England." And another statute was then made, "for making more effectual provision for the government of the province of Quebec, &c." All which statutes are impolitic, unjust, cruel, as well as unconstitutional, and most dangerous and destructive of American rights.

And whereas, Assemblies have been frequently dissolved, contrary to the rights of the people, when they attempted to deliberate on grievances; and their dutiful, humble, loyal, & reasonable petitions to the crown for redress, have been repeatedly treated with contempt, by his majesty's ministers of state:

The good people of the several Colonies of New-hampshire, Massachusetts-bay, Rhode-island and Providence plantations, Connecticut, New-York, New-Jersey, Pennsylvania, Newcastle, Kent and Sussex on Delaware, Maryland, Virginia, North Carolina, and South Carolina, justly alarmed at these arbitrary proceedings of parliament and administration, have severally elected, constituted, and appointed deputies to meet and sit in general congress, in the city of Philadelphia, in order to obtain such establishment, as that their religion, laws, and liberties, may not be subverted:

Whereupon the deputies so appointed being now assembled, in a full and free representation of these Colonies, taking into their most serious consideration, the best means of attaining the ends aforesaid, do, in the first place, as Englishmen, their ancestors in like cases have usually done, for asserting and vindicating their rights and liberties, declare,

That the inhabitants of the English Colonies in North America, by the immutable laws of nature, the principles of the English constitution, and the several charters or compacts, have the following Rights:

*Resolved*, N.C.D.1. That they are entitled to life, liberty, & property, and they have never ceded to any sovereign power whatever, a right to dispose of either without their consent.

*Resolved*, N.C.D.2. That our ancestors, who first settled these colonies, were at the time of their emigration from the mother country, entitled to all the rights, liberties, and immunities of free and natural-born subjects, within the realm of England.

*Resolved*, N.C.D.3. That by such emigration they by no means forfeited, surrendered, or lost any of those rights, but that they were, and their descendants now are, entitled to the exercise and enjoyment of all such of them, as their local and other circumstances enable them to exercise and enjoy.

*Resolved*, 4. That the foundation of English liberty, and of all free government, is a right in the people to participate in their legislative council: and as the English colonists are not represented, and from their local and other circumstances, cannot properly be represented in the British parliament, they are entitled to a free and exclusive power of legislation in their several provincial legislatures, where their right of representation can alone be preserved, in all cases of taxation and internal polity, subject only to the negative of their sovereign, in such manner as has been heretofore used and accustomed. But, from the necessity of the case, and a regard to the mutual interest of both countries, we cheerfully consent to the operation of such acts of the British parliament, as are bona fide, restrained to the regulation of our external commerce, for the purpose of securing the commercial advantages of the whole empire to the mother country, and the commercial benefits of its respective members; excluding every idea of taxation, internal or external, for raising a revenue on the subjects in America, without their consent.

*Resolved*, N.C.D.5. That the respective colonies are entitled the common law of England, and more especially to the great and inestimable privilege of being tried by their peers of the vicinage, according to the course of that law.

*Resolved*, 6. That they are entitled to the benefit of such of the English statutes as existed at the time of their colonization; and which they have, by experience, respectively found to be applicable to their several local and other circumstances.

*Resolved*, N.C.D.7. That these, his majesty's colonies, are likewise entitled to all the immunities and privileges granted & confirmed to them by royal charters, or secured by their several codes of provincial laws.

*Resolved*, N.C.D.8. That they have a right peaceably to assemble, consider of their grievances, and petition the King; and that all prosecutions, prohibitory proclamations, and commitments for the same, are illegal.

*Resolved*, N.C.D.9. That the keeping a Standing army in these colonies, in times of peace, without the consent of the legislature of that colony, in which such army is kept, is against law.

*Resolved*, N.C.D.10. It is indispensably necessary to good government, and rendered essential by the English constitution, that the constituent branches of the legislature be independent of each other; that therefore, the exercise of legislative power in several colonies, by a council appointed, during pleasure, by the crown, is unconstitutional, dangerous, and destructive to the freedom of American legislation.

All and each of which the aforementioned deputies, in behalf of themselves and their constituents, do claim, demand, and insist on, as their indubitable rights and liberties; which cannot be legally taken from them, altered or abridged by any power whatever, without their own consent, by their representatives in their several provincial legislatures.

In the course of our inquiry, we find many infringements and violations of the foregoing rights, which, from an ardent desire, that harmony and mutual intercourse of affection and interest may be restored, we pass over for the present, and proceed to state such acts and measures as have been adopted since the last war, which demonstrate a system formed to enslave America.

*Resolved*, N.C.D. That the following acts of Parliament are infringements and violations of the rights of the colonists; and that the repeal of them is essentially necessary in order to restore harmony between Great-Britain and the American colonies, viz:

The several acts of 4 Geo. 3. ch. 15, & ch. 34.-5 Geo. 3. ch. 25.-6 Geo. 3. ch. 52.-7 Geo. 3. ch. 41, & ch. 46.-8 Geo. 3. ch. 22, which impose duties for the purpose of raising a revenue in America, extend the powers of the admiralty courts beyond their ancient limits, deprive the American subject of trial by jury, authorize the judges' certificate to indemnify the prosecutor from damages, that he might otherwise be liable to, requiring oppressive security from a claimant of ships and goods seized, before he shall be allowed to defend his property, and are subversive of American rights.

Also the 12 Geo. 3. ch. 24, entituled "An act for the better securing his Majesty's dock-yards, magazines, ships, ammunition, and stores," which declares a new offence in America, and deprives the American subject of a constitutional trial by jury of the vicinage, by authorizing the trial of any person, charged with the committing any offence described in the said act, out of the realm, to be indicted and tried for the same in any shire or county within the realm.

Also the three acts passed in the last session of parliament, for stopping the port and blocking up the harbour of Boston, for altering the charter & government of the Massachusetts-bay, and that which is entituled "An act for the better administration of Justice," &c.

Also the act passed in the same session for establishing the Roman Catholick Religion in the province of Quebec, abolishing the equitable system of English laws, and erecting a tyranny there, to the great danger, from so total a dissimilarity of Religion, law, and government of the neighbouring British colonies, by the assistance of whose blood and treasure the said country was conquered from France.

Also the act passed in the same session for the better providing suitable quarters for officers and soldiers in his Majesty's service in North-America.

Also, that the keeping a standing army in several of these colonies, in time of peace, without the consent of the legislature of that colony in which such army is kept, is against law.

To those grievous acts and measures, Americans cannot submit, but in hopes that their fellow subjects in Great-Britain will, on a revision of them, restore us to that state in which both countries found happiness and prosperity, we have for the present only resolved to pursue the following peaceable measures:

...

1st.    To enter into a non-importation, non-consumption, and non-exportation agreement or association.

2.    To prepare an address to the people of Great-Britain, and a memorial to the inhabitants of British America, &

3.    To prepare a loyal address to his Majesty; agreeable to Resolutions already entered into.


## 12.    New Hampshire Non-Importation Agreement, 1774[12]

*Congress proposed a commercial boycott, the Continental Association, as the means to seek redress for its grievances and to bring about the repeal of the Coercive Acts. Under the terms of the Continental Association, Americans should refuse to import goods from Britain and Ireland after December 1, 1774, and should cease exporting their own goods and produce after September 10, 1775. Boycotts and non-importation agreements had emerged as a crucial weapon of protest since the days of the Stamp Act and had been particularly effective in response to the Townshend Duties. This document presents a Non-Importation Agreement which was circulated in New Hamshire. By signing such agreements, colonists publicly pledged to support the protest movement and brought pressure to bear on Parliament.*

WE the Subscribers, Inhabitants of the Town of        having taken into our serious Consideration, the precarious State of the LIBERTIES of NORTH-AMERICA, and more especially the present distressed Condition of our Sister-Colony of the Massachusetts-Bay, embarrassed as it is by several Acts of the British Parliament, tending to the entire Subversion of their natural and Charter Rights; among which is the *Act for blocking up the Harbour of* BOSTON: And being fully sensible of our indispensable Duty to lay hold on every Means in our Power to preserve and recover the much injured Constitution of our Country; and conscious at the same Time of no Alternative between the Horrors of Slavery, or the Carnage and Desolation of a civil War, but a Suspension of all commercial Intercourse with the Island of Great-Britain, DO, in the Presence of GOD, solemnly and in good Faith, covenant and engage with each other.

1. That from henceforth we will suspend all commercial Intercourse with the said Island of Great-Britain, until the Parliament shall cease to enact Laws imposing Taxes upon the Colonies, without their Consent, or until the pretended Right of Taxing is dripped. And

2. That there may be less Temptation to others to continue in the said now dangerous Commerce; and in order to promote Industry, Oeconomy, Arts and Manufactures among ourselves, which are of the last Importance to the Welfare and Well-being of a Community; we do, in like Manner, solemnly covenant that we will not buy, purchase or consume, or suffer any Person, by, or under us, to purchase, nor will we use in our Families in any Manner whatever, any Goods, Wares or Merchandise which shall arrive in America from Great-Britain aforesaid, from and after the last Day of August next ensuing (except only such Articles as shall be judged absolutely necessary by the Majority of the Signers hereof;- and as much as in us lies, to prevent our being interrupted and defeated in this only peaceable Measure entered into for the Recovery and Preservation of our Rights, and the Rights of our Brethren in our Sister Colonies, We agree to break of all Trade and Commerce, with all Persons, who prefering their private Interest to the Salvation of their now almost perishing Country, as shall still continue to import Goods from Great-Britain, or shall purchase of those who import after the said last Day of August, until the aforesaid pretended Right of Taxing the Colonies shall be given up or dropped.

3. As a Refusal to come into any Agreement which promises Deliverance of our Country from the Calamities it now feels, and which, like a Torrent, are rushing upon it with increasing Violence, must, in our Opinion, evidence a Disposition enemical to, or criminally negligent of the common Safety: —It is agreed, that all such ought to be considered, and shall by us be esteemed, as Encouragers of contumacious Importers.

Lastly, We hereby further engage, that we will use every Method in our Power, to encourage and promote the Production of Manufactures among ourselves, that this Covenant and Engagement may be as little detrimental to ourselves and Fellow Countrymen as possible.

### Notes

1. *The Statutes at Large, from the fifth year of King George the Third, to the tenth year of King George the Third, inclusive. To which is prefixed, a table of the titles of all the statutes during that time. With a copious index. Volume the eighth* (London, 1771), 17, 22–23. This document has been edited for

length. The full version can be found at the book's website (http://www.routledge.com/textbooks/revolutionaryamerica/).

2.  *Maryland Gazette* (Annapolis), July 4, 1765.
3.  *Proceedings of the Congress at New York* (Annapolis, MD: Jonas Green, 1766), 15–16.
4.  *Pennsylvania Journal* (Philadelphia), October 31, 1765. Image from the Granger Collection, New York.
5.  *Pennsylvania Gazette* (Philadelphia), November 7, 1765.
6.  *The Examination of Doctor Benjamin Franklin, before an August Assembly, relating to the Repeal of the Stamp Act, &c.* (Philadelphia: Hall and Sellers, 1766), 1–4, 6, 8–9, 11–13, 16. This document has been edited for length. The full version can be found at the book's website (http://www.routledge.com/textbooks/revolutionaryamerica/).
7.  *The Statutes at Large, from the fifth year of King George the Third, to the tenth year of King George the Third, inclusive. To which is prefixed, a table of the titles of all the statutes during that time. With a copious index. Volume the eighth* (London, 1771), 183.
8.  *The Statutes at Large, from the fifth year of King George the Third, to the tenth year of King George the Third, inclusive. To which is prefixed, a table of the titles of all the statutes during that time. With a copious index. Volume the eighth* (London, 1771), 183.
9.  *Boston Gazette and Country Journal*, March 12, 1770.
10. The Granger Collection, New York.
11. Worthington C. Ford et al, eds., *Journals of the Continental Congress, 1774–1789*, 34 vols. (Washington, DC, 1904–37), 1:63–73.
12. Library of Congress Printed Ephemera Collection; Portfolio 87, Folder 16 [No publisher or place of publication provided].

# CHAPTER 4

# Revolution, 1775–1776

## Introduction

Over the course of approximately eighteen months in 1775 and 1776, British rule collapsed in mainland British North America—with the exception of Quebec and the Floridas. Over the previous decade colonists had organized protests and boycotts, articulated increasingly refined constitutional arguments to justify their resistance, and exercised increased, often extralegal, autonomy. In so doing they laid the foundation for their future independence. Patrick Henry's speech in March 1775 (document 1) before the Virginia Convention, in which he called for the colony to take charge of its own defense—against British encroachments—reflects the increased autonomy, militancy, and confidence in the colonies. A month later British soldiers and Massachusetts militia began killing each other, and the War of Independence commenced (documents 2, 3, 4, 5). With the outbreak of the War the British-American dispute entered a new phase. No longer did the controversy concern taxation but more fundamental issues of authority and governance. The Continental Congress began to act as a national government for the rebels. In so doing it presented the colonists' grievances to the wider world, issuing a Declaration of the Causes and Necessity of Taking Up Arms (document 6) on July 6, 1775, to justify the use of force in Massachusetts. Two days later Congress sent the Olive Branch Petition (document 7) to King George III beseeching the sovereign to intervene to stop the conflict and address colonial grievances. The king, faced with armed resistance to his authority, was in no mood to treat with the killers of his soldiers and proclaimed the colonists to be in a state of rebellion (document 8).

By the end of 1775 reconciliation between the rebellious colonists and Britain seemed unlikely. The fundamental question facing the rebels was whether to declare independence formally or not. Despite the war, many Americans still favored Britain or were neutrally inclined. Even among rebel supporters independence seemed a step too far. In January 1776, Common Sense (document 9) was published anonymously in Philadelphia. Thomas Paine, a radical émigré from Britain made a passionate and persuasive case which helped to persuade many Americans to support independence. Congress voted in favor of independence on July 2, 1776, and set about editing Jefferson's draft declaration of independence (document 10) before formally adopting the Declaration of Independence (appendix) on July 4. In 1825 Jefferson averred that the object of the Declaration of Independence was, "Not to find new principles, or new arguments, never before thought of, not merely to say things which had never been said before; but to place before mankind the common sense of the subject, in terms so plain and firm as to command their assent, and to justify ourselves in the independent stand we are compelled to take."[1] We have included Jefferson's version of the Declaration so that interested readers might compare it to the version adopted by Congress in order to assess the stylistic and ideological differences between the two documents. In declaring independence Americans were required to jettison their loyalty to George III. This was the reason for the long indictment against the king in the Declaration of Independence. They committed figurative regicide in adopting the Declaration. New Yorkers did so symbolically on July 9, 1776, when they destroyed a statue of the king (document 11).

### 1.   Patrick Henry, Give Me Liberty or Give Me Death, March 23, 1775[2]

*As British authority broke down in America during the spring of 1775, Patriots began to assume greater authority. On March 20, 1775, the Second Virginia Convention began sitting in Richmond in defiance of the colony's royal governor. On March 23, Patrick Henry (1736–1799), who had been radical opponent of British rule—a decade before with his introduction of the Virginia Resolves in opposition to the Stamp Act (see chapter 3, document 2)—introduced a resolution calling for the raising of militia companies in every Virginia county to oppose the British. In his speech, which is an expression of the radical position on the eve of the Revolution, Henry famously declared, "Give me liberty, or give me death!" No contemporary transcription of the speech exists. Henry's early nineteenth-century biographer, William Wirt (1772–1834) reconstructed the oration by interviewing witnesses, including Thomas Jefferson.*

No man [thinks] more highly than [I do] of the patriotism, as well as abilities, of the very worthy gentlemen who [have] just addressed the house. But different men often [see] the same subject in different lights; and, therefore, [I hope] it [will] not be thought disrespectful to those gentlemen, if, entertaining as [I do] opinions of a character very opposite to theirs, [I shall] speak forth [my] sentiments freely, and without reserve. This [is] no time for ceremony. The question before the house [is] one of awful moment to the country. For [my] own part, [I consider] it as nothing less than a question of freedom or slavery: And in proportion to the magnitude of the subject, ought to be the freedom of the debate. It is only in this way that [we can] hope to arrive at the truth, and fulfill the great responsibility which [we hold] to God and [our] country. Should [I] keep back [my] opinions at such a time, through fear of giving offense, [I] should consider [myself] as guilty of treason towards [my] country, and of an act of disloyalty toward the majesty of heaven, which [I revere] above all earthly kings.

Mr. President, it is natural to man to indulge in the illusions of hope. We are apt to shut our eyes against a painful truth—and listen to the song of that siren, till she transforms us into beasts. Is this the part of wise men, engaged in a great and arduous struggle for liberty? [Are] we disposed to be of the numbers of those, who having eyes, see not, and, having ears, hear not, the things which so nearly concern their temporal salvation? For [my] part, whatever anguish of spirit it may cost, [I] am willing to know the whole truth, to know the worst, and to provide for it.

[I have] but one lamp by which [my] feet [are] guided, and that [is] the lamp of experience. [I know] of no way of judging of the future but by the past. And judging by the past, [I wish] to know what there has been in the conduct of the British ministry for the last ten years, to justify those hopes with which gentlemen [have] been pleased to solace themselves and the House. Is it that insidious smile with which our petition has been lately received? Trust it not, sir; it will prove a snare to your feet. Suffer not yourselves to be betrayed with a kiss. Ask yourselves how this gracious reception of our petition comports with those warlike preparations which cover our waters and darken our land. Are fleets and armies necessary to a work of love and reconciliation? Have we shown ourselves so unwilling to be reconciled, that force must be called in to win back our love? Let us not deceive ourselves, sir. These are the implements of war and subjugation—the last arguments to which kings resort. I ask gentlemen, sir, what means this martial array, if its purpose be not to force us to submission? Can gentlemen assign any other possible motive for it? Has Great Britain any enemy in this quarter of the world, to call for all this accumulation of navies and armies? No, sir, she has none. They are meant for us: they can be meant for no other. They are sent over to bind and rivet upon us those chains which the British ministry have been so long forging. And what have we to oppose to them? Shall we try argument? Sir, we have been trying that for the last ten years. Have we anything new to offer upon the subject? Nothing. We have held the subject up in every light of which it is capable; but it has been all in vain. Shall we resort to entreaty and humble supplication? What terms shall we find, which have not been already exhausted? Let us not, I beseech you, sir, deceive ourselves longer. Sir, we have done every thing that could be done, to avert the storm which is now coming on. We have petitioned—we have remonstrated; we have supplicated; we have prostrated ourselves before the throne, and have implored its interposition to arrest the tyrannical hands of the ministry and parliament.

Our petitions have been slighted; our remonstrances have produced additional violence and insult; our supplications have been disregarded; and we have been spurned, with contempt, from the foot of the throne! In vain, after these things, may we indulge the fond hope of peace and reconciliation. *There is no longer any room for hope.* If we wish to be free—if we mean to preserve inviolate those inestimable privileges for which we have been so long contending—if we mean not basely to abandon the noble struggle in which we have been so long engaged, and which we have pledged ourselves never to abandon until the glorious object of our contest shall be obtained—we must fight! I repeat it, sir, we must fight!! An appeal to arms and to the God of hosts is all that is left us!

They tell us, sir, that we are weak; unable to cope with so formidable an adversary. But when shall we be stronger? Will it be the next week, or the next year? Will it be when we are totally disarmed, and when a British guard shall be stationed in every house? Shall we gather strength but irresolution and inaction? Shall we acquire the means of effectual resistance by lying supinely on our backs and hugging the delusive phantom of hope, until our enemies shall have bound us hand and foot? Sir, we are not weak if we make a proper use of those means which the God of nature hath placed in our power. Three millions of people, armed in the holy cause of liberty, and in such a country as that which we possess, are invincible by any force which our enemy can send against us. Besides, sir, we shall not fight our battles alone. There is a just God who presides over the destinies of nations, and who will raise up friends to fight our battles for us. The battle, sir, is not to the strong alone; it is to the vigilant, the active, the brave. Besides, sir, we have no election. If we were base enough to desire it, it is now too late to retire from the contest. There is no retreat but in submission and slavery! Our chains are forged. Their clanking may be heard on the plains of Boston! The war is inevitable—and let it come!! I repeat it, sir, let it come!!!

It is in vain, sir, to extentuate the matter. Gentlemen may cry, peace, peace—but there is no peace. The war is actually begun! The next gale that sweeps from the north will bring to our ears the clash of resounding arms! Our brethren are already in the field! Why stand we here idle? What is it that gentlemen wish? What would they have? Is life so dear, or peace so sweet, as to be purchased at the price of chains and slavery? Forbid it, Almighty God! I know not what course others may take; but as for me, give me liberty or give me death!

## 2.   The Battles of Lexington and Concord, April 19, 1775[3]

*Isaac Merrill (1708–1787) was a Massachusetts militia colonel. In this letter, written on the day that the War of Independence began, Merrill wrote to John Currier, a militia captain in Amesbury, Massachusetts, providing a brief account of the skirmishing at Lexington and Concord and urging him to mobilize his troops. In the aftermath of the fighting on April 19, nearly twenty-thousand New England militia descended on Boston and undertook an impromptu siege of the British forces in the city.*

…this Day I have received intiligence that the ministeriel troops under the Command of General Gage did Last evening march out of Boston and marched to Lexington & there Killed a Number of our American Soldiers & thence proceed to Concord Killing and Destroying our men and interest. These are therefore to Order you forthwith to Mobilize and muster as many of your under officers and Soldiers as you can possible to meet immedially to Some Suitable place: and then to march of forthwith to Concord or Else where as in your Descretion you Shall think best to the reliefe of our Friend and Country: and also to order those who are now absent & out of the way to Follow after and ioin you as Soon as they shall be apprized of the Alaram and when you have marched your men to Some part of our army you are to appoint some officer to head them in case you return home your Self: till Some Further Order may be taken: in this Faile Not…

### 3. Battle of Lexington, 1775[4]

*Among the militiamen who descended on Boston was Amos Doolittle (1754–1832), a silversmith from New Haven, Connecticut. Doolittle's company joined the siege of Boston on April 29, 1775. Doolittle visited Lexington and Concord and interviewed survivors of the battle on the 19th before producing a series of engravings, which are the only contemporary visual representations of the fighting on the war's first*

**Figure 4.1** The Battle of Lexington, 1775. Courtesy of the Granger Collection, New York.

*day. This image shows the Patriot militia firing on columns of British troops from behind stone walls, a practice which had deadly effect yet was disdained by the British as dishonorable (see Thomas Gage's proclamation, document 4).*

### 4. General Gage's Proclamation, June 12, 1775[5]

*Although British soldiers and American militia had killed each other and the rebellious colonists were besieging the British in Boston, the two sides found themselves suspended between peace and open war during the spring of 1775. On June 12, General Thomas Gage (1720–1787), the governor of Massachusetts and commander of British forces in North America, issued a proclamation which sought to resolve the conflict by offering an amnesty to all who would lay down their arms, except Samuel Adams and John Hancock, believed to be the leaders of the rebellion in Massachusetts. The proclamation was ineffective in part because of its patronizing tone.*

WHEREAS the infatuated Multitudes, who have long suffered themselves to be conducted by certain well known Incendiaries and Traitors, in a fatal Progression of Crimes, against the constitutional Authority of the State, have at length proceeded to avowed Rebellion; and the good Effects which were expected arise from the Patience and Lenity of the King's Government, have been often frustrated, and are now rendered hopeless, by the Influence of the same evil Counsels; it only remains for those who are entrusted with supreme Rule, as well for the Punishment of the guilty, as the Protection of the well-affected, to prove they do not bear the Sword in vain.

The Infringements which have been committed upon the most sacred Rights of the Crown and People of Great-Britain, are too many to enumerate on one Side, and are all too atrocious to be palliated on the other. All unprejudiced People who have been Witnesses of the late Transactions, in this and the neighbouring Provinces, will find upon a transient Review, Marks of Premeditation and Conspiracy that would justify the fulness of Chastisement: And even those who are least acquainted with Facts, cannot fail to receive a just Impression of their Enormity, in Proportion as they discover the Arts and Assiduity by which they have been falsified or concealed. The Authors of the present unnatural Revolt never daring to trust their Cause or their Actions, to the Judgment of an impartial Public, or even to the dispassionate Reflection of their Followers, have uniformly placed their chief Confidence in the Suppression of Truth: And while indefatigable and shameless Pains have been taken to obstruct every Appeal to the real Interest of the People of America; the grossest Forgeries, Calumnies and Absurdities that ever insulted human Understanding, have been imposed upon their Credulity. The Press, that distinguished Appendage of public Liberty, and when fairly and impartially employed its best Support, has been invariably prostituted to the most contrary Purposes: The animated Language of ancient and virtuous Times, calculated to vindicate and promote the just Rights and

Interest of Mankind, have been applied to countenance the most abandoned Violation of those sacred Blessings; and not only from the flagitious Prints, but from the popular Harrangues of the Times, Men have been taught to depend upon Activity in Treason, for the Security of their Persons and properties; 'till to compleat the horrid Profanation of Terms, and of Ideas, the Name of GOD, has been introduced in the Pulpits to excite and justify Devastation and Massacre.

The Minds of Men have been thus gradually prepared for the worst Extremities, a Number of armed Persons, to the amount of many Thousands assembled on the 19th of April last, and from behind Walls, and lurking Holes, attacked a Detachment of the King's Troops who not expecting so consummate an Act of Phrenzy, unprepared for Vengeance, and willing to decline it, made use of their Arms only in their own Defence. Since that Period, the Rebels, deriving Confidence from Impunity, have added Insult to Outrage; have repeatedly fired upon the King's Ships and Subjects, with Cannon and small Arms, have possessed the Roads, and other Communications by which the Town of Boston was supplied with Provisions; and with a preposterous Parade of Military Arrangement, they affect to hold the Army besieged; while Part of their Body make daily and indiscriminate Invasions upon private Property, and with a Wantonness of Cruelty ever incident to lawless Tumult, carry Depredation and Distress wherever they turn their Steps. The Actions of the 19th of April are of such Notoriety, as must baffle all Attempts to contradict them, and the Flames of Buildings and other Property from the Islands, and adjacent Country, for some Weeks past, spread a melancholy Confirmation of the subsequent Assertions.

In this Exigency of complicated Calamities, I avail myself of the last Effort within the Bounds of my Duty, to spare the Effusion of Blood; to offer, and I do hereby in his Majesty's Name, offer and promise, his most gracious Pardon to all Persons who shall forthwith lay down their Arms, and return to the Duties of peaceable Subjects, excepting only from the Benefit of such Pardon, *Samuel Adams* and *John Hancock*, whose Offences are of too flagitious a Nature to admit of any other Consideration about that of condign Punishment.

And to the End that no Person within the Limits of this proffered Mercy, may plead Ignorance of the Conseqences of refusing it, I by these Presents proclaim not only the Persons above-named and excepted, but also all their Adherents, Associates, and Abettors, meaning to comprehend in those Terms, all and every Person, and Persons of what Class, Denomination or Description soever, who have appeared in Arms against the King's Government, and shall not lay down the same as afore-mentioned; and likewise all such as shall so take Arms after the Date hereof, or who shall in any-wise protect or conceal such Offenders, or assist them with Money, Provision, Cattle, Arms, Ammunition, Carriages, or any other Necessary for Subsistence or Offence; or shall hold secret Correspondence with them by Letter, Message, Signal, or otherwise, to be Rebels and Traitors, and as such to be treated.

AND WHEREAS, during the Continuance of the present unnatural Rebellion, Justice cannot be administered by the common Law of the Land, the Course whereof has, for a long Time past been violently impeded, and wholly interrupted; from whence results a Necessity for using and exercising the Law Martial; I have therefore thought fit, by the Authority vested in me, by the Royal Charter to this Province, to publish, and I do hereby publish, proclaim and order the Use and Exercise of the Law Martial, within and throughout this Province, for so long Time as the present unhappy Occasion shall necessarily require; whereof all Persons are hereby required to take Notice, and govern themselves, as well to maintain Order and Regularity among the peaceable Inhabitants of the Province, as to resist, encounter, and subdue the Rebels and Traitors above-described by such as shall be called upon those Purposes.

To these inevitable, but I trust salutary Measures, it is a far more pleasing Part of my Duty, to add the Assurances of Protection and Support, to all who in so trying a Crisis, shall manifest their Allegiance to the King, and Affection to the Parent State. So that such Persons as may have been intimidated to quit their Habitations in the Course of this Alarm, may return to their respective Callings and Professions; and stand distinct and separate from the Parricides of the Constitution, till GOD in his Mercy shall restore to his Creatures, in this distracted Land, that System of Happiness from which they have be seduced, the Religion of Peace, and Liberty founded upon Law.

## 5. Bunker's Hill or America's Head Dress, 1776[6]

*Gage's proclamation went unheeded and on June 17, 1775, the British stormed the rebel positions in Charlestown achieving a pyrrhic victory at the Battle of Bunker*

**Figure 4.2** Bunker's Hill Cartoon, 1776. Courtesy of the Granger Collection, New York.

*Hill at the cost of more than a thousand men killed and wounded. This satirical cartoon appeared the next year in London. It presents Bunker (sic, Breed's) Hill as a fashionable hairstyle, the "High Roll" favored by some wealthy American women. The cartoon likened the American rebellion to the hairstyle—which is traversed by British soldiers—frivolous, impractical, and short-lived.[7]*

## 6. Declaration of the Causes and Necessity of Taking Up Arms, July 6, 1775[8]

*Faced with war in New England and the collapse of British authority throughout the mainland colonies, the Second Continental Congress began to direct the rebellion. In June it created the Continental Army and appointed George Washington as its commander. Nonetheless, its authority to govern the rebellious colonies was dubious. On July 6, 1775, it issued this Declaration to justify the rebellion and to offer terms for reconciliation. The main authors of the Declaration were Thomas Jefferson (1743–1826) of Virginia and John Dickinson (1732–1808) of Pennsylvania. When compared to Gage's proclamation of June 12 (document 4), the differences between the British and rebel positions in the summer of 1775—and the unlikelihood of a rapprochement between the two—become apparent.*

If it was possible for men, who exercise their reason, to believe, that the Divine Author of our existence intended a part of the human race to hold an absolute property in, and an unbounded power over others, marked out by his infinite goodness and wisdom, as the objects of a legal domination never rightfully resistible, however severe and oppressive, the Inhabitants of these Colonies might at least require from the Parliament of Great Britain some evidence, that this dreadful authority over them, has been granted to that body. But a reverence for our great Creator, principles of humanity, and the dictates of common sense, must convince all those who reflect upon the subject, that government was instituted to promote the welfare of mankind, and ought to be administered for the attainment of that end. The legislature of Great Britain, however, stimulated by an inordinate passion for a power, not only unjustifiable, but which they know to be peculiarly reprobated by the very constitution of that kingdom, and desperate of success in any mode of contest, where regard should be had to truth, law, or right, have at length, deserting those, attempted to effect their cruel and impolitic purpose of enslaving these Colonies by violence, and have thereby rendered it necessary for us to close with their last appeal from Reason to Arms.—Yet, however blinded that assembly may be, by their intemperate rage for unlimited domination, so to slight justice and the opinion of mankind, we esteem ourselves bound, by obligations of respect to the rest of the world, to make known the justice of our cause.

Our forefathers, inhabitants of the island of Great Britain, left their native land, to seek on these shores a residence for civil and religious freedom. At the expence of their blood, at the hazard of their fortunes, without the least charge to the country from which they removed, by unceasing labor, and an unconquerable spirit, they effected settlements in the distant and inhospitable wilds of America, then filled with numerous and warlike nations of barbarians. Societies or governments, vested with perfect legislatures, were formed under charters from the crown, and an harmonious intercourse was established between the colonies and the kingdom from which they derived their origin. The mutual benefits of this union became in a short time so extraordinary, as to excite astonishment. It is universally confessed, that the amazing increase of the wealth, strength, and navigation of the realm, arose from this source; and the minister, who so wisely and successfully directed the measures of Great Britain in the late war, publicly declared, that these colonies enabled her to triumph over her enemies…From that fatal moment, the affairs of the British empire began to fall into confusion, and gradually sliding from the summit of glorious prosperity, to which they had been advanced by the virtues and abilities of one man, are at length distracted by the convulsions, that now shake it to its deepest foundations…

These devoted colonies were judged to be in such a state, as to present victories without bloodshed, and all the easy emoluments of statuteable plunder.—The uninterrupted tenor of their peaceable and respectful behaviour from the beginning of colonization, their dutiful, zealous, and useful services during the war, though so recently and amply acknowledged in the most honorable manner by his majesty, by the late king, and by Parliament, could not save them from the meditated innovations.—Parliament was influenced to adopt the pernicious project, and assuming a new power over them, have, in the course of eleven years, given such decisive specimens of the spirit and consequences attending this power, as to leave no doubt concerning the effects of acquiescence under it. They have undertaken to give and grant our money without our consent, though we have ever exercised an exclusive right to dispose of our own property; statutes have been passed for extending the jurisdiction of courts of Admiralty and Vice-Admiralty beyond their ancient limits; for depriving us of the accustomed and inestimable privilege of trial by jury, in cases affecting both life and property; for suspending the legislature of one of the colonies; for interdicting all commerce to the capital of another; and for altering fundamentally the form of government established by charter, and secured by acts of its own legislature solemnly confirmed by the crown; for exempting the "murderers" of colonists from legal trial, and in effect, from punishment; for erecting in a neighboring province, acquired by the joint arms of Great Britain and America, a despotism dangerous to our very existence; and for quartering soldiers upon the colonists in time of profound peace. It has also been resolved in parliament, that colonists charged with committing certain offences, shall be transported to England to be tried.

But why should we enumerate our injuries in detail? By one statute it is declared, that parliament can "of right make laws to bind us IN ALL CASES WHATSOEVER." What is to defend us against so enormous, so unlimited a power? Not a single man of those who assume it, is chosen by us; or is subject to our controul or influence; but, on the contrary, they are all of them exempt from the operation of such laws, and an American revenue, if not diverted from the ostensible purposes for which it is raised, would actually lighten their own burdens in proportion as they increase ours. We saw the misery to which such despotism would reduce us. We for ten years incessantly and ineffectually besieged the Throne as supplicants; we reasoned, we remonstrated with parliament, in the most mild and decent language. But Administration, sensible that we should regard these oppressive measures as freemen ought to do, sent over fleets and armies to enforce them. The indignation of the Americans was roused, it is true; but it was the indignation of a virtuous, loyal, and affectionate people...We have pursued every temperate, every respectful measure: we have even proceeded to break off our commercial intercourse with our fellow-subjects, as the last peaceable admonition, that our attachment to no nation upon earth should supplant our attachment to liberty.—This, we flattered ourselves, was the ultimate step of the controversy: But subsequent events have shewn, how vain was this hope of finding moderation in our enemies.

Several threatening expressions against the colonies were inserted in his Majesty's speech; our petition, though we were told it was a decent one, and that his Majesty had been pleased to receive it graciously, and to promise laying it before his Parliament, was buddled into both houses amongst a bundle of American papers, and there neglected. The Lords and Commons in their address, in the month of February, said, that "a rebellion at that time actually existed within the province of Massachusetts bay; and that those concerned in it, had been countenanced and encouraged by unlawful combinations and engagements, entered into by his Majesty's subjects in several of the other colonies; and therefore they besought his Majesty, that he would take the most effectual measures to enforce due obedience to the laws and authority of the supreme legislature."—Soon after, the commercial intercourse of whole colonies, with foreign countries, and with each other, was cut off by an act of Parliament; by another, several of them were entirely prohibited from the fisheries in the seas near their coasts, on which they always depended for their sustenance; and large re-inforcements of ships and troops were immediately sent over to General Gage...

Soon after the intelligence of these proceedings arrived on this continent, General Gage, who in the course of the last year had taken possession of the town of Boston, in the province of Massachusetts Bay, and still occupied it as a garrison, on the 19th day of April, sent out from that place a large detachment of his army, who made an unprovoked assault on the inhabitants of the said province, at the town of Lexington, as appears by the affidavits of a great number of persons, some of whom were officers and soldiers of that detachment, murdered eight of the inhabitants, and wounded many others. From thence the troops proceeded in warlike array to the town of Concord, where they set upon another party of the inhabitants of the same province, killing several and wounding more, until compelled to retreat by the country people suddenly assembled to repel this cruel aggression. Hostilities, thus commenced by the British troops, have been since prosecuted by them without regard to faith or reputation...

The General, further emulating his ministerial masters, by a proclamation bearing date on the 12th day of June, after venting the grossest falsehoods and calumnies against the good people of these colonies, proceeds to "declare them all, either by name or description, to be rebels and traitors, to supersede the course of the common law, and instead thereof to publish and order the use and exercise of the law martial."—His troops have butchered our countrymen, have wantonly burnt Charles-Town, besides a considerable number of houses in other places; our ships and vessels are seized; the necessary supplies of provisions are intercepted, and he is exerting his utmost power to spread destruction and devastation around him.

We have received certain intelligence that General Carleton, the Governor of Canada, is instigating the people of that province and the Indians to fall upon us; and we have but too much reason to apprehend, that schemes have been formed to excite domestic enemies against us. In brief, a part of these colonies now feels, and all of them are sure of feeling, as far as the vengance of administration can inflict them, the complicated calamities of fire, sword, and famine.—We are reduced to the alternative of chusing an unconditional submission to the tyranny of irritated ministers, or resistance by force.—The latter is our choice.—We have counted the cost of this contest, and find nothing so dreadful as voluntary slavery.—Honor, justice, and humanity, forbid us tamely to surrender that freedom which we received from our gallant ancestors, and which our innocent posterity have a right to receive from us. We cannot endure the infamy and guilt of resigning succeeding generations to that wretchedness which inevitably awaits them, if we basely entail hereditary bondage upon them.

Our cause is just. Our union is perfect. Our internal resources are great, and, if necessary, foreign assistance is undoubtedly attainable.—We gratefully acknowledge, as signal instances of the Divine favour towards us, that his Providence would not permit us to be called into this severe controversy, until we were grown up to our present strength, had been previously exercised in warlike operation, and possessed of the means of defending ourselves.—With hearts fortified with these animating reflections, we most solemnly, before God and the world, declare, that, exerting the utmost energy of those powers, which our beneficent Creator hath graciously bestowed upon us, the arms we have been compelled by our enemies to assume, we will, in defiance of every hazard, with unabating firmness and perseverance, employ for the preservation of our liberties; being with our [one] mind resolved to dye Free-men rather than live Slaves.

Lest this declaration should disquiet the minds of our friends and fellow-subjects in any part of the empire, we assure them that we mean not to dissolve that Union which has so long and so happily subsisted between us, and which we sincerely wish to see restored.—Necessity has not yet driven us into that desperate measure, or induced us to excite any other nation to war against them.—We have not raised armies with ambitious designs of separating from Great Britain, and establishing independent states. We fight not for glory or for conquest. We exhibit to mankind the remarkable spectacle of a people attacked by unprovoked enemies, without any imputation or even suspicion of offence. They boast of their privileges and civilization, and yet proffer no milder conditions than servitude or death.

In our own native land, in defence of the freedom that is our birth-right, and which we ever enjoyed till the late violation of it—for the protection of our property, acquired solely by the honest industry of our fore-fathers and ourselves, against violence actually offered, we have taken up arms. We shall lay them down when hostilities shall cease on the part of the aggressors, and all danger of their being renewed shall be removed, and not before.

With an humble confidence in the mercies of the supreme and impartial Judge and Ruler of the universe, we most devoutly implore his divine goodness to protect us happily through this great conflict, to dispose our adversaries to reconciliation on reasonable terms, and thereby to relieve the empire from the calamities of civil war.

### 7.   Olive Branch Petition, July 8, 1775[9]

*At the same time that Congress was justifying American resistance in the* Declaration of the Causes and Necessity of Taking Up Arms *it also prepared a direct appeal to George III. Two days after issuing the* Declaration of the Causes and Necessity of Taking Up Arms, *it formally adopted the Olive Branch Petition which was a direct appeal to George III. The petition claimed that the colonists had no desire for independence but sought to negotiate solutions to the trade and tax disputes between the colonies and Britain. The petition was largely drafted by John Dickinson, who adopted a conciliatory tone beseeching the king to intervene to restore peace to the empire.*

*To the king's most excellent Majesty:*
MOST GRACIOUS SOVEREIGN,

We, your Majesty's faithful subjects of the colonies of new Hampshire, Massachusetts bay, Rhode island and Providence Plantations, Connecticut, New York, New Jersey, Pennsylvania, the counties of New Castle, Kent, and Sussex, on Delaware, Maryland, Virginia, North Carolina, and South Carolina in behalf of ourselves, and the inhabitants of these colonies, who have deputed us to represent them in general Congress, entreat your Majesty's gracious attention to this our humble petition.

The union between our Mother country and these colonies, and the energy of mild and just government, produced benefits so remarkably important, and afforded such an assurance of their permanency and increase, that the wonder and envy of other Nations was excited, while they beheld Great Britain riseing to a power the most extraordinary the world has ever known.

Her rivals, observing that there was no probability of this happy connextion being broken by civil dissensions, and apprehending its future effects, it left any longer undisturbed, resolved to prevent her receiving such continual and formidable accessions of wealth and strength, by checking the growth of these settlements from which they were to be derived.

In the prosecution of this attempt, events so unfavourable to the design took place, that every friend to the interests of Great Britain and these colonies, entertaining pleasing and reasonable expectations of seeing an additional force and extention immediately given to the operations of the union hitherto experienced, by an enlargement of the dominions of the Crown, and the removal of ancient and warlike enemies to a greater distance.

At the conclusion, therefore, of the late war, the most glorious and advantageous that ever had been carried on by British arms, your loyal colonists having contributed to its success, by such repeated and strenuous exertions, as frequently procured them the distinguished approbation of your Majesty, of the late king, and of parliament, doubted not but that they should be permitted, with the rest of the empire, to share in the blessings of peace, and the emoluments of victory and conquest. While these recent and honorable acknowledgements of their merits remained on record in the journals and acts of that august legislature, the Parliament, undefaced by the imputation or even the suspicion of any offence, they were alarmed by the imputation or even the suspicion of any offence, they were alarmed by a new system of statutes and regulations adopted for the administration of the colonies, that filled their minds with the most painful fears and jealousies; and, to their inexpressible astonishment, perceived the dangers of a foreign quarrel quickly succeeded by domestic dangers, in their judgment, of a more dreadful kind.

Nor were their anxieties alleviated by any tendency in this system to promote the welfare of the Mother country. For tho' its effects were more immediately felt by them, yet its influence appeared to be injurious to the commerce and prosperity of Great Britain.

We shall decline the ungrateful task of describing the irksome variety of artifices, practiced by many of your Majesty's Ministers, the delusive pretences, fruitless terrors, and unavailing severities, that have, from time to time, been dealt out by them, in their attempts to execute this impolitic plan, or of traceing, thro' a series of years past, the progress of the unhappy differences between Great Britain and these colonies, which have flowed from this fatal source.

Your Majesty's Ministers, persevering in their measures, and proceeding to open hostilities for enforcing them, have compelled us to arm in our own defence, and have engaged us in a controversy so peculiarly abhorrent to the affections of your still faithful colonists, that when we consider whom we must oppose in this contest, and if it continues, what may be the consequences, our own particular misfortunes are accounted by us only as parts of our distress.

Knowing to what violent resentments and incurable animosities, civil discords are apt to exasperate and inflame the contending parties, we think ourselves required by indispensable obligations to Almighty God, to your Majesty, to our fellow subjects, and to ourselves, immediately to use all the means in our power, not incompatible with our safety, for stopping the further effusion of blood, and for averting the impending calamities that threaten the British Empire.

Thus called upon to address your Majesty on affairs of such moment to America, and probably to all your dominions, we are earnestly desirous of performing this office, with the utmost deference for your Majesty; and we therefore pray, that your royal magnanimity and benevolence may make the most favourable construction of our expressions on so uncommon an occasion. Could we represent in their full force, the sentiments that agitate the minds of us your dutiful subjects, we are persuaded your Majesty would ascribe any seeming deviation from reverence in our language, and even in our conduct, not to any reprehensible intention, but to the impossibility of reconciling the usual appearances of respect, with a just attention to our own preservation against those artful and cruel enemies, who abuse your royal confidence and authority, for the purpose of effecting our destruction.

Attached to your Majesty's person, family, and government, with all devotion that principle and affection can inspire, connected with Great Britain by the strongest ties that can unite societies, and deploring every event that tends in any degree to weaken them, we solemnly assure your Majesty, that we not only most ardently desire the former harmony between her and these colonies may be restored, but that a concord may be established between them upon so firm a basis as to perpetuate its blessings, uninterrupted by any future dissentions, to succeeding generations in both countries, and to transmit your Majesty's Name to posterity, adorned with that signal and lasting glory, that has attended the memory of those illustrious personages, whose virtues and abilities have extricated states from dangerous convulsions, and, by securing happiness to others, have erected the most noble and durable monuments to their own fame.

We beg leave further to assure your Majesty, that notwithstanding the sufferings of your loyal colonists, during the course of the present controversy, our breasts retain too tender a regard for the kingdom from which we derive our origin, to request such a reconciliation as might in any manner be inconsistent with her dignity or her welfare. These, related as we are to her, honor and duty, as well as inclination, induce us to support and advance; and the apprehensions that now oppress our hearts with unspeakable grief, being once removed, your Majesty will find your faithful subjects on this continent ready and willing at all times, as they ever have been, with their lives and fortunes, to assert and maintain the rights and interests of your Majesty, and of our Mother country.

We, therefore, beseech your Majesty, that your royal authority and influence may be graciously interposed to procure us relief from our afflicting fears and jealousies, occasioned by the system before mentioned, and to settle peace through every part of your dominions, with all humility submitting to your Majesty's wise consideration whether it may not be expedient for facilitating those important purposes, that your Majesty be pleased to direct some mode, by which the united applications of your faithful colonists to the throne, in pursuance of their common councils, may be improved into a happy and permanent reconciliation; and that, in the main time, measures may be taken for preventing the further destruction of the lives of your Majesty's subjects; and that such statutes as more immediately distress any of your Majesty's colonies may be repealed.

For by such arrangements as your Majesty's wisdom can form, for collecting the united sense of your American people, we are convinced your Majesty would receive such satisfactory proofs of the disposition of the colonists toward their sovereign and parent state, that the wished for opportunity would soon be restored to them, of envincing the sincerity of their professions, by every testimony of devotion becoming the most dutiful subjects, and the most affectionate colonists.

That your Majesty may enjoy a long and prosperous reign, and that your descendants may govern your dominions with honor to themselves and happiness to their subjects, is our sincere and fervent prayer.

### 8. George III Proclaims the Americans in a State of Rebellion, August 23, 1775[10]

*King George III refused to accept the Olive Branch Petition. On August 23, 1775, he issued this proclamation which declared that the colonies were in a state of rebellion and called upon all the civil and military officers of the British state as well as his loyal subjects in America to assist in suppressing the insurrection.*

WHEREAS many of Our Subjects in divers Parts of Our Colonies and Plantations in *North America*, misled by dangerous and ill designing Men, and forgetting the Allegiance which they owe to the Power that has protected and supported them; after various disorderly Acts committed in Disturbance of the Publick Peace, to the Obstruction of lawful Commerce, and to the Oppression of Our Loyal Subjects carrying on the same; have at length proceeded to open and avowed Rebellion, by arraying themselves in a hostile Manner to withstand the Execution of the Law, and traitorously preparing, ordering and levying War against Us: And whereas there is Reason to apprehend that such Rebellion hath been much promoted and encouraged by the traitorous Correspondence, Counsels, and Comfort of divers wicked and desperate Persons within this Realm: To the End therefore that none of Our subjects may neglect or violate their Duty through Ignorance thereof, or through any Doubt of the Protection which the Law will afford to their Loyalty and Zeal; We have thought fit, by and with the

Advice of Our Privy Council, to issue this Our Royal Proclamation, hereby declaring that not only all Our Officers, Civil and Military, are obliged to exert their utmost Endeavours to suppress such Rebellion, and to bring the Traitors to Justice; but that all Our Subjects of this Realm and the Dominions thereunto belonging are bound by Law to be aiding and assisting in the Suppression of such Rebellion, and to disclose and make known all traitorous Conspiracies and attempts against Us, Our Crown and Dignity; And We do accordingly strictly charge and command all Our Officers as well as Civil and Military and all other Our obedient and loyal Subjects, to use their utmost Endeavours to withstand and suppress such Rebellion, and to disclose and make known all Treasons and traitorous Conspiracies which they shall know to be against Us, Our Crown and Dignity; and for that Purpose, that they transmit to One of Our Principal Secretaries of State, or other proper Officer, due and full Information of all Persons who shall be found carrying on Correspondence with, or in any Manner or Degree aiding or abetting the Persons now in open Arms and Rebellion against Our Government within any of Our Colonies and Plantations in *North America*, in order to bring to condign Punishment the Authors, Perpetrators, and Abetters of such traitorous Designs.

### 9. Thomas Paine, *Common Sense*, 1776[11]

*During the autumn of 1775 the war between the British and the rebellious colonists spread. The Royal Navy burned Falmouth (now Portland), Maine, on October 18. On November 7 Lord Dunmore, the Royal Governor of Virginia offered freedom to any slaves who fled rebel masters to serve the British (see chapter 6, document 2). On January 1, 1776, the Royal Navy burned Norfolk, Virginia. Against this backdrop an increasingly passionate debate occurred concerning the rebels' war aims. On January 10, 1776, Robert Bell, a Philadelphia printer published an anonymous pamphlet,* Common Sense, *which argued in forthright and passionate language that the colonies must declare independence from Britain. Thomas Paine (1737–1809), a recently arrived British radical, was the author of the pamphlet which became a best-seller. Paine wrote in vivid, colloquial, language and drew his imagery from the Bible, rather than the Classics, which made his pamphlet accessible to a mass audience.* Common Sense *helped to clarify the thinking of many Americans and persuaded them to embrace independence.*

…The cause of America is in a great measure the cause of all mankind. Many circumstances have, and will arise, which are not local, but universal, and through which the principles of all lovers of mankind are affected, and in the event of which, their affections are interested. The laying of a country desolate with fire and sword, declaring war against the natural rights of all mankind, and extirpating the defenders thereof from the face of the earth, is the concern of every man to whom nature hath given the power of feeling…

I know it is difficult to get over local or long standing prejudices, yet if we will suffer ourselves to examine the component parts of the English constitution, we shall find them to be the base remains of two ancient tyrannies, compounded with some new republican materials.

*First.* The remains of Monarchical tyranny in the person of the King.

*Secondly.* The remains of Aristocratical tyranny in the persons of the Peers.

*Thirdly.* The new republican materials, in the persons of the Commons, on whose virtue depends the freedom of England.

The two first, by being hereditary, are independent of the People; wherefore in a *Constitutional Sense* they contribute nothing towards the freedom of the State.

To say that the constitution of England is a *Union* of three powers reciprocally *checking* each other, is farcical, either the words have no meaning, or they are flat contradictions.

To say that the Commons is a check upon the King, presupposes two things.

*First.*—That the King is not to be trusted without being looked after; or in other words, that a thirst for absolute power is the natural disease of Monarchy.

*Secondly.*—That the Commons by being appointed for that purpose, are either wiser or more worthy of confidence than the Crown.

But as the same constitution which gives the Commons a power to check the King by with-holding the supplies, gives afterwards the King a power to check the Commons, by empowering him to reject their other bills; it again supposes that the King is wiser than those, whom it has already supposed to be wiser than him. A mere absurdity!

There is something exceedingly ridiculous in the composition of Monarchy, it first excludes a man from the means of information yet empowers him to act in cases where the highest judgment is required.—The state of a King shuts him from the World; yet the business of a King requires him to know it thoroughly: wherefore the different parts by unnaturally opposing and destroying each other, prove the whole character to be absurd and useless…

That the crown is this overbearing part in the English constitution needs not be mentioned, and that it derives its whole consequence merely from being the giver of places and pensions is self-evident; wherefore, tho' we have been wise enough to shut and lock a door against absolute Monarchy, we at the same time have been foolish enough to put the Crown in possession of the key.

The prejudice of Englishmen in favour of their own government by King, Lords and Commons, arises as much or more from national pride than reason. Individuals are undoubtedly safer in England than in some other Countries; but the *will* of the King is as much the *law* of the land in Britain as in France, with this difference, that instead of proceeding directly from his mouth, it is handed to the People under the more formidable shape of an act of Parliament. For the fate of Charles the first hath only made Kings more subtle—not more just.

Wherefore laying aside all national pride and prejudice in favour of modes and forms, the plain truth is, that *it is wholly owing to the constitution of the people, and not to the constitution of the government* that the Crown is not as oppressive in England as in Turkey…

Government by Kings was first introduced into the World by the Heathens, from whom the children of Israel copied the custom. It was the most prosperous invention the Devil ever set on foot for the promotion of idolatry. The Heathens paid divine honors to their deceased Kings, and the Christian World hath improved on the plan by doing the same to their living ones. How impious is the title of sacred Majesty applied to a worm, who in the midst of his splendor is crumbling into dust!

As the exalting one man so greatly above the rest cannot be justified on the equal right of nature, so neither can it be defended on the authority of scripture; for the will of the Almighty, as declared by Gideon and the prophet Samuel, expressly disapproves of Government by Kings. All anti-monarchical parts of scripture have been very smoothly glossed over in monarchical governments, but they undoubtedly merit the attention of Countries which have their governments yet to form. *"Render unto Cesar the things which are Cesar's,"* is the scripture doctrine of Courts, yet it is no support of monarchical government, for the Jews at that time were without a King, and in a state of vassalage to the Romans.

Near three thousand years passed away from the Mosaic account of the creation, till the Jews under a national delusion requested a king. Till then their form of government (except in extraordinary cases, where the Almighty interposed) was a kind of republic administered by a judge and the elders of the tribes. Kings they had none, and it was held sinful to acknowledge any Being under that title but the Lord of Hosts. And when a man seriously reflects on the idolatrous homage which is paid to the persons of kings, he need not wonder that the Almighty, ever jealous of his honor, should disapprove of a form of government which so impiously invades the prerogative of Heaven.

Monarchy is ranked in scripture as one of the sins of the Jews, for which a curse in reserve is denounced against them. The history of that transaction is worth attending to.

The children of Israel being oppressed by the Midianites, Gideon marched against them with a small army, and victory thro' the Divine interposition decided in his favour. The Jews elate with success, and attributing it to the generalship of Gideon, proposed making him a king; saying, *Rule thou over us, thou and thy son and thy son's son.* Here was temptation in its fullest extent; not a kingdom only, but an hereditary one, but Gideon in the piety of his soul replied, *I will not rule over you, neither shall my son rule over you.* THE LORD SHALL RULE OVER YOU. Words need not be more explicit; Gideon doth not *decline* the honor, but denieth their right to give it; neither doth he compliment them with invented declarations of his thanks, but in the positive stile of a prophet charges them with disaffection to their proper Sovereign, the King of Heaven…

To the evil of monarchy we have added that of hereditary succession; and as the first is a degradation and lessening of ourselves, so the second, claimed as a matter of right, is an insult and an imposition on posterity. For all men being originally equals, no *one* by *birth* could have a right to set up his own family in perpetual preference to all others for ever, and tho' himself might deserve *some* decent degree of honors of his cotemporaries, yet his descendants might be far too unworthy to inherit them. One of the strongest *natural* proofs of the folly of hereditary right in kings, is, that nature disapproves it, otherwise, she would not so frequently turn it into ridicule by giving mankind an *ass for a lion.*

Secondly, as no man at first could possess any other public honors than were bestowed upon him, so the givers of those honors could have no power to give away the right of posterity, and though they might say "We choose you for *our* head," they could not without manifest injustice to their children, say "that your children and your children's children shall reign over *our's* for ever." Because such an unwise, unjust, unnatural compact might (perhaps) in the next succession put them under the government of a rogue or a fool. Most wise men in their private sentiments have ever treated hereditary right with contempt; yet it is one of those evils, which when once established is not easily removed: many submit from fear, others from superstition, and the more powerful part shares with the king the plunder of the rest.

This is supposing the present race of kings in the world to have had an honorable origin: whereas it is more than probable, that could we take off the dark covering of antiquity and trace them to their first rise, that we should find the first of them nothing better than the principal ruffian of some restless gang, whose savage manners or pre-eminence in subtility obtained him the title of chief among plunderers; and who by increasing in power, and extending his depredations, over-awed the quiet and defenceless to purchase their safety by frequent contributions. Yet his electors could have no idea of giving hereditary right to his descendants, because such a perpetual exclusion of themselves was incompatible with the free and unrestrained principles they professed to live by. Wherefore, hereditary succession in the early ages of monarchy could not take place as a matter of claim, but as something casual or complimental; but as few or no records were extant in those days, and traditionary history stuff'd with fables, it was very easy after the lapse of a few generations, to trump up some superstitious tale conveniently timed, Mahomet like, to cram hereditary right down the throats of the vulgar. Perhaps the disorders which threatened, or seemed to threaten, on the decease of a leader and the choice of a new one (for elections among ruffians could not be very orderly) induced many at first to favor hereditary pretensions; by which means it happened, as it hath happened since, that what at first was submitted to as a convenience, was afterwards claimed as a right…

But it is not so much the absurdity as the evil of hereditary succession which concerns mankind. Did it ensure a race of good and wise men it would have the seal of divine authority, but as it opens a door to the *foolish*, the *wicked*, and the *improper,* it hath in it the nature of oppression. Men who look upon themselves born to reign, and others to obey, soon grow insolent—selected from the rest of mankind their minds are early poisoned by importance; and the world they act in differs so materially from the world at large, that they have but little opportunity of knowing its true interests, and when they succeed to the government are frequently the most ignorant and unfit of any throughout the dominions.

Another evil which attends hereditary succession is, that the throne is subject to be possessed by a minor at any age; all which time the regency acting under the cover of a king, have every opportunity and inducement to betray their trust. The same national misfortune happens when a king worn out with age and infirmity enters the last stage of human weakness. In both these cases the public becomes a prey to every miscreant, who can tamper successfully with the follies either of age or infancy...

The Sun never shined on a cause of greater worth. 'Tis not the affair of a City, a Country, a Province, or a Kingdom; but of a Continent—of at least one eighth part of the habitable globe. 'Tis not the concern of a day, a year, or an age; posterity are virtually involved in the contest, and will be more or less affected even to the end of time by the proceedings now. Now is the seed time of continental union, faith and honor. The least fracture now, will be like a name engraved with the point of a pin on the tender rind of a young oak; The wound will enlarge with the tree, and posterity read it in full grown characters.

By referring the matter from argument to arms, a new era for politics is struck—a new method of thinking hath arisen. All plans, proposals, &c. prior to the 19th of April, *i.e.* to the commencement of hostilities, are like the almanacks of the last year; which tho' proper then, are superceded and useless now. Whatever was advanced by the advocates on either side of the question then, terminated in one and the same point, viz. a union with Great Britain; the only difference between the parties, was the method of effecting it; the one proposing force, the other friendship; but it hath so far happened that the first hath failed, and the second hath withdrawn her influence.

As much hath been said of the advantages of reconciliation, which, like an agreeable dream, hath passed away and left us as we were, it is but right, that we should examine the contrary side of the argument, and enquire into some of the many material injuries which these colonies sustain, and always will sustain, by being connected with, and dependant on Great Britain. To examine that connection and dependance on the principles of nature and common sense, to see what we have to trust to if separated, and what we are to expect if dependant.

I have heard it asserted by some, that as America hath flourished under her former connection with Great Britain, that the same connection is necessary towards her future happiness and will always have the same effect—Nothing can be more fallacious than this kind of argument; we may as well assert that because a child has thrived upon milk, that it is never to have meat, or that the first twenty years of our lives is to become a precedent for the next twenty. But even this is admitting more than is true, for I answer roundly, that America would have flourished as much, and probably much more, had no European power taken any notice of her. The commerce, by which she hath enriched herself are the necessaries of life, and will always have a market while eating is the custom of Europe...

It hath lately been asserted in Parliament, that the colonies have no relation to each other but through the parent country, *i.e.* that Pennsylvania and the Jerseys and so on for the rest, are sister colonies by the way of England; this is certainly a very round about way of proving relationship, but it is the nearest and only true way of proving enemyship, if I may so call it. France and Spain never were, nor perhaps ever will be our enemies as *Americans*, but as our being the *subject of Great Britain*.

But Britain is the parent country, say some. Then the more shame upon her conduct. Even brutes do not devour their young, nor savages make war upon their families; wherefore the assertion, if true, turns to her reproach; but it happens not to be true, or only partly so, and the phrase *parent* or *mother country* hath been jesuitically adopted by the King and his parasites, with a low papistical design of gaining an unfair bias on the credulous weakness of our minds. Europe and not England is the parent country of America. This new world hath been the asylum for the persecuted lovers of civil and religious liberty from *every part* of Europe. Hither have they fled, not from the tender embraces of the mother, but from the cruelty of the monster; and it is so far true of England, that the same tyranny which drove the first emigrants from home, pursues their descendants still.

In this extensive quarter of the globe, we forget the narrow limits of three hundred and sixty miles (the extent of England) and carry our friendship on a larger scale; we claim brotherhood with every European Christian, and triumph in the generosity of the sentiment...

## 10. Jefferson's Original Rough Draft of the Declaration of Independence[12]

*On June 7, 1776, the Continental Congress began debating a resolution on independence. On June 10 it created a committee to draft a declaration of independence should it be necessary. The members of the committee were Thomas Jefferson of Virginia, John Adams of Massachusetts, Benjamin Franklin of Pennsylvania, Roger Sherman of Connecticut, and Robert Livingston of New York. The committee charged Jefferson with the task of preparing the draft declaration. The committee made some minor changes to Jefferson's draft which was submitted to Congress on June 28. After Congress voted in favor of independence on July 2, it edited and amended Jefferson's draft. Jefferson's draft, below, was a more radical document than that adopted by Congress.*

A Declaration of the Representatives of the UNITED STATES OF AMERICA, in General Congress assembled.

When in the course of human events it becomes necessary for a people to advance from that subordination in which they have hitherto remained, & to assume among the powers of the earth the equal & independant station to which the laws of nature & of nature's god entitle them, a decent respect to the opinions of mankind requires that they should declare the causes which impel them to the change.

We hold these truths to be sacred & undeniable; that all men are created equal & independant, that from that equal creation they derive rights inherent & inalienable, among which are the preservation of life, & liberty, & the pursuit of happiness; that to secure these ends, governments are instituted among men, deriving their just powers from the consent of the governed; that whenever any form of government shall become destructive of these ends, it is the right of the people to alter or to abolish it, & to institute new government, laying it's foundation on such principles & organising it's powers in such form, as to them shall seem most likely to effect their safety & happiness. prudence indeed will dictate that governments long established should not be changed for light & transient causes: and accordingly all experience hath shewn that mankind are more disposed to suffer while evils are sufferable, than to right themselves by abolishing the forms to which they are accustomed. but when a long train of abuses & usurpations, begun at a distinguished period, & pursuing invariably the same object, evinces a design to subject them to arbitrary power, it is their right, it is their duty, to throw off such government & to provide new guards for their future security. such has been the patient sufferance of these colonies; & such is now the necessity which constrains them to expunge their former systems of government. the history of his present majesty, is a history of unremitting injuries and usurpations, among which no one fact stands single or solitary to contradict the uniform tenor of the rest, all of which have in direct object the establishment of an absolute tyranny over these states. to prove this, let facts be submitted to a candid world, for the truth of which we pledge a faith yet unsullied by falsehood.

he has refused his assent to laws the most wholesome and necessary for the public good:

he has forbidden his governors to pass laws of immediate & pressing importance, unless suspended in their operation till his assent should be obtained; and when so suspended, he has neglected utterly to attend to them.

he has refused to pass other laws for the accomodation of large districts of people unless those people would relinquish the right of representation, a right inestimable to them, & formidable to tyrants alone:

he has dissolved Representative houses repeatedly & continually, for opposing with manly firmness his invasions on the rights of the people:

he has refused for a long space of time to cause others to be elected, whereby the legislative powers, incapable of annihilation, have returned to the people at large for their exercise, the state remaining in the mean time exposed to all the dangers of invasion from without, & convulsions within:

he has endeavored to prevent the population of these states; for that purpose obstructing the laws for naturalization of foreigners; refusing to pass others to encourage their migrations hither; & raising the conditions of new appropriations of lands:

he has suffered the administration of justice totally to cease in some of these colonies, refusing his assent to laws for establishing judiciary powers:

he has made our judges dependant on his will alone, for the tenure of their offices, and amount of their salaries:

he has erected a multitude of new offices by a self-assumed power, & sent hither swarms of officers to harrass our people & eat out their substance:

he has kept among us in times of peace standing armies & ships of war:

he has affected to render the military, independant of & superior to the civil power:

he has combined with others to subject us to a jurisdiction foreign to our constitutions and unacknoleged by our laws; giving his assent to their pretended acts of legislation, for quartering large bodies of armed troops among us;

for protecting them by a mock-trial from punishment for any murders they should commit on the inhabitants of these states;

for cutting off our trade with all parts of the world;

for imposing taxes on us without our consent;

for depriving us of the benefits of trial by jury;

for transporting us beyond seas to be tried for pretended offences: for taking away our charters, & altering fundamentally the forms of our governments;

for suspending our own legislatures & declaring themselves invested with power to legislate for us in all cases whatsoever:

he has abdicated government here, withdrawing his governors, & declaring us out of his allegiance & protection:

he has plundered our seas, ravaged our coasts, burnt our towns & destroyed the lives of our people:

he is at this time transporting large armies of foreign merce naries to compleat the works of death, desolation & tyranny, already begun with circumstances of cruelty & perfidy unworthy the head of a civilized nation:

he has endeavored to bring on the inhabitants of our frontiers the merciless Indian savages, whose known rule of warfare is an undistinguished destruction of all ages, sexes, & conditions of existence:

he has incited treasonable insurrections in our fellow-subjects, with the allurements of forfeiture & confiscation of our property:

he has waged cruel war against human nature itself, violating it's most sacred rights of life & liberty in the persons of a distant people who never offended him, captivating & carrying them into slavery in another hemisphere, or to incur miserable death in their transportation thither. this piratical warfare, the opprobrium of *infidel* powers, is the warfare of the CHRISTIAN king of Great Britain. determined to keep open a market where MEN should be bought & sold, he has prostituted his negative for suppressing every legislative attempt to prohibit or to restrain this execrable commerce: and that this assemblage of horrors might want no fact of distinguished die, he is now exciting those very people to rise in arms among us, and to purchase that liberty of which *he* has deprived them, & murdering the people upon whom *he* also obtruded them; thus paying off former crimes committed against the *liberties* of one people, with crimes which he urges them to commit against the *lives* of another.

in every stage of these oppressions we have petitioned for redress in the most humble terms; our repeated petitions have been answered by repeated injury. a prince whose character is thus marked by every act which may define a tyrant, is unfit to be the ruler of a people who mean to be free. future ages will scarce believe that the hardiness of one man, adventured within the short compass of 12 years only, on so many acts of tyranny without a mask, over a people fostered & fixed in principles of liberty.

Nor have we been wanting in attentions to our British brethren. we have warned them from time to time of attempts by their legislature to extend a jurisdiction over these our states. we have reminded them of the circumstances of our emigration & settlement here, no one of which could warrant so strange a pretension: that these were effected at the expence of our own blood & treasure, unassisted by the wealth or the strength of Great Britain: that in constituting indeed our several forms of government, we had adopted one common king, thereby laying a foundation for perpetual league & amity with them: but that submission to their parliament was no part of our constitution, nor ever in idea, if history may be credited: and we appealed to their native justice & magnanimity, as well as to the ties of our common kindred to disavow these usurpations which were likely to interrupt our correspondence & connection. they too have been deaf to the voice of justice & of consanguinity, & when occasions have been given them, by the regular course of their laws, of removing from their councils the disturbers of our harmony, they have by their free election re-established them in power. at this very time too they are permitting their chief magistrate to send over not only soldiers of our common blood, but Scotch & foreign mercenaries to invade & deluge us in blood. these facts have given the last stab to agonizing affection, and manly spirit bids us to renounce for ever these unfeeling brethren. we must endeavor to forget our former love for them, and to hold them as we hold the rest of mankind, enemies in war, in peace friends. we might have been a free & great people together; but a communication of grandeur & of freedom it seems is below their dignity. be it so, since they will have it: the road to glory & happiness is open to us too; we will climb it in a separate state, and acquiesce in the necessity which pronounces our everlasting Adieu!

We therefore the representatives of the United States of America in General Congress assembled do, in the name & by authority of the good people of these states, reject and renounce all allegiance & subjection to the kings of Great Britain & all others who may hereafter claim by, through, or under them; we utterly dissolve & break off all political connection which may have heretofore subsisted between us & the people or parliament of Great Britain; and finally we do assert and declare these a colonies to be free and independant states, and that as free & independant states they shall hereafter have power to levy war, conclude peace, contract alliances, establish commerce, & to do all other acts and things which independent states may of right do. And for the support of this declaration we mutually pledge to each other our lives, our fortunes, & our sacred honour.

## 11. Statue of George III Demolished, July 9, 1776[13]

*Declaring independence required Americans to discard their allegiance to King George III. For much of the previous decade Americans had attacked Parliament's authority. Independence meant severing ties with the British monarchy as well, which is why the Declaration of Independence contained a lengthy indictment of the monarch. This proved effective. After a public reading of the Declaration of Independence in New York City on July 9, 1776, New Yorkers symbolically overthrew the King when they destroyed an equestrian statue of the him. This is an early nineteenth-century image of the incident.*

**Figure 4.3** The Statue of George III Demolished, 1776. Courtesy of the Granger Collection, New York.

# Notes

1. "Thomas Jefferson to Henry Lee, May 8, 1825," Merrill D. Peterson, ed. *Thomas Jefferson: Writings* (New York: Library of America, 1984), 1501.
2. William Wirt, *Sketches of the Life and Character of Patrick Henry* (Philadelphia: Desilver Thomas, 1836), 138–142.
3. Gilder Lehrman Collection, New-York Historical Society. This document has been edited for length. The full version can be found at the book's website (http://www.routledge.com/textbooks/ revolutionaryamerica/).
4. The Granger Collection, New York.
5. Hon. Thomas Gage, Esq., *A Proclamation* (New York: n.p., 1775). Library of Congress Printed Ephemera Collection; Portfolio 38, Folio 17.
6. The Granger Collection, New York.
7. For the "High Roll" see Kate Haulman, "A Short History of the High Roll," *Common-Place*, 2 (2001); http://www.historycooperative.org/journals/cp/vol-02/no-01/lessons/
8. Worthington C. Ford et al., eds., *Journals of Continental Congress, 1774–1779*, 34 vols. (Washington DC: Government Printing Office, 1904–37), 2:140–157. This document has been edited for length. The full version can be found at the book's website (http://www.routledge.com/textbooks/ revolutionaryamerica/).
9. Worthington C. Ford et al., eds., *Journals of Continental Congress, 1774–1779*, 34 vols. (Washington DC: Government Printing Office, 1904–37), 2:158–161.
10. By the King, A Proclamation, For suppressing Rebellion and Sedition (London: Charles Eyre and William Straban, 1775).
11. Thomas Paine, *Common Sense* (Philadelphia: Robert Bell, 1776), ii, 4–9, 11–15, 17–20. The full text of this pamphlet can be found at the book's website (http://www.routledge.com/textbooks/ revolutionaryamerica/).
12. Thomas Jefferson, June 1776, Rough Draft of the Declaration of Independence, Thomas Jefferson Papers, Series 1: General Correspondence, 1651–1827. Library of Congress, Manuscript Division, Washington, DC.
13. The Granger Collection, New York.

# CHAPTER 5

# Winning Independence
## *The Wars of the American Revolution*

## Introduction

The War of Independence was *the* decisive turning point in British-American relations. Once British Americans and Britons began killing each other, compromise over the political and constitutional issues became infinitely more difficult. Ultimately, the rebel victory in the prolonged and bloody struggle confirmed the independence which Congress declared in July 1776. Britain recognized the independence of the United States in the 1783 Peace of Paris which changed the course of international relations (document 8).

The early days of the conflict were marked by uncertainty as the rebels undertook an *ad hoc* siege of the British in Boston (documents 1, 2, 4). Soon the rebels realized that they would have to raise a standing army if they were to win their independence (documents 1, 4, 6). Although the war featured regular soldiers from Britain, North America, and mainland Europe engaging in set-piece battles, it was also a bloody civil war which pitted British Americans against each other, leading to unprecedented violence and intimidation involving civilians, militias and irregular soldiers (documents 3 and 5). Loyalists and suspected loyalists were subject to physical intimidation and were sometimes killed. Some, like Samuel Curwen, went into exile during the war (document 9). Curwen's experience underscores the fact that the War of Independence, like all wars, was experienced by individuals each of whom had their own story to tell. The letters of William Russell—soldier, privateersman, and British prisoner provide an insight into the war from the perspective of an ordinary man caught up in extraordinary circumstances (document 7).

## 1. A British View of the Siege of Boston[1]

*In the aftermath of the fighting at Lexington and Concord, rebel militiamen subjected the British in Boston to an impromptu siege. This letter from a British naval surgeon reflects British attitudes toward the early stages of the uprising. The author is contemptuous of the rebels and confident in the ability of British forces to withstand the siege and suppress the rebellion.*

...There is a large body of them in arms near the town of Boston. Their camp and quarters are plentifully supplied with all sorts of provisions, and the roads are crouded with carts and carriages, bringing them rum cyder, &c., from the neighbouring towns, for without New-England rum, a New-England army could not be kept together; they could neither fight nor say their prayers, one with another; they drink at least a bottle of it a man a day. I had the honour to see several of their great Generals, and among the rest, General Judadiah Pribble: He is a stout looking old fellow, seems to be turned of 70. This army, which you will hear to much said, and see so much wrote about, is truly nothing but a drunken, canting, lying, praying, hypocritical rabble, without order, subjection, discipline, or cleanliness; and must fall to pieces of itself in the course of three months, notwithstanding every endeavour of their leaders, teachers, and preachers, though the last are the most canting, hypocritical, lying scoundrels that this or any other country ever afforded. You are mistaken, if you think they are Presbyterian, they are Congregationalists, divided and subdivided into a variety of distinctions, the descendants of Oliver Cromwell's army, who truly inherit the spirit which was the occasion of so much bloodshed in your country from the year 1642, till the Restoration, but these people are happily placed at a distance from you, and though they may occasion a little expence of men and money before they are reduced to order, yet they cannot extend the calamities of war to your island. They have not been hitherto the least molested since the affair at Lexington. Time has been given for their passions to subside, but I do not suppose that the General's patience will continue much longer, he is at present confined to the town of Boston, and all supplies from the country stopped, and both the navy and the army live upon salt provisions of that sort; I am well informed, there are nine months provisions in the town.

## 2. George Washington Reflects on his Appointment to Command the Continental Army[2]

*As the siege of Boston dragged on, Congress took responsibility for the ad hoc collection of militiamen surrounding the port. In June of 1775 it created the Continental Army and appointed George Washington (1732–1799) as its commander. The creation of the army and Washington's appointment as its commander signalled that Congress believed the war would be lengthy and would include most of the British colonies which had participated in the resistance to British taxation. In this letter written to his wife Martha Custis Washington (1731–1802) immediately after his appointment, Washington reflects on the conflict and considers the impact it will have on he and his wife.*

My Dearest:

I am now set down to write to you on a subject, which fills me with inexpressible concern, and this concern is greatly aggravated and increased, when I reflect upon the uneasiness I know it will give you. It has been determined in Congress, that the whole army raised for the defence of the American cause shall be put under my care, and that it is necessary for me to proceed immediately to Boston to take upon me the command of it.

You may believe me, my dear Patsy, when I assure you, in the most solemn manner that, so far from seeking this appointment, I have used every endeavour in my power to avoid it, not only from my unwillingness to part with you and the family, but from a consciousness of its being a trust too great for my capacity, and that I should enjoy more real happiness in one month with you at home, than I have the most distant prospect of finding abroad, if my stay were to be seven times seven years. But as it has been a kind of destiny, that has thrown me upon this service, I shall hope that my undertaking it is designed to answer some good purpose. You might, and I suppose did perceive, from the tenor of my letters, that I was apprehensive I could not avoid this appointment, as I did not pretend to intimate when I should return. That was the case. It was utterly out of my power to refuse this appointment, without exposing my character to such censures, as would have reflected dishonor upon myself, and given pain to my friends. This, I am sure, could not, and ought not, to be pleasing to you, and must have lessened me considerably in my own esteem. I shall rely, therefore, confidently on that Providence, which has heretofore preserved and been bountiful to me, not doubting but that I shall return safe to you in the fall. I shall feel no pain from the toil or the danger of the campaign; my unhappiness will flow from the uneasiness I know you will feel from being left alone. I therefore beg, that you will summon your whole fortitude, and pass your time as agreeably as possible. Nothing will give me so much sincere satisfaction as to hear this, and to hear it from your own pen. My earnest and ardent desire is, that you would pursue any plan that is most likely to produce content, and a tolerable degree of tranquillity; as it must add greatly to my uneasy feelings to hear, that you are dissatisfied or complaining at what I really could not avoid.

As life is always uncertain, and common prudence dictates to every man the necessity of settling his temporal concerns, which it is in his power, and while the mind is calm and undisturbed, I have, since I came to this place (for I had not time to do it before I left home) got Colonel Pendleton to draft a will for me, by the directions I gave him, which will I now enclose, The provision made for you in case of my death will, I hope, be agreeable.

I shall add nothing more, as I have several letters to write, but to desire that you will remember me to your friends, and to assure you that I am with the most unfeigned regard, my dear Patsy, your affectionate, &c.

### 3.   Harassment of Loyalists in South Carolina[3]

*From the outset the War of Independence was a violent struggle which often pitted neighbors against each other and divided families. In this letter, William Campbell (1730–1778), the last royal governor of South Carolina, describes the lynching of a free African American and the tarring and feathering of a suspected Loyalist. Written at the beginning of the war, Campbell's letter suggests that British authority and law and order collapsed quite quickly in South Carolina.*

…This is a very disagreable subject for me to dwell on, but my Duty requires I should represent the true state of this Province, and of my unfortunate Vicinage of N. Carolina, and Georgia, which is equally neglected, equally abandon'd. Your Lordship will I am sure excuse my warmth when I acquaint you, that yesterday under colour of Law, they hanged & burned, an unfortunate wretch, a free Negroe, of considerable property, one of the most valuable, useful men in his way, in the Province, on suspicion of instigating an Insurrection, for which I am convinced there was not the least ground. I could not save him My Lord! the very reflection Harrows my Soul! I have only the comfort to think I left no means untried to preserve him.

They have now dipt their hands in Blood, God Almighty knows where it is will end, but I am determined to remain till the last extremity in hope to promote the King's Service, 'tho my familys being here, adds not a little to my distress. Another Act of Barbarity, tho happily of not so tragical a Nature, was committed a few days ago on a poor man, the Gunner of Fort Johnson, who for expressing his Loyalty was tarr'd, & feather'd 10 or 12 times, in different parts of the Town, & otherwise treated with great cruelty, stopping him at the doors of those Crown officers who were most obnoxious; & the Mob so grossly insulted Mr. Milligan in particular who is Surgeon, to the Forts, & Garrisons in this Province, that he was under a necessity of taking refuge on board the King's ship till the Packet Boat sails.

### 4.   Observations of a New Hampshire Loyalist[4]

*Benjamin Thompson (1753–1814) was a New Hampshire Loyalist who fled to the British lines after his home was attacked by a Patriot mob. In this letter he provides a detailed description of the Continental Army. He astutely reflects on the difficulty which the imposition of military discipline posed to the rebels who took up arms to defend their rights.*

The army in general is not very badly accoutred, but most wretchedly clothed, and as dirty a set of mortals as ever disgraced the name of a soldier. They have no clothes of any sort provided for them by the Congress (except the detachment of 1,333 that are gone to Canada under Col. Arnold, who had each of them a new coat a linen frock served out to them before they set out), tho' the army in general, and the Massachusetts forces in particular, had encouragement of having coats given them by way of bounty for inlisting. And the neglect of the Congress to fulfil their promise in this respect has been the source of not a little uneasiness among the soldiers.

They have no women in the camp to do washing for the men, and they in general not being used to doing things of this sort, and thinking it rather a disparagement to them, choose rather to let their linen, &c., rot upon their backs than to be at the trouble of cleaning 'em themselves. And to this nasty way of life, and to the change of their diet from milk, vegetables, &c. to living almost intirely upon flesh, must be attributed those putrid, malignant, and infectious disorders which broke out among them soon after their taking the field, and which have prevailed with unabating fury during the whole summer.

The leading men among them (with their usual art and cunning), have been indefatigable in their endeavours to conceal the real state of the army in this respect, and to convince the world that the soldiers were tolerably heavy. But the contrary has been apparent, even to a demonstration, to every person that had but the smallest acquaintance with their camp. And so great was the prevalence of these disorders in the month of July that out of 4,207 men who were stationed upon Prospect Hill no more than 2,227 were returned fit for duty.

The mortality among them must have been very great, and to this in a great measure must be attributed the present weakness of their regiments; many of which were must [much] stronger when they came into the field. But the number of soldiers that have died in the camp is comparatively small to those vast numbers that have gone off in the interior parts of the country. For immediately upon being taken down these disorders they have in general been carried back into the country to their own homes, where they have not only died themselves, but by spreading the infection among their relatives and friends have introduced such a general mortality throughout New England as was never known since its first planting. Great numbers have been carried off in all parts of the country. Some towns 'tis said have lost near one-third of their inhabitants; and there is scarce a village in New England but has suffered more or less from the raging virulence of these dreadful disorders.

Perhaps the intolerable heats and continual droughts during the late summer by inclining the blood to a putrid state, and rendering it more easily susceptible of the infection, may have contributed not a little to the spread of these diseases.

Every article of provision that is the natural produce of the country is extremely cheap in the camp, except the article of bread, which is very far from being so, as the price of corn of every sort is much raised on account of a very great scarcity of it, occasioned by the late drought…

The soldiers in general are most heartily sick of the service, and I believe it would be with the utmost difficulty that they could be prevailed upon to serve another campaign. The Continental Congress are very sensible of this, and have lately sent a Committee to the camp to consult with the General Officers upon some method of raising the necessary forces to serve during the winter season, as the greatest part of the army that is now in the filed is to be disbanded upon the last day of December.

Whether they will be successful in their endeavours to persuade the soldiers to re-inlist or not, I cannot say, but am rather inclined to think that they will. For as they are men possessed of every species of cunning and artifice, and as their political existence depends upon the existence of the army, they will leave no stone unturn'd to accomplish their designs.

Notwithstanding the indefatigable indeavours of Mr. Washington, and the other Generals, and particularly of Adjutant General Gates, to arrange and discipline the army, yet any tolerable degree of order and subordination is what they are totally acquainted with in the rebel camp. And the doctrines of independence and levellism have been so effectually sown throughout the country, and so universally imbibed by all ranks of men, that I apprehend it will be with the greatest difficulty that the interior officers and soldiers will be ever brought to any tolerable degree of subjection to the commands of their superiors.

Many of their leading men are not insensible of this, and I have often heard them lament that the existence of that very spirit which induced the common people to take up arms, and resist the authority of Great Britain, should induce them to resist the authority of their own officers, and by that means effectually prevent their ever making good soldiers.

Another great reason why it is impossible to introduce a proper degree of subordination in the rebel army is the great degree of equality as to birth, fortune and education, that universally prevails among them. For men cannot bear to be commanded by others that are their superiors in nothing but in having had the good fortune to get a superior commission, for which perhaps they stood equally fair. And in addition to this, the officers and men are not only in general very nearly upon a par as to birth, fortune, &c., but in particular regiments are most commonly neighbours and acquaintances, and as such can with less patience submit to that degree of absolute submission and subordination which is necessary to form a well-disciplined corps.

Another reason why the army can never be well united and regulated is the disagreement and jealousies between the different troops from the different Colonies; which must ever fail to create disaffection and uneasiness among them. The Massachusetts forces already complain very loudly of the partiality of the General to the Virginians, and have even gone so far as to tax him with taking pleasure in bringing their officers to Court Martials, and having them cashiered that he may fill their places with his friends from that quarter. The gentlemen from the Southern Colonies, in their turn, complain of the enormous proportion of New England officers in the army, and particularly of those belonging to the province of Massachusetts Bay, and say, as the cause is now become a common one, and the expence is general, they ought to have an equal chance for command with their neighbours.

Thus have these jealousies and uneasiness already begun which I think cannot fail to increase, and grow every day more and more interesting, and if they do not finally destroy the very existence of the army (which I think they bid very fair to do), yet must unavoidably render it much less formidable than it otherways might have been.

Of all useless sets of men that ever incumbered an army, surely the boasted riflemen are certainly the most so. When they came to the camp they had every liberty and indulgence allow'd them that they could possibly wish for. They had more pay than any other soldiers; did no duty; were under no constraint from the commands of their officers, but went when and where they pleased, without being subject to be stopped or examined by any one, and did almost intirely as they pleased in every respect whatever. But they have not answered the end for which they were designed in any one article whatever. For instead of being the best marksmen in the world, and picking off every regular that was to be seen, there is scarcely a regiment in camp but can produce men that can beat them at shooting, and the army is now universally convinced that the continual fire which they kept up by the week and month together has had no other effect than to waste their ammunition, and convince the King's troops that they are not really not so formidable adversaries as they would wish to be thought…

## 5. Congress Resolves to Protect Loyalists, June 18, 1776[5]

*The persecution of loyalists posed a political problem for the Patriots who sought to win the allegiance of loyalist- and neutrally-inclined Americans. The question of loyalty was particularly complex prior to the adoption of the Declaration of Independence. On the eve of independence Congress adopted this resolution intended to protect loyalists from attacks and, presumably, to eventually win their allegiance.*

Resolved, That no man in these colonies, charged with being a tory, or unfriendly to the cause of American liberty, be injured in his person or property, or in any manner whatever disturbed, unless the proceeding against him be founded on an order of this Congress, or the Assembly, convention, council or committee of safety of the colony, or committee of inspection and observation, of the district wherein he resides; provided, that this resolution shall not prevent the apprehending any person found in the commission of some act destructive of American liberty, or justly suspected of a design to commit such act, and intending to escape, and bringing such person before proper authority for examination and trial.

## 6. Washington Reflects on the Challenges Facing the Continental Army[6]

*During the summer of 1776 the British captured New York City, which they occu-pied until 1783. In the aftermath of the defeat Washington wrote to John Hancock (1737–1793), the President of the Continental Congress describing the state of Continental Army. The commander argues that civilian concerns about stand-ing armies will need to be overcome if the rebels are to be successful. His letter highlights the problems, as he sees them, of trying to wage war against the British using militias.*

…We are now as it were, upon the eve of another dissolution of our Army: the remembrance of the difficulties which heppened upon that occasion last year, the consequences which might have followed the change, if proper advantages had been taken by the Enemy; added to a knowledge of the present temper and Situation of the Troops, reflect but a very gloomy prospect upon the appear-ance of things now, and satisfie me, beyond the possibility of doubt, that unless some speedy, and effectual measures are adopted by Congress, our cause will be lost.

It is in vain to expect, that any (or more than a trifling) part of this Army will again engage in the Service on the encouragement offered by Congress. When Men find that their Townsmen and Companions are receiving 20, 30, and more Dollars, for a few Months Service, (which is truely the case) it cannot be expected; without using compulsion; and to force them into the Service would answer no valuable purpose. When Men are irritated, and the Passions inflamed, they fly hastely and chearfully to Arms; but after the first emotions are over, to expect, among such People, as compose the bulk of an Army, that they are influenced by any other principles than those of Interest, is to look for what never did…

A Soldier reasoned with upon the goodness of the cause he is engaged in, and the inestimable rights he is contending for, hears you with patience, and acknowledges the truth of your observations, but adds, that it is of no more Importance to him than others. The Officer makes you the same reply, with this further remark, that his pay will not support him, and he cannot ruin himself and Family to serve his Country, when every Member of the community is equally Interested and benefitted by his Labours. The few therefore, who act upon Principles of disinterestedness, are, comparatively speaking, no more than a drop in the Ocean. It becomes evidently clear then, that as this Contest is not likely to be the Work of a day; as the War must be carried on systematically, and to do it, you must have good Officers, there are, in my Judgment, no other pos-sible means to obtain them but by establishing your Army upon a permanent footing; and giving your Officers good pay; this will induce Gentlemen, and Men of Character to engage; and till the bulk of your Officers are composed of such persons as are actuated by Principles of honour, and a spirit of enterprize, you have little to expect from them. —They ought to have such allowances as will enable them to live like, and support the Characters of Gentlemen; and not be driven by a scanty pittance to the low, and dirty arts which many of them practice, to filch the Public of more than the difference of pay would amount to upon an ample allowe. besides, something is due to the Man who puts his life in his hands, hazards his health, and forsakes the Sweets of domestic enjoyments. Why a Captn. in the Continental Service should receive no more than 5/. Curry per day, for performing the same duties that an officer of the same Rank in the British Service receives 10/. Sterlg. for, I never could conceive; especially when the latter is provided with every necessary he requires, upon the best terms, and the former can scarce procure them, at any Rate. There is nothing that gives a Man consequence, and renders him fit for Command, like a support that renders him Independant of every body but the State he Serves.

With respect to the Men, nothing but a good bounty can obtain them upon a permanent establishment; and for no shorter time than the continuance of the War, ought they to be engaged; as Facts incontestibly prove, that the difficulty, and cost of Inlistments, increase with time. When the Army was first raised at Cambridge, I am persuaded the Men might have been got without a bounty for the War: after this, they began to see that the Contest was not likely to end so speedily as was immagined, and to feel their consequence, by remarking, that to get the Militia In, in the course of last year, many Towns were induced to give them a bounty. Foreseeing the Evils resulting from this, and the destructive consequences which unavoidably would follow short Inlistments, I took the Liberty in a long Letter, written by myself (date not now recollected, as my Letter Book is not here) to recommend the Inlistments for and during the War; assigning such Reasons for it, as experience has since convinced me were well founded. At that time twenty Dollars would, I am persuaded, have engaged the Men for this term. But it will not do to look back, and if the present opportunity is slip'd, I am perswaded that twelve months more will Increase our difficulties fourfold. I shall therefore take the freedom of giving it as my opinion, that a good Bounty be immediately offered, aided by the proffer of at least 100, or 150 Acres of Land and a suit of Cloaths and Blankt, to each non-Comd. Officer and Soldier; as I have good authority for saying, that however high the Men's pay may appear, it is barely sufficient in the present scarcity and dearness of all kinds of goods, to keep them in Cloaths, much less afford support to their Families. If this encouragement then is given to the Men, and such Pay allowed the Officers as will induce Gentlemen of Character and liberal Sentiments to engage; and proper care and precaution are used in the nomination (having more regard to the Characters of Persons, than the Number of Men they can Inlist) we should in a little time have an Army able to cope with any that can be opposed to it, as there are excellent Materials to form one out of: but while the only merit an Officer possesses is his ability to raise Men; while those Men consider, and treat him as an equal; and (in the Character of an Officer) regard him no more than a broomstick, being mixed together as one common herd; no order, nor no discipline can prevail; nor will the Officer ever meet with that respect which is essentially necessary to due subordination.

To place any dependance upon Militia, is, assuredly, resting upon a broken staff. Men just dragged from the tender Scenes of domestick life; unaccustomed to the din of Arms; totally unacquainted with every kind of Military skill, which being followed by a want of confidence in themselves, when opposed to Troops regularly train'd, disciplined, and appointed, superior in knowledge, and superior in Arms, makes them timid, and ready to fly from their own shadows. Besides, the sudden change in their manner of living, (particularly in the lodging) brings on sickness in many; impatience in all, and such an unconquerable desire of returning to their respective homes that it not only produces shameful, and scandalous Desertions among themselves, but infuses the like spirit in others. Again, Men accustomed to unbounded freedom, and no controul, cannot not brook the Restraint which is indispensably necessary to the good order and Government of an Army; without which, licentiousness, and every kind of disorder triumpantly reign. To bring Men to a proper degree of Subordination, is not the work of a day, a Month or even a year; and unhappily for us, and the cause we are Engaged in, the little discipline I have been labouring to establish in the Army under my immediate Command, is in a manner done away by having such a mixture of Troops as have been called together within these few Months.

Relaxed, and unfit, as our Rules and Regulations of War are, for the Government of an Army, the Militia (those properly so called, for of these we have two sorts, the Six Months Men and those sent in as a temporary aid) do not think themselves subject to 'em, and therefore take liberties, which the Soldier is punished for; this creates jealousy; jealousy begets dissatisfaction, and these by degrees ripen into Mutiny; keeping the whole Army in a confused, and disordered State; rendering the time of those who wish to see regularity and good Order prevail more unhappy than Words can describe. Besides this, such repeated changes take place, that all arrangement is set at nought, and the constant fluctuation of things, deranges every plan, as fast as adopted.

These Sir, Congress may be assured, are but a small part of the Inconveniences which might be enumerated and attributed to Militia; but there is one that merits particular attention, and that is the expence. Certain I am, that it would be cheaper to keep 50, or 100,000 Men in constant pay than to depend upon half the number, and supply the other half occasionally by Militia. The time the latter is in pay before and after they are in Camp, assembling and Marching; the waste of Ammunition; the consumption of Stores, which in spite of every Resolution, and requisition of Congress they must be furnished with, or sent home, added to other incidental expences consequent upon their coming, and conduct in Camp, surpasses all Idea, and destroys every kind of regularity and œconomy which you could establish among fixed and Settled Troops; and will, in my opinion prove (if the scheme is adhered to) the Ruin of our Cause.

The Jealousies of a standing Army, and the Evils to be apprehended from one, are remote; and in my judgment, situated and circumstanced as we are, not at all to be dreaded; but the consequence of wanting one, according to my Ideas, formed from the present view of things, is certain, and inevitable Ruin; for if I was called upon to declare upon Oath, whether the Militia have been most serviceable or hurtful upon the whole; I should subscribe to the latter. I do not mean by this however to arraign the Conduct of Congress, in so doing I should equally condemn my own measures, (if I did not my judgment); but experience, which is the best criterion to work by, so fully, clearly, and decisively reprobates the practice of trusting to Militia, that no Man who regards order, regularity, and œconomy; or who has any regard for his own honour, Character, or peace of Mind, will risk them upon this Issue.

No less attention should be paid to the choice of Surgeons than other Officers of the Army; they should undergo a regular examination; and if not appointed by the Director Genl. and Surgeons of the Hospital, they ought to be subordinate to, and governed by his directions; the Regimental Surgeons I am speaking of, many of whom are very great Rascals, countenancing the Men in sham Complaints to exempt them from duty, and often receiving Bribes to Certifie Indispositions, with a view to procure discharges or Furloughs; but independant of these practices, while they are considered as unconnected with the Genl. Hospital there will be nothing but continual Complaints of each other: The Director of the Hospital charging them with enormity in their drafts for the Sick; and they him, for denying such things as are necessary. In short, there is a constant bickering among them, which tends greatly to the Injury of the Sick; and will always subsist till the Regimental Surgeons are made to look up to the Director Genl. of the Hospital as a Superior. Whether this is the case in regular Armies, or not, I cannot undertake to say; but certain I am there is a necessity for it in this, or the Sick will suffer; the Regimental Surgeons are aiming, I am persuaded, to break up the Genl. Hospital, and have, in numberless Instances, drawn for Medic'roes, Stores &ca. in the most profuse and extravagant manner, for private purposes.

Another matter highly worthy of attention, is, that other Rules and Regulation's may be adopted for the Government of the Army than those now in existence, otherwise the Army, but for the name, might as well be disbanded. For the most attrocious offences, (one or two Instances only excepted) a Man receives no more than 39 Lashes; and these perhaps (thro' the collusion of the Officer who is to see it inflicted), are given in such a manner as to become rather a matter of sport than punishment; but when inflicted as they ought, many hardend fellows who have been the Subjects, have declared that for a bottle of Rum they would undergo a Second operation; it is evident therefore that this punishment is inadequate to many Crimes it is assigned to, as a proof of it, thirty and 40 Soldiers will desert at a time; and of late, a practice prevails, (as you will see by my Letter of the 22d) of the most alarming nature; and which will, if it cannot be checked, prove fatal both to the Country and Army; I mean the infamous practice of Plundering, for under the Idea of Tory property, or property which may fall into the hands of the Enemy, no Man is secure in his effects, and scarcely in his Person; for in order to get at them, we have several Instances of People being frightned out of their Houses under pretence of those Houses being ordered to be burnt; and this is done with a view of siezing the Goods; nay, in order that the villany may be more effectually concealed, some Houses have actually been burnt to cover the theft...

## 7.   Letters from a Rebel Prisoner[7]

*William Russell (1748–1784) was a Boston schoolteacher and an early supporter of the Patriot cause. He participated in the Boston Tea Party and enlisted in the Massachusetts forces which unsuccessfully laid siege to the British in Newport, Rhode Island, in 1778. He then joined the crew of a rebel privateer and was captured and imprisoned by the British in Mill Prison, near Plymouth, England. Russell was held captive for several years. While in prison he kept a journal and wrote letters to his family and friends. The first letter here is to Benjamin Edes (1732–1801), a radical Boston newspaper printer. Russell reacts to the capture of Charleston in June 1780 and comments on the morale of his fellow prisoners. In the second letter, written in 1781, Russell wrote to his wife, Mary Richardson Russell (1753–1814), describing conditions in Mill Prison and expressing doubts about his hopes that he will be freed in a prisoner exchange. Russell was eventually freed in an exchange in June 1782. He was subsequently recaptured and imprisoned on the* Jersey *prison ship in New York harbor. He was freed at the end of the war and died of ill-health contracted while in captivity in 1784.*

### 7a.  William Russell to Benjamin Edes, July 1780

…When I wrote my first letter to you, I was in hopes soon to follow, but vain are the hopes of man, & especially in this place for when the 'Cartiel' came from France she brought no prisoners back, and then all our hopes of being exchanged was, and still is at an end, for it planely does appear that our friends have forsaken us, and don't care anything about us, for if they did they would not suffer English prisoners to enter into their service and keep us confined here as dead to our country, and lost to our distressed families, and God only knows, when we shall be able to avenge the wrongs that our families and we have received.

I am extremely sorry to hear that Charleston is taken from us, you can't think what an alteration it has made here. Some time before the news came here we were informed by some Gentlemen of Plymouth (good friends to our Country) that if we beat the English at Carolina, America would immediately be declared Independant, in short it was the general talk in England, but as I said before about the alteration, the cry now is America is coming in, their money is bad 40 paper for 1 silver; General Washington has but 4000 Troops and Congress is broke up &c. which news and knowing of Charleston being taken, greatly affects us, and what still adds to our grief is, that we are not likely to be exchanged to assist our much injured Country.

Some of my fellow prisoners have lain here almost four years, and if something is not done soon for us, I think the greater part will enter into the English service...

### 7b. William Russell to Mary Richardson Russell, March 4, 1781

Notwithstanding my long confinement, I bless God I have not experienced the want of any of the necessaries of life in this Prison, for with my industry and what I am allowed I live comfortably for a Prisoner.

The usage we receive (if I am a judge) is very good for we are allowed the liberty of the yard all day, and an open Market at the gate, to buy or sell from 9 o'clock in the morning to two in the afternoon, beside we have some comfortable lodgings. I have never been in the black hole once, nor on a half diet, for I have made it my study to behave as a prisoner ought, and am treated accordingly.

Last year before this time we had the pleasing prospect of an exchange and one hundred went, but to my inexpressible grief, I see but little hope of being exchanged now till the war is at an end, and where to lay the blame I'm at a loss, tho' I think our People might do more than they do; however I keep up good spirits, and still live in hopes, as we are informed something is doing for us tho' slowly. Write soon and direct to the care of Jonathan Williams and Nantz as I do understand from Capt Manley he is there. Give my duty to my mother &c. &c.

P.S. Give my love to Billy and Sammy and run them to school. Inform Mr James Brewer (Block Maker) that his son & grandson are here and well &c.

### 8. Treaty of Paris, 1783[8]

*After Cornwallis's surrender at Yorktown in October 1781, the British suspended major military operations in North America—though the war continued against the French and Spanish in the West Indies. American and British diplomats engaged in prolonged negotiations which resulted in the Treaty of Paris, signed on September 3, 1783. Under the terms of the treaty the British recognized the independence of the United States, gave the new republic generous boundaries, and the signatories agreed to honor pre-war debt claims. The United States undertook to urge the states to make restitution to loyalists for property seized and to prevent future seizures. The British pledged to withdraw their forces from the United States without taking the property of Americans, including slaves, with them. The British also signed treaties with France, Spain, and the Netherlands thereby bringing the War of Independence to an end.*

...Art 1. His Brittanic Majesty acknowledges the said United States, viz., New-Hampshire, Massachusetts Bay, Rhode-Island and Providence Plantations, Connecticut, New York, New Jersey, Pennsylvania, Delaware, Maryland, Virginia,

North-Carolina, South-Carolina and Georgia, to be free, sovereign and independent states; that he treats with them as such, and for himself, his heirs, and successors, relinquishes all claims to the government, propriety, and territorial rights of the same and every part thereof.

Art 2. And that all disputes which might arise in future on the subject of the boundaries of the said United States may be prevented, it is hereby agreed and declared, that the following are and shall be their boundaries, viz.; from the northwest angle of Nova Scotia, viz., that angle which is formed by a line drawn due north from the source of St. Croix River to the Highlands; along the said Highlands, which divide those rivers that empty themselves into the river St. Lawrence, from those which fall into the Atlantic Ocean, to the north-westernmost head of Connecticut River; thence down along the middle of that river to the forty-fifth degree of north latitude; from thence by a line due west on said latitude, until it strikes the river Iroquois or Cataraquy; thence along the middle of said river into Lake Ontario; through the middle of the said lake until it strikes the communication by water between that lake and Lake Erie; thence along the middle of said communication into Lake Erie, through the middle of said lake until it arrives at the water communication between that lake and Lake Huron; thence along the middle of said water communication into Lake Huron, thence through the middle of said lake to the water communication between that lake and Lake Superior; thence through Lake Superior, northward of the Isles Royal and Phelipeaux to the Long Lake; thence through the middle of said Long Lake and the water communication between it and the Lake of the Woods, to the said Lake of the Woods; thence through the said lake to the most north-westernmost point thereof, and from thence on a due west course to the river Mississippi; thence by a line to be drawn along the middle of the said river Mississippi until it shall intersect the northernmost part of the thirty-first degree of north latitude, South, by a line to be drawn due east from the determination of the line last mentioned in the latitude of thirty-one degrees of the equator, to the middle of the river Apalachicola or Catahouche; thence along the middle thereof to its junction with the Flint River; thence straight to the head of St. Mary's River; and thence down along the middle of St. Mary's River to the Atlantic Ocean; east, by a line to be drawn along the middle of the River St. Croix, from its mouth in the Bay of Fundy to its source, and from its source directly north to the aforesaid Highlands which divide the rivers that fall into the Atlantic Ocean from those which fall into the River St. Lawrence; comprehending all islands within twenty leagues of any part of the shores of the United States, and lying between lines to be drawn due east from the points where the aforesaid boundaries between Nova Scotia on the one part and East Florida on the other, shall respectively, touch the Bay of Fundy and the Atlantic Ocean, excepting such islands as now are or heretofore have been within the limits of the said province of Nova Scotia.

Art 3. It is agreed that the people of the United States shall continue to enjoy unmolested the right to take fish of every kind on the Grand Bank, and on all the other banks of Newfoundland, also in the gulpf of St. Lawrence, and all other places in the sea, where the inhabitants of both countries used at any time heretofore to fish. And also that the inhabitants of the United States shall have liberty to take fish of every kind on such part of the coast of Newfoundland as British fishermen shall use, (but not to dry or cure the same on that island) and also on the coasts, bays and creeks of all other of his Brittanic Majesty's dominions in America; and that the American fishermen shall have liberty to dry and cure fish in any of the unsettled bays, harbors, and creeks of Nova Scotia, Magdalen Islands, and Labrador, so long as the same shall remain unsettled: but so soon as the same or either of them shall be settled, it shall not be lawful for the said fishermen to dry or cure fish at such settlement without a previous agreement for that purpose with the inhabitants, proprietors, or possessors of the ground.

Art 4. It is agreed that creditors on either side shall meet with no lawful impediment to the recovery of the full value in sterling money of all bona fide debts heretofore contracted.

Art 5. It is agreed that Congress shall earnestly recommend it to the legislatures of the respective states to provide for the restitution of all estates, rights, and properties, which have been confiscated belonging to real British subjects; and also of the estates, rights, and properties of persons resident in districts in the possession on his Majesty's arms and who have not borne arms against the said United States: and that persons of any other description shall have free liberty to go to any part or parts of any of the Thirteen United States, and therein to remain twelve months unmolested in their endeavors to obtain the restitution of such of their estates, rights, and properties as may have been confiscated; and that Congress shall also earnestly recommend to the several states a reconsideration and revision of all acts or laws regarding the premises, so as to render the said laws or acts perfectly consistent, not only with justice and equity, but with that spirit of conciliation, which, on the return of the blessings of peace should universally prevail: and that Congress shall also earnestly recommend to the several states, that the estates, rights, and properties, of such last mentioned persons shall be restored to them, they refunding to any persons who may be now in possession the bona fide price (where any has been given) which such persons may have paid on purchasing any of the said lands, rights, or properties since the confiscation.

And it is agreed that all persons who have any interest in confiscated lands, either by debts, marriage settlements, or otherwise, shall meet with no lawful impediment in the prosecution of their just rights.

Art 6. That there shall be no future confiscations made, nor any prosecutions commenced against any person or persons for, or by reason of the part which he or they may have taken in the present war: and that no person shall, on that account suffer any future loss or damage; either in his person, liberty, or property: and that those who may be in confinement on such charges at the time of the ratification of the treaty in America, shall be immediately set at liberty, and the prosecutions so commenced be discontinued.

Art 7. There shall be a firm and perpetual peace between his Brittanic Majesty and the said states, and between the subjects of the one and the citizens of the other; wherefore all hostilities both by sea and land shall from henceforth cease: all prisoners on both sides shall be set at liberty, and his Brittanic majesty shall, with all convenient speed, and without causing any destruction, or carrying away any negroes or other property of the American inhabitants, withdraw all his armies, garrisons, and fleets from the said United States, and from every post, place, and harbour, within the same, leaving in all fortifications the American artilery that may be therein; and shall also order and cause all archives, records, deeds, and papers belonging to any of the said states, or their citizens, which in the course of the war may have fallen into the hands of his officers, to be forthwith restored and delivered to the proper states and persons to whom they belong.

Art 8. The navigation of the river Mississippi, from its source to the ocean, shall forever remain free and open to the subjects of Great Britain and the citizens of the United States.

Art 9. In case it so shou'd happen that any place or territory belonging to Great Britain, or to the United States should have been conquered by the arms of either from the other, before the arrival of the said provisional articles in America, it is agreed, that the same shall be restored without difficulty and without requiring any compensation.

Art 10. The solemn ratifications of the present treaty, expedited in good and due form shall be exchanged between the Contracting Parties in the space of six months, or sooner, if possible, to be computed from the day of the signature of the present treaty. In Witness whereof, we the undersigned, their ministers plenipotentiary, have in their name and in virtue of our full powers, signed with our hands the present Definitive Treaty, and caused the seals of our arms to be affixed thereto.

## 9.  A Loyalist Returns[9]

*With the end of the War of Independence, thousands of Loyalists had to choose whether to remain in (or return to) the new United States or to go into permanent exile. The choice was a difficult one as evidenced by this letter from Samuel Curwen (1715–1802) written after the conclusion of the Treaty of Paris. Curwen was a Loyalist merchant from Salem, Massachusetts, who went into exile when the War of Independence began. At the end of the war Curwen contemplated a return to Massachusetts. In his letter to William Pynchon, he reveals his anxieties about returning home and provides an account of John Adams's arrival in London as the first American ambassador to Britain. Eventually Samuel Curwen returned to Salem. His brief diary entry recounts his return after nearly nine and half years' exile. It speaks to the human cost of the war.*

### 9a. Samuel Curwen to William Pynchon, London, November 28, 1783

However unfavorable to my wishes the result of the American Assemblies may be, I shall be gratified by receiving the earliest advices. Capt. Nathaniel West brings me a message from the principal merchants and citizens of Salem, proposing and encouraging my return; which instance of moderation I view as an honor to the town and respectful to myself, and I wish to return my thanks through you. It affords me pleasure, and I would cheerfully accept the offer; but should the popular dislike rise against me, especially if co-operating with governmental resolves, to what a plight should I be reduced, being at present (but for how long is a painful uncertainty) on the British government list for £100 a year, (a competency for a single person exercising strict economy,) to surrender this precarious allowance without public assurances of personal security.

It would be little short of madness, should the popular rage combine with the public decisions to prevent our future residence; deprived of all assistance, and even the last refuge of the wretched, hope here, expelled there. Imagine to yourself the distress of an old man, without health, under such adverse circumstances, and you will advise me to wait with resignation till the several Assemblies shall have taken decisive measures on congressional recommendation, agreeably to the provisional treaty, if that body shall deem it prudent to conform to what their commissioners have agreed to. But enough of this. One of your Massachusetts public ministers, Mr. John Adams, is here in all the pride of American independence; by Mr. Gorham I am told he uttered to him the following speech, that *"together with the war he had buried all animosity against the absentees."* Though he is of a rigid temper, and a thorough-paced republican, candor obliges me to give him credit for the humanity of the sentiment, being spoken in private, and to one of his own party, and probably without an intention to be published abroad. In a conversation with my informant, he further replied, that he chose to consider himself as a plain American republican; his garb plain, without a sword, which is carrying his transatlantic ideas, I fear, a little too far. Should he have the curiosity, or his public character render it expedient, to attend at a royal levee, or at a drawing-room at St. James's on a court day, I hope he will not deserve and meet with as mortifying a repulse as our late chancellor, Lord Thurlow, at the court of Versailles; whose surly pertinacity in wearing a bob-wig occasioned his being refused admittance into the king's presence. However frivolous a part of dress soever a sword may appear to one of Mr. Adams's scholar-like turn, he is by this time, I fancy, too well acquainted with the etiquette of courts to neglect so necessary an appendage, without which no one can find admittance out of the clerical line...

## 9b. Samuel Curwen, Diary, September 25, 1784

Arrived at Boston, and at half past three o'clock landed at the end of Long-wharf, after an absence of nine years and five months, occasioned by a lamented civil war, excited by ambitious, selfish men here and in England, to the disgrace, dishonor, distress and disparagement of these extensive territories. By plunder and rapine some few have accumulated wealth, but many more are greatly injured in their circumstances; some have to lament over the wreck of their departed wealth and estates, of which pitiable number I am; my affairs having sunk into irretrievable ruin.

## Notes

1. Margaret Wheeler Willard (ed.), *Letters on the American Revolution, 1774–1776* (Port Washington, NY: Kennikat, 1968), 120–121. This document has been edited for length. The full version can be found at the book's website (http://www.routledge.com/textbooks/revolutionaryamerica/).
2. "George Washington to Martha Washington, Philadelphia, June 18, 1775," in John C. Fitzpatrick (ed.), *The Writings of George Washington*, Vol. 3 (Washington, DC: United States Government Printing Office, 1931), 293–295.
3. *Manuscripts of the Earl of Dartmouth*, Vol. 2 (London: HMSO, 1887–1896), 354. This document has been edited for length.
4. "Observations by Benjamin Thompson (afterwards Count Rumford)," *Report on The Manuscripts of Mrs. Stopford Sackville of Northamptonshire*, Vol. 2 (Hereford, England: Hereford Times Co. Ltd., 1910), 15–18. This document has been edited for length.
5. *Pennsylvania Gazette*, June 19, 1776.
6. "George Washington to the President of Congress, September 24, 1776" in Fitzpatrick (ed.), *Writings of Washington*, Vol. 6, 106–114. This document has been edited for length. The full version can be found at the book's website ((http://www.routledge.com/textbooks/revolutionaryamerica/).
7. James Kimball, *A Journal giving an account of the sufferings & privations of the American Prisoners confined in the 'Old Mill Prison' Plymouth, England made prisoners, whilst serving under the American Flat, Written by William Russell of Boston, Clerk to John Manley Esq, Commander of the Continental Ship Jason, Also Appended a list of Prisoners; with the names of vessels in which taken; during the whole period of the American War. With notes and annotations from British and American State Papers.* This document has been edited for length.
8. Treaty of Paris, 1783, *The Definitive Treaty between Great-Britain and the United States, signed at Paris the 3rd Day of September, 1783* (Baltimore, MD: J. Hayes and J. A. Killen, 1783). This document has been edited for length. The full version can be found at the book's website (http://www.routledge.com/textbooks/revolutionaryamerica/).
9. George Atkinson Ward (ed.), *Journal and Letters of the late Samuel Curwen, Judge of Admiralty, Etc., An American Refugee in England, from 1775 to 1784, Comprising Remarks on the Prominent Men and Measures of that Period To Which Are Added, Biographical Notices of Many American Loyalists and Other Eminent Persons* (New York: C.S. Francis and Co., 1842), 393–394, 415.

# African Americans in the Age of Revolution

## Introduction

"How is it that we hear the loudest yelps for liberty among the drivers of Negroes?" So asked the English lexicographer Samuel Johnson at the height of the imperial crisis. Johnson directly addressed the contradiction at the heart of the American Revolution. When the American revolutionaries committed themselves to independence and republicanism premised on an assertion of equal rights, they did so despite the fact that one-fifth of the American population was enslaved and denied the legal and political rights for which the rebels fought. Some Americans argued that the right to hold human beings as property was among the rights for which they fought, as the November 1775 petition from Patriots in Halifax Virginia suggests (document 1). The Revolution and the War of Independence presented African-American slaves with opportunities to win their liberty. In many cases, particularly in the South, the British presented slaves with the best chance of attaining freedom. Early in the war Lord Dunmore, the last royal governor of Virginia, offered freedom to the slaves of rebels who fled their masters, like those in Halifax County, and supported the British war effort (document 2). This set a precedent which the British often followed during the war; many slaves associated the British with freedom.

A Virginian, Thomas Jefferson, perhaps more than any other American, epitomized the contradiction criticized by Samuel Johnson. Documents 3a–d reflect the range of Jefferson's thinking on the subject. Included are his condemnation of the slave trade in his draft of the Declaration of Independence, his notorious theories on racial differences as well as his analysis of the impact of slavery on whites from *Notes on the State of Virginia* and an exchange of letters between Jefferson and the African American astronomer, Benjamin Banneker.

In the northern states slaves sought to apply political and legal pressure to end slavery through petitions and lawsuits as well as service in the rebel forces. These efforts met with qualified success as each of the northern states abolished slavery, mainly through the adoption of gradual emancipation laws such as the 1780 act adopted in Pennsylvania (documents 4–6). Others sought freedom outside of the United States. At the end of the War of Independence, among the thousands of Loyalists that the British removed from the United States were many former slaves who were relocated throughout the British Empire. Many went to Nova Scotia (document 7).

In the face of a growing abolition movement in Britain and in the wake of the American and French Revolutions, slavery was under increasing pressure throughout the Atlantic world as the eighteenth century drew to a close. A nascent abolition movement developed in the new American republic (document 8). Meanwhile, in the French colony of Saint-Domingue, slaves rebelled and established a republic during the 1790s (documents 9–10). Dominguan refugees reinforced the deep-seated fear of slave rebellion in the United States. That fear seemed to be realized in the abortive Virginia uprising in August 1800 known as Gabriel's Rebellion (documents 11–12).

## 1. Virginia Revolutionaries Defend Slavery[1]

*Terms like "liberty," "tyranny," and "slavery" appeared regularly in the dispute over British rule in America in the decade before the War of Independence began. This rhetoric caused some Patriots to question slavery and even to take action to limit or abolish the institution. Anti-slavery sentiment was limited, however. This Virginia petition from supporters of the Revolution invokes biblical authority and property rights to defend slavery against a proposed abolition bill.*

When the British Parliament usurped a Right to dispose of our Property without our Consent, we dissolved the Union with our Parent Country, and established a Constitution and Form of Government of our own, that our Property might be secure in Future. In Order to effect this, we risked our Lives and fortunes, and waded through Seas of Blood. Divine Providence smiled on our Enterprize, and crowned it with Success. And our Rights of Liberty and Property are now as well secured to us, as they can be by any human Constitution and Form of Government.

But notwithstanding this, we understand, a very subtle and daring Attempt is on Foot to deprive us of a very important Part of our Property. An Attempt carried on by the Enemies of our Country, Tools of the British Administration, and supported by a Number of deluded Men among us, to wrest from us our Slaves by an act of the Legislature for a general Emancipation of them. They have the Address, indeed to cover their Design, with the Veil of Piety and Liberality of Sentiment. But is unsupported by the Word of God, and will be ruinous to Individuals and to the Public.

It is unsupported by the World of God. Under the Old Testament Dispensation, Slavery was permitted by the Deity himself. Thus it is recorded, in Levit. Chap. 25. Ver. 44, 45, 46. 'Both they Bond-men, and Bond-maids, which thou shalt have, shall be of the Heathen that are round about you; of them shall ye buy Bond-men and Bond-maids. Moreover, of the Children of the Strangers, that do sojourn among you of them shall ye buy, and of their Families that are with you, which they beget in your Land, and they shall be your Possession, and ye shall take them, as an Inheritance for your Children after you, to inherit them for a Possession; they shall be your Bond-men forever.' This Permission to possess and inherit Bond Servants, we have Reason to conclude, was continued through all the Revolutions of the Jewish Government, down to the Advent of our Lord. And we do not find, that either he or his Apostles abridged it. On the Contrary, the Freedom which the Followers of Jesus were taught to expect, was a Freedom from the Bondage of Sin and Satan, and from the Dominion of their Lusts and Passions; but as to their outward Condition, whatever that was, wether Bond or Free, when they embraced Christianity, it was to remain the same afterwards. This Saint Paul hath expressly told us 1 Cor. Chap. 7. Ver. 20th. where he is speaking directly to this very Point; 'Let every Man abide in the same Calling, wherein he is called'; and at Ver. 24. 'Let every Man wherein he is called therein abide with God.' Thus it is evident the above Attempt is unsupported by the Divine Word.

It is also ruinous to Individuals and to the Public. For it involves in it, and is productive of Want, Poverty, Distress, and Ruin to the Free Citizen; Neglect, Famine, and Death to the helpless black Infant and superannuated Parent; the Horrors of all the Rapes, Murders, and Outrages, which a vast Multitude of unprincipled, unpropertied, vindictive, and remorseless Banditti are capable of perpetrating; inevitable Bankruptcy to the Revenue, and consequently Breach of public Faith, and Loss of Credit with foreign nations; and lastly Ruin to this now free and flourishing Country.

We therefore your Remonstrants and Petitioners do solemnly abjure and humble pray you, that you will discountenance and utterly reject every Motion and Proposal for emancipating our Slaves; that as the Act lately made, empowering the Owners of Slaves to liberate them has been and is still productive, in some Measure, of sundry of the above pernicious Effects, you will immediately and totally repeal it; and that as many of the Slaves, liberated by the said Act, have been guilty of Thefts and Outrages, Insolence and Violences destructive to the Peace, Safety, and Happiness of Society, you will make effectual Provision for the due Government of them.

## 2. Lord Dunmore Promises Freedom to Virginia Slaves[2]

*As the preceding document suggests, slaves had little hope of achieving liberty at the hands of the Virginia Patriots. In contrast, just four days later, John Murray, Earl of Dunmore (1732–1809), the last royal governor of Virginia, issued this proclamation promising freedom to all slaves who fled rebel masters to support the British war effort.*

As I have ever entertained hopes, that an accommodation might have taken Place between *Great Britain* and this colony, without being compelled, *by my duty* to this most disagreeable, but now absolutely necessary step, rendered so by a body of armed men, unlawfully assembled, firing on his majesty's troops, and the formation of an army, and that army now on their march to attack his majesty's troops and destroy the well disposed subjects of this colony: To defeat such treasonable purposes, and that all such traitors, and their abetters, may be brought to justice, and that the peace and good order of this colony may be again restored, which the ordinary course of the civil law is unable to effect, I have thought fit to issue this my proclamation, hereby declaring, that until the aforesaid good purposes can be obtained, I do in virtue of the power and authority to me given, *by his majesty*, determine to execute martial law, and cause the same to be executed throughout this colony; and to the end that *peace* and *good order* may the sooner be restored, I do require every person capable of bearing arms, to resort to his majesty's STANDARD, or be looked upon as traitors to his majesty's crown and government, and thereby become liable to the penalty the law inflicts upon such offences; such as *forfeiture of life, confiscation of lands,* &c. &c. And I do hereby further declare all *indented servants, negroes,* or others, (appertaining to Rebels) *free,* that are able and willing to bear arms, they *joining his majesty's troops,* as soon as may be, for the more speedily reducing this colony to a *proper sense* of their duty, to his majesty's liege subjects to retain their quitrents, or any other taxes due, or that may become due, in their own custody, till such time as peace may be again restored to this at present most unhappy country, or demanded of them for their former salutary purposes, by officers properly authorised to receive the fame.

### 3. Thomas Jefferson on Slavery and African Americans

*As the author of the Declaration of Independence and a slaveholder, Thomas Jefferson embodied the moral contradiction at the heart of the American Revolution. During his lifetime Jefferson owned approximately 600 slaves, only a few of whom he freed when he died. Jefferson was aware of the ethical challenge which slavery posed to the new republic. He condemned slavery even though he took little meaningful action against the institution. The following selections reveal Jefferson's ambivalence with respect to slavery. The first, a clause from Jefferson's draft of the Declaration of Independence (excised by Congress), condemned the Atlantic slave trade and recognized the "rights of life & liberty" of Africans. The next passages from* Notes on the State of Virginia *(the only book Jefferson ever published) discuss Jefferson's opposition to slavery, based largely on its effect on the morality and character of slaveholders. While he opposed slavery, Jefferson believed that Africans were inferior to Europeans. In the* Notes *he enumerated the racial differences between blacks and whites, anticipating the scientific racism of the nineteenth century. Notwithstanding his belief in African inferiority, Jefferson was presented with evidence to the contrary as his exchange with the African American astronomer and publisher, Benjamin Banneker (1731–1806) attests. In response to Jefferson's claims concerning the racial differences between Africans and Europeans, Banneker presented Jefferson with a copy of his almanac. In his reply Jefferson conceded that differences in attainment between whites and blacks might be explained by environmental rather than racial differences.*

### 3a.  Rough Draft of the Declaration of Independence, July 1, 1776[3]

…he has waged cruel war against human nature itself, violating it's most sacred rights of life & liberty in the persons of a distant people who never offended him, captivating & carrying them into slavery in another hemisphere, or to incur miserable death in their transportation thither. this piratical warfare, the opprobium of *infidel* powers, is the warfare of the *Christian* king of Great Britain. *determined* to keep open a market where MEN should be bought & sold he has prostituted his negative for suppressing every legislative attempt to prohibit or to restrain this execrable commerce [~~determining to keep open a market where MEN should be bought and sold~~]: and that this assemblage of horrors might want no fact of distinguished die, he is now exciting those very people to rise in arms among us, and to purchase that liberty of which *he* has deprived them, by murdering the people upon whom he also obtruded them: thus paying off former crimes committed against the *liberties* of one people, with crimes which he urges them to commit against the *lives* of another…

### 3b.  Notes on the State of Virginia, 1781–1782[4]

Query 14: "Laws" The administration of justice and description of the laws? Many of the laws which were in force during the monarchy being relative merely to that form of government , or inculcating principles inconsistent with republicanism, the first assembly which met after the establishment of the commonwealth appointed a committee to revise the whole code, to reduce it into proper form and volume, and report it to the assembly…

The following are the most remarkable alterations proposed…

To emancipate all slaves born after passing the act. The bill reported by the revisors does not itself contain this proposition; but an amendment containing it was prepared, to be offered to the legislature whenever the bill should be taken up, and further directing, that they should continue with their parents to a certain age, then be brought up, at the public expence, to tillage, arts or sciences, according to their geniusses, till the females should be eighteen, and the males twenty-one years of age, when they should be colonized to such place as the circumstances of the time should render most proper, sending them out with arms, implements of houshold and of the handicraft arts, feeds, pairs of the useful domestic animals, &c. to declare them a free and independant people, and extend to them our alliance and protection, till they have acquired strength; and to send vessels at the same time to other parts of the world for an equal number of white inhabitants; to induce whom to migrate hither, proper encouragements were to be proposed. It will probably be asked, Why not retain and incorporate the blacks into the state, and thus save the expence of supplying, by importation of white settlers, the vacancies they will leave? Deep rooted prejudices entertained by the whites; ten thousand recollections, by the blacks, of the injuries they have sustained; new provocations; the real distinctions which nature has made; and many other circumstances, will divide us into parties, and produce convulsions which will probably never end but in the extermination of the one or the other race. —To these objections, which are political, may be added others, which are physical and moral. The first difference which strikes us is that of colour. Whether the black of the negro resides in the reticular membrane between the skin and scarf-skin, or in the scarf-skin itself; whether it proceeds from the colour of the blood, the colour of the bile, or from that of some other secretion, the difference is fixed in nature, and is as real as if its seat and cause were better known to us. And is this difference of no importance? Is it not the foundation of a greater or less share of beauty in the two races? Are not the fine mixtures of red and white, the expressions of every passion by greater or less suffusions of colour in the one, preferable to that eternal monotony, which reigns in the countenances, that immoveable veil of black which covers all the emotions of the other race? Add to these, flowing hair, a more elegant symmetry of form, their own judgment in favour of the whites, declared by their preference of them, as uniformly as is the preference of the Oranootan for the black women over those of his own species. The circumstance of superior beauty, is thought worthy attention in the propagation of our horses, dogs, and other domestic animals; why not in that of man? Besides those of colour, figure, and hair, there are other physical distinctions proving a difference of race. They have less hair on the face and body. They secrete less by the kidnies, and more by the glands of the skin, which gives them a very strong and disagreeable odour. This greater degree of transpiration renders them more tolerant of heat, and less so of cold, than the whites. Perhaps too a difference of structure in the pulmonary apparatus, which a late ingenious experimentalist has discovered to be the principal regulator of animal heat, may have disabled them from extricating, in the act of inspiration, so much of that fluid from the outer air, or obliged them in expiration, to part with more of it. They seem to require less sleep. A black after hard labour through the day, will be induced by the slightest amusements to sit up till midnight or later, though knowing he must be out with the first dawn of the morning. They are at least as brave, and more adventuresome. But this may perhaps proceed from a want of fore-thought, which prevents their seeing a danger till it be present. When present, they do not go through it with more coolness or steadiness than the whites. They are more ardent after their female: but love seems with them to be more an eager desire, than a tender delicate mixture of sentiment and sensation. Their griefs are transient. Those numberless afflictions, which render it doubtful whether heaven has given life to us in mercy or in wrath, are less felt, and sooner forgotten with them. In general, their existence appears to participate more of sensation than reflection. To this must be ascribed their disposition to sleep when abstracted from their diversions, and unemployed in labour. An animal whose body is at rest, and who does not reflect, must be disposed to sleep of course. Comparing them by their faculties of memory, reason, and imagination, it appears to me, that in memory they are equal to the whites; in reason much inferior, as I think one could scarcely be found capable of tracing and comprehending the investigations of Euclid; and that in imagination they are dull, tasteless, and anomalous. It would be unfair to follow them to Africa for this investigation. We will consider them here, on the same stage with the whites, and where the facts are not apocryphal on which a judgment is to be formed. It will be right to make great allowances for the difference of condition, of education, of conversation, of the sphere in which they move. Many millions of them have been brought to, and born in America. Most of them indeed have been confined to tillage, to their own homes, and their own society: yet many have been so situated, that they might have availed themselves of the conversation of their masters; many have been brought up to the handicraft arts, and from that circumstance have always been associated with the whites. Some have been liberally educated, and all have lived in coun-tries where the arts and sciences are cultivated to a considerable degree, and have had before their eyes samples of the best works from abroad...But never yet could I find that a black had uttered a thought above the level of plain nar-ration; never see even an elementary trait of painting or sculpture. In music they are more generally gifted than the whites with accurate ears for tune and time, and they have been found capable of imagining a small catch. Whether they will be equal to the composition of a more extensive run of melody, or of compli-cated harmony, is yet to be proved. Misery is often the parent of the most affect-ing touches in poetry. —Among the blacks is misery enough, God knows, but no poetry. Love is the peculiar cestrum of the poet. Their love is ardent, but it kindles the senses only, not the imagination. Religion indeed has produced a Phyllis Whately; but it could not produce a poet. The compositions published under her name are below the dignity of criticism...The improvement of the blacks in body and mind, in the first instance of their mixture with the whites, has been observed by every one, and proves that their inferiority is not the effect merely of their condition of life. We know that among the Romans, about the Augustan age especially, the condition of their slaves was much more deplorable than that of the blacks on the continent of America...Yet...their slaves were often their rarest artists. They excelled too in science, insomuch as to be usu-ally employed as tutors to their master's children. Epictetus, Terence, and Phaedrus, were slaves. But they were of the race of whites. It is not their condition then, but nature, which has produced the distinction.—Whether further observation will or will not verify the conjecture, that nature has been less bountiful to them in the endowments of the head, I believe that in those of the heart she will be found to have done them justice…we find among them numerous instances of the most rigid integrity, and as many as among their better instructed masters, of benevolence, gratitude, and unshaken fidelity…It is not against experience to suppose, that different species of the same genus, or varieties of the same species, may possess different qualifications. Will not a lover of natural history then, one who views the gradations in all the races of animals with the eye of philosophy, excuse an effort to keep those in the department of man as distinct as nature has formed them? This unfortunate difference of colour, and perhaps of faculty, is a powerful obstacle to the emancipation of these people. Many of their advocates, while they wish to vindicate the liberty of human nature, are anxious also to preserve its dignity and beauty. Some of these, embarrassed by the question 'What further is to be done with them?' join themselves in opposition with those who are actuated by sordid avarice only. Among the Romans emancipation required but one effort. The slave, when made free, might mix with, without staining the blood of his master. But with us a second is necessary, unknown to history. When freed, he is to be removed beyond the reach of mixture.

Query 18 "Manners": The particular customs and manners that may happen to be received in that state?
…There must doubtless be an unhappy influence on the manners of our people produced by the existence of slavery among us. The whole commerce between master and slave is a perpetual exercise of the most boisterous passions, the most unremitting despotism on the one part, and degrading submissions on the other. Our children see this, and learn to imitate it; for man is an imitative animal. This quality is the germ of all education in him. From his cradle to his grave he is learning to do what he sees others do…The man must be a prodigy who can retain his manners and morals undepraved by such circumstances. And with what execration should the statesman be loaded, who permitting one half the citizens thus to trample on the rights of the other, transforms those into despots, and these into enemies, destroys the morals of the one part, and the amor patriae of the other. For if a slave can have a country in this world, it must be any other in preference to that in which he is born to live and labour for another: in which he must lock up the faculties of his nature, contribute as far as depends on his individual endeavours to the evanishment of the human race, or entail his own miserable condition on the endless generations proceeding from him. With the morals of the people, their industry also is destroyed. For in a warm climate, no man will labour for himself who can make another labour for him. This is so true, that of the proprietors of slaves a very small proportion indeed are ever

seen to labour. And can the liberties of a nation be thought secure when we have removed their only firm basis, a conviction in the minds of the people that these liberties are of the gift of God? That they are not to be violated but with his wrath? Indeed I tremble for my country when I reflect that God is just: that his justice cannot sleep for ever: that considering numbers, nature and natural means only, a revolution of the wheel of fortune, an exchange of situation, is among possible events: that it may become probable by supernatural interference!...I think a change already perceptible, since the origin of the present revolution. The spirit of the master is abating, that of the slave rising from the dust, his condition mollifying, the way I hope preparing, under the auspices of heaven, for a total emancipation, and that this is disposed, in the order of events, to be with the consent of the masters, rather than by their extirpation.

### 3c. Benjamin Banneker to Thomas Jefferson, Baltimore County, August 19, 1791[5]

I AM fully sensible of the greatness of that freedom, which I take with you on the present occasion; a liberty which seemed to me scarcely allowable, when I reflected on that distinguished and dignified station in which you stand, and the almost general prejudice and prepossession, which is so prevalent in the world against those of my complexion.

I suppose it is a truth too well attested to you, to need a proof here, that we are a race of beings, who have long labored under the abuse and censure of the world; that we have long been looked upon with an eye of contempt; and that we have long been considered rather as brutish than human, and scarcely capable of mental endowments.

Sir, I hope I may safely admit, in consequence of that report which hath reached me, that you are a man far less inflexible in sentiments of this nature, than many others; that you are measurably friendly, and well disposed towards us; and that you are willing and ready to lend your aid and assistance to our relief, from those many distresses, and numerous calamities, to which we are reduced. Now Sir, if this is founded in truth, I apprehend you will embrace every opportunity, to eradicate that train of absurd and false ideas and opinions, which so generally prevails with respect to us; and that your sentiments are concurrent with mine, which are, that one universal Father hath given being to us all; and that he hath not only made us all of one flesh, but that he hath also, without partiality, afforded us all the same sensations and endowed us all with the same faculties; and that however variable we may be in society or religion, however diversified in situation or color, we are all of the same family, and stand in the same relation to him.

Sir, if these are sentiments of which you are fully persuaded, I hope you cannot but acknowledge, that it is the indispensible duty of those, who maintain for themselves the rights of human nature, and who possess the obligations of Christianity, to extend their power and influence to the relief of every part of the human race, from whatever burden or oppression they may unjustly labor under; and this, I apprehend, a full conviction of the truth and obligation of these principles should lead all to. Sir, I have long been convinced, that if your love for yourselves, and for those inestimable laws, which preserved to you the rights of human nature, was founded on sincerity, you could not but be solicitous, that every individual, of whatever rank or distinction, might with you equally enjoy the blessings thereof; neither could you rest satisfied short of the most active effusion of your exertions, in order to their promotion from any state of degradation, to which the unjustifiable cruelty and barbarism of men may have reduced them.

Sir, I freely and cheerfully acknowledge, that I am of the African race, and in that color which is natural to them of the deepest dye; and it is under a sense of the most profound gratitude to the Supreme Ruler of the Universe, that I now confess to you, that I am not under that state of tyrannical thraldom, and inhuman captivity, to which too many of my brethren are doomed, but that I have abundantly tasted of the fruition of those blessings, which proceed from that free and unequalled liberty with which you are favored; and which, I hope, you will willingly allow you have mercifully received, from the immediate hand of that Being, from whom proceedeth every good and perfect Gift.

Sir, suffer me to recal to your mind that time, in which the arms and tyranny of the British crown were exerted, with every powerful effort, in order to reduce you to a state of servitude: look back, I entreat you, on the variety of dangers to which you were exposed; reflect on that time, in which every human aid appeared unavailable, and in which even hope and fortitude wore the aspect of inability to the conflict, and you cannot but be led to a serious and grateful sense of your miraculous and providential preservation; you cannot but acknowledge, that the present freedom and tranquility which you enjoy you have mercifully received, and that it is the peculiar blessing of Heaven.

This, Sir, was a time when you cleary saw into the injustice of a state of slavery, and in which you had just apprehensions of the horrors of its condition. It was now that your abhorrence thereof was so excited, that you publicly held forth this true and invaluable doctrine, which is worthy to be recorded and remembered in all succeeding ages: "We hold these truths to be self-evident, that all men are created equal; that they are endowed by their Creator with certain unalienable rights, and that among these are, life, liberty, and the pursuit of happiness." Here was a time, in which your tender feelings for yourselves had engaged you thus to declare, you were then impressed with proper ideas of the great violation of liberty, and the free possession of those blessings, to which you were entitled by nature; but, Sir, how pitiable is it to reflect, that although you were so fully convinced of the benevolence of the Father of Mankind, and of his equal and impartial distribution of these rights and privileges, which he hath conferred upon them, that you should at the same time counteract his mercies, in detaining by fraud and violence so numerous a part of my brethren, under groaning captivity and cruel oppression, that you should at the same time be found guilty of that most criminal act, which you professedly detested in others, with respect to yourselves.

I suppose that your knowledge of the situation of my brethren, is too extensive to need a recital here; neither shall I presume to prescribe methods by which they may be relieved, otherwise than by recommending to you and all others, to wean yourselves from those narrow prejudices which you have imbibed with respect to them, and as Job proposed to his friends, "put your soul in their souls' stead;" thus shall your hearts be enlarged with kindness and benevolence towards them; and thus shall you need neither the direction of myself or others, in what manner to proceed herein. And now, Sir, although my sympathy and affection for my brethren hath caused my enlargement thus far, I ardently hope, that your candor and generosity will plead with you in my behalf, when I make known to you, that it was not originally my design; but having taken up my pen in order to direct to you, as a present, a copy of an Almanac, which I have calculated for the succeeding year, I was unexpectedly and unavoidably led thereto.

This calculation is the production of my arduous study, in this my advanced stage of life; for having long had unbounded desires to become acquainted with the secrets of nature, I have had to gratify my curiosity herein, through my own assiduous application to Astronomical Study, in which I need not recount to you the many difficulties and disadvantages, which I have had to encounter.

And although I had almost declined to make my calculation for the ensuing year, in consequence of that time which I had allotted therefor, being taken up at the Federal Territory, by the request of Mr. Andrew Ellicott, yet finding myself under several engagements to Printers of this state, to whom I had communicated my design, on my return to my place of residence, I industriously applied myself thereto, which I hope I have accomplished with correctness and accuracy; a copy of which I have taken the liberty to direct to you, and which I humbly request you will favorably receive; and although you may have the opportunity of perusing it after its publication, yet I choose to send it to you in manuscript previous thereto, that thereby you might not only have an earlier inspection, but that you might also view it in my own hand writing.

### 3d.   *Thomas Jefferson to Benjamin Banneker, August 30, 1791*[6]

I THANK you, sincerely, for your letter of the 19th instant, and for the Almanac it contained. No body wishes more than I do, to see such proofs as you exhibit, that nature has given to our black brethren talents equal to those of the other colors of men; and that the appearance of the want of them, is owing merely to the degraded condition of their existence, both in Africa and America. I can add with truth, that no body wishes more ardently to see a good system commenced, for raising the condition, both of their body and mind, to what it ought to be, as far as the imbecility of their present existence, and other circumstances, which cannot be neglected, will admit.

I have taken the liberty of sending your Almanac to Monsieur de Condozett, Secretary of the Academy of Sciences at Paris, and Member of the Philanthropic Society, because I considered it as a document, to which your whole color had a right for their justification, against the doubts which have been entertained of them.

## 4. Massachusetts Slaves Petition for Freedom[7]

*Slaves were at the forefront of the effort to end slavery during the era of the American Revolution. In the northern states slaves brought political, legal, and moral pressure to bear on the institution through protests, lawsuits, and petitions. In Massachusetts slaves petitioned the legislature to end slavery as early as 1773. This, later, petition shows that slaves in Massachusetts were fully conversant with the ideology at the heart of the Revolution and sought to use it to secure their liberty.*

The petition of A Great Number of Blackes detained in a State of Slavery in the Bowels of a free & christian Country Humbly shuwith that your Petitioners Apprehend that Thay have in Common with all other men a Natural and Unaliable Right to that freedom which the Grat - Parent of the Unavese hath Bestowed equalley on all menkind and which they have Never forfuted by Any Compact or Agreement whatever—but thay wher Unjustly Dragged by the hand of cruel Power from their Derest frinds and sum of them Even torn from the Embraces of their tender Parents—from A popolous Plasant And plentiful cuntry And in Violation of Laws of Nature and off Nations And in defiance of all the tender feelings of humanity Brough hear Either to Be sold Like Beast of Burthen & Like them Condemnd to Slavery for Life—among A People Profesing the…Religion of Jesus A people Not Insensible of the Secrets of Rationable Being Nor without spirit to Resent the unjust endeavours of others to Reduce them to A state of Bondage and Subjection your honouer Need not to be informed that A Life of Slavery Like that of your Petioners Deprived of Every social Priviledge of Every thing Requiset to Render Life Tolable is far… worse then Nonexistance.

[In imita ]tion of [the] Lawdable Example of the Good People of these States your petiononers have Long and Patiently waited the Evnt of petition after petition By them presented to the Legislative Body of this state And cannot but with Grief Reflect that their Sucess hath ben but too similar they Cannot but express their Astonisments that It has Never Bin Consirdered that Every Principle from which Amarica has Acted in the Cours Of their unhappy Deficultes with Great Briton Pleads Stronger than A thousand arguments in favowrs of Your petioners thay therfor humble Beseech your Honours to give this petion its due weight & consideration and cause an act of the Legislatur to be past Wherby they may Be Restored to the Enjoyments of that Which is the Naturel Right of all men—and their—Children who wher Born in this Land of Liberty may not be heald as Slaves after they arive at the age of Twenty one years so may the Inhabitance of thes State No longer chargeable with the inconsistancey of acting themselves the part which thay condem and oppose in Others Be prospered in their present Glorious Struggle for Liberty and have those Blessing to them &c.

**Figure 6.1** *Soldiers in Uniform*, 1781–1784, by Jean Baptiste Antoine de Verger. Courtesy of Anne S.K. Brown Military Collection, Brown University Library, Providence, RI.

## 5.  Rebel Soldiers[8]

*Slaves also took up arms to secure their freedom. While the British offered liberty to slaves who fought against the rebellion from the beginning of the war, the rebels were more reluctant to arm slaves. Eventually, the Continental Army began accepting African-American soldiers in 1777. By the end of the war every state north of Maryland accepted African-American soldiers in its Continental regiments and state militias. Slaves who enlisted received their freedom in exchange for their service. This watercolor, by a Swiss officer in French service, shows typical rebel soldiers at the end of the war including an enlisted slave.*

## 6.  Gradual Abolition in Pennsylvania[9]

*Owing to the pressure brought by black and white abolitionists, as well as the contributions of slaves to the successful rebel war effort, and the contradiction inherent between republicanism premised on notions of equality and chattel slavery, all of the northern states took steps to end slavery during and after the American Revolution. One of the earliest states to act was Pennsylvania whose government adopted a gradual emancipation act in 1780.*

When we contemplate our abhorrence of that condition to which the arms and tyranny of Great Britain were exerted to reduce us, when we look back on the variety of dangers to which we have been exposed, and how miraculously our wants in many instances have been supplied, and our deliverances wrought, when even hope and human fortitude have become unequal to the conflict, we are unavoidably led to a serious and grateful sense of the manifold blessings which we have undeservedly received from the hand of that Being from whom every good and perfect gift cometh. Impressed with these ideas, we conceive that it is our duty, and we rejoice that it is in our power, to extend a portion of that freedom to others which has been extended to us, and release them from the state of thraldom, to which we ourselves were tyrannically doomed, and from which we have now every prospect of being delivered. It is not for us to inquire why, in the creation of mankind, the inhabitants of the several parts of the earth were distinguished by a difference in feature or complexion. It is sufficient to know that all are the work of the Almighty Hand. We find in the distribution of the human species, that the most fertile as well as the most barren parts of the earth are inhabited by men of complexions different from ours, and different from each other; from whence we may reasonably as well as religiously infer, that He, who placed them in their various situations, has extended equally his care and protection to all, and that it becomes not us to counteract His mercies.

We esteem it a peculiar blessing granted to us that we are enabled this day to add one more step to universal civilization by removing as much as possible, the sorrows of those who have lived in undeserved bondage, and from which, by the assumed authority of the Kings of Great Britain, no effectual legal relief could be obtained. Weaned by a long course of experience from those narrow prejudices and partialities we had imbibed, we find our hearts enlarged with kindness and benevolence toward all men of all conditions and nations, and we conceive ourselves at this particular period particularly called upon, by the blessings which we have received, to manifest the sincerity of our profession, and to give a substantial proof of our gratitude…

### 7.   Freedom Certificate, 1783[10]

*At the end of the War of Independence, the British transported approximately 100,000 loyalists out of the new United States. Approximately 20,000 of the refugees were black. A small minority of these were former slaves had who won their freedom through military service (the balance were the slaves of loyalists). Below is a certificate allowing a former slave who fled to the British lines to leave the United States and resettle in Nova Scotia or elsewhere within the British Empire.*

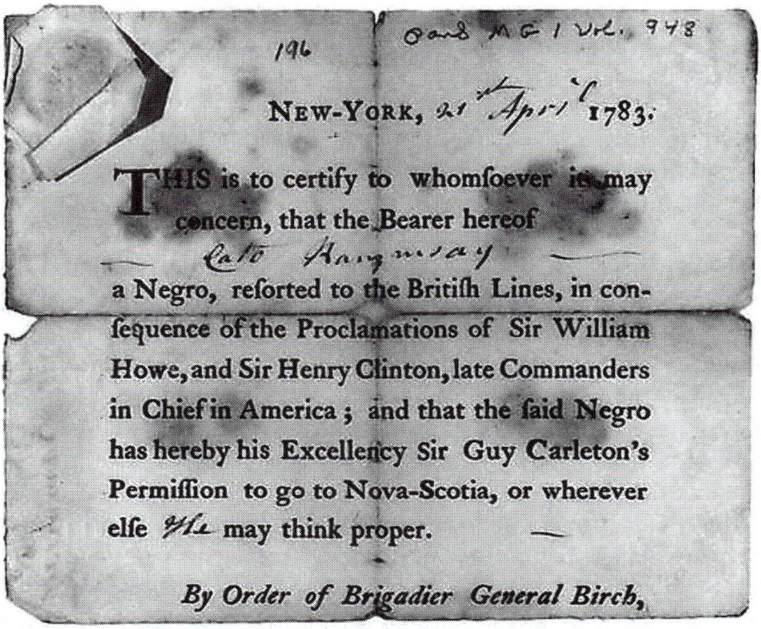

196

NEW-YORK, 21 April 1783.

THIS is to certify to whomsoever it may concern, that the Bearer hereof Cato [illegible] a Negro, resorted to the British Lines, in consequence of the Proclamations of Sir William Howe, and Sir Henry Clinton, late Commanders in Chief in America; and that the said Negro has hereby his Excellency Sir Guy Carleton's Permission to go to Nova-Scotia, or wherever else He may think proper.

*By Order of Brigadier General Birch,*

**Figure 6.2** Freedom Certificate, 1783. Courtesy of the Nova Scotia Archives and Records Management, Halifax, Canada.

## 8. Pennsylvania Abolitionists Petition Congress, 1790[11]

*With the gradual abolition of slavery across the northern states in the wake of independence, slavery became a source of sectional tension. Sectional differences manifested themselves in the series of compromises made over slavery in the federal constitution. After the ratification of the constitution, abolitionists sought to pressure the federal government to end slavery and the slave trade. This is an early petition to Congress seeking abolition.*

The memorial of the Pennsylvania Society for promoting the Abolition of Slavery, the relief of free Negroes unlawfully held in bondage, & the Improvement of the Condition of the African Race.

Respectfully Sheweth, That from a regard for the happiness of Mankind an Association was formed several years since in this State by a number of her Citizens of various religious denominations for promoting the Abolition of Slavery & for the relief of those unlawfully held in bondage. A just & accurate Conception of the true Principles of liberty, as it spread through the land, produced accessions to their numbers, many friends to their Cause, & a legislative

Co-operation with their views, which, by the blessing of Divine Providence, have been successfully directed to the relieving from bondage a large number of their fellow Creatures of the African Race. They have also the Satisfaction to observe, that in Consequence of that Spirit of Philanthropy & genuine liberty which is generally diffusing its beneficial Influence, similar Institutions are gradually forming at home & abroad.

That mankind are all formed by the same Almighty being, alike objects of his Care & equally designed for the Enjoyment of Happiness the Christian Religion teaches us to believe, & the Political Creed of America fully coincides with the Position. Your Memorialists, particularly engaged in attending to the Distresses arising from Slavery, believe it their indispensible Duty to present this Subject to your notice. They have observed with great Satisfaction, that many important & salutary Powers are vested in you for "promoting the Welfare & securing the blessings of liberty to the People of the United States." And as they conceive, that these blessings ought rightfully to be administered, without distinction of Color, to all descriptions of People, so they indulge themselves in the pleasing expectation, that nothing, which can be done for the relief of the unhappy objects of their care will be either omitted or delayed.

From a persuasion that equal liberty was originally the Portion, & is still the Birthright of all Men, & influenced by the strong ties of Humanity & the Principles of their Institution, your Memorialists conceive themselves bound to use all justifiable endeavours to loosen the bands of Slavery and promote a general Enjoyment of the blessings of Freedom. Under these Impressions they earnestly entreat your serious attention to the Subject of Slavery, that you will be pleased to countenance the Restoration of liberty to those unhappy Men, who alone, in this land of Freedom, are degraded into perpetual Bondage, and who, amidst the general Joy of Surrounding Freemen, are groaning in Servile Subjection, that you will devise means for removing this Inconsistency from the Character of the American People, that you will promote Mercy and Justice towards the distressed Race, & that you will step to the very verge of the Powers vested in you, for discouraging every Species of Traffick in the Persons of our fellow Men.

## 9.   An Account of Toussaint L'Ouverture[12]

*In 1791 slaves on the Caribbean island of San Domingue rebelled against their French masters. After a bloody struggle that lasted more than a decade, the Haitian Republic was established. Haiti posed a challenge for the new United States. On one hand the two nations shared a common heritage as republicans born of bloody independence struggles against European imperialism. On the other, the United States as a slaveholding nation was uncomfortable with a republic whose citizens were former slaves who had won their freedom by overthrowing and killing their masters. This letter from Tobias Lear (1762–1816) to Secretary of State, James Madison describes diplomatic and commercial relations between Saint-Domingue and the United States. Saint-Domingue was a major trading partner of the United States, and Lear had been appointed as the American commercial agent to the island. He described Toussaint L'Ouverture (1743–1803), who was a leader of the Haitian Revolution and sought to establish improved trade and diplomatic relations with the United States.*

...On my arrival I delivered your letter to Dr. Stevens, and received from him every mark of polite attention. He went with me to General Toussaint Louverture, to whom he introduced me as the person who was to succeed him in his Office. I handed my Commission to the General, who asked me if I had not a letter for him from the President, or from the Government. I told him I had not, and explained the reason, as not being customary in missions of this kind, where I should be introduced by my Predecessor, and exhibit my Commission as an evidence of my Appointment. He immediately returned my Commission without opening it, expressing his disappointment and disgust in strong terms, saying that his colour was the cause of his being neglected, and not thought worthy of the Usual attentions. I explained to him, with temper and candour, the nature of the Appointment as not requiring those particular introductions which are given to Diplomatic Characters, and assured him of the President's respect & consideration. He became more cool—said he would consider the matter, and desired me to see him at 9 o'clock the next morning. I went accordingly, and found with him Genl. Moyese and Genl. Christolphe, two of the principal Generals. He repeated the observations which he had made the Evening before, and added, that it must hurt him in the eyes of his Chief Officers, when it was found that he was not thot. worthy of having a letter from the President of the Governmt. I gave the same explainations wh. I had offered before. He appeared to be much hurt; but after some further conversation, said, that, notwithstanding the mortification he felt, he would give an evidence of his sincere desire to preserve harmony and a good understanding with the United States, by received me, and giving me all the countenance and protection, in the execution of my Office, which I could desire. I left my Commission with him to be translated and recorded, and received it back the same evening. Since that time I have had no cause to complain of a want of attention.

I enclose you several papers printed here, by, which you will see the Arretes which have been passed at different times respecting Commerce. That of the 18h of Floriel seemed to bear hard upon the American Merchants settled in this Island. Dr. Stevans had remonstrated against it. Several Americans were put upon the list of Consignees; byt many remained without that priviledge. On the 18th instant I wrote to the General on the subject in strong but temperate terms. His answer was expressive of warm wishes to favour the Commerce of the United

States; but still reserving to himself the right of judging of the qualifications of those who were desireous of being allowed to become Consignees. Since that time he has, however, granted permission to all the Americans settled here (about 20) excepting two or three, and I have reason to suppose that the same has been extended to those settled in other parts of the Island.

I have heard of no Captures by the British since I have been here, and do not learn that they have any Cruizers on this side of the Island. There are 32 American Vessels now in this Port. Flour, Fish and Dry Goods constitute almost all their Cargoes...

I have not been long enough here to form a correct opinion of the state of things in this Island. The General in Chief expresses, on all occasions, his strong wishes for a friendly intercourse with the United States.

A new and important Symbol Aera has commenced here. A Constitution has been formed for the Government of this Island, by Deputies called together for that purpose by the General in Chief. It was read in public, with great parade, on the 7th instant. The papers which I send you will shew the Addresses which preceded and followed the reading. It is not yet printed from the public. It declares Genl. Toussaint Louverture Governor for life, with the power of naming his successor. It is to be submitted to the French Republic for approbation; but in the meantime, it is to have effect here in the Island.

I shall have the honor of writing to you more fully in a few days, by the Brig Neptune, in which I came out, and which returns directly to Alexandria. By that time I hope to get a Copy of the Constitution which I shall forward to you. At present I shall only add, that I have this moment received a letter from the Governor informing me that provisions are much wanting at Port Republican, and requesting that I would communicate it to the Merchants here. The consequence of which I expect will be to drain this market, which is at present full, and create a demand in this place. With the highest respect & sincere Attachment I have the honor to be Sir, Your most obedient Servant.

## 10.   Revolution in Haiti[13]

*In the aftermath of the Haitian Revolution, Napoleon Bonaparte sent an army to re-conquer Saint-Domingue in 1802. The campaign failed but was attended by considerable bloodshed, and atrocities were committed by both parties on both sides. This image, published in the United States in 1805, attests to the violence in Haiti while fueling the fears of American slaveholders of the consequences of slave rebellion.*

**Figure 6.3** Revenge taken by the Black Army for the Cruelties practiced on them by the French. Courtesy of JCB Archive of Early American Images, The John Carter Brown Library, Brown University, Providence, RI.

## 11. Ben Woolfolk, Testimony in the Trial of Gabriel, October 6, 1800[14]

*The fears of American slaveholders seemed borne out in August 1800 when a putative slave rebellion was uncovered in Richmond, Virginia. The leader of the plot was Gabriel Prosser (1776–1800), an enslaved blacksmith. The rebels, possibly influenced by events in Saint-Domingue, planned to kill all the whites in Richmond except those recognized as opponents of slavery—Quakers, Methodists, and the French. The plot failed owing to poor weather and a slave revealing the plan to his master. Below is testimony by one of the conspirators, describing the plot, at Gabriel's trial.*

The prisoner was present at the meeting at Mr Youngs who came to get persons to join him to carry on the War against the white people—That after meeting they adjourned to the spring and held a consultation when it was concluded that in 3 Weeks the business should commence—Gabriel said he had 12 dozen of swords made, and had worn out 2 pair of Bullet moulds in runing bullets, and pulling a third pair of his pocket observed that was nearly worn out—That Bob Cooley and Mr Tinsleys Jim was to let them into the Capitol to get the arms out—That the lower part of the town towards Rocketts was to be fired, which would draw forth the Citizens (that part of the town being of little value) this would give an opportunity to the negro's to seize on the arms and ammunition, and then they would commence the attack upon them—After the Assembling of the negroes near Prossers and previous to their coming to Richmond a Company was to be sent to Gregories Tavern to take possession of some arms there Deposited—The prisoner said at the time of meeting the witness at Mr Youngs, that he had the evening before received six Guns, one of which he had delivered to Colonel Wilkinson's Sam—That he was present when Gabriel was appointed General and George Smith second in Command That none were to be spared of the Whites, except quakers Methodists and French people—The prisoner and Gilbert concluded to purchase a piece of Silk for a flag on which they would have written *death or liberty*, and they would kill all except as before excepted unless they agreed to the freedom of the Blacks, in which case they would at least cut off one of their Arms—That the prisoner told the Witness that Bob Cooley had told him if he would call on him about a week before the time of the Insurrection, he would untie the Key of the room in which the Arms and Ammunition were kept at the Capitol and give it to him or if he did not come, then on the night of the Insurrection being commenced he would hand him Arms out as fast as he could arm his men, and that he had on sunday previous to this been shown by Cooley every room in the Capitol.

### 12.   Rebel's Statement from Gabriel's Conspiracy, September 25, 1804[15]

*Gabriel and twenty-six others were tried and executed for their involvement in the conspiracy. This is a statement made by one of the rebels during his trial. The rebel makes a clear link between the cause of Virginia's slaves and those Virginians who rebelled against British rule a generation before. The Haitian Revolution and Gabriel's Rebellion led to a backlash in favor of slavery in Virginia and across the South. Manumission laws were tightened and greater restrictions were imposed on free blacks.*

I pursued my way to Richmond in the mail stage, through a beautiful country, but clouded and debased by Negro slavery. At the house where I breakfasted,

which is called the Bowling-green, I was told that the owner had in his possession 200 slaves. In one field near the house, planted with tobacco, I counted
nearly 20 women and children, employed in picking grubs from the plant. In
the afternoon I passed by a field in which several poor slaves had lately been
executed, on the charge of having an intention to rise against their masters. A
lawyer who was present at their trials at Richmond, informed me that on one of
them being asked, what he had to say to the court on his defence, he replied, in
a manly tone of voice: "I have nothing more to offer than what General Washington would have had to offer, had he been taken by the British and put to trial
by them. I have adventured my life in endeavouring to obtain the liberty of my
countrymen, and am a willing sacrifice in their cause: and I beg, as a favour, that
I may be immediately led to execution. I know that you have pre-determined to
shed my blood, why then all this mockery of a trial?"

## Notes

1. Proslavery Petition, November 10, 1785, Library of Virginia (taken from transcription on library website).
2. *Virginia Gazette* [Purdie], November 24, 1775.
3. Thomas Jefferson, June 1776, Rough draft of the Declaration of Independence, Thomas Jefferson Papers, Series 1: General Correspondence, 1651–1827. Washington, DC: Library of Congress, Manuscript Division.
4. Thomas Jefferson, *Notes on the State of Virginia* (Philadelphia: Prichard and Hall, 1788), 145–154, 172–174. This document has been edited for length. The full version can be found at the book's website (http://www.routledge.com/textbooks/revolutionaryamerica/).
5. Copy of a letter from Benjamin Banneker to the secretary of state, with his answer (Philadelphia: Daniel Lawrence, 1792).
6. Ibid.
7. "Petition for Freedom to the Massachusetts Council and House of Representatives, January 13, 1777," Belknap Papers, Boston: Massachusetts Historical Society
8. Jean Baptiste Antoine de Verger, *Soldiers in Uniform (1781–1784)*, Anne S.K. Brown Military Collection, Brown University Library, Providence, RI.
9. James T. Mitchell and Henry Flanders, *The Statutes at Large of Pennsylvania from 1682 to 1801, Vol. 10: 1779 to 1781* (Harrisburg, PA: Wm. Stanley Ray, 1904), 67–68, This document has been edited for length. The full version can be found at the book's website (http://www.routledge.com/textbooks/revolutionaryamerica/).
10. Certificate of Freedom, Halifax, Canada: Nova Scotia Archives and Records Management.
11. Records of the United States Senate, Center for Legislative Archives (Washington, DC: National Archives).
12. "Tobias Lear to James Madison, Cape Francoise, July 17, 1801," Miscellaneous Letters, General Records of the Department of State, Record Group 59; National Archives, Washington, DC.
13. J. Barlow and Marcus Rainford, *Revenge taken by the Black Army for the Cruelties practiced on them by the French* (London: James Cundee, 1805). JCB Archive of Early American Images, The John Carter Brown Library, Brown University, Providence, RI.
14. Governor's Office, Letters Received, James Monroe, Record Group 3, Library of Virginia (available from transcription on library website)
15. Robert Sutcliffe, *Travels in Some Parts of North America in the years 1804, 1805 and 1806* (York, England: C. Peacock, 1811), 50.

# CHAPTER 7

# The Confederation Era

## Introduction

By waging war and declaring independence, the new American states raised vital questions concerning their constitutional and legal status. Nine months before the Declaration of Independence, John Adams called for the colonies to form new governments and suggested how this might be done (document 1). Much of the most important experiments with constitution-making took place at the state level. Pennsylvania acted relatively quickly and adopted one of the most radical constitutions of the era (document 2). When lawmakers in Massachusetts attempted to act with similar rapidity they were opposed by the voters and the proposed constitution was rejected. A special convention was convened and it proposed a new frame of government which found favour with the voters (documents 3–4). Of course, while the individual states grappled with constitutional questions, the states collectively had to draft a frame of government, while waging war for their existence. The result was the Articles of Confederation (document 5), which created a relatively weak central government. The apparent weaknesses of the Articles of Confederation frustrated some politicians and theorists who sought to create a stronger federal government (document 6).

Despite its flaws, the United States was governed under the Articles of Confederation for nearly a decade from 1781 to 1789. While the United States enjoyed some successes during this period—notably the successful conclusion of the War of Independence—the nation was beset by considerable problems as well during the 1780s. Notable among these was economic instability. Under the Articles of Confederation Congress did not have the power to levy taxes. In order to pay for the war it resorted to printing paper money as did many of the states (document 7), resulting in runaway inflation. When Massachusetts sought to implement a deflationary currency program hard-pressed farmers took up arms and closed the courts in a public disorder known as Shays's Rebellion (documents 8, 9, and 10). While some, such as Thomas Jefferson, took a benign view of Shays's Rebellion as a normal feature of political life in a republic (document 11), others viewed it as an indication that the American republic was in danger and called for political reform.

## 1. John Adams Calls for New Constitutions, 1775[1]

*Soon after the War of Independence began, John Adams recalled in his autobiography that he advocated the colonies draft new constitutions. In this passage he enumerated the practical advantages drafting new constitutions would have. He also stressed that in his view the appropriate format was for the states to hold special conventions to draft the constitutions so that they would have popular legitimacy, which was crucial in a republic.*

…I embraced with joy the opportunity of haranguing on the Subject at large, and of urging Congress to resolve on a general recommendation to all the States to call Conventions and institute regular Governments. I reasoned from various Topicks, many of which perhaps I could not now recollect. Some I remember as

1. The danger of the Morals of the People, from the present loose State of Things and general relaxation of Laws and Government through the Union.
2. The danger of Insurrections in some of the most disaffected parts of the Colonies, in favour of the Enemy or as they called them, the Mother Country, an expression that I thought it high time to erase out of our Language.
3. Communications and Intercourse with the Ennemy, from various parts of the Continent could not be wholly prevented, while any of the Powers of Government remained, in the hands of the King's servants.
4. It could not be well considered as a Crime to communicate Intelligence, or to Act as Spies or Guides to the Ennemy, without assuming all the Powers of Government.
5. The People of America, would never consider our Union as compleat, but our Friends would always suspect divisions among Us, and our Ennemies who were scattered in larger or smaller Numbers not only in every State and City, but in every Village through the whole Union, would forever represent Congress as divided and ready to break to pieces, and in this Way would intimidate and discourage multitudes of our People who wished Us well.
6. The absurdity of carrying on War, against a King, When so many Persons were daily taking Oaths and Affirmations of Allegeance to him.
7. We could not expect that our Friends in Great Britain would believe Us United and in earnest, or exert themselves very strenuously in our favour, while We acted such a wavering, hesitating Part.

8. Foreign nations particularly France and Spain would not think Us worthy of ~~attending~~ their attention while We appeared to be deceived by such fallacious hopes of redress of Grievances, of pardon for our Offences, and of Reconciliation with our Enemies.

9. We could not command the natural Resources of our own Country; We could ~~not~~ establish Manufactories of Arms, Cannon, Salt Petre, Powder, Ships, &c. Without the Powers of Government, and all these and many other preparations ought to be going on in every State or Colony, if you will, in the Country.

Although the Opposition was still inveterate, many Members of Congress began to hear me with more Patience, and some began to ask me civil questions. How can the People institute Governments? My Answer was, By Conventions of Representatives, freely, fairly, and proportionally chosen. When the convention has fabricated a Government, or a Constitution rather, how do We know the People will submit to it? If there is any doubt of that, the Convention may send out their Project of a Constitution, to the People in their several Towns, Counties, or districts, and the People may make the Acceptance of it their own Act. But the People know nothing about Constitutions. I believe you are much mistaken in that Supposition; if you are not, they will not oppose a Plan prepared by their own chosen Friends; but I believe that in every considerable portion of the People, there will be found some Men, who will understand the Subject as well as their representatives, and these will assist in enlightening the rest…But what Plan of a Government, would you advise? A Plan as nearly resembling the Government under which We were born and have lived as the Circumstances of the Country will admit. Kings We never had among Us. Nobles We never had. Nothing hereditary ever existed in the Country: Nor will the Country require or admit of any such Thing: but Governors, and Councils We have always had as Well as Representatives. A Legislature in three Branches ought to be preserved, and independent judges. Where and how will you get your Governors and Councils? By elections. How, who shall elect? The Representatives of the People in a Convention will be the best qualified to contrive a Mode…

## 2. Pennsylvania's New Constitution—A Critical View[2]

*In the immediate aftermath of the Declaration of Independence, a special convention, dominated by political radicals, met in Philadelphia to draft a new constitution for Pennsylvania. The Pennsylvania constitution of 1776 vested powers in an unicameral legislature, annually elected according to a broad franchise, and a twelve-man executive council rather than an individual governor. In this letter the conservative patriot, Benjamin Rush (1745–1813) offered a critique of the constitution.*

I wish I could add here that the declaration of independence had produced the same happy effects in Pensylvania that it has in the rest of the united States. Our people (intoxicated with the must or first flowings of liberty) have formed a government that is absurd in its principles and incapable of execution without the most alarming influence upon liberty. The wisest and I believe the major part of the people are dissatisfied with it, but they have suspended all opposition to it for the present, as the enemy are now at our gates. A happy constitution is a most powerful inducement to press on a soldier to the toils and dangers of a campaign. He anticipates the pleasure with which he will forget them both in the perfect security he will enjoy hereafter for his property, liberty, and life. I wish I could animate you with such prospects in our native province. No, my friend, you will find when you lay down your arms and seek to refresh yourself under the shade of your own vine and fig tree, that the one will want fruits and the other leaves to support and shelter you against the rude influence of slavery.

The public testimony I bore against our domestic tyranny cost me my seat in Congress. Our Assembly (who are the only unaccountable body of men that ever existed in a free country) displaced me about two months ago. I thanked them for it, having previously determined to join the army in the line of my profession.

Adieu, my friend. I have no higher wish than to be once again more free and happy with you and the few choice spirits who began the opposition in Pensylvania.

### 3. Massachusetts Voters Reject a Constitution[3]

*In 1778 the Massachusetts legislature drafted a constitution which it submitted to the various towns in the state for ratification. The constitution was rejected in part because the legislature had not followed John Adams's advice, or the example of Pennsylvania, and called a special convention to draft the state's constitution. Others, like the voters in Brookline, rejected the constitution because it did not contain a bill of rights.*

At a legal meeting of the Inhabitants of the Town of Brookline on Thursday May 21, 1778.

Upon reading and considering the proposed new Form of Government; Voted, that the same is not calculated and adapted, to promote and secure in the best manner attainable, the true and lasting Happiness and Freedom of the People of this State, that it is essential to a Constitution designed for that most important and desirable End, that a full and express Declaration of the Rights of the People, be made a part thereof, and that the powers of Rulers should be accurately defined and properly limited, that as the Form proposed is almost totally deficient in those Respects and imperfect and intricate in many parts, it ought therefore to be Rejected, and this meeting consisting of forty five persons do unanimously and absolutely reject the same.

### 4.   Massachusetts Tries Again, 1780[4]

*Having failed in their first effort at constitution-making, revolutionaries in Massachusetts called a constitutional convention which met from September 1779 to February 1780. The convention considered a draft constitution which was largely the work of John Adams. The proposed constitution was circulated to every town in the state for ratification with this address, which justified the structure and content of the constitution as well as the procedure by which it was drafted and would be ratified.*

Having had your Appointment and Instruction, we have undertaken the arduous Task of preparing a civil Constitution for the People of Massachusetts Bay; and we now submit it to your candid Consideration. It is your *Interes*t to revise it with the greatest Care and Circumspection, and it is your undoubted *Right*, either to propose such Alternations and Amendments as you shall judge proper, or, to give it your own Sanction in its present Form, or, totally to reject it…

A *Government* without Power to exert itself, is at best, but an useless Piece of Machinery. It is probable, that for the want of Energy, it would speedily lose even the Appearance of Government, and sink into Anarchy. Unless a due Proportion of Weight is given to each of the Powers of Government, there will soon be a Confusion of the whole. An Overbearing of any of its Parts on the rest, would destroy the Balance and accelerate its Dissolution and Ruin: And, a Power without *any* Restraint is Tyranny. The Powers of Government must then be balanced: To do this accurately requires the highest Skill in political Architecture. Those who are to be invested with the Administration, should have such Powers given to them, as are requisite to render them useful in their respective Places; and such *Checks* should be added to every Branch of Power as maybe sufficient to prevent its becoming formidable and injurious to the Common wealth. If we have been so fortunate as to succeed in this point of the greatest Importance, our Happiness will be compleat, in the Prospect of having laid a good Foundation for many Generations. *You* are the Judges how far we have succeeded; and whether we have raised our Superstructure, agreeably to our profess'd Design; upon the Principles of a *Free Common Wealth*.

In order to assist your Judgments, we have thought it necessary, briefly to explain to you the Grounds and Reasons upon which we have formed our Plan. In the third article of the Declaration of Rights, we have, with as much Precision as we are capable of, provided for the free exercise of *the Rights of Conscience*: We are very sensible that our Constituents hold those Rights infinitely more valuable than all others; and we flatter ourselves, that while we have considered Morality and the public Worship of GOD, as important to the happiness of

Society, we have sufficiently guarded the rights of Conscience from every possible infringement...

In the form now presented to you, there are no more Departments of Government than are absolutely necessary for the free and full Exercise of the Powers thereof. The House of Representatives is intended as the Representative of the Persons and the Senate, of the property of the Common Wealth. These are to be annually chosen, and to sit in separate Bodies, each having a Negative upon the Acts of the other. This Power of a Negative in each must ever be necessary; for all Bodies of Men, assembled upon the same occasion and united by one common Interest of Rank, Honor, or Estate, are liable, like an individual, to mistake bias and prejudice. These two Houses are vested with the Powers of Legislation, and are to be chosen by the Male Inhabitants who are Twenty one Years of age, and have a Freehold of the small annual income of Three Pounds or Sixty Pounds in any Estate. Your Delegates considered that Persons who are Twenty one Years of age, and have no Property, are either those who live upon a part of a Paternal estate, expecting the Fee thereof, who are but just entering into business, or those whose Idleness of Life and profligacy of manners will forever barr them from acquiring and possessing Property. And we will submit it to the former Class, whether they would not think it safer for them to have their right of Voting for a Representative suspended for small space of Time, than forever hereafter to have their Privileges liable to the control of Men, who will pay less regard to the Rights of Property because they have nothing to loose.

The Power of Revising, and stating objections to any Bill or Resolve that shall be passed by the two Houses, we were of the opinion ought to be lodged in the hands of some *one* person; not only to preserve the Laws from being unsystematical and inaccurate, but that a due balance may be preserved in the three capital powers of Government. The Legislative, the Judicial and Executive Powers naturally exhist in every Government: And the History of the rise and fall of the Empires of the World affords us ample proof, that when the Man or Body of Men enact, interpret and execute the Laws, property becomes too precarious to be valuable, and a People are finally borne down with the force of corruption resulting from the Union of those Powers. The Governor is emphatically the Representative of the whole People, being chosen not by one Town or County, but by the People at large. We have therefore thought it safest to rest this Power in his hands; and as the Safety of the Common wealth requires, that there should be one Commander in Chief over the Militia, we have given the Governor that Command for the same reason, that we thought him the only proper Person that could be trusted with the power of revising the Bills and Resolves of the General Assembly; but the People may if they please choose their own Officers.

You will observe that we have resolved, that Representation ought to be founded on the Principle of equality; but it cannot be understood thereby that each Town in the Commonwealth shall have Weight and importance in a just proportion to its Numbers and property. An exact Representation would be unpracticable even in a System of Government arising from the State of Nature, and much more so in a state already divided into nearly three hundred Corporations...

To prevent the governor from abusing the Power which is necessary to be put into his hands we have provided that he shall have a Council to advise him at all Times and upon all important Occasions, and he with the advice of his Council is to have the Appointment of Civil Officers. This was very readily agreed to by your Delegates, and will undoubtedly be agreeable to their Constituents; for if those Officers who are to interpret and execute the Laws are to be dependent upon the Election of the people it must forever keep them under the Controul of ambitious, artful and interested men, who can obtain most Votes for them. —If they were to be Appointed by the Two Houses or either of them, the persons appointing them would be too numerous to be accountable for putting weak or wicked Men into office. Besides the House is designed as the Grand Inquest of the Common Wealth, and are to impeach Officers for male Conduct, the Senate are to try the Merits of such impeachments; it would be therefore unfit that they should have the Creation of those Officers which the one may impeach and the other remove: but we conceive there is the greatest propriety in Vesting the Governor with this Power, he being as we have observed, the compleat representative of all the People, and at all Times liable to be impeached by the House before the Senate for male Administration. And we would here observe that all the Powers which we have given the Governor are necessary to be lodged in the hands of one Man, as the General of the Army and first Magistrate, and none to be entitled to it but he who has the Annual and United Suffrages of the whole Common Wealth.

You will readily conceive it to be necessary for your own Safety, that your Judges should hold their Offices during good behaviour; for Men who hold their places upon so precarious a Tenure as annual or other frequent Appointments will never so assiduously apply themselves to study as will be necessary to the filling their places with dignity. Judges should at all Times feel themselves independent and free.

YOUR Delegates have further provided that the Supreme Judicial Department, by fixed and ample Salaries, may be enabled to devote themselves wholly to the Duties of their important Office. And for this reason, as well as to keep this Department separate from the others in Government have excluded them from a Seat in the Legislature; and when our Constituents consider that the final Decision of their Lives and Property must be had in this Court, we conceive they will universally approve the measure...

## 5.  The Articles of Confederation, 1777[5]

*When Congress began debating whether to declare independence, it also created a committee to draft a frame of government for the new states. Owing to the demands of the war, Congress did not approve the Articles of Confederation until November 15, 1777. It was then sent to the individual states for ratification which had to be unanimous. The Articles, which created a relatively confederacy of states, were not ratified until February 1781, officially taking effect on March 1, 1781.*

To all to whom these Presents shall come, we, the undersigned, Delegates of the States affixed to our Names, send greeting: Whereas the Delegates of the United States of America in Congress assembled, did on the fifteenth day of November, in the year of our Lord one thousand seven hundred and seventy seven, and in the second year of the Independence of America, agree to certain articles of Confederation and perpetual Union between the states of New Hampshire, Massachusetts-bay, Rhode Island and Providence Plantations, Connecticut, New York, New Jersey, Pennsylvania, Delaware, Maryland, Virginia, North Carolina, South Carolina, and Georgia, in the words following, viz. Articles of Confederation and perpetual Union between the States of New Hampshire, Massachusetts-bay, Rhode Island and Providence Plantations, Connecticut, New York, New Jersey, Pennsylvania, Delaware, Maryland, Virginia, North Carolina, South Carolina, and Georgia.

Article I. The stile of this confederacy shall be, "The United States of America."

Article II. Each State retains its sovereignty, freedom, and independence, and every power, jurisdiction, and right, which is not by this confederation, expressly delegated to the United States, in Congress assembled.

Article III. The said States hereby severally enter into a firm league of friendship with each other, for their common defence, the security of their liberties, and their mutual and general welfare, binding them-selves to assist each other against all force offered to, or attacks made upon them, or any of them, on account of religion, sovereignty, trade, or any other pretence whatever.

Article IV. The better to secure and perpetuate mutual friendship and intercourse among the people of the different States in this union, the free inhabitants of each of these States, paupers, vagabonds, and fugitives from justice excepted, shall be entitled to all privileges and immunities of free citizens in the several States; and the people of each State shall have free ingress and regress to and from any other State, and shall enjoy therein all the privileges of trade and commerce, subject to the same duties, impositions, and restrictions, as the inhabitants thereof respectively; provided that such restrictions shall not extend so far as to prevent the removal of property imported into any State, to any other State, of which the owner is an inhabitant; provided also, that no imposition, duties, or restriction, shall be laid by any State on the property of the United States, or either of them.

If any person guilty of, or charged with, treason, felony, or other high misdemeanor in any State, shall flee from justice, and be found in any of the united States, he shall, upon demand of the governor or executive power of the State from which he fled, be delivered up, and re-moved to the State having jurisdiction of his offence.

Full faith and credit shall be given, in each of these States, to the records, acts, and judicial proceedings of the courts and magistrates of every other State.

Article V. For the more convenient management of the general interests of the united States, delegates shall be annually appointed in such manner as the legislature of each State shall direct, to meet in Congress on the first Monday in November, in every year, with a power reserved to each State to recall its delegates, or any of them, at any time within the year, and to send others in their stead, for the remainder of the year.

No State shall be represented in Congress by less than two, nor by more than Seven Members; and no person shall be capable of being delegate for more than three years, in any term of Six years; nor shall any person, being a delegate, be capable of holding any office under the united States, for which he, or another for his benefit, receives any salary, fees, or emolument of any kind.

Each State shall maintain its own delegates in a meeting of the States, and while they act as members of the committee of the States.

In determining questions in the united States in Congress assembled, each State shall have one vote…

Article XIII. Every State shall abide by the determinations of the united States, in congress assembled, on all questions which by this confederation are submitted to them. And the articles of this confederation shall be inviol-ably observed by every State, and the Union shall be perpetual; nor shall any alteration at any time hereafter be made in any of them, unless such alteration be agreed to in a congress of the united States, and be afterwards con-firmed by the legislatures of every State…

## 6. Alexander Hamilton Decries the Weakness of Congress[6]

*Congress governed the United States according to Articles of Confederation even before the Articles were formally ratified in 1781. In this 1780 letter Alexander Hamilton (1755–1804) offered a critique of the weakness of Congress, which he feared endangered the republic.*

…The fundamental defect is a want of power in Congress. It is hardly worth while to show in what this consists, as it seems to be universally acknowleged; or to point out how it has happened, as the only question is how to remedy it. It may, however, be said that it has originated from three causes: an excess of the spirit of liberty, which has made the particular States show a jealousy of all power not in their own hands,—and this jealousy has led them to exercise a right of judging in the last resort of the measures recommended by Congress, and of acting according to their own opinions of their propriety or necessity; a diffidence, in Congress, of their own powers, by which they have been timid and indecisive in their resolutions, constantly making concessions to the States, till they have scarcely left themselves the shadow of power; a want of sufficient means at their disposal to answer the public exigencies, and of vigor to draw forth those means; which have occasioned them to depend on the States individually to fulfil their engagements with the army,—and the consequence of which has been to ruin their influence and credit with the army, to establish its dependence on each State separately rather than *on them*—that is rather than on the whole collectively.

It may be pleaded that Congress had never any definite powers granted them, and of course could exercise none, could do nothing more than recommend. The manner in which Congress was appointed would warrant, and the public good required that they should have considered themselves as vested with full power *to preserve the republic from harm*. They have done many of the highest acts of sovereignty, which were always cheerfully submitted to: The declaration of independence, the declaration of war, the levying an army, creating a navy, emitting money, making alliances with foreign powers, appointing a dictator etc. All these implications of a complete sovereignty were never disputed, and ought to have been a standard for the whole conduct of administration. Undefined powers are discretionary powers, limited only by the object for which they were given; in the present case, the independence and freedom of America…

But the Confederation itself is defective, and requires to be altered. It is neither fit for war nor peace. The idea of an uncontrollable sovereignty in each State over its internal police will defeat the other powers given to Congress, and make our union feeble and precarious. There are instances without number, where acts necessary for the general good, and which rise out of the powers given to Congress, must interfere with the internal police of the States; and there are as many instances in which the particular States, by arrangements of internal police, can effectually, though indirectly, counteract the arrangements of Congress…

The Confederation gives the States, individually, too much influence in the affairs of the army. They should have nothing to do with it. The entire formation and disposal of our military forces ought to belong to Congress. It is an essential cement of the union; and it ought to be the policy of Congress to destroy all ideas of State attachments in the army, and make it look up wholly to them. For this purpose all appointments, promotions, and provisions, whatsoever, ought to be made by them. It may be apprehended that this may be dangerous to liberty. But nothing appears more evident to me than that we run much greater risk of having a weak and disunited federal government, than one which will be able to usurp upon the rights of the people…

The forms of our State constitutions must always give them great weight in our affairs, and will make it too difficult to bend them to the pursuit of a common interest, too easy to oppose whatever they do not like, and to form partial combinations subversive of the general one. There is a wide difference between our situation and that of an empire under one simple form of government, distributed into counties, provinces, or districts, which have no Legislatures, but merely magistratical bodies to execute the laws of a common sovereign. Here the danger is that the sovereign will have too much power, and oppress the parts of which it is composed. In our case, that of an empire composed of confederated States, each with a government completely organized within itself, having all the means to draw its subjects to a close dependence on itself, the danger is directly the reverse. It is that the common sovereign will not have power sufficient to unite the different members together, and direct the common forces to the interest and happiness of the whole…

The Confederation, too, gives the power of the purse too entirely to the State Legislatures. It should provide perpetual funds, in the disposal of Congress, by a land tax, poll tax, or the like. All imposts upon commerce ought to be laid by Congress, and appropriated to their use. For, without certain revenues, a government can have no power. That power which holds the purse strings absolutely, must rule. This seems to be a medium which, without making Congress altogether independent, will tend to give reality to its authority.

Another defect in our system is want of method and energy in the administration. This has partly resulted from the other defect; but in a great degree from prejudice, and the want of a proper executive. Congress have kept the power too much into their own hands, and have meddled too much with details of every sort. Congress is, properly, a deliberative corps, and it forgets itself when it attempts to play the executive. It is impossible such a body, numerous as it is, constantly fluctuating, can ever act with sufficient decision or with system. Two thirds of the members, one half the time, cannot know what has gone before them, or what connection the subject in hand has to what has been transacted on former occasions. The members who have been more permanent, will only give information that promotes the side they espouse in the present case, and will as often mislead as enlighten. The variety of business must distract, and the proneness of every assembly to debate must at all times delay…

I shall now propose the remedies which appear to me applicable to our circumstances, and necessary to extricate our affairs from their present deplorable situation.

The first step must be to give Congress powers competent to the public exigencies. This may happen in two ways: one by resuming and exercising the discretionary powers I suppose to have been originally vested in them for the safety of the States, and resting their conduct on the candor of their countrymen and the necessity of the conjuncture; the other, by calling immediately a Convention of all the States, with full authority to conclude finally upon a General Confederation, stating to them beforehand, explicitly, the evils arising from a want of power in Congress, and the impossibility of supporting the contest on its present footing, that the delegates may come possessed of proper sentiments as well as proper authority to give to the meeting. Their commission should include a right of vesting Congress with the whole, or a proportion, of the unoccupied lands, to be employed for the purpose of raising a revenue; reserving the jurisdiction to the States by whom they are granted.

The first plan, I expect, will be thought too bold an expedient by the generality of Congress; and, indeed, their practice hitherto has so riveted the opinion of their want of power, that the success of this experiment may very well be doubted.

I see no objection to the other mode, that has any weight in competition with the reasons for it. The Convention should assemble the first of November next. The sooner the better. Our disorders are too violent to admit of a common or lingering remedy. The reasons for which I require them to be vested with plenipotentiary authority are that the business may suffer no delay in the execution, and may, in reality come to effect. A Convention may agree upon a Confederation; the States individually hardly ever will. We must have one at all events, and a vigorous one, if we mean to succeed in the contest and be happy hereafter…I ask that the Convention should have a power of vesting the whole, or a part, of the unoccupied land in Congress; because it is necessary that body should have some property as a fund for the arrangements of finance; and I know of no other kind that can be given them.

The Confederation, in my opinion, should give Congress complete sovereignty, except as to that part of internal police which relates to the rights of property and life among individuals, and to raising money by internal taxes. It is necessary that every thing belonging to this should be regulated by the State Legislatures. Congress should have complete sovereignty in all that relates to war; peace, trade, finance; and to the management of foreign affairs; the right of declaring war; of raising armies, officering, paying them, directing their motions in every respect; of equipping fleets, and doing the same with them; of building fortifications, arsenals, magazines etc., etc., of making peace on such conditions as they think proper; of regulating trade, determining with what countries it shall be carried on; granting indulgencies; laying prohibitions on all the articles of export or import; imposing duties; granting bounties and premiums for raising, exporting, importing, and applying to their own use, the product of these duties—only giving credit to the States on whom they are raised in the general account of revenues and expences; instituting Admiralty Courts etc., of coining money; establishing banks on such terms, and with such privileges as they think proper; appropriating funds, and doing whatever else relates to the operations of finance; transacting every thing with foreign nations, making alliances, offensive and defensive, treaties of commerce, etc., etc…

## 7. Banknotes[7]

*One of the major weaknesses of the government under the Articles of Confederation was its inability to raise revenue. Congress did not have the power to tax, but rather issued requisitions to the individual states which they may or may not have*

**Figure 7.1** (above, right) Massachusetts Banknote, 1780 (below, right) Georgia Banknote, 1777. Courtesy of the Granger Collection, New York.

**EIGHT DOLLARS**

## State of Massachusetts-Bay.

No. 25480 EIGHT DOLLARS.

THE Poffeffor of this Bill shall be paid
EIGHT Spanish milled DOLLARS by the Thirty-first
Day of December, One Thousand Seven Hundred and Eigh-
ty-fix, with Interest in like MONEY, at the Rate of Five
per Centum per Annum, by the State of MASSACHUSETTS-
BAY, according to an Act of the Legiflature of the faid
State, of the Fifth Day of May, 1780.

Interest.  s. d. q.
Annually, 2 4 3
Monthly, 0 2 1½

4 DOL.                          4 DOL.

Georgia.  1777.              No.
THIS CERTIFICATE, for the Support
of the Continental Troops, and other Ex-
pences of Government, entitles the Bearer to
FOUR DOLLARS in CONTINENTAL
Currency, according to the Refolution of
Affembly, September 10, 1777.

DOL.  4 DOL.

**Figure 7.1** (continued) Continental Currency, 1779. Courtesy of the Granger Collection, New York.

*honoured. In response, Congress and the individual states printed their own currency which led to rampant inflation during and after the war. Figure 7.1 shows examples of three different banknotes—one congressional and two from the states (Massachusetts and Georgia).*

## 8. Shays's Rebellion[8]

*After the ratification of the 1780 constitution, the Massachusetts government pursued a deflationary policy, constricting the money supply, requiring that taxes be paid with specie, and prosecuting debtors. Farmers in the western part of the state were especially hard-hit by these policies, and, during the summer of 1786, farmers in Hampshire County, many of whom were veterans of the War of Independence, such as Daniel Shays, who gave his name to the resistance, took up arms and closed the courts so that debt cases could not be prosecuted. Faced with widespread civil unrest the state's governor, James Bowdoin (1726–1790), declared the protestors to be in rebellion and called out the militia to suppress the unrest on September 2, 1786.*

WHEREAS information has been given to the Supreme Executive of this Commonwealth, that on Tuesday last, the 29th of August, being the day appointed by law for the sitting of the Court of Common Pleas and Court of General Sessions of the Peace, at *Northampton* in the county of *Hampshire*, within this Commonwealth, a large concourse of people, from several parts of that county, assembled at the Court-House in *Northampton*, many of whom were armed with guns, swords, and other deadly weapons, and with drums beating and fifes playing, in contempt and open defiance of the authority of this Government, did, by their threats of violence and keeping possession of the Court-House until twelve o'clock on the night of the same day, prevent the sitting of the Court, and the orderly administration of justice in that county:

AND WHEREAS this high-handed offence is fraught with the most fatal and pernicious consequences, must tend to subvert all law and government; to dissolve our excellent Constitution, and introduce universal riot, anarchy and confusion, which would probably terminate in absolute despotism, and consequently destroy the fairest prospects of political happiness, that any people was ever favoured with:

I HAVE therefore thought fit, by and with the advice of the Council, to issue this Proclamation, calling upon all Judges, Justices, Sheriffs, Constables, and other officers, civil and military, within this Commonwealth, to prevent and suppress all such violent and riotous proceedings if they should be attempted in their several counties.

AND I DO hereby, pursuant to the indispensable duty I owe to the good people of this Commonwealth, most solemnly call upon them, as they value the blessings of freedom and independence, which at the expense of so much blood and treasure they have purchased—as they regard their faith, which in the sight of GOD and the world, they pledged to one another and to the people of the United States, when they adopted the present Constitution of Government—as they would not disappoint the hopes, and thereby become contemptible in the eyes of other nations, in the view of whom they have risen to glory and empire—as they would not deprive themselves of the security derived from well-regulated Society, to their lives, liberties and property; and as they would not devolve upon their children, instead of peace, freedom and safety, a state of anarchy, confusion and slavery, I do most earnestly and most solemnly call upon them to aid and assist with their utmost efforts the aforesaid officers, and to unite in preventing and suppressing all such treasonable proceedings, and every measure that has a tendency to encourage them…

### 9. The Shaysites Make Their Case

*Shays's Rebellion lasted throughout the autumn and winter of 1786–1787 when Massachusetts troops fired on Shaysites attempting to seize the state armory at Springfield. Over the next several months the rebellion collapsed. The rebels enjoyed widespread support among the debt-ridden farmers of the United States. These two letters were published in local newspapers and stated the rebels' grievances for which they sought redress.*

*To the Printer of the Hampshire Herald.*[9]

Sir,

IT has some how or other fallen to my lot to be employed in a more conspicuous manner than some others of my fellow citizens, in stepping forth in defence of the rights and privileges of the people, more especially of the county of *Hampshire.*

THEREFORE, upon the desire of the people now at arms, I take this method to publish to the world of mankind in general, particularly the people of this Commonwealth, some of the principal grievances we complain of, and of which we are now seeking redress, and mean to contend for, until a redress can be obtained, which we hope, will soon take place; and if so, our brethren in this Commonwealth, that do not see with us as yet, shall find we shall be as peaceable as they be.

IN the first place, I must refer you to a draught of grievances drawn up by a committee of the people, now at arms, under the signature of *Daniel Gray*, chairman, which is heartily approved of; some others also are here added, viz.

1st.  The General Court, for certain obvious reasons, must be removed out of the town of *Boston.*

2d.  A revision of the constitution is absolutely necessary,

3d.  All kinds of governmental securities, now on interest, that have been bought of the original owners for two shillings, three shillings, four shillings, and the highest for six shillings and eight pence on the pound, and have received more interest than the principal cost the speculator who purchased them – that if justice was done, we verily believe, nay positively know, it would save this Commonwealth thousands of pounds.

4th.  Let the lands belonging to this Commonwealth, at the eastward, be sold at the best advantage, to pay the remainder of our domestick debt.

5th.  Let the monies arising from impost and excise be appropriated to discharge the foreign debt.

6th.  Let that act, passed by the General Court last *June*, by a small majority of only seven, called the Supplementary Aid, for twenty five years to come, be repealed.

7th.  The total abolition of the Inferiour Court of Common Pleas and General Sessions of the Peace.

8th.  Deputy Sheriffs totally set aside, as a useless set of officers in the community; and Constables who are really necessary, be empowered to do the duty, by which means a large swarm of lawyers will be banished from their wonted haunts, who have been more damage to the people at large, especially the common farmers, than the savage beasts of prey.

To this I boldly sing my proper name, as a hearty wellwisher to the rights of the people.

THOMAS GROVER
*Worcester, December 7, 1786.*

An ADDRESS to the PEOPLE of the several towns in the county of Hampshire, from the Body now at arms[10]

*Gentlemen,*
We have thought proper to inform you of some of the principal causes of the late risings of the people, and also of their present movement, viz.

1st.   The present expensive mode of collecting debts, which, by the reason of the great scarcity of cash, will of necessity fill our gaols with unhappy debtors, and thereby render a reputable body of people incapable of being serviceable either to themselves or the community.

2d.   The monies raised by impost and excise being appropriated to discharge the interest of governmental securities, and not the foreign debt, when these securities are not subject to taxation.

3d.   A suspension of the Writ of Habeus corpus, by which those persons who have stepped forth to assert and maintain the rights of the people, are liable to be taken and conveyed even to the most distant part of the commonwealth, and thereby subjected to an unjust punishment.

4th.   The unlimited power granted to Justices of the Peace and Sheriffs, Deputy Sheriffs, and Constables, by the Riot Act, indemnifying them to the protection thereof; when perhaps, wholly actuated from a principle of revenge, hatred and envy.

*Furthermore,* Be assured, that this body, now at arms, despise the idea of being instigated by British emissaries, which is so strenuously propagated by the enemies of our liberties: We also wish the most proper and speedy measures may be taken to discharge both our foreign and domestic debt.

Per Order,
DANIEL GRAY, *Chairman of the Committee, for the above purpose.*

## 10.   Massachusetts Pursues a Contradictory Strategy in Response to the Rebels[11]

*Governor James Bowdoin faced a particularly difficult challenge in dealing with Shays's Rebellion. On one hand the rebels were challenging the authority of the lawfully elected government. On the other, there was public sympathy with the grievances of the rebels. As a consequence the government pursued a contradictory policy with regard to the rebellion, offering pardons to those who would lay down their arms and take a loyalty oath while at the same time threatening to bring the force of the state upon those who continued to resist. This rather bellicose declaration was issued in February 1787 as the rebellion petered out. Although the rebels seemed to have failed to achieve redress of their grievances, the government subsequently relaxed the financial measures which caused the uprising and Bowdoin lost his bid for re-election in large part because of his response to the rebellion.*

Whereas the doings of the General Court at their last session, relative to the Insurgents against the Government and Authority of the State, in several Counties within this Commonwealth; were lenient and mercifull, were intended to quiet the minds of the disaffected, and ought to have had the effect they were design,d to produce

And Whereas every complaint of Grievance was carefully attended to with a disproportion to grant all that relief which could be afforded, consistant with equal justice and the dignity of Government; ~~and measures were adopted accordingly~~ and the General Court so far as they were A. able adopted measures accordingly—ᴬ

And Whereas a full and free pardon, for all the outrageous proceedings against the Government, whereof the Insurgents had been guilty, was tender,d them, upon this mild condition alone, that they should be guilty of such outrages no more, and as evidence of their intentions to demean themselves in future, as good and faithful ~~subjects~~ Citizens, should before the first day of January AD 1787 take and subscribe the oath of Allegiance, ᴮ And B as *a full and clear information was given to them Insurgents as well as others of the general situation of public affairs, and that everything had been done for their relief consistent with the safety and justice of the State* ᶜ it manifestly appears, from the subsequent conduct of the leaders of the Insurgents, that their opposition to Government has not arisen, from a misapprehension, as to the views and disposition of Government; as from a temporary invitation, arising from the pressure of supposed grievances, or from a misguided zeal to promote the public happiness, as has been insidiously asserted; but from a settled determination to subvert the Constitution and put an end to the Government of this Commonwealth. —it is also abundantly manifest, that the conduct of the Insurgents, in Stopping the Courts of Justice in the Counties of Worcester, and Hampshire—in Assembling in Arms avowedly to commit the same outrages in the County of Middlesex,—in calling upon the Towns in some Counties, to furnish themselves with Arms and ammunition—in appointing Committees to form ~~them~~ their adherents into regular military Companies properly Officer'd, thereby to establish within this Commonwealth, a Standing Force, beyond the controul of, and for the express purpose of apposing in arms, the Constitutional government of the State—in endeavouring to increase the Commotions in the Counties aforesaid, by publicly inviting and allowing others to throw off their allegiance and join their body; in Subversion of all order and government, absolutely incompatible with the public safety and happiness; And is an open, unnatural, unprovoked, and wicked Rebellion; against the dignity authority and government of this Commonwealth—And the Legislature in duty to their Constituents, in conformity to their oaths, And by virtue of the authority vested in them by the Constitution, (having ineffectually try,d every lenient measure to reclaim them,) do hereby solemnly ~~pronounce and~~ declare, that a horrid and unnatural Rebellion and War, has been openly and traitorously raised and levied against this Commonwealth, and is still continued, and now exists within the same, with design to subvert and overthrow the Constitution and form of Government thereof which has been most solemnly agreed to, and established by the Citizens of this Commonwealth; And that Government ought and will, with the greatest energy and force, exert and bring forth, all the powers of the Commonwealth for the Suppression thereof; and all the horrors and evils, that may follow in the consequence of this Rebellion, must be imputed to those men, who have, contrary to the duty of their allegiance, and every principle of law and Justice, been the fomenters, Abetters, and Supporters of the same

A.  insert and gave full & clear information, to the Insurgents as well as others, of the general Situation of public Affairs
B.  dele from B. to C-

## 11.  "A Little Rebellion Now and Then Is a Good Thing": Jefferson Reacts to Shays's Rebellion[12]

*Many wealthy Americans were alarmed by Shays's Rebellion. Indeed, the turmoil in Massachusetts was the catalyst for the calling of the Constitutional Convention in the summer of 1787. Thomas Jefferson, writing from Paris, was more sanguine about events in Massachusetts, viewing them as a necessary feature of republican government.*

...I am impatient to learn your sentiments on the late troubles in the Eastern states. So far as I have yet seen, they do not appear to threaten serious consequences. Those states have suffered by the stoppage of the channels of their commerce, which have not yet found other issues. This must render money scarce, and make the people uneasy. This uneasiness has produced acts absolutely unjustifiable; but I hope they will provoke no severities from their governments. A consciousness of those in power that their administration of the public affairs has been honest, may perhaps produce too great a degree of indignation: and those characters wherein fear predominates over hope may apprehend too much from these instances of irregularity. They may conclude too hastily that nature has formed man insusceptible of any other government but that of force, a conclusion not founded in truth, nor experience. Societies exist under three forms sufficiently distinguishable.

1.  Without government, as among our Indians.
2.  Under governments wherein the will of every one has a just influence,

as is the case in England in a slight degree, and in our states, in a great one.

3.  Under governments of force: as is the case in all other monarchies and in most of the other republics.

To have an idea of the curse of existence under these last, they must be seen. It is a government of wolves over sheep. It is a problem, not clear in my mind, that the 1st condition is not the best. But I believe it to be inconsistent with any great degree of population. The second state has a great deal of good in it. The mass of mankind under that enjoys a precious degree of liberty & happiness. It has it's evils too: the principal of which is the turbulence to which it is subject. But weigh this against the oppressions of monarchy, and it becomes nothing... Even this evil is productive of good. It prevents the degeneracy of government, and nourishes a general attention to the public affairs. I hold it that a little rebellion now and then is a good thing, & as necessary in the political world as storms in the physical. Unsuccessful rebellions indeed generally establish the encroachments on the rights of the people which have produced them. An observation of this truth should render honest republican governors so mild in their punishment of rebellions, as not to discourage them too much. It is a medicine necessary for the sound health of government. If these transactions give me no uneasiness, I feel very differently at another piece of intelligence, to wit, the possibility that the navigation of the Mississippi may be abandoned to Spain. I never had any interest Westward of the Alleghaney; & I never will have any. But I have had great opportunities of knowing the character of the people who inhabit that country. And I will venture to say that the act which abandons the navigation of the Mississippi is an act of separation between the Eastern & Western country. It is a relinquishment of five parts out of eight of the territory of the United States, an abandonment of the fairest subject for the paiment of our public debts, & the chaining those debts on our own necks in perpetuum...If they declare themselves a separate people, we are incapable of a single effort to retain them. Our citizens can never be induced, either as militia or as souldiers, to go there to cut the throats of their own brothers & sons, or rather to be themselves the subjects instead of the perpetrators of the parricide. Nor would that country requite the cost of being retained against the will of it's inhabitants, could it be done. But it cannot be done. They are able already to rescue the navigation of the Mississippi out of the hands of Spain, & to add New Orleans to their own territory. They will be joined by the inhabitants of Louisiana. This will bring on a war between them & Spain; and that will produce the question with us whether it will not be worth our while to become parties with them in the war, in order to reunite them with us, & thus correct our error? & were I to permit my forebodings to go one step further, I should predict that the inhabitants of the US would force their rulers to take the affirmative of that question. I wish I may be mistaken in all these opinions...

# Notes

1. John Adams autobiography, part 1, "John Adams," through 1776, sheet 29 of 53 [electronic edition]. *Adams Family Papers: An Electronic Archive.* Boston: Massachusetts Historical Society, http://www. masshist.org/digitaladams/

2. L.H. Butterfield (ed.), *Letters of Benjamin Rush*, Vol. 1 (Princeton, NJ: Princeton University Press, 1951), 136–137.

3. "Return of Brookline (Suffolk County), May 21, 1778," in Robert J. Taylor (ed.), *Massachusetts, Colony to Commonwealth: Documents on the Formation of Its Constitution, 1775–1780* (Chapel Hill: University of North Carolina Press, 1961), 70.

4. *An Address of the Convention, for framing a new constitution of government, for the state of Massachusetts-Bay, to their Constituents* (Boston: White and Adams, 1780), 5, 8–17.

5. Engrossed and corrected copy of the Articles of Confederation, showing amendments adopted, November 15, 1777, Papers of the Continental Congress, 1779–1789; Records of the Continental and Conferation Congresses and the Constitutional Convention, 1779–1789, Record Group 360; National Archives.

6. September 3, 1780. Letter to Duane on Government. Alexander Hamilton, The Works of Alexander Hamilton, ed. Henry Cabot Lodge (Federal Edition) (New York: G. P. Putnam's Sons, 1904). In 12 vols. Vol. 1 Chapter: "The Government and the Constitution." Available from http://oll.libertyfund. org/title/1378/64139/1590430 on 2009-10-09.

7. The Granger Collection, New York.

8. *By His Excellency James Bowdoin Esquire, A Proclamation. September 2, 1786* (Boston: Adams and Nourse, 1786).

9. George Richard Minot, *The History of the Insurrections, in Massachusetts, In the Year 1786, and the Rebellion Consequent Thereon* (Worcester, MA: Isaiah Thomas, 1788), 85–87.

10. *The Cumberland Gazette*, January 12, 1787.

11. Declaration of the General Court, February 4, 1787, Massachusetts State Archives, Boston.

12. Thomas Jefferson to James Madison, January 30, 1787, with List of Decoded Passages, The Thomas Jefferson Papers, Series 1: General Correspondence, 1651–1827. Washington, DC: Library of Congress, Manuscript Division.

# CHAPTER 8

# Creating the Constitution

## Introduction

In the aftermath of Shays's Rebellion and the apparent failure of the United States under the Articles of Confederation, many leading republicans in the United States desired significant constitutional change. Among these, one of the most important was James Madison (1751–1836) of Virginia. Madison had served in the Virginia Convention which called for independence from Great Britain and helped to draft his state's constitution after independence was declared. He served in Congress during the early 1780s and became acutely aware of the limitations of the national government under the Articles of Confederation. This experience convinced him of the need for a stronger national government. During the winter of 1786–1787, he prepared for the Constitutional Convention to be held in Philadelphia during the summer of 1787. In April he produced a lengthy memorandum (document 1) outlining the flaws in the national government under the Articles of Confederation. This memo laid the groundwork for the Virginia Plan (document 2), his proposed new constitution for the United States which would replace the Articles of Confederation. For some delegates to the Convention, the Virginia Plan went too far and they sought simply to modify the Articles of Confederation. The opposition to the Virginia Plan coalesced around William Paterson's New Jersey Plan (document 3). Eventually, a series of compromises were made over key elements of Madison's plan, particularly with respect to sovereignty and representation, and a modified version of the Virginia Plan was submitted to the states for approval. As Benjamin Franklin reflected at the close of the convention (document 4), the proposed constitution, while imperfect, represented the best efforts of the convention. It remained to be seen whether nine state ratifying conventions would approve the proposed constitution. As documents 5–8 show the debate over the Constitution was vibrant, divisive, and passionate. It took place on various levels from constitutional and political theory to sarcasm and derision. The debate over the Constitution marked a high point in American political culture and public engagement with the meaning of the Revolution. Apart from subjecting the Constitution to rigorous scrutiny, it also gave it a measure of popular legitimacy which was essential for a document drafted in secret. A more concrete outcome of the debate was the Bill of Rights (document 9), which was the Antifederalists' contribution to the American constitutional tradition and a crucial legacy of the ratification process.

### 1. Madison on the Flaws of the Articles of Confederation[1]

*In advance of the Constitutional Convention, James Madison wrote a memorandum, "Vices of the Political System of the United States," which provided a detailed analysis of the faults in, and problems arising from, the Articles of Confederation. Madison had read widely in republican political history and theory and sought in the "Vices of the Political System" to identify the major flaws in the American political system. Among the problems he identified were the relative impotence of the national government and the danger posed by the state governments, the policies of which were often antithetical to national interests. In Madison's view, the constant bickering between the states endangered America's republican experiment. Madison circulated this memorandum among key members of the Constitutional Convention. In so doing he laid the groundwork for proposing radical constitutional change rather than simple amendments to the Articles of the Confederation. He set the agenda for the Constitutional Convention during the summer of 1787.*

1. Failure of the States to comply with the Constitutional requisitions.

This evil has been so fully experienced both during the war and since the peace, results so naturally from the number and independent authority of the States and has been so uniformly examplified in every similar Confederacy, that it may be considered as not less radically and permanently inherent in, than it is fatal to the object of, the present System.

2. Encroachments by the States on the federal authority.

…Among these examples are the wars and Treaties of Georgia with the Indians—The unlicensed compacts between Virginia and Maryland, and between Pena. & N. Jersey—the troops raised and to be kept up by Massts.

3. Violations of the law of nations and of treaties.

From the number of Legislatures, the sphere of life from which most of their members are taken, and the circumstances under which their legislative business is carried on, irregularities of this kind must frequently happen…

As yet foreign powers have not been rigorous in animadverting on us. This moderation however cannot be mistaken for a permanent partiality to our faults, or a permanent security agst. those disputes with other nations…

4. Trespasses of the States on the rights of each other.

...Paper money, instalments of debts, occlusion of Courts, making property a legal tender, may likewise be deemed aggressions on the rights of other States. As the Citizens of every State aggregately taken stand more or less in the relation of Creditors or debtors, to the Citizens of every other States, Acts of the debtor State in favor of debtors, affect the Creditor State, in the same manner, as they do its own citizens who are relatively creditors towards other citizens. This remark may be extended to foreign nations. If the exclusive regulation of the value and alloy of coin was properly delegated to the federal authority, the policy of it equally requires a controul on the States in the cases above mentioned. It must have been meant 1. to preserve uniformity in the circulating medium throughout the nation. 2. to prevent those frauds on the citizens of other States, and the subjects of foreign powers, which might disturb the tranquility at home, or involve the Union in foreign contests.

The practice of many States in restricting the commercial intercourse with other States, and putting their productions and manufactures on the same footing with those of foreign nations, though not contrary to the federal articles, is certainly adverse to the spirit of the Union, and tends to beget retaliating regulations, not less expensive & vexatious in themselves, than they are destructive of the general harmony.

5. want of concert in matters where common interest requires it.

This defect is strongly illustrated in the state of our commercial affairs. How much has the national dignity, interest, and revenue suffered from this cause? Instances of inferior moment are the want of uniformity in the laws concerning naturalization & literary property; of provision for national seminaries, for grants of incorporation for national purposes, for canals and other works of general utility, wch. may at present be defeated by the perverseness of particular States whose concurrence is necessary.

6. want of guaranty to the States of their Constitutions & laws against internal violence.

The confederation is silent on this point and therefore by the second article the hands of the federal authority are tied. According to Republican Theory, Right and power being both vested in the majority, are held to be synonimous. According to fact and experience a minority may in an appeal to force, be an overmatch for the majority. 1. If the minority happen to include all such as possess the skill and habits of military life, & such as possess the great pecuniary resources, one third only may conquer the remaining two thirds. 2. One third of those who participate in the choice of the rulers, may be rendered a majority by the accession of those whose poverty excludes them from a right of suffrage, and who for obvious reasons will be more likely to join the standard of sedition than that of the established Government. 3. Where slavery exists the republican Theory becomes still more fallacious.

7. want of sanction to the laws, and of coercion in the Government of the Confederacy.

A sanction is essential to the idea of law, as coercion is to that of Government. The federal system being destitute of both, wants the great vital principles of a Political Cons[ti]tution. Under the form of such a Constitution, it is in fact nothing more than a treaty of amity of commerce and of alliance, between independent and Sovereign States…It is no longer doubted that a unanimous and punctual obedience of 13 independent bodies, to the acts of the federal Government, ought not be calculated on. Even during the war, when external danger supplied in some degree the defect of legal & coercive sanctions, how imperfectly did the States fulfil their obligations to the Union? In time of peace, we see already what is to be expected. How indeed could it be otherwise? In the first place, Every general act of the Union must necessarily bear unequally hard on some particular member or members of it. Secondly the partiality of the members to their own interests and rights, a partiality which will be fostered by the Courtiers of popularity, will naturally exaggerate the inequality where it exists, and even suspect it where it has no existence. Thirdly a distrust of the voluntary compliance of each other may prevent the compliance of any, although it should be the latent disposition of all. Here are causes & pretexts which will never fail to render federal measures abortive. If the laws of the States, were merely recommendatory to their citizens, or if they were to be rejudged by County authorities, what security, what probability would exist, that they would be carried into execution?..

8. Want of ratification by the people of the articles of Confederation.

In some of the States the Confederation is recognized by, and forms a part of the constitution. In others however it has received no other sanction than that of the Legislative authority. From this defect two evils result: 1. Whenever a law of a State happens to be repugnant to an act of Congress, particularly when the former is of posterior date to the former, it will be at least questionable whether the latter must not prevail; and as the question must be decided by the Tribunals of the State, they will be most likely to lean on the side of the State. 2. As far as the Union of the States is to be regarded as a league of sovereign powers, and not as a political Constitution by virtue of which they are become one sovereign power, so far it seems to follow from the doctrine of compacts, that a breach of any of the articles of the confederation by any of the parties to it, absolves the other parties from their respective obligations, and gives them a right if they chuse to exert it, of dissolving the Union altogether.

9. Multiplicity of laws in the several States.

In developing the evils which viciate the political system of the U. S. it is proper to include those which are found within the States individually, as well as those which directly affect the States collectively, since the former class have an indirect influence on the general malady and must not be overlooked in forming a compleat remedy…As far as laws are necessary, to mark with precision the duties of those who are to obey them, and to take from those who are to administer them a discretion, which might be abused, their number is the price of liberty. As far as the laws exceed this limit, they are a nuisance: a nuisance of the most pestilent kind. Try the Codes of the several States by this test, and what a luxuriancy of legislation do they present. The short period of independency has filled as many pages as the century which preceded it…

10. mutability of the laws of the States.

…We daily see laws repealed or superseded, before any trial can have been made of their merits: and even before a knowledge of them can have reached the remoter districts within which they were to operate. In the regulations of trade this instability becomes a snare not only to our citizens but to foreigners also.

11. Injustice of the laws of States.

If the multiplicity and mutability of laws prove a want of wisdom, their injustice betrays a defect still more alarming: more alarming not merely because it is a greater evil in itself, but because it brings more into question the fundamental principle of republican Government, that the majority who rule in such Governments, are the safest Guardians both of public Good and of private rights. To what causes is this evil to be ascribed?

These causes lie

1. in the Representative bodies.
2. in the people themselves.

1. Representative appointments are sought from 3 motives. 1. ambition 2. personal interest. 3. public good. Unhappily the two first are proved by experience to be most prevalent. Hence the candidates who feel them, particularly, the second, are most industrious, and most successful in pursuing their object: and forming often a majority in the legislative Councils, with interested views, contrary to the interest, and views, of their Constituents, join in a perfidious sacrifice of the latter to the former…

2. A still more fatal if not more frequent cause lies among the people themselves. All civilized societies are divided into different interests and factions, as they happen to be creditors or debtors—Rich or poor—husbandmen, merchants or manufacturers—members of different religious sects—followers of different political leaders—inhabitants of different districts—owners of different kinds of property &c &c. In republican Government the majority however composed, ultimately give the law. Whenever therefore an apparent interest or common passion unites a majority what is to restrain them from unjust violations of the rights and interests of the minority, or of individuals? Three motives only 1. a prudent regard to their own good as involved in the general and permanent good of the Community. This consideration although of decisive weight in itself, is found by experience to be too often unheeded…2dly. respect for character. However strong this motive may be in individuals, it is considered as very insufficient to restrain them from injustice. In a multitude its efficacy is diminished in proportion to the number which is to share the praise or the blame…3dly. will

Religion the only remaining motive be a sufficient restraint? It is not pretended to be such on men individually considered. Will its effect be greater on them considered in an aggregate view? quite the reverse. The conduct of every popular assembly acting on oath, the strongest of religious Ties, proves that individuals join without remorse in acts, against which their consciences would revolt if proposed to them under the like sanction, separately in their closets…

The great desideratum in Government is such a modification of the Sovereignty as will render it sufficiently neutral between the different interests and factions, to controul one part of the Society from invading the rights of another, and at the same time sufficiently controuled itself, from setting up an interest adverse to that of the whole Society…

An auxiliary desideratum for the melioration of the Republican form is such a process of elections as will most certainly extract from the mass of the Society the purest and noblest characters which it contains; such as will at once feel most strongly the proper motives to pursue the end of their appointment, and be most capable to devise the proper means of attaining it.

12. Impotence of the laws of the States

## 2. The Virginia Plan[2]

*Having identified the flaws in the American constitutional system in the "Vices of the Political System of the United States" (document 1), Madison proposed a solution—the creation of a continental super-republic with the authority to over-ride the states, which he believed were the greatest single source of political instability. Madison prepared a draft constitution in advance of the convention. He caucused with the other members of the Virginia delegation and won their support for the plan, which came to be known as the Virginia Plan. On May 29, 1787, Edmund Randolph (1753–1813) of Virginia presented the plan as a series of resolutions to the Convention. If adopted, the Virginia Plan would radically alter the fundamental constitution of the United States, replacing the Articles of Confederation with a more powerful, centralized government.*

State of the resolutions submitted to the consideration of the House by the honorable Mr. Randolph, as altered, amended, and agreed to, in a Committee of the whole House.

1.  Resolved that it is the opinion of this Committee that a national government ought to be established consisting of a Supreme Legislative, Judiciary, and Executive.
2.  Resolved that the national Legislature ought to consist of Two Branches.
3.  Resolved that the members of the first branch of the national Legislature ought to be elected by the People of the several States for the term of Three years. to receive fixed stipends, by which they may be compensated for the devotion of their time to public service to be paid out of the National

Treasury. to be ineligible to any Office established by a particular State or under the authority of the United-States (except those peculiarly belonging to the functions of the first branch) during the term of service, and under the national government for the space of one year after it's expiration.

4.  Resolved that the members of the second Branch of the national Legislature ought to be chosen by the individual Legislatures. to be of the age of thirty years at least. to hold their offices for a term sufficient to ensure their independency, namely seven years. to receive fixed stipends, by which they may be compensated for the devotion of their time to public service—to be paid out of the National Treasury to be ineligible to any office established by a particular State, or under the authority of the United States (except those peculiarly belonging to the functions of the second branch) during the term of service, and under the national government, for the space of one year after it's expiration.

5.  Resolved that each branch ought to possess the right of originating acts.

6.  Resolved that the national Legislature ought to be empowered to enjoy the legislative rights vested in Congress by the confederation—and moreover to legislate in all cases to which the separate States are incompetent: or in which the harmony of the United States may be interrupted by the exercise of individual legislation. to negative all laws passed by the several States contravening, in the opinion of the national Legislature, the articles of union, or any treaties subsisting under the authority of the union.

7.  Resolved that the right of suffrage in the first branch of the national Legislature ought not to be according to the rule established in the articles of confederation: but according to some equitable ratio of representation— namely, in proportion to the whole number of white and other free citizens and inhabitants of every age, sex, and condition including those bound to servitude for a term of years, and three fifths of all other persons not comprehended in the foregoing description, except Indians, not paying taxes in each State.

8.  Resolved that the right of suffrage in the second branch of the national Legislature ought to be according to the rule established for the first.

9.  Resolved that a national Executive be instituted to consist of a single person. to be chosen by the National Legislature. for the term of seven years. with power to carry into execution the national Laws, to appoint to Offices in cases not otherwise provided for to be ineligible a second time, and to be removable on impeachment and conviction of mal practice or neglect of duty. to receive a fixed stipend, by which he may be compensated for the devotion of his time to public service to be paid out of the national Treasury.

10.  Resolved that the national executive shall have a right to negative any legislative act: which shall not be afterwards passed unless by two third parts of each branch of the national Legislature.

11. Resolved that a national Judiciary be established to consist of One Supreme Tribunal. The Judges of which to be appointed by the second Branch of the National Legislature. to hold their offices during good behaviour to receive, punctually, at stated times, a fixed compensation for their services: in which no encrease or diminution shall be made so as to affect the persons actually in office at the time of such encrease or diminution.

12. Resolved that the national Legislature be empowered to appoint inferior Tribunals.

13. Resolved that the jurisdiction of the national Judiciary shall extend to cases which respect the collection of the national revenue: impeachments of any national officers: and questions which involve the national peace and harmony.

14. Resolved that provision ought to be made for the admission of States, lawfully arising within the limits of the United States, whether from a voluntary junction of government and territory, or otherwise, with the consent of a number of voices in the national Legislature less than the whole.

15. Resolved that provision ought to be made for the continuance of Congress and their authorities until a given day after the reform of the articles of Union shall be adopted; and for the completion of all their engagements.

16. Resolved that a republican constitution, and its existing laws, ought to be guaranteed to each State by the United States.

17. Resolved that provision ought to be made for the amendment of the articles of Union, whensoever it shall seem necessary.

18. Resolved that the Legislative, Executive, and Judiciary powers within the several States ought to be bound by oath to support the articles of Union.

19. Resolved that the amendments which shall be offered to the confederation by the Convention, ought at a proper time or times, after the approbation of Congress to be submitted to an assembly or assemblies of representatives, recommended by the several Legislatures, to be expressly chosen by the People to consider and decide thereon.

## 3. The New Jersey Plan[3]

*The Virginia Plan (document 2) would strike at the authority of the states—both because it would vest so much authority in the federal government and because representation within the proposed bicameral congress would be apportioned according to population. Under the Continental Congress and the Articles of Confederation, each of the states were equal and possessed one vote. On June 14 and 15, 1787, William Paterson (1745–1806) of New Jersey presented an alternative to the Virginia Plan. According to Paterson's plan, which had the support of several small states which feared they would be overwhelmed under the Virginia Plan,*

*Congress would have increased powers but it would retain a unicameral structure and each state delegation would have one vote. Paterson's plan was closer to the original intention of the Constitutional Convention in so far as it recommended modifications to the Articles of Confederation rather than their replacement by a new constitution. The New Jersey Plan prompted a debate about the nature of representation in the new government, and a compromise emerged whereby representation in the lower house of Congress, the House of Representatives, would be according to state population but each of the states would be equal in the upper house having two votes in the Senate.*

1.   Resd. that the articles of Confederation ought to be so revised, corrected & enlarged, as to render the federal Constitution adequate to the exigencies of Government, & the preservation of the Union.

2.   Resd. that in addition to the powers vested in the U. States in Congress, by the present existing articles of Confederation, they be authorized to pass acts for raising a revenue, by levying a duty or duties on all goods or merchandizes of foreign growth or manufacture, imported into any part of the U. States, by Stamps on paper, vellum or parchment, and by a postage on all letters or packages passing through the general post-Office, to be applied to such federal purposes as they shall deem proper & expedient; to make rules & regulations for the collection thereof; and the same from time to time, to alter & amend in such manner as they shall think proper: to pass Acts for the regulation of trade & commerce as well with foreign nations as with each other: provided that all punishments, fines, forfeitures & penalties to be incurred for contravening such acts rules and regulations shall be adjudged by the Common law Judiciaries of the State in which any offense contrary to the true intent & meaning of such Acts rules & regulations shall have been committed or perpetrated, with liberty of commencing in the first instance all suits & prosecutions for that purpose in the superior Common law Judiciary in such State, subject nevertheless, for the correction of all errors, both in law & fact in rendering judgment, to an appeal to the Judiciary of the U. States.

3.   Resd. that whenever requisitions shall be necessary, instead of the rule for making requisitions mentioned in the articles of Confederation, the United States in Congs. be authorized to make such requisitions in proportion to the whole number of white & other free citizens & inhabitants of every age sex and condition including those bound to servitude for a term of years & three fifths of all other persons not comprehended in the foregoing description, except Indians not paying taxes; that if such requisitions be not complied with, in the time specified therein, to direct the collection thereof in the non complying States & for that purpose to devise and pass acts directing & authorizing the same; provided that none of the powers hereby vested in the U. States in Congs shall be exercised without the

consent of at least States, and in that proportion if the number of Confederated States should hereafter be increased or diminished.

4. Resd. that the U. States in Congs be authorized to elect a federal Executive to consist of persons, to continue in office for the term of years, to receive punctually at stated times a fixed compensation for their services, in which no increase or diminution shall be made so as to affect the persons composing the Executive at the time of such increase or diminution, to be paid out of the federal treasury; to be incapable of holding any other office or appointment during their time of service and for years thereafter; to be ineligible a second time, & removeable by Congs on application by a majority of the Executives of the several States; that the Executives besides their general authority to execute the federal acts ought to appoint all federal officers not otherwise provided for, & to direct all military operations; provided that none of the persons composing the federal Executive shall on any occasion take command of any troops, so as personally to conduct any enterprise as General or in other capacity.

5. Resd. that a federal Judiciary be established to consist of a supreme Tribunal the Judges of which to be appointed by the Executive, & to hold their offices during good behaviour, to receive punctually at stated times a fixed compensation for their services in which no increase or diminution shall be made, so as to affect the persons actually in office at the time of such increase or diminution; that the Judiciary so established shall have authority to hear & determine in the first instance on all impeachments of federal officers, & by way of appeal in the dernier resort in all cases touchung the rights of Ambassadors, in all cases of captures from an enemy, in all cases of piracies & felonies on the high Seas, in all cases in which foreigners may be interested, in the construction of any treaty or treaties, or which may arise on any of the Acts for regulation of trade, or the collection of the federal Revenue: that none of the Judiciary shall during the time they remain in Office be capable of receiving or holding any other office or appointment during their time of service, or for thereafter.

6. Resd. that all Acts of the U. States in Congs. made by virtue & in pursuance of the powers hereby & by the articles of confederation vested in them, and all Treaties made & ratified under the authority of the U. States shall be the supreme law of the respective States so far forth as those Acts or Treaties shall relate to the said States or their Citizens, and that the Judiciary of the several States shall be bound thereby in their decisions, any thing in the respective laws of the Individual States to the contrary notwithstanding; and that if any State, or any body of men in any State shall oppose or prevent ye carrying into execution such acts or treaties, the federal Executive shall be authorized to call forth ye power of the Confederated States, or so much thereof as may be necessary to enforce and compel an obedience to such Acts, or an observance of such Treaties.

7.  Resd. that provision be made for the admission of new States into the Union.
8.  Resd. the rule for naturalization ought to be the same in every State.
9.  Resd. a Citizen of one State committing an offense in another State of the Union, shall be deemed guilty of the same offense as if it had been committed by a Citizen of the State in which the Offense was committed.

## 4.   Franklin Addresses the Constitutional Convention[4]

*The two best-known delegates to the Constitutional Convention were George Washington and Benjamin Franklin. In this address to the Convention as it came to an end on September 17, Franklin expressed qualified support for the proposed Constitution. This address was important as an expression of moderate Federalist support for the Constitution and because it was widely reprinted in the press during the debates over ratification.*

I confess that there are several parts of this constitution which I do not at present approve, but I am not sure I shall never approve them: For having lived long, I have experienced many instances of being obliged by better information or fuller consideration, to change opinions even on important subjects, which I once thought right, but found to be otherwise. It is therefore that the older I grow, the more apt I am to doubt my own judgment, and to pay more respect to the judgment of others. Most men indeed as well as most sects in Religion, think themselves in possession of all truth, and that whereever others differ from them it is so far error. Steele, a Protestant in a Dedication tells the Pope, that the only difference between our Churches in their opinions of the certainty of their doctrines is, the Church of Rome is infallible and the Church of England is never in the wrong. But though many private persons think almost as highly of their own infallibility as of that of their sect, few express it so naturally as a certain french lady, who in a dispute with her sister, said "I don't know how it happens, Sister but I meet with no body but myself, that's always in the right"—*Il n'y a que moi qui a toujours raison.*

In these sentiments, Sir, I agree to this Constitution with all its faults, if they are such; because I think a general Government necessary for us, and there is no form of Government but what may be a blessing to the people if well administered, and believe farther that this is likely to be well administered for a course of years, and can only end in Despotism, as other forms have done before it, when the people shall become so corrupted as to need despotic Government, being incapable of any other. I doubt too whether any other Convention we can obtain may be able to make a better Constitution. For when you assemble a number of men to have the advantage of their joint wisdom, you inevitably assemble with those men, all their prejudices, their passions, their errors of opinion, their local interests, and their selfish views. From such an Assembly can a perfect production be expected? It therefore astonishes me, Sir, to find this system approaching so near to perfection as it does; and I think it will astonish our enemies, who are waiting with confidence to hear that our councils are confounded like those of the Builders of Babel; and that our States are on the point of separation, only to meet hereafter for the purpose of cutting one another's throats. Thus I consent, Sir, to this Constitution because I expect no better, and because I am not sure, that it is not the best. The opinions I have had of its errors, I sacrifice to the public good—I have never whispered a syllable of them abroad—Within these walls they were born, and here they shall die—If every one of us in returning to our Constituents were to report the objections he has had to it, and endeavor to gain partizans in support of them, we might prevent its being generally received, and thereby lose all the salutary effects & great advantages resulting naturally in our favor among foreign Nations as well as among ourselves, from our real or apparent unanimity. Much of the strength & efficiency of any Government in procuring and securing happiness to the people, depends on opinion, on the general opinion of the goodness of the Government, as well as well as of the wisdom and integrity of its Governors. I hope therefore that for our own sakes as a part of the people, and for the sake of posterity, we shall act heartily and unanimously in recommending this Constitution (if approved by Congress & confirmed by the Conventions) wherever our influence may extend, and turn our future thoughts & endeavors to the means of having it well administered.

On the whole, Sir, I cannot help expressing a wish that every member of the Convention who may still have objections to it, would with me, on this occasion doubt a little of his own infallibility—and to make manifest our unanimity, put his name to this instrument."—He then moved that the Constitution be signed by the members and offered the following as a convenient form viz. "Done in Convention, by the unanimous consent of *the States* present the 17th. of Sepr. &c—In Witness whereof we have hereunto subscribed our names."

## 5.  Federalist Number 10[5]

*In the debate over the ratification of the Constitution, Federalists and Antifederalists produced hundreds of essays which appeared in newspapers and pamphlets. Among these, the most famous are the eighty-five* Federalist *essays which appeared in New York newspapers between October 1787 and August 1788. The essays, published under the pseudonym "Publius," were written by James Madison, Alexander Hamilton, and John Jay. Madison wrote twenty-seven essays, Hamilton fifty-one, and Jay five. Taken together, they constitute the most coherent explication of the Federalist principles during the ratification debate.* Federalist No. 10 *is, perhaps, the most famous of the essays. In it, Madison addressed the widespread belief, derived from Montesquieu's* Spirit of the Laws, *that republics must be geographically small to thrive. On the contrary Madison argued, republics were ideally suited to large nations because the large number of competing interest groups in a large republic would ensure that no one faction or group could dominate and oppress the others. Rather than endangering liberty, Madison argued, a large republic was better suited to preserving and protecting minority views.*

To the People of the State of New York:

AMONG the numerous advantages promised by a well constructed Union, none deserves to be more accurately developed than its tendency to break and control the violence of faction…The instability, injustice, and confusion introduced into the public councils, have, in truth, been the mortal diseases under which popular governments have everywhere perished; as they continue to be the favorite and fruitful topics from which the adversaries to liberty derive their most specious declamations. The valuable improvements made by the American constitutions on the popular models, both ancient and modern, cannot certainly be too much admired; but it would be an unwarrantable partiality, to contend that they have as effectually obviated the danger on this side, as was wished and expected. Complaints are everywhere heard from our most considerate and virtuous citizens, equally the friends of public and private faith, and of public and personal liberty, that our governments are too unstable, that the public good is disregarded in the conflicts of rival parties, and that measures are too often decided, not according to the rules of justice and the rights of the minor party, but by the superior force of an interested and overbearing majority…

By a faction, I understand a number of citizens, whether amounting to a majority or a minority of the whole, who are united and actuated by some common impulse of passion, or of interest, adversed to the rights of other citizens, or to the permanent and aggregate interests of the community.

There are two methods of curing the mischiefs of faction: the one, by removing its causes; the other, by controlling its effects.

There are again two methods of removing the causes of faction: the one, by destroying the liberty which is essential to its existence; the other, by giving to every citizen the same opinions, the same passions, and the same interests.

It could never be more truly said than of the first remedy, that it was worse than the disease. Liberty is to faction what air is to fire, an aliment without which it instantly expires. But it could not be less folly to abolish liberty, which is essential to political life, because it nourishes faction, than it would be to wish the annihilation of air, which is essential to animal life, because it imparts to fire its destructive agency.

The second expedient is as impracticable as the first would be unwise. As long as the reason of man continues fallible, and he is at liberty to exercise it, different opinions will be formed…The diversity in the faculties of men, from which the rights of property originate, is not less an insuperable obstacle to a uniformity of interests. The protection of these faculties is the first object of Government. From the protection of different and unequal faculties of acquiring property, the possession of different degrees and kinds of property immediately results; and from the influence of these on the sentiments and views of the respective proprietors, ensues a division of the society into different interests and parties.

The latent causes of faction are thus sown in the nature of man; and we see them everywhere brought into different degrees of activity, according to the different circumstances of civil society. A zeal for different opinions concerning religion, concerning Government, and many other points, as well of speculation as of practice; an attachment to different leaders ambitiously contending for pre-eminence and power; or to persons of other descriptions whose fortunes have been interesting to the human passions, have in turn divided mankind into parties, inflamed them with mutual animosity, and rendered them much more disposed to vex and oppress each other than to co-operate for their common good. So strong is this propensity of mankind to fall into mutual animosities, that where no substantial occasion presents itself, the most frivolous and fanciful distinctions have been sufficient to kindle their unfriendly passions and excite their most violent conflicts. But the most common and durable source of factions has been the various and unequal distribution of property. Those who hold and those who are without property have ever formed distinct interests in society. Those who are creditors, and those who are debtors, fall under a like discrimination. A landed interest, a manufacturing interest, a mercantile interest, a moneyed interest, with many lesser interests, grow up of necessity in civilized nations, and divide them into different classes, actuated by different sentiments and views. The regulation of these various and interfering interests forms the principal task of modern Legislation, and involves the spirit of party and faction in the necessary and ordinary operations of Government.

No man is allowed to be a judge in his own cause; because his interest would certainly bias his judgment, and, not improbably, corrupt his integrity. With equal, nay with greater reason, a body of men are unfit to be both judges and parties at the same time; yet what are many of the most important acts of legislation, but so many judicial determinations, not indeed concerning the rights of single persons, but concerning the rights of large bodies of citizens; and what are the different classes of legislators, but advocates and parties to the causes which they determine? Is a law proposed concerning private debts? It is a question to which the creditors are parties on one side and the debtors on the other. Justice ought to hold the balance between them. Yet the parties are, and must be, themselves the judges; and the most numerous party, or, in other words, the most powerful faction must be expected to prevail…

It is in vain to say, that enlightened statesmen will be able to adjust these clashing interests, and render them all subservient to the public good. Enlightened statesmen will not always be at the helm. Nor, in many cases, can such an adjustment be made at all, without taking into view indirect and remote considerations, which will rarely prevail over the immediate interest which one party may find in disregarding the rights of another or the good of the whole.

The inference to which we are brought is, that the *causes* of faction cannot be removed, and that relief is only to be sought in the means of controlling its *effects*.

If a faction consists of less than a majority, relief is supplied by the republican principle, which enables the majority to defeat its sinister views by regular vote: It may clog the administration, it may convulse the society; but it will be unable to execute and mask its violence under the forms of the Constitution. When a majority is included in a faction, the form of popular government, on the other hand, enables it to sacrifice to its ruling passion or interest both the public good and the rights of other citizens. To secure the public good and private rights against the danger of such a faction, and at the same time to preserve the spirit and the form of popular government, is then the great object to which our inquiries are directed...

By what means is this object attainable? Evidently by one of two only. Either the existence of the same passion or interest in a majority at the same time must be prevented; or the majority, having such coexistent passion or interest, must be rendered, by their number and local situation, unable to concert and carry into effect schemes of oppression. If the impulse and the opportunity be suffered to coincide, we well know that neither moral nor religious motives can be relied on as an adequate control...

From this view of the subject it may be concluded that a pure Democracy, by which I mean a Society, consisting of a small number of citizens, who assemble and administer the Government in person, can admit of no cure for the mischiefs of faction. A common passion or interest will, in almost every case, be felt by a majority of the whole; a communication and concert result from the form of Government itself; and there is nothing to check the inducements to sacrifice the weaker party or an obnoxious individual. Hence it is that such Democracies have ever been spectacles of turbulence and contention; have ever been found incompatible with personal security or the rights of property; and have in general been as short in their lives as they have been violent in their deaths. Theoretic politicians, who have patronized this species of government, have erroneously supposed that by reducing mankind to a perfect equality in their political rights, they would, at the same time, be perfectly equalized and assimilated in their possessions, their opinions, and their passions.

A Republic, by which I mean a Government in which the scheme of representation takes place, opens a different prospect, and promises the cure for which we are seeking. Let us examine the points in which it varies from pure Democracy, and we shall comprehend both the nature of the cure and the efficacy which it must derive from the Union.

The two great points of difference between a Democracy and a Republic are: first, the delegation of the Government, in the latter, to a small number of citizens elected by the rest; secondly, the greater number of citizens, and greater sphere of country, over which the latter may be extended.

The effect of the first difference is, on the one hand, to refine and enlarge the public views, by passing them through the medium of a chosen body of citizens, whose wisdom may best discern the true interest of their country, and whose patriotism and love of justice will be least likely to sacrifice it to temporary or partial considerations. Under such a regulation, it may well happen that the public voice, pronounced by the representatives of the people, will be more consonant to the public good than if pronounced by the people themselves, convened for the purpose. On the other hand, the effect may be inverted. Men of factious tempers, of local prejudices, or of sinister designs, may, by intrigue, by corruption, or by other means, first obtain the suffrages, and then betray the interests, of the people. The question resulting is, whether small or extensive republics are more favorable to the election of proper guardians of the public weal: and it is clearly decided in favor of the latter by two obvious considerations:

In the first place, it is to be remarked that, however small the Republic may be, the Representatives must be raised to a certain number, in order to guard against the cabals of a few; and that, however large it may be, they must be limited to a certain number, in order to guard against the confusion of a multitude. Hence, the number of Representatives in the two cases not being in proportion to that of the Constituents, and being proportionally greater in the small Republic, it follows, that if the proportion of fit characters, be not less in the large than in the small Republic, the former will present a greater option, and consequently a greater probability of a fit choice.

In the next place, as each Representative will be chosen by a greater number of citizens in the large than in the small Republic, it will be more difficult for unworthy candidates to practice with success the vicious arts by which elections are too often carried; and the suffrages of the people being more free, will be more likely to centre in men who possess the most attractive merit and the most diffusive and established characters.

It must be confessed, that in this, as in most other cases, there is a mean, on both sides of which inconveniences will be found to lie. By enlarging too much the number of electors, you render the representatives too little acquainted with all their local circumstances and lesser interests; as by reducing it too much, you render him unduly attached to these, and too little fit to comprehend and pursue great and national objects. The Federal Constitution forms a happy combination in this respect; the great and aggregate interests being referred to the national, the local and particular to the State legislatures.

The other point of difference is, the greater number of citizens and extent of territory; which may be brought within the compass of Republican, than of Democratic Government; and it is this circumstance principally which renders factious combinations less to be dreaded in the former than in the latter. The smaller the society, the fewer probably will be the distinct parties and interests composing it; the fewer the distinct parties and interests, the more frequently will a majority be found of the same party; and the smaller the number of individuals composing a majority, and the smaller the compass within which they are placed, the more easily will they concert and execute their plans of oppression. Extend the sphere, and you take in a greater variety of parties and interests; you make it less probable that a majority of the whole will have a common motive to invade the rights of other citizens; or if such a common motive exists, it will be more difficult for all who feel it to discover their own strength, and to act in unison with each other. Besides other impediments, it may be remarked that, where there is a consciousness of unjust or dishonorable purposes, communication is always checked by distrust in proportion to the number whose concurrence is necessary.

Hence, it clearly appears, that the same advantage which a Republic has over a Democracy, in controlling the effects of faction, is enjoyed by a large over a small Republic,—is enjoyed by the Union over the States composing it. Does the advantage consist in the substitution of Representatives whose enlightened views and virtuous sentiments render them superior to local prejudices and schemes of injustice? It will not be denied that the Representation of the Union will be most likely to possess these requisite endowments. Does it consist in the greater security afforded by a greater variety of parties, against the event of any one party being able to outnumber and oppress the rest? In an equal degree does the encreased variety of parties comprised within the Union, encrease this security. Does it, in fine, consist in the greater obstacles opposed to the concert and accomplishment of the secret wishes of an unjust and interested majority? Here, again, the extent of the Union gives it the most palpable advantage.

The influence of factious leaders may kindle a flame within their particular States, but will be unable to spread a general conflagration through the other States; a religious sect, may degenerate into a political faction in a part of the Confederacy; but the variety of sects dispersed over the entire face of it must secure the national councils against any danger from that source; a rage for paper money, for an abolition of debts, for an equal division of property, or for any other improper or wicked project, will be less apt to pervade the whole body of the Union than a particular member of it; in the same proportion as such a malady is more likely to taint a particular county or district, than an entire State.

In the extent and proper structure of the Union, therefore, we behold a Republican remedy for the diseases most incident to Republican Government. And according to the degree of pleasure and pride we feel in being Republicans, ought to be our zeal in cherishing the spirit and supporting the character of Federalists.

## 6. Political Creed of Every Federalist[6]

*This sarcastic passage highlights the bitter tone the debate over the Constitution sometimes engendered. One of the most powerful criticisms made by the Antifederalists was that the Federalists were aristocrats bent upon implementing despotism over the people of the United States. Since the proposed Constitution was drafted in secret and would limit the power of the states, this accusation resonated with many people.*

I BELIEVE in the infallibility, all sufficient wisdom, and infinite goodness of the late convention; or, in other words, I believe that some men are of so perfect a nature, that it is absolutely impossible for them to commit error, or design villainy.

I believe that the great body of the people are incapable of judging in their nearest concerns; and that therefore, they ought to be guided by the opinions of their superiors.

I believe that it is totally unnecessary to secure the rights of mankind in the formation of a constitution.

I believe that aristocracy is the best form of government.

I believe that the people of America are cowards and unable to defend themselves, and that, consequently, standing armies are absolutely necessary.

I believe that the trial by jury, and the freedom of the press ought to be exploded from every wise government.

I believe that the new constitution will not affect the state constitutions, yet that the state officers will oppose it, because it will abridge their power.

I believe that the new constitution will prove the bulwark of liberty—the balm of misery—the essence of justice, and the astonishment of all mankind. In short, I believe (in the words of that inimitable reasoner Attorney Wilson) that it is the best form of government which has ever been offered to the world.

I believe, that to speak, write, read, think, or hear any thing against the proposed government, is damnable heresy, execrable rebellion, and high treason against the sovereign majesty of the convention—And lastly, I believe that every person, who differs from me in belief, is an infernal villain. AMEN.

## 7. Opposition to the Constitution in Pennsylvania[7]

*On December 12, 1787, Pennsylvania became the second state to ratify the Constitution, a mere five days after neighboring Delaware had endorsed the plan. The Pennsylvania ratifying convention acted swiftly and decisively—the vote in favour of the constitution was 46 to 23. Pennsylvania had a distinguished history of constitutional debate going back at least as far as the state's first constitution, the most radical of the revolutionary state constitutions, adopted in 1776. In this extract from the proceedings of the convention which was published in the* Pennsylvania

Packet, *the opponents of the Constitution articulated many of the criticisms which became common among Antifederalists over the subsequent eighteen months.*

...[W]e entered on the examination of the proposed system of government, and found it to be such as we could not adopt, without, as we conceived, surrendering up your dearest rights. We offered our objections to the convention, and opposed those parts of the plan, which, in our opinion, would be injurious to you, in the best manner we were able; and closed our arguments by offering the following propositions to the convention.

1. The right of conscience shall be held inviolable; and neither the legislative, executive nor judicial powers of the United States shall have authority to alter, abrogate, or infringe any part of the constitution of the several states, which provide for the preservation of liberty in matters of religion.

2. That in controversies respecting property, and in suits between man and man, trial by jury shall remain as heretofore, as well in the federal courts, as in those of the several states.

3. That in all capital and criminal prosecutions, a man has a right to demand the cause and nature of his accusation, as well in the federal courts, as in those of the several states; to be heard by himself and his counsel; to be confronted with the accusers and witnesses; to call for evidence in his favor, and a speedy trial by an impartial jury of his vicinage, without whose unanimous consent, he cannot be found guilty, nor can he be compelled to give evidence against himself; and that no man be deprived of his liberty, except by the law of the land or the judgment of his peers.

4. That excessive bail ought not to be required, nor excessive fines imposed, nor cruel nor unusual punishments inflicted.

5. That warrants unsupported by evidence, whereby any officer or messenger may be commanded or required to search suspected places, or to seize any person or persons, his or their property, not particularly described, are grievous and oppressive, and shall not be granted either by the magistrates of the federal government or others.

6. That the people have a right to the freedom of speech, of writing and publishing their sentiments, therefore, the freedom of the press shall not be restrained by any law of the United States.

7. That the people have a right to bear arms for the defense of themselves and their own state, or the United States, or for the purpose of killing game; and no law shall be passed for disarming the people or any of them, unless for crimes committed, or real danger of public injury from individuals; and as standing armies in the time of peace are dangerous to liberty, they ought not to be kept up: and that the military shall be kept under strict subordination to and be governed by the civil powers.

8. The inhabitants of the several states shall have liberty to fowl and hunt in seasonable times, on the lands they hold, and on all other lands in the United States not inclosed, and in like manner to fish in all navigable waters, and others not private property, without being restrained therein by any laws to be passed by the legislature of the United States.

9. That no law shall be passed to restrain the legislatures of the several states from enacting laws for imposing taxes, except imposts and duties on goods imported or exported, and that no taxes, except imposts and duties upon goods imported and exported, and postage on letters shall be levied by the authority of Congress.

10. That the house of representatives be properly increased in number; that elections shall remain free; that the several states shall have power to regulate the elections for senators and representatives, without being controuled either directly or indirectly by any interference on the part of the Congress; and that elections of representatives be annual.

11. That the power of organizing, arming and disciplining the militia (the manner of disciplining the militia to be prescribed by Congress) remain with the individual states, and that Congress shall not have authority to call or march any of the militia out of their own state, without the consent of such state, and for such length of time only as such state shall agree.

    That the sovereignty, freedom and independency of the several states shall be retained, and every power, jurisdiction and right which is not by this constitution expressly delegated to the United States in Congress assembled.

12. That the legislative, executive, and judicial powers be kept separate; and to this end that a constitutional council be appointed, to advise and assist the president, who shall be responsible for the advice they give, hereby the senators would be relieved from almost constant attendance; and also that the judges be made completely independent.

13. That no treaty which shall be directly opposed to the existing laws of the United States in Congress assembled, shall be valid until such laws shall be repealed, or made conformable to such treaty; neither shall any treaties be valid which are in contradiction to the constitution of the United States, or the constitutions of the several states.

14. That the judiciary power of the United States shall be confined to cases affecting ambassadors, other public ministers and consuls; to cases of admiralty and maritime jurisdiction; to controversies to which the United States shall be a party; to controversies between two or more states—between a state and citizens of different states—between citizens claiming lands under grants of different states; and between a state or the citizens thereof and foreign states, and in criminal cases, to such only as are expressly enumerated in the constitution, & that the United States in Congress assembled, shall not have power to enact laws, which shall alter the laws of descents

and distribution of the effects of deceased persons, the titles of lands or goods, or the regulation of contracts in the individual states...

Our objections are comprised under three general heads of dissent, viz.

WE Dissent, first, because it is the opinion of the most celebrated writers on government, and confirmed by uniform experience, that a very extensive territory cannot be governed on the principles of freedom, otherwise than by a confederation of republics, possessing all the powers of internal government; but united in the management of their general, and foreign concerns...

We dissent, secondly, because the powers vested in Congress by this constitution, must necessarily annihilate and absorb the legislative, executive, and judicial powers of the several states, and produce from their ruins one consolidated government, which from the nature of things will be *an iron banded despotism*, as nothing short of the supremacy of despotic sway could connect and govern these United States under one government...

The powers of Congress under the new constitution, are complete and unlimited over the *purse* and the *sword*, and are perfectly independent of, and supreme over, the state governments; whose intervention in these great points is entirely destroyed...

We dissent, Thirdly, Because if it were practicable to govern so extensive a territory as these United States includes, on the plan of a consolidated government, consistent with the principles of liberty and the happiness of the people, yet the construction of this constitution is not calculated to attain the object, for independent of the nature of the case, it would of itself, necessarily produce a despotism, and that not by the usual gradations, but with the celerity that has hitherto only attended revolutions effected by the sword.

To establish the truth of this position, a cursory investigation of the principles and form of this constitution will suffice.

The first consideration that this review suggests, is the emission of a BILL of RIGHTS ascertaining and fundamentally establishing those unalienable and personal rights of men, without the full, free, and secure enjoyment of which there can be no liberty, and over which it is not necessary for a good government to have the controul. The principal of which are the rights of conscience, personal liberty by the clear and unequivocal establishment of the writ of *habeas corpus*, jury trial in criminal and civil cases, by an impartial jury of the vicinage or county, with the common law proceedings, for the safety of the accused in criminal prosecutions and the liberty of the press, that scourge of tyrants; and the grand bulwark of every other liberty and privilege; the stipulations heretofore made in saving of them in the state constitutions, are entirely superceded by this constitution...

The next consideration that the constitution presents, is the undue and dangerous mixture of the powers of government: the same body possessing legislative, executive, and judicial powers. The senate is a constituent branch of the legislature, it has judicial power in judging on impeachments, and in this case unites in some measure the characters of judge and party as all the principal officers are appointed by the president-general with the concurrence of the senate and therefore they derive their offices in part from the senate. This may biass the judgments of the senators, and tend to screen great delinquents from punishment. And the senate has, moreover, various and great executive powers, viz. in concurrence with the president-general, they form treaties with foreign nations, that may controul and abrogate the constitutions and laws of the several states. Indeed, there is no power, privilege or liberty of the state governments, or of the people, but what may be affected by virtue of this power. For all treaties, made by them, are to be the "supreme law of the land: any thing in the constitution or laws of any state, to the contrary notwithstanding..."

## 8.  The Grand Federal Edifice[8]

*The Massachusetts ratifying convention approved the Constitution on February 6, 1788, by a relatively narrow vote of 187 in favor of the Constitution and 168 against. Several days later this cartoon appeared in the* Massachusetts Centinel. *It portrays the states that had ratified the Constitution: Delaware, Pennsylvania, New Jersey, Georgia, Connecticut, and Massachusetts as columns supporting the*

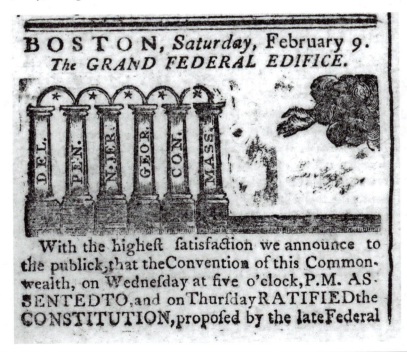

**Figure 8.1** The Grand Federal Edifice. Courtesy of the Massachusetts Historical Society, Boston.

*"Federal edifice." Nine states were required to approve the Constitution, and the crucial large states of Virginia and New York had yet to vote, leaving the edifice still incomplete.*

## 9.  Bill of Rights, 1789[9]

*One of the most common Antifederalist criticisms of the Constitutions was that it lacked a Bill of Rights. Some Federalists were opposed to enumerating individual rights because they felt that the Constitution provided sufficient safeguards for personal liberty. Nonetheless, after the Massachusetts ratifying convention agreed to recommend proposed amendments as a condition of ratification, moderate Antifederalists were won over, and the same condition was adopted by most subsequent states when they ratified the Constitution. More than two hundred amendments were submitted to Congress by the state ratifying conventions. James Madison pared the list down to twelve—mainly derived from a list submitted by the Virginia ratifying convention—and these were approved by Congress in September 1789. These twelve were submitted to the states for ratification and ten were approved by December 1791 (see appendix).*

Congress of the United States begun and held at the City of New-York, on Wednesday the fourth of March, one thousand seven hundred and eighty nine.

THE Conventions of a number of the States, having at the time of their adopting the Constitution, expressed a desire, in order to prevent misconstruction or abuse of its powers, that further declaratory and restrictive clauses should be added: And as extending the ground of public confidence in the Government, will best ensure the beneficent ends of its institution.

RESOLVED by the Senate and House of Representatives of the United States of America, in Congress assembled, two thirds of both Houses concurring, that the following Articles be proposed to the Legislatures of the several States, as amendments to the Constitution of the United States, all, or any of which Articles, when ratified by three fourths of the said Legislatures, to be valid to all intents and purposes, as part of the said Constitution; viz.

ARTICLES in addition to, and Amendment of the Constitution of the United States of America, proposed by Congress, and ratified by the Legislatures of the several States, pursuant to the fifth Article of the original Constitution.

Article the first... After the first enumeration required by the first article of the Constitution, there shall be one Representative for every thirty thousand, until the number shall amount to one hundred, after which the proportion shall be so regulated by Congress, that there shall be not less than one hundred Representatives, nor less than one Representative for every forty thousand persons, until the number of Representatives shall amount to two hundred; after which the proportion shall be so regulated by Congress, that there shall not be less than two hundred Representatives, nor more than one Representative for every fifty thousand persons.

Article the second... No law, varying the compensation for the services of the Senators and Representatives, shall take effect, until an election of Representatives shall have intervened.

Article the third... Congress shall make no law respecting an establishment of religion, or prohibiting the free exercise thereof; or abridging the freedom of speech, or of the press; or the right of the people peaceably to assemble, and to petition the Government for a redress of grievances.

Article the fourth... A well regulated Militia, being necessary to the security of a free State, the right of the people to keep and bear Arms, shall not be infringed.

Article the fifth... No Soldier shall, in time of peace be quartered in any house, without the consent of the Owner, nor in time of war, but in a manner to be prescribed by law.

Article the sixth... The right of the people to be secure in their persons, houses, papers, and effects, against unreasonable searches and seizures, shall not be violated, and no Warrants shall issue, but upon probable cause, supported by Oath or affirmation, and particularly describing the place to be searched, and the persons or things to be seized.

Article the seventh... No person shall be held to answer for a capital, or otherwise infamous crime, unless on a presentment or indictment of a Grand Jury, except in cases arising in the land or naval forces, or in the Militia, when in actual service in time of War or public danger; nor shall any person be subject for the same offence to be twice put in jeopardy of life or limb; nor shall be compelled in any criminal case to be a witness against himself, nor be deprived of life, liberty, or property, without due process of law; nor shall private property be taken for public use, without just compensation.

Article the eighth... In all criminal prosecutions, the accused shall enjoy the right to a speedy and public trial, by an impartial jury of the State and district wherein the crime shall have been committed, which district shall have been previously ascertained by law, and to be informed of the nature and cause of the accusation; to be confronted with the witnesses against him; to have compulsory process for obtaining witnesses in his favor, and to have the Assistance of Counsel for his defence.

Article the ninth... In Suits at common law, where the value in controversy shall exceed twenty dollars, the right of trial by jury shall be preserved, and no fact tried by a jury, shall be otherwise re-examined in any Court of the United States, than according to the rules of the common law.

Article the tenth... Excessive bail shall not be required, nor excessive fines imposed, nor cruel and unusual punishments inflicted.

Article the eleventh... The enumeration in the Constitution, of certain rights, shall not be construed to deny or disparage others retained by the people.

Article the twelfth... The powers not delegated to the United States by the Constitution, nor prohibited by it to the States, are reserved to the States respectively, or to the people.

## Notes

1.  William T. Hutchison et al. (eds.), *The Papers of James Madison*, Vol. 9 (Chicago: University of Chicago Press, 1975), 348–357.
2.  From Virginia (Randolph) Plan as Amended (National Archives Microfilm Publication M866, 1 roll); The Official Records of the Constitutional Convention; Records of the Continental and Confederation Congresses and the Constitutional Convention, 1774–1789, Record Group 360 (Washington, DC: National Archives).
3.  Max Farrand (ed.), *The Records of the Federal Convention of 1787*, Vol. 1. (New Haven, CT: Yale University Press, 1911), 242–245.
4.  Max Farrand (ed.), *The Records of the Federal Convention of 1787*, Vol. 2 (New Haven, CT: Yale University Press, 1911), 641–643.
5.  *Daily Advertiser* (New York), November 22, 1787. This document has been edited for length. The full version can be found at the book's website (http://www.routledge.com/textbooks/revolution-aryamerica/).
6.  *The New-York Journal, and Weekly Patriotic Register*, Wednesday, December 12, 1787.
7.  *Pennsylvania Packet and Daily Advertiser* (Philadelphia), December 18, 1787. This document has been edited for length. The full version can be found at the book's website (http://www.routledge.com/textbooks/revolutionaryamerica/).
8.  *Massachusetts Centinel* (Boston), February 9, 1788 (Boston: Massachusetts Historical Society).
9.  Engrossed Bill of Rights, September 25, 1789; General Records of the United States Government; Record Group 11 (Washington, DC: National Archives).

# CHAPTER 9

# American Women in the Age of Revolution

## Introduction

Women played a central role in the history of the American Revolution. Without the support of women the resistance to the British taxation policies prior to the War of Independence would not have been possible. The first documents in this chapter examine aspects of the pre-war resistance from the perspective of women. Deborah Franklin's letter (document 1) from Philadelphia to her husband Benjamin, who was serving as a colonial agent in London, describes the rioting which accompanied the resistance to the Stamp Act. In a subsequent letter (document 2) Benjamin Franklin reports the repeal of the Stamp Act and resumption of transatlantic trade. He enumerates in detail the types of articles traded between Britain and the colonies and gives us an insight into the buying habits of urban women in America on the eve of the Revolution. These women would be essential to the later success of colonial boycotts when they opted to forego imported goods in support of the resistance movement against British taxation, as demonstrated in documents 4 and 5, which present two views of female colonial resistance. The extract from the *Boston Evening Post* (document 4) presents an account of 300 Boston women signing a pledge to boycott tea, while a famous British cartoon (document 5) mocked North Carolina women for signing a similar non-importation agreement at the "Edenton Tea Party." Owing to Benjamin Franklin's prolonged absences, Deborah Franklin exercised the power of attorney in looking after his business interests (document 3). This legal document, in which she signed over the power of attorney to James Wilson, shows how the resistance movement required women to exercise increased public authority.

The War of Independence presented American women with numerous challenges and opportunities. The letter from Abigail Adams to John Adams during the siege of Boston (document 6) reveals the dangers the war posed to women and their families, particularly from disease. Women were not simply victims of the conflict, they helped to sustain the war effort on both sides of the conflict. Esther Reed's *Sentiments of an American Woman* (document 7) was a broadside which appeared in a successful campaign to raise funds among Philadelphia women in support of the Continental Army. The letter from Baron Ottendorf to Henry Clinton (document 8) includes a deposition from a female spy, identified only as "Miss Jenny," who sought to infiltrate the French and Continental ranks. Women's support for the war often came at great sacrifice to themselves as Rachel Well's 1786 petition to Congress (document 9) shows. Wells had loaned significant sums of money to the rebels and had fallen on hard times after the war, in part because of the failure of the government to repay her.

Rachel Wells's difficulties epitomized the post-war challenges which confronted American women. Many women had supported the rebel war effort but had little to show for their sacrifices. While American men were now citizens of an independent republic, the place of women in the new polity was not clearly defined. Theorists and commentators, mostly male, sought to define a new place for women in the new republic and articulated a view, Republican Motherhood, which stressed women's primary role as the protectors and promoters of virtue. Benjamin Rush's *Thoughts upon Female Education* (document 10) is an early expression of Republican Motherhood. Hannah Callender's diary (document 11) shows that some women, especially upper-class women, embraced and accepted Republican Motherhood. Not all women were content with being defined as the promoters of republican virtue and sought to exercise a more direct role in public life. On the eve of the Declaration of Independence, Abigail Adams was determined that Congress should "remember the ladies" when drafting the new constitutions necessitated by independence (document 6). A loophole in the New Jersey Constitution (document 12) allowed women to vote, and women in the state exercised the franchise for two decades before being disenfranchised. Their disenfranchisement was confirmed in a later clause in the constitution adopted in 1844. The American Revolution, however, provided women with the language to demand greater rights as evidenced by the 1848 Declaration of Sentiments (document 13) which deliberately followed the Declaration of Independence to advance a claim for female equality.

## 1.   Deborah Franklin Describes the Stamp Act Riots[1]

*Deborah Franklin (1708–1774) wrote to her husband Benjamin Franklin (1706–1790) in September 1765 describing the riots in opposition to the Stamp Act which had taken place in Philadelphia. At the time Benjamin Franklin was acting as an agent in London representing the interests of several colonies. Throughout the course of their long marriage, Benjamin and Deborah Franklin were often separated for long periods of time when he was abroad in Europe.*

My Dear child

I have reseved yours by Capt. Friend and one which was to a Cume by N yorke and by the packit and yisterday by Capt. Cotin they all give me pleshuer indead and I love to hear from you I am so verey poor a writer that I donte undertake to say aney thing a bought the dis[order] in this porte of the world but to me it semes we air verey wicked and so is the pepel in in London and other plases on your sid the watter I pray god mend us all.

You will se by the papers what worke has hapened in other plases and sumthing has bin sed relaiteing to raising a mob in this plase. I was for 9 day keep in one Contineued hurrey by pepel to removef and Salley was porswaided to go to burlinton for saiftey but on munday laste we had verey graite rejoysing on a Count of the Chang of the Ministrey and a preyperaition for binfiers [bonfires] att night and several houses thretened to be puled down. Cusin Davenporte Come and told me that more then twenty pepel had told him it was his Duty to be with me. I sed I was plesed to reseve Civility from aney bodey so he staid with me sum time to words night I sed he shold fech a gun or two as we had none. I sente to aske my Brother to Cume and bring his gun all so so we maid one room into a Magazin. I ordored sum sorte of defens up Stairs such as I Cold manaig my self. I sed when I was advised to remove that I was verey shuer you had dun nothing to hurte aney bodey nor I had not given aney ofense to aney person att all nor wold I be maid unesey by aney bodey nor wold I stir or show the leste uneseynis but if aney one Came to disturbe me I wold show a proper resentement and I shold be very much afrunted with aney bodey. Salley was gon with Miss Ross to see Cap. Reals Dafter and heard the reporte thair and Came home to be with me but I had sente her word not to Come. I was told that thair was 8 hundred men readey to asiste aney one that shold be molisted. This minit gorge Cumes and ses the packit is to saile on tasday I did not think it wold go so sune. I will run and aske hough poor Mr. Hughes is and tell you. On freyday Mr. Parker brough Mrs. and Miss Parker down to spend a week with us he went to Burlinton this day Billey Come agan to aske us up to Burlinton I Consented to Salley going but I will not stir as I rely donte think it wold be right in me to stir or show the leste uneseynes att all. Salley did not go but will when Mrs. Parker returnes. I have bin to see mr. Hughes he is verey ill indead but I beleve his son is to write to you. I am afraid his Complainte is like Mr. Plumsteds our poor nabors Sumaines has bin verey ill indead. I though Shee wold adeyed for severel day but Shee is a litel better but not abel to set up at all it has bin sickley for sume time paste but it begins to be Cold and we make fiers and I hope we shall drive away the bad air with Smoke of the Chimneyes. When I begon to write this letter I had no thoughtes of the packites Sailing but only wrote as I had time I am in hopes to tell you by Friend that the Lott is setteld and the wale finished but it leyes open on that sid indead I was afraid to have it dun as we had bin ajected of wold it not a bin a trespase indead I am afraid of giveing aney ofens and Contente my self with thinking what ever is, is beste.

My Compleymentes to good Mrs. Stephenson I will write to her by friend I like the Curtins verey well and everey thing that is sente and I due beleve befor this time you muste a reseved letters from me which will tell you that and a boute the house all so but if I waite to tel you aney more the poste will be gon. My brother bring this letter yisterday and I get him to make the drafte of the house and lott for you thought we Joyned on Mr. Keepley but thair is 33 feet betwen us and his. It is paste three a clock I have only to tell you who was so good as to visit me on laste munday night Cusin Davenporte my Brother J Foxcrofte Mr. Whorton sener he Come paste 8 a Clocke on horse back his son Samey Mr. Banton Mr. S Rodes thay ofred to Stay all night but I beged thay wold not leste thay shold get Sick my three Cusins Lakockes and Mr. Hall nabor Shumakers sones nabor Whisters Son and more of the nabors young Dr. Tenent who Came home in Friend Came and ofred me all the asistens in his power. I thanked him. I shold not for get Mr. John Ross and Brother Swore it is Mr. Saml Smith that is a seting the pepel a-mading by teling them that it was you that had pland the Stampe ackte and that you air indevering to get the teste ackte brought over hear but as I donte go much to town I mabey shall be esey for a while after the eleckshon is over but tel that I muste be disturbed. I shal send your letter by friend god bles you and keep you is the prayer of yours forever
D Franklin

## 2.   Benjamin Franklin to Deborah Franklin, London, April 6, 1766[2]

*Writing from London to his wife Deborah, Benjamin Franklin discusses the resumption of trade following the repeal of the Stamp Act. His letter suggests the range of trade goods exchanged across the Atlantic, and he discusses the anti-government cartoons circulating in Britain during the Stamp Act crisis.*

My dear Child,
As the Stamp Act is at length repeal'd, I am willing you should have a new Gown, which you may suppose I did not send sooner, as I knew you would not like to be finer than your Neighbours, unless in a Gown of your own Spinning. Had the Trade between the two Countries totally ceas'd, it was a Comfort to me to recollect that I had once been cloth'd from Head to Foot in Woollen and Linnen of my Wife's Manufacture, that I never was prouder of any Dress in my Life, and that she and her Daughter might do it again if it was necessary. I told the Parliament that it was my Opinion, before the old Cloaths of the Americans were worn out, they might have new ones of their own making. And indeed if they had all as many old Clothes as your old Man has, that would not be very unlikely; for I think you and George reckon'd when I was last at home, at least 20 pair of old Breeches. Joking apart, I have sent you a fine Piece of Pompador Sattin, 14 Yards cost 11s. per Yard. A Silk Negligee and Petticoat of brocaded Lutestring for my dear Sally, with 2 Doz. Gloves, 4 Bottles of Lavender Water, and two little

Reels. The Reels are to screw on the Edge of a Table, when she would wind Silk or Thread, the Skein is to be put over them, and winds better than if held in two Hands. There is also an Ivory Knob to each, to which she may with a Bit of Silk Cord hang a Pinhook to fasten her plain Work to like the Hooks on her Weight. I send you also Lace for two Lappet Caps, 3 Ells of Cambrick (the Cambrick by Mr. Yates) 3 Damask Table Cloths, a Piece of Crimson Morin for Curtains, with Tassels, Line and Binding. A large true Turkey Carpet cost 10 Guineas, for the Dining Parlour. Some oil'd Silk; and a Gimcrack Corkscrew which you must get some Brother Gimcrack to show you the Use of. In the Chest is a Parcel of Books for my Friend Mr. Coleman, and another for Cousin Colbert. Pray did he receives those I sent him before? I send you also a Box with three fine Cheeses. Perhaps a Bit of them may be left when I come home. Mrs. Stevenson has been very diligent and serviceable in getting these things together for you, and presents her best Respects, as does her Daughter, to both you and Sally. There are too Boxes included in your Bill of Lading for Billy.

I received your kind Letter of Feb. 20. It gives me great Pleasure to hear that our good old Friend Mrs. Smith is on the Recovery. I hope she has yet many happy Years to live. My Love to her.

I fear, from the Account you give of Brother Peter that he cannot hold it long. If it should please God that he leaves us before my Return; I would have the Post Office remain under the Management of their Son, till Mr. Foxcroft and I agree how to settle it.

There are some Droll Prints in the Box, which were given me by the Painter; and being sent when I was not at home, were pack'd up without my Knowledge. I think he was wrong to put in Lord Bute, who had nothing to do with the Stamp Act. But it is the Fashion here to abuse that Nobleman as the Author of all Mischief. I send you a few Bush Beans, a new Sort for your Garden. I shall write to my Friends per Packet, that goes next Saturday. I am very well, and hope this will find you and Sally so with all our Relations and Friends, to whom my Love. I am, as ever, Your affectionate Husband,

B Franklin

p.s. A Young Man, by name Joseph Wharton, came to me the other day, said he had been sick and was in distress for Money, and beg'd me to take a Draft on his Brother at Philadelphia for Twelve Guineas. I did not remember or know him, but could refuse nothing to the Name of my Friend. So I let him have the Money, and enclose his Bill. You will present it for Payment.

## 3.  Deborah Franklin: Power of Attorney, October 14, 1768[3]

*Owing to his prolonged absences in Europe, Benjamin Franklin gave his wife power of attorney to manage his business interests. In this document Deborah Franklin, who had exercised the power of attorney for more than eleven years, signed the power over to James Wilson.*

Whereas my Husband Benjamin Franklin late of this City of Philadelphia but now of London Esqr. by his Letter of Attorney dated the Fourth Day of April, A Domi. 1757, did constitute and appoint me the Subscriber his Attorney to negotiate settle and transact all his private Affairs and Business in America with power to substitute an Attorney under me for that purpose Now in pursuance of the said power to me given I do hereby substitute authorize and appoint James Wilson of Reading in Berks County Esqr. to acknowledge Satisfaction on Record of the Mortgage Moneys due to the said Benjamin Franklin from the Estate of William Maugridge deceased by Virtue of an Indenture of Mortgage executed by the said William Maugridge bearing Date the Ninth Day of December ADomi. 1763 provided always and upon this Condition that Sarah Drury doth before the said Acknowledgement of Satisfaction pay unto my said Attorney the Sum of One hundred and four pounds and doth assign over so many Bonds to the said Benjamin Franklin to be payable to him from [*blank*] Ferree purchaser of the Mortgaged premises as shall amount in Value to the Sum due to the said B. Franklin. In Witness whereof I have hereunto set my hand and Seal this fourteenth Day of October 1768.
D Franklin

Sealed and Delivered In the presence of Nicholas Waln Berks ss. The 14 Day of Octr. 1768 appeared the abovenamed Deborah Franklin and acknowledged the above writing to be her Act and Deed Coram
John Patton

Berks County ss Entered of Record in the office for Recording of Deeds at Reading in and for the said County of Berks in Mortgage Book B a[t?] page 165 In Testimony Whereof I have hereunto set my Hand and the seal of the said County the Twenty first Day of November Anno Domini 1768.
James Read Rec. ib.
*Endorsed:* Power of Attorney from Mrs Franklin to Jas Wilson

### 4. Boston Women Boycott Tea, 1770[4]

*This extract from the Boston Evening-Post describes an agreement to boycott tea by three hundreed Boston women. The boycott was adopted in response to the Townshend Duties. The extract notes that Virginia women have supported boycotts in their colony by producing home-made clothes and calls on Massachusetts women to do the same.*

*The following Agreement has lately been come into by upwards of 300 Mistresses of Families in this Town; in which Number the Ladies of the highest Rank and Influence, that could be waited upon in so short a Time, are included.*
*Boston, January 31, 1770.*

AT a Time when our invaluable Rights and Privileges are attacked in an unconstitutional and most alarming Manner, and as we find we are reproached for not being so ready as could be desired, to lend our Assistance, we think it our Duty perfectly to concur with the true Friends of Liberty, in all the Measures they have taken to save this abused Country from Ruin and Slavery: And particularly, we join with the very respectable Body of Merchants and other Inhabitants of this Town, who met in Faneuil-Hall the 23d of this Instant, in their Resolutions, *totally* to abstain from the Use of TEA: And as the greatest Part of the Revenue arising by Virtue of the late Acts, is produced from the Duty paid upon Tea, which Revenue is wholly expended to support the American Board of Commissioners: We the Subscribers do strictly engage, that we will *totally* abstain from the Use of that Article, (Sickness excepted) not only in our respective Families; but that we will absolutely refuse it, if it should be offered to us upon any Occasion whatsoever. This Agreement we chearfully come into, as we believe the very distressed Situation of our Country requires it, and we do hereby oblige ourselves religiously to observe it, till the late Revenue Acts are repealed.

NEW TOASTS
THE patriotic Ladies of Virginia, who have nobly distinguished themselves by appearing in the Manufactures of America, and may those of the Massachusetts be laudably ambitious of not being out-done even by Virginians.

The wise and virtuous part of the Fair Sex in Boston and other Towns, who being at length sensible that by the consumption of Teas they are supporting the Commissioners & other Tools of Power, have voluntarily agreed not to give or receive any further Entertainments of that Kind, until those Creatures, together with the Boston Standing Army, are removed, and the Revenue Acts repealed.

May the Disgrace which a late venal & corrupt Assembly as brought upon a Sister Colony, be wiped away by a Dissolution.

## 5. The Edenton Tea Party, 1774[5]

*One of the most famous instances of women's resistance prior to independence was the "Edenton Tea Party," which took place in Edenton, North Carolina. On October 25, 1774, fifty-one women led by Mrs. Penelope Barker gathered at the home of Elizabeth King to sign a pledge not to consume imported tea. This satirical print appeared in England to mock the women's efforts.*

**Figure 9.1** Boycott of British Tea. Courtesy of Granger Collection, New York.

### 6. Abigail Adams to John Adams[6]

*In these letters, written in the spring of 1776, Abigail Adams (1744–1818)wrote from Braintree, Massachusetts, to her husband, John (1735–1826), who was serving in the Continental Congress. She describes life in Massachusetts during the siege of Boston and asserts a claim for women's rights as a consequence of the impending Declaration of Independence.*

March 31, 1776

I wish you would ever write me a Letter half as long as I write you; and tell me if you may where your Fleet are gone? What sort of Defence Virginia can make against our common Enemy? Whether it is so situated as to make an able Defence? Are not the Gentery Lords and the common people vassals, are they not like the uncivilized Natives Brittain represents us to be? I hope their Riffel Men who have shewen themselves very savage and even Blood thirsty; are not a specimen of the Generality of the people.

I [illegible] am willing to allow the Colony great merrit for having produced a Washington but they have been shamefully duped by a Dunmore.

I have sometimes been ready to think that the passion for Liberty cannot be Eaquelly Strong in the Breasts of those who have been accustomed to deprive their fellow Creatures of theirs. Of this I am certain that it is not founded upon that generous and christian principal of doing to others as we would that others should do unto us.

Do not you want to see Boston; I am fearfull of the small pox, or I should have been in before this time. I got Mr. Crane to go to our House and see what state it was in. I find it has been occupied by one of the Doctors of a Regiment, very dirty, but no other damage has been done to it. The few things which were left in it are all gone. Cranch has the key which he never deliverd up. I have wrote to him for it and am determined to get it cleand as soon as possible and shut it up. I look upon it a new acquisition of property, a property which one month ago I did not value at a single Shilling, and could with pleasure have seen it in flames.

The Town in General is left in a better state than we expected, more oweing to a percipitate flight than any Regard to the inhabitants, tho some individuals discoverd a sense of honour and justice and have left the rent of the Houses in which they were, for the owners and the furniture unhurt, or if damaged sufficent to make it good.

Others have committed abominable Ravages. The Mansion House of your President is safe and the furniture unhurt whilst both he House and Furniture of the Solisiter General have fallen a prey to their own merciless party. Surely the very Fiends feel a Reverential awe for Virtue and patriotism, whilst they Detest the paricide and traitor.

I feel very differently at the approach of spring to what I did a month ago. We knew not then whether we could plant or sow with safety, whether when we had toild we could reap the fruits of our own industery, whether we could rest in our own Cottages, or whether we should not be driven from the sea coasts to seek shelter in the wilderness, but now we feel as if we might sit under our own vine and eat the good of the land.

I feel a gaieti de Coar to which before I was a stranger. I think the Sun looks brighter, the Birds sing more melodiously, and Nature puts on a more chearfull countanance. We feel a temporary peace, and the poor fugitives are returning to their deserted habitations.

Tho we felicitate ourselves, we sympathize with those who are trembling least the Lot of Boston should be theirs. But they cannot be in similar circumstances unless pusilanimity and cowardise should take possession of them. They have time and warning given them to see the Evil and shun it. —I long to hear that you have declared an independency—and by the way in the new Code of Laws which I suppose it will be necessary for you to make I desire you would Remember the Ladies, and be more generous and favourable to them than your ancestors. Do not put such unlimited power into the hands of the Husbands. Remember all

Men would be tyrants if they could. If perticuliar care and attention is not paid to the Laidies we are determined to foment a Rebelion, and will not hold ourselves bound by any Laws in which we have no voice, or Representation.

That your Sex are Naturally Tyrannical is a Truth so thoroughly established as to admit of no dispute, but such of you as wish to be happy willingly give up the harsh title of Master for the more tender and endearing one of Friend. Why then, not put it out of the power of the vicious and the Lawless to use us with cruelty and indignity with impunity. Men of Sense in all Ages abhor those customs which treat us only as the vassals of your Sex. Regard us then as Beings placed by providence under your protection and in immitation of the Supreem Being make use of that power only for our happiness.

April 5

Not having an opportunity of sending this I shall add a few lines more; tho not with a heart so gay. I have been attending the sick chamber of our Neighbour Trot whose affliction I most sensibly feel but cannot discribe, striped of two lovely children in one week. Gorge the Eldest died on wednesday and Billy the youngest on fryday, with the Canker fever, a terible disorder so much like the throat distemper, that it differs but little from it. Betsy Cranch has been very bad, but upon the recovery. Becky Peck they do not expect will live out the day. Many grown persons are now sick with it, in this street. It rages much in other Towns. The Mumps too are very frequent. Isaac is now confined with it. Our own little flock are yet well. My Heart trembles with anxiety for them. God preserve them.

I want to hear much oftener from you than I do. March 8 was the last date of any that I have yet had.—You inquire of whether I am making Salt peter. I have not yet attempted it, but after Soap making believe I shall make the experiment. I find as much as I can do to manufacture cloathing for my family who would else be Naked. I know of but one person in this part of the Town who has made any, that is Mr. Tertias Bass as he is calld who has got very near an hundred weight which has been found to be very good. I have heard of some others in the other parishes. Mr. Reed of Weymouth has been applied to, to go to Andover to the mills which are now at work, and has gone. I have lately seen a small Manuscrip describing the proportions for the various sorts of powder, such as fit for cannon, small arms and pistols [illegible]. If it would be of any Service your way I will get it transcribed and send it to you. —Every one of your Friends send their Regards, and all the little ones. Your Brothers youngest child lies bad with convulsion fitts. Adieu. I need not say how much I am Your ever faithfull Friend.

### 7. The Sentiments of an American Woman, 1780[7]

*This broadside, probably written by Esther De Berdt Reed (1746–1780), was published to raise funds in support of the Continental Army among the women of Philadelphia. Aimed at women, it makes a direct appeal to women's patriotism and asks them to make sacrifices in the name of the rebel cause.*

On the commencement of actual war, the Women of America manifested a firm resolution to contribute as much as could depend on them, to the deliverance of their country. Animated by the purest patriotism, they are sensible of sorrow at this day, in not offering more than barren wishes for the success of so glorious a Revolution. They aspire to render themselves more really useful; and this sentiment is universal from the north to the south of the Thirteen United States. Our ambition is kindled by the same of those heroines of antiquity, who have rendered their sex illustrious, and have proved to the universe, that, if the weakness of our Constitution, if opinion and manners did not forbid us to march to glory by the same paths as the Men, we should at least equal, and sometimes surpass them in our love for the public good. I glory in all that which my sex has done great and commendable. I call to mind with enthusiasm and admiration, all those acts of courage, or constancy and patriotism, which history has transmitted to us: The people favoured by Heaven, preserved from destruction by the virtues, the zeal and the resolution of Deborah, of Judith, of Esther! The fortitude of the mother of the Macchabees, in giving up her sons to die before her eyes: Rome saved from the fury of a victorious enemy by the efforts of Volumnia, and other Roman Ladies: So many famous sieges where the Women have been seen forgetting the weakness of their sex, building new walls, digging trenches with their feeble hands; furnishing arms to their defenders, they themselves darting the military weapons on the enemy, resigning the ornaments of their apparel, and their fortune, to fill the public treasury; and to hasten the deliverance of their country; burying themselves under its ruins; throwing themselves into the flames rather than submit to the disgrace of humiliation before a proud enemy.

Born for liberty, disdaining to bear the irons of a tyrannic Government, we associate ourselves to the grandeur of those Sovereigns, cherished and revered, who have held with so much splendour the scepter of the greatest States. The Batildas, the Elizabeths, the Maries, the Catherines, who have extended the empire of liberty, and contented to reign by sweetness and justice, have broken the chains of slavery, forged by tyrants in the times of ignorance and barbarity. The Spanish Women, do they not make, at this moment, the most patriotic sacrifices, to encrease the means of victory in the hands of their Sovereign. He is a friend to the French Nation. They are our allies. We call to mind, doubly interested, that it was a French Maid who kindled up amongst our fellow-citizens, the flame of patriotism buried under long misfortunes: it was the Maid of Orleans who drove from the kingdom of France the ancestors of those same British, whose odious yoke we have just shaken off; and whom it is necessary that we drive from this Continent.

But I must limit myself to the recollection of this small number of atchievements. Who knows if persons disposed to censure, and sometimes too severely with regard to us, may not disapprove our appearing acquainted even with the actions of which our sex boasts? We are at least certain, that he cannot be a good citizen who will not applaud our efforts for the relief of the armies which defend our lives, our possessions, our liberty? The situation of our soldiery has been represented to me; the evils inseparable from war, and the firm and generous spirit which has enabled them to support these. But it has been said, that they may apprehend, that, in the course of a long war, the view of their distress may be lost, and their services be forgotten. Forgotten! never; I can answer in the name of all my sex. Brave Americans, your disinteredness, your courage, and your constancy will always be dear to America, as long as she shall preserve her virtue.

We know that at a distance from the theatre of war, if we enjoy any tranquility, it is the fruit of your watchings, your labours, your dangers. If I live happy in the midst of my family; if my husband cultivates his field, and reaps his harvest in peace; if, surrounded with my children, I myself nourish the youngest, and press it to my bosom, without being affraid of seeing myself separated from it, by a ferocious enemy; if the house in which we dwell; if our barns, our orchards are safe at the present time from the hands of those incendiaries, it is to you that we owe it. And shall we hesitate to evidence to you our gratitude? Shall we hesitate to wear a cloathing more simple; hair dressed less elegant, while at the price of this small privation, we shall deserve your benedictions. Who, amongst us, will not renounce with the highest pleasure, those vain ornaments, when she shall consider that the valiant defenders of America will be able to draw some advantage from the money which she may have laid out in these; that they will be better defended from the rigours of the seasons, that after their painful toils, they will receive some extraordinary and unexpected relief; that these presents will perhaps be valued by them at a greater price, when they will have it in their power to say: *This is the offering of the Ladies.* The time is arrived to display the same sentiments which animated us at the beginning of the Revolution, when we renounced the use of teas, however agreeable to our taste, rather than receive them from our persecutors; when we made it appear to them that we placed former necessities in the rank of superfluities, when our liberty was interested; when our republican and laborious hands spun the flux, prepared the linen intended for the use of our soldiers; when exiles and fugitives we supported with courage all the evils which are the concomitants of war. Let us not lose a moment; let us be engaged to offer the homage of our gratitude at the alter of military valour, and you, our brave deliverers, while mercenary slaves combat to cause you to share with them, the irons with which they are loaded, receive with a free hand our offering, the purest which can be presented to your virtue.

## 8.  The Deposition of a Female Spy, 1781[8]

*Nicholas Dietrich, Baron de Ottendorf, was a German mercenary who had been commissioned in the Continental Army in 1776. He was relieved of his command by George Washington in 1777 and eventually enlisted in the British army. In this letter to General Henry Clinton, Ottendorf presents the deposition of female spy, Miss Jenny, who infiltrated the rebel and French lines in the Hudson River Valley in August 1781 while the Franco-American army marched to Virginia to confront Cornwallis. Her deposition suggests the opportunities and dangers which the War of Independence presented to women.*

*Debriefing of Miss Jenny, upon return from the French camp*

Miss Jenny left here on Thursday the 9th of this month in the evening, she slept in Kingsbridge and passed the lines in the morning between 3 and 4 o'clock having walked more or less 3 miles Our refugees came upon her stopped her and brought her back to Kingsbridge to Colonel Warn who sent her back directly with a passport. having followed the main road keeping always to the right, she came across an officer on a horse coming from the woods, of whom she asked Mr. can you show me the French camp, He answered her why are you French, Yes, Mr. come with me I will take you there, the officer led her to the first guard post after having proposed an amorous liaison to her, even desiring to force her, which she did not wish according to [her instructions?] arrived at the main guard post, the Capt. asked her whom she sought, she answered that she came from the direction of York having learned that her father was there, and that she will be delighted to come see him, that she was a seamstress and that her mother was a laundress, and that they found out that their father returned from France with the troops, seeing that it was six years since he went to France from Canada, the Capt of the guard sent her to the headquarters of Mr. de Rochambeau and Mr. L. V. Cl. de Laval had orders to question her, seeing he was not able to get anything from her, and asked her several times, whether she knew Hend. and that surely he had promised her money for coming to spy, she answered him that she did not know what he meant, upon which she was sent to Mr. de Roch. who asked several questions and in the end said Mad. I will send you to Gen. Wahit. which he did, arrived there she was interrogated by Mr. Smidt and Mr. Cooper, finding nothing against her, they held her two days, and she was sent back to the French camp, while Mr. Smidt and Cooper questioned her, she was asked several time whether she knew me and that I was responsible for the desertion of the French and that I would be the first one hanged if ever York were ever taken. after all that, she was sent back Upon arrival at the French camp, she was handed over to the Provost nevertheless, she was treated well enough, the Chief Provost questioned her several times over the course of two days, and insisted that she must know me, using guile and intimidation to make her talk. Seeing that nothing could be got from her, the order arrived on Tuesday in the evening on the 14th for her to depart on Wednesday at daybreak, and beforehand, to have her Hair cut in such a fashion that she could be recognised another time, which was done, then [for her] to be set on a horse with neither bonnet nor hair covering, sitting on a cloak between two archers and [for her] to be led in this manner outside of the lines with the order not to return unless she wants to run the risk of being severely punished.

She says that everything is ready for them to march and that the general opinion is that they want to come and attack in two places, as soon as their fleet arrives the troop was paid yesterday, the 14th Aug. She saw some of our Jägers arrive, around 4 or 5. They were not retained, they were sent immediately to Philadelphia When these Jägers arrived at Wach.n's, he had them given something to drink and to eat informing them that soon all of our people will come, and that in a short while he will be in York...

Monsieur Major, Miss Jeny has just arrived this moment. I will have her stay here until evening, and I beg you if your business allows you to stop by for a little while. You can be sure that no one will know you, and you will be perhaps happy to hear from her lips the agreeable statement which she has just made, she will not know who you are. Until such time I have the honour to be respectfully, Your very humble and very obedient servant B. Ottendorf

### 9.   Petition of Rachel Wells to the Continental Congress, 1786[9]

*Rachel Wells (c.1735–c. 1796), a wax sculptor, was a widow who supported the rebel war effort by loaning money to the state of New Jersey. After the war she faced difficult circumstances and petitioned the state for payment. Owing to a technicality, the state rejected her petitions and refused to repay her. In desperation she petitioned Congress for restitution. It is not known whether her petition was successful or not. Her petition is testimony to the sacrifices made by women, on both sides, to support the war effort as well as the vulnerable position of women, particularly single or widowed women, in the wake of independence.*

To the Honnorabell Congress I Rachel do make this Complaint Who am a Widow far advanced in years & dearly have ocasion of ye Interest for that Cash I Lent the Stats.

I was a Sitizen in ye jearsey when I Lent ye Stats a Considreabell Sum of moneys & had I justice don me it mite be Suficant to Suporte me in ye whear I am now near bordenton I Lived hear Then when Mr Joseph Borden Capt of office for the State but being torn to peases & so Robd by the Britans & others I went to Phi[ladephi]a to try to git a Living as I Cant doe Nothing in Bordentown in my way So after ye English Left their [?]. I went to Phila & was Their in the year 1783 when our assembly was pleasd to pas a Law that no one Should have aney Interest that Livd out of jearsey State I have Sent in a petition To ye asembley They Say it Lies in your brest as the Cash was Lent to you They give me a form of an oath which Runs Thus that I was a Resedentor when I put ye Cash into the office & was in ye year 83 & am Still I can Swair that I was then & am now but in 83 I was not Now gentlemen in this Liberty had it bin advertisd that he or She that moved out of the State Should Louse his or her Interest you mite have Sum plea against me But I am Innocent Suspectd no trick I have don as much to Carrey on the warr as maney that Sett nowe at ye healm of government & No Notice taken of me before this one of your asembley Borrowed £300 in gould of me jest as the warr Comencd & Now I can Nither git Intrest nor principell Nor Even Security why, because they have pasd a Law that no officer Shall be troubled under five years after peace Comencd Not onley So but one of our Chaplens to our armey I believe has Robd me of one hundred & eighty six pounds & My acount was provd & causd into ye office opinted for that Purpose of what I had Sufferd by ye English which Came to Two Thousand Eight hundred 7 five pounds hard Cash But this I Can bair but to be Robd by my Contrey men is verey trying to nature My dr Sister Wright wrote to me to be thankfull that I had it in my Power to Help on the warr which is well enough but then this is to be Considerd that others gits their Intrest & why then a poor old widow to be put of who am thus Stript I often think of a text in Scripture Ecclesiastes ye 9 & 15th their was in the City a poor man that by his wisdom deliverd the City yet No one Rememberd that Same poor man

had their bin given to Sister wright only one quarter of an ackor of ground to have Laid her bones in I Should not have thought I beleve of the text as it was her desire to be buried hear how did She make her Cuntrey her whole atention her Letters gave us ye first alarm She was Lock in the parelement house with 5 other Ladyes & heard govener Hutchings Letters Red…& went home & wrote ameadetly She wrote to our printers & to persons of note…(She Sent Letters in buttons & picturs heads to me) ye first in Congress atended Constantly To me for them in that perilous hour

ask Doctr Rogan & generall Mackdugall Mr Hancock Cornell Floyd Mr. Shearman Mr Adams & Numbers Doctr Frankland with whome she was Intimate & gave him Inteligence as She could git accounts where [s]he not they coud not goe…

I think gentlemen that I Can ask for my Intrust as an individal on Her acount now she is no more, I only want my one, Cant their be order given to our asembly that the widow Rachel Wells in and of the jarsey Stats may have the Intrust of her Cash that She Lent ye Stats in 1778 & not make good that Law maid in Eighty Three…I hartely pity others that ar in my Case that Cant speak for themselves may god direct you there is bread Enough & to Spair god has Spred a plentifull table for us & you gentlemen ar ye Carvors for us pray forgit not the poor weaklings at the fut of the table ye poor Sogers has got Sum Crumbs that fall from their masters tables Sum 2/6 Sum 2/3 in ye pound why not Rachel Wells have a littel intrust if she did not fight She threw in all her mite which bought ye Sogers food & Clothing & Let Them have Blankets & Since that She has bin obliged to Lay upon Straw & glad of that

And as to my Carracter ask Doctor Rogers & generall mackdugell…

I am no Stranger in york & was not before the warr But numbers of my old frind ar Sins dead & I doe Expect to hear Sumthing To my Satisfaction very Soon that I may Say before I Leave This world that the States did me justice tho Never Expect to See the principall is the prayer of your humble Servent Rachel Wells

## 10. Benjamin Rush, *Thoughts upon Female Education*, 1787[10]

*Benjamin Rush (1745–1813) was a Philadelphia physician and educator and a leading supporter of the of the American Revolution in Pennsylvania. The advent of Republican Motherhood required improvements in women's education. Rush's* Thoughts upon Female Education *was delivered as a speech before Philadelphia's Young Ladies' Academy in 1787 and published in the city. It presents an early articulation of Republican Motherhood and presents both the promise and limits of the doctrine for American women.*

I HAVE yielded with diffidence to the solicitations of the Principal of the Academy, in undertaking to express my regard for the prosperity of this Seminary of Learning, by submitting to your candor, a few Thoughts upon Female Education.

The first remark that I shall make upon this subject is, that female education should be accommodated to the state of society, manners, and government of the country, in which it is conducted.

This remark leads me at once to add, that the education of young ladies, in this country, should be conducted upon principles very different from what it is in Great Britain, and in some respects different from what it was when we were part of a monarchical empire.

There are several circumstances in the situation, employments, and duties of women in America, which require a peculiar mode of education.

I. The early marriages of our women, by contracting the time allowed for education, renders it necessary to contract its plan, and to confine it to the more useful branches of literature.

II. The state of property, in America, renders it necessary for the greatest part of our citizens to employ themselves, in different occupations, for the advancement of their fortunes. This cannot be done without the assistance of the female members of the community. They must be the steward, and guardians of their husbands' property. That education, therefore, will be most proper for our women, which teaches them to discharge the duties of those offices with the most success and reputation.

III. From the numerous avocations to which a professional life exposes gentlemen in America from their families, a principal share of the instruction of children naturally devolves upon the women. It becomes us therefore to prepare them by a suitable education, for the discharge of this most important duty of mothers.

IV. The equal share that every citizen has in the liberty, and the possible share that he may have in the government of our country, make it necessary that our ladies should be qualified to a certain degree by a peculiar and suitable education, to concur in instructing their sons in the principles of liberty and government.

V. In Great-Britain the business of servants is a regular occupation; but in America this humble station is the usual retreat of unexpected indigence; hence the servants in this country possess less knowledge and subordination than are required from them; and hence, our ladies are obliged to attend more to the private affairs of their families, than ladies generally do, of the same rank in Great Britain...

The branches of literature most essential for a young lady in this country, appear to be,

I. A knowledge of the English language. She should not only read, but speak and spell it correctly. And to enable her to do this, she should be taught the English grammar, and be frequently examined in applying its rules in common conversation.

II. Pleasure and interest conspire to make the writing of a fair and legible hand, a necessary branch of female education. For this purpose she should be taught not only to shape every letter properly, but to pay the strictest regard to points and capitals...

III. Some knowledge of figures and book-keeping is absolutely necessary to qualify a young lady for the duties which await her in this country. There are certain occupations in which she may assist her husband with this knowledge; and should she survive him, and agreeably to the custom of our country be the executix of his will, she cannot fail of deriving immense advantages from it.

IV. An acquaintance with geography and some instruction in chronology will enable a young lady to read history, biography, and travels, with advantage; and thereby qualify her not only for a general intercourse with the world, but, to be an agreeable companion for a sensible man. To these branches of knowledge may be added, in some instances, a general acquaintance with the first principles of astronomy, and natural philosophy, particularly with such parts of them as are calculated to prevent superstition, by explaining the causes, or obviating the effects of natural evil.

V. Vocal music should never be neglected, in the education of a young lady, in this country. Besides preparing her to join in that part of public worship which consists in psalmody, it will enable her to soothe the cares of domestic life. The distress and vexation of a husband—the noise of a nursery, and, even, the sorrows that will sometimes intrude into her own bosom, may all be relieved by a song, where sound and sentiment unite to act upon the mind...

VI. DANCING is by no means an improper branch of education for an American lady. It promotes health, and renders the figure and motions of the body easy and agreeable. I anticipate the time when the resources of conversation shall be so far multiplied, that the amusement of dancing shall be wholly confined to children. But in our present state of society and knowledge, I conceive it to be an agreeable substitute for the ignoble pleasures of drinking, and gaming, in our assemblies of grown people.

VII. The attention of our young ladies should be directed, as soon as they are prepared for it, to the reading of history—travels—poetry—and moral essays. These studies are accommodated, in a peculiar manner, to the present state of society in America, and when a relish is excited for them, in early life, they subdue that passion for reading novels, which so generally prevails among the fair sex. I cannot dismiss this species of writing and reading without observing, that the subjects of novels are by no means accommodated to our present manners. They hold up *life*, it is true, but it is not as yet *life*, in America...As yet the intrigues of a British novel, are as foreign to our manners, as the refinements of Asiatic vice. Let it not be said, that the tales of distress, which fill modern novels, have a tendency to soften the female heart into acts of humanity. The fact is the reverse of this. The abortive sympathy which is excited by the recital of imaginary distress, blunts the heart to that which is real; and, hence, we sometimes see instances of young ladies, who weep away a whole forenoon over the criminal sorrows of a fictitious Charlotte or Werter, turning with disdain at two o'clock from the sight of a beggar, who solicits in feeble accents of signs, a small portion only, of the crumbs which fall from their fathers' tables.

VIII. It will be necessary to connect all these branches of education with regular instruction in the Christian religion. For this purpose the principles of the different sects of Christians should be taught and explained, and our pupils should early be furnished with some of the most simple arguments in favour of the truth of Christianity. A portion of the bible (of late improperly banished from our schools) should be read by them every day, and such questions should be asked, after reading it, as are calculated to imprint upon their minds the interesting stories contained in it...

IX. If the measures that have been recommended for inspiring our pupils with a sense of religious and moral obligation be adopted, the government of them will be easy and agreeable. I shall only remark under this head, that *strictness* of discipline will always render *severity* unnecessary, and that there will be the most instruction in that school, where there is the most order.

A philosopher once said "let me make all the ballads of a country and I care not who makes its laws." He might with more propriety have said, let the ladies of a country be educated properly, and they will not only make and administer its laws, but form its manners and character. It would require a lively imagination to describe, or even to comprehend, the happiness of a country, where knowledge and virtue, were generally diffused among the female sex...The influence of female education would be still more extensive and useful in domestic life. The obligations of gentlemen to qualify themselves by knowledge and industry to discharge the duties of benevolence, would be encreased by marriage; and the patriot—the hero—and the legislator, would find the sweetest reward of their toils, in the approbation and applause of their wives. Children would discover the marks of maternal prudence and wisdom in every station of life; for it has been remarked that there have been few great or good men who have not been blessed with wise and prudent mothers.

### 11.    Diary of Hannah Callender, July 4, 1788[11]

*As the wife of a Philadelphia merchant, Hannah Callender (1737–1801) might be seen as an archetypal Republican Mother. In this entry from her diary Callender describes attending the parade in Philadelphia to celebrate the ratification of the Constitution.*

Elliston Sally, & Josey Sansom went to town, Josey to mind house, and they be at the grand procession for the Federal government, mon epouse come to me, and we let the whole family go to the place of destination, union green, at bush hill. I was well pleased with dear little Sam thinking myself better employed to raise I hope a good and happy subject to a constitution built on a stable foundation.

### 12.    Extracts from the New Jersey Constitution, 1776, 1844[12]

*The 1776 New Jersey Constitution allowed women, who could meet the property and residence requirements, to vote in the state. They did so for the better part of two decades. During the antebellum period, a clause was adopted which restricted the franchise to white men while removing property requirements. The first clause might be read as an expression of the egalitarian radicalism of 1776, limited by class as reflected in the property requirement. The 1844 clause, while limiting "universal" suffrage to white males, reflects the boundaries of democracy in antebellum America.*

1776
IV. That all inhabitants of this Colony, of full age, who are worth fifty pounds proclamation money, clear estate in the same, and have resided within the county in which they claim a vote for twelve months immediately preceding the election, shall be entitled to vote for Representatives in Council and Assembly; and also for all other public officers, that shall be elected by the people of the county at large.

1844
One. Every white male citizen of the United States, of the age of twenty-one years, who shall have been a resident of this State one year, and of the county in which he claims his vote five months, next before the election, shall be entitled to vote for all officers that now are, or hereafter may be, elective by the people:

*Provided,* That no person in the military, naval, or marine service of the United States shall be considered a resident in this State, by being stationed in any garrison, bar-rack, or military or naval place or station within this State; and no pauper, idiot, insane person, or person convicted of a crime which now excludes him from being a witness, unless pardoned or restored by law to the right of suffrage, shall enjoy the right of an elector.

## 13. Declaration of Sentiments, 1848[13]

*Jefferson's Declaration of Independence asserted that "all men are created equal." In 1848 the first women's rights convention in the United States, held at Seneca Falls, New York, adopted the "Declaration of Sentiments." The principal author of the Declaration of Sentiments was the feminist activist Elizabeth Cady Stanton (1815–1902). Stanton deliberately followed the Declaration of Independence in asserting a claim to equal rights for American women. In so doing Stanton and the Seneca Falls Convention sought to draw a rhetorical contrast between the egalitarian principles of the Revolution and the unequal position of women in mid-nineteenth-century America.*

When, in the course of human events, it becomes necessary for one portion of the family of man to assume among the people of the earth a position different from that which they have hitherto occupied, but one to which the laws of nature and of nature's God entitle them, a decent respect to the opinions of mankind requires that they should declare the causes that impel them to such a course.

We hold these truths to be self-evident: that all men and women are created equal; that they are endowed by their Creator with certain inalienable rights, that among these are life, liberty, and the pursuit of happiness; that to secure these rights governments are instituted, deriving their just powers from the consent of the governed. Whenever any form of Government becomes destructive of these ends, it is the right of those who suffer from it to refuse allegiance to it, and to insist upon the institution of a new government, laying its foundation on such principles, and organizing its powers in such form as to them shall seem most likely to effect their safety and happiness. Prudence, indeed, will dictate that governments long established should not be changed for light and transient causes; and accordingly, all experience hath shown that mankind are more disposed to suffer, while evils are sufferable, than to right themselves by abolishing the forms to which they are accustomed. But when a long train of abuses and usurpations, pursuing invariably the same object evinces a design to reduce them under absolute despotism, it is their duty to throw off such government, and to provide new guards for their future security. Such has been the patient sufferance of the women under this government, and such is now the necessity which constrains them to demand the equal station to which they are entitled.

The history of mankind is a history of repeated injuries and usurpations on the part of man toward woman, having in direct object the establishment of an absolute tyranny over her. To prove this, let facts be submitted to a candid world.

He has never permitted her to exercise her inalienable right to the elective franchise.

He has compelled her to submit to laws, in the formation of which she had no voice.

He has withheld from her rights which are given to the most ignorant and degraded men—both natives and foreigners.

Having deprived her of this first right of a citizen, the elective franchise, thereby leaving her without representation in the halls of legislation, he has oppressed her on all sides.

He has made her, if married, in the eye of the law, civilly dead.

He has taken from her all right in property, even to the wages she earns.

He has made her, morally, an irresponsible being, as she can commit many crimes with impunity, provided they be done in the presence of her husband. In the covenant of marriage, she is compelled to promise obedience to her husband, he becoming, to all intents and purposes, her master—the law giving him power to deprive her of her liberty, and to administer chastisement.

He has so framed the laws of divorce, as to what shall be the proper causes of divorce; in case of separation, to whom the guardianship of the children shall be given; as to be wholly regardless of the happiness of women—the law, in all cases, going upon the false supposition of the supremacy of man, and giving all power into his hands.

After depriving her of all rights as a married woman, if single and the owner of property, he has taxed her to support a government which recognizes her only when her property can be made profitable to it.

He has monopolized nearly all the profitable employments, and from those she is permitted to follow, she receives but a scanty remuneration.

He closes against her all the avenues to wealth and distinction, which he considers most honorable to himself. As a teacher of theology, medicine, or law, she is not known.

He has denied her the facilities for obtaining a thorough education—all colleges being closed against her.

He allows her in Church as well as State, but a subordinate position, claiming Apostolic authority for her exclusion from the ministry, and with some exceptions, from any public participation in the affairs of the Church.

He has created a false public sentiment, by giving to the world a different code of morals for men and women, by which moral delinquencies which exclude women from society, are not only tolerated but deemed of little account in man.

He has usurped the prerogative of Jehovah himself, claiming it as his right to assign for her a sphere of action, when that belongs to her conscience and her God.

He has endeavored, in every way that he could to destroy her confidence in her own powers, to lessen her self-respect, and to make her willing to lead a dependent and abject life.

Now, in view of this entire disfranchisement of one-half the people of this country, their social and religious degradation,—in view of the unjust laws above mentioned, and because women do feel themselves aggrieved, oppressed, and fraudulently deprived of their most sacred rights, we insist that they have immediate admission to all the rights and privileges which belong to them as citizens of these United States.

In entering upon the great work before us, we anticipate no small amount of misconception, misrepresentation, and ridicule; but we shall use every instrumentality within our power to effect our object. We shall employ agents, circulate tracts, petition the State and national Legislatures, and endeavor to enlist the pulpit and the press in our behalf. We hope this Convention will be followed by a series of Conventions, embracing ever part of the country.

Firmly relying upon the final triumph of the Right and the True, we do this day affix our signatures to this declaration.

## Notes

1. "Deborah Franklin to Benjamin Franklin, Philadelphia, September 22, 1765," in Leonard W. Labaree et al. (eds.), *The Papers of Benjamin Franklin*, 39 vols. to date (New Haven, CT; Yale University Press, 1959-), 12:270–274.
2. "Benjamin Franklin to Deborah Franklin, London, April 6, 1766," in Leonard W. Labaree et al. (eds.), *The Papers of Benjamin Franklin*, 39 vols. to date (New Haven, CT; Yale University Press, 1959-), 13:233–243.
3. "Deborah Franklin: Power of Attorney, October 14, 1768," in William B. Willcox et al. (eds.) *The Papers of Benjamin Franklin*, 39 vols. to date (New Haven, CT: Yale University Press, 1959–), 15:227–228.
4. *Boston Evening Post*, February 12, 1770.
5. The Granger Collection, New York.
6. Letter from Abigail Adams to John Adams, 31 March–5 April 1776 [electronic edition]. *Adams Family Papers: An Electronic Archive*. Boston: Massachusetts Historical Society, http://www.masshist.org/digitaladams/
7. *Sentiments of An American Woman* (Philadelphia: John Dunlap, 1780). This document has been edited for length. The full version can be found at the book's website.
8. From Sir Henry Clinton Collection, Clements Library, Ann Arbor, MI. Translated and transcribed by Nora Allavoine Duncan.
9. "Petition of Rachel Wells to the Continental Congress, 1786," Petitions Address to Congress, 1775-1789, *Papers of the Continental Congress* (M-247), Roll 56, Vol. 8, Item 42, 354–355.
10. From Benjamin Rush, *Thoughts Upon Female Education* (Philadelphia: Prichard & Hall, 1787), 5–12, 14, 19–20. This document has been edited for length. The full version can be found at the book's website (http://www.routledge.com/textbooks/revolutionaryamerica/).
11. George Vaux Collection, American Philosophical Society, Philadelphia.
12. New Jersey State Library, Trenton, NJ.
13. *First Convention Ever Called to Discuss the Civil and Political Rights of Women, Seneca Falls, New York, July 19, 20, 1848*, Miller NAWSA Suffrage Scrapbooks, 1897–1911, Washington, DC: Library of Congress, Rare Book and Special Collections Division.

# CHAPTER 10

# The Federalist Era

## Introduction

After the election of George Washington as the first president in January 1789, his supporters and political allies called themselves Federalists. The Federalists won successive elections in 1792 and 1796 and they did not lose the presidency until the election of 1800. A major area of contention between the Federalists and their adversaries, who came to be known as Republicans, was political economy. Economic instability was, perhaps, the biggest problem facing the new government. Washington's Treasury Secretary, Alexander Hamilton, developed a comprehensive economic program under the terms of which the federal government would assume the public debts of the states and promote manufacturing (document 1). Hamilton believed that the United States should emulate Britain's economic model. Opposition to Hamilton's program coalesced in and out of Congress (document 2). The Republicans opposed state-supported manufacturing and sought to maintain the United States as an agricultural nation of independent small farmers. The leading exponent of this view was Thomas Jefferson who served as Secretary of State under Washington and as Vice President to John Adams. In his *Notes on the State of Virginia,* Jefferson articulated a vision of republican political economy which eschewed manufacturing in favor of agriculture (document 3).

Hamilton sought, in part, to finance his fiscal program—which was meant to strengthen the federal government as well as the economy—through an excise tax on whiskey. In 1794 the excise duty, which was very unpopular, especially in frontier areas, led to a rebellion in western Pennsylvania. The Whiskey Rebellion was a direct challenge to the authority of the federal government and seemed to threaten the authority of the new constitution. As a consequence, the Federalists used the army to suppress the disorder (document 4). Washington's presidency coincided with the early stages of the French Revolution, which bitterly divided

Americans. Although Washington proclaimed the United States neutral in the wars of the French Revolution, the Federalists were sympathetic to Britain and the Republicans to France. In his 1796 "Farewell Address" (document 5), Washington warned Americans against political partisanship and entangling alliances with foreign powers. Notwithstanding this warning, partisanship and international tensions increased during the administration of Washington's successor, John Adams. During Adams's administration the United States and France waged a "quasi-war" at sea. In anticipation of a formal declaration of war, the Federalists in Congress adopted a series of measures, the Alien and Sedition Acts (document 6) which sought to limit the right to free speech and to extend the period of time which immigrants would have to wait to become American citizens. Republicans objected to these measures. As the leaders of the Republicans, Madison and Jefferson arranged for the legislatures of Virginia and Kentucky to adopt a series of resolutions denouncing the Alien and Sedition Acts and raising the specter that individual states might nullify federal legislation (document 7). Although no other states endorsed these resolutions, the Alien and Sedition Acts were unpopular and contributed to the defeat of the Federalists in 1800.

## 1. A Federalist Vision of Economic Development[1]

*As Washington's Treasury Secretary, Alexander Hamilton (1755–1804) came into office with an activist agenda to transform the federal government and the United States. He issued a series of reports outlining his vision for the economic development of the United States. The first of these, The Report on Public Credit (1790), proposed that the federal government assume the responsibility for all public debt in the United States—that owed by the federal government and the states, as well as the debt owed to foreign governments and private individuals. Hamilton proposed to pay this debt through import duties, land sales, and an excise tax on whiskey. In so doing he intended to undermine state sovereignty and unite the interests of the wealthy and the federal government. Having strengthened the federal government, Hamilton intended that the government should use its power to promote manufacturing in the United States. In his Report on Manufactures (1791), Hamilton argued that the United States should promote manufacturing by protecting infant industries, thereby guaranteeing the future health and prosperity of the United States.*

### 1a. The Report on Public Credit

...Every breach of the public engagements, whether from choice or necessity, is, in different degrees, hurtful to public credit. When such a necessity does truly exist, the evils of it are only to be palliated by a scrupulous attention, on the part of the Government, to carry the violation no further than the necessity absolutely requires, and to manifest, if the nature of the case admit of it, a sincere disposition to make reparation whenever circumstances shall permit. But, with every possible mitigation, credit must suffer, and numerous mischiefs ensue...

This reflection derives additional strength from the nature of the debt of the United States. It was the price of liberty. The faith of America has been repeatedly pledged for it, and with solemnities that give peculiar force to the obligation. There is, indeed, reason to regret that it has not hitherto been kept; that the necessities of the war, conspiring with inexperience in the subjects of finance, produced direct infractions; and that the subsequent period has been a continued scene of negative violation or non-compliance. But a diminution of this regret arises from the reflection, that the last seven years have exhibited an earnest and uniform effort, on the part of the Government of the Union, to retrieve the national credit, by doing justice to the creditors of the nation; and that the embarrassments of a defective constitution, which defeated this laudable effort, have ceased.

From this evidence of a favorable disposition given by the former Government, the institution of a new one, clothed with powers competent to calling forth the resources of the community, has excited correspondent expectations. A general belief accordingly prevails, that the credit of the United States will quickly be established on the firm foundation of an effectual provision for the existing debt. The influence which this has had at home is witnessed by the rapid increase that has taken place in the market value of the public securities...

It cannot but merit particular attention, that, among ourselves, the most enlightened friends of good government are those whose expectations are the highest.

To justify and preserve their confidence; to promote the increasing respectability of the American name; to answer the calls of justice; to restore landed property to its due value; to furnish new resources, both to agriculture and commerce; to cement more closely the union of the States; to add to their security against foreign attack; to establish public order on the basis of an upright and liberal policy;—these are the great and invaluable ends to be secured by a proper and adequate provision, at the present period, for the support of public credit...

The advantage to the public creditors, from the increased value of that part of their property which constitutes the public debt, needs no explanation.

But there is a consequence of this, less obvious, though not less true, in which every other citizen is interested. It is a well-known fact, that, in countries in which the national debt is properly funded, and an object of established confidence, it answers most of the purposes of money. Transfers of stock or public debt are there equivalent to payments in specie; or, in other words, stock, in the principal transactions of business, passes current as specie. The same thing would, in all probability, happen here under the like circumstances.

The benefits of this are various and obvious:

*First.* Trade is extended by it, because there is a larger capital to carry it on, and the merchant can, at the same time, afford to trade for smaller profits; as his stock, which, when unemployed, brings him an interest from the Government, serves him also as money when he has a call for it in his commercial operations.

*Secondly.* Agriculture and manufactures are also promoted by it, for the like reason, that more capital can be commanded to be employed in both; and because the merchant, whose enterprise in foreign trade gives to them activity and extension, has greater means for enterprise.

*Thirdly.* The interest of money will be lowered by it; for this is always in a ratio to the quantity of money, and to the quickness of circulation. This circumstance will enable both the public and individuals to borrow on easier and cheaper terms.

And from the combination of these effects, additional aids will be furnished to labor, to industry, and to arts of every kind. But these good effects of a public debt are only to be looked for, when, by being well funded, it has acquired an adequate and stable value; till then, it has rather a contrary tendency. The fluctuation and insecurity incident to it, in an unfunded state, render it a mere commodity, and a precarious one. As such, being only an object of occasional and particular speculation, all the money applied to it is so much diverted from the more useful channels of circulation, for which the thing itself affords no substitute; so that, in fact, one serious inconvenience of an unfunded debt is, that it contributes to the scarcity of money…

Having now taken a concise view of the inducements to a proper provision for the public debt, the next inquiry which presents itself is, What ought to be the nature of such a provision?…

The Secretary, concluding that a discrimination between the different classes of creditors of the United States cannot, with propriety, be made, proceeds to examine whether a difference ought to be permitted to remain between them and another description of public creditors—those of the States, individually. The Secretary, after mature reflection on this point, entertains a full conviction, that an assumption of the debts of the particular States by the Union, and a like provision for them as for those of the Union, will be a measure of sound policy and substantial justice.

It would, in the opinion of the Secretary, contribute, in an eminent degree, to an orderly, stable, and satisfactory arrangement of the national finances. Admitting, as ought to be the case, that a provision must be made, in some way or other, for the entire debt, it will follow that no greater revenues will be required whether that provision be made wholly by the United States, or partly by them and partly by the States separately.

The principal question, then, must be whether such a provision cannot be more conveniently and effectually made, by one general plan, issuing from one authority, than by different plans, originating in different authorities? In the first case there can be no competition for resources; in the last there must be such a competition. The consequences of this, without the greatest caution on both sides, might be interfering regulations, and thence, collision and confusion. Particular branches of industry might also be oppressed by it…

If all the public creditors receive their dues from one source, distributed with an equal hand, their interest will be the same. And, having the same interests, they will unite in the support of the fiscal arrangements of the Government—as these, too, can be made with more convenience where there is no competition. These circumstances combined will insure to the revenue laws a more ready and more satisfactory execution...

There are several reasons which render it probable that the situation of the State creditors would be worse than that of the creditors of the Union, if there be not a national assumption of the State debts. Of these it will be sufficient to mention two: one, that a principal branch of revenue is exclusively vested in the Union; the other, that a State must always be checked in the imposition of taxes on articles of consumption, from the want of power to extend the same regulation to the other States, and from the tendency of partial duties to injure its industry and commerce...

The general principle of it seems to be equitable: for it appears difficult to conceive a good reason why the expenses for the particular defence of a part, in a common war, should not be a common charge, as well as those incurred professedly for the general defence. The defence of each part is that of the whole; and unless all the expenditures are brought into a common mass, the tendency must be to add to the calamities suffered, by being the most exposed to the ravages of war, an increase of burthens...

### 1b.   *The Report on Manufactures*[2]

...The expediency of encouraging manufactures in the United States, which was not long since deemed very questionable, appears at this time to be pretty generally admitted. The embarrassments which have obstructed the progress of our external trade, have led to serious reflections on the necessity of enlarging the sphere of our domestic commerce. The restrictive regulations, which, in foreign markets, abridge the vent of the increasing surplus of our agricultural produce, serve to beget an earnest desire that a more extensive demand for that surplus may be created at home; and the complete success which has rewarded manufacturing enterprise in some valuable branches, conspiring with the promising symptoms which attend some less mature essays in others, justify a hope that the obstacles to the growth of this species of industry are less formidable than they were apprehended to be, and that it is not difficult to find, in its further extension, a full indemnification for any external disadvantages, which are or may be experienced, as well as an accession of resources, favorable to national independence and safety...

It ought readily be conceded that the cultivation of the earth, as the primary and most certain source of national supply, as the immediate and chief source of subsistence to a man, as the principal source of those materials which constitute the nutriment of other kinds of labor, as including a state most favorable to the freedom and independence of the human mind—one, perhaps, most conducive to the multiplication of the human species, has intrinsically a strong claim to pre-eminence over every other kind of industry.

But, that it has a title to any thing like an exclusive predilection, in any country, ought to be admitted with great caution; that it is even more productive than every other branch of industry, requires more evidence than has yet been given in support of the position. That its real interests, precious and important as, without the help of exaggeration, they truly are, will be advanced, rather than injured, by the due encouragement of manufactures, may, it is believed, be satisfactorily demonstrated. And it is also believed that the expediency of such encouragement, in a general view, may be shown to be recommended by the most cogent and persuasive motives of national policy...

To affirm that the labor of the manufacturer is unproductive, because he consumes as much of the produce of land as he adds value to the raw material which he manufactures, is not better founded than it would be to affirm that the labor of the farmer, which furnishes materials to the manufacturer, is unproductive, because he consumes an equal value of manufactured articles. Each furnishes a certain portion of the produce of his labor to the other, and each destroys a corresponding portion of the produce of the labor of the other. In the meantime, the maintenance of two citizens, instead of one, is going on; the State has two members instead of one; and they, together, consume twice the value of what is produced from the land...

Considering how fast and how much the progress of new settlements in the United States must increase the surplus produce of the soil, and weighing seriously the tendency of the system which prevails among most of the commercial nations of Europe, whatever dependence may be placed on the force of natural circumstances to counteract the effects of an artificial policy, there appear strong reasons to regard the foreign demand for that surplus as too uncertain a reliance, and to desire a substitute for it in an extensive domestic market.

To secure such a market there is no other expedient than to promote manufacturing establishments. Manufacturers, who constitute the most numerous class, after the cultivators of land, are for that reason the principal consumers of the surplus of their labor.

This idea of an extensive domestic market for the surplus produce of the soil, is of the first consequence. It is, of all things, that which most effectually conduces to a flourishing state of agriculture. If the effect of manufactories should be to detach a portion of the hands which would otherwise be engaged in tillage, it might possibly cause a smaller quantity of lands to be under cultivation; but, by their tendency to procure a more certain demand for the surplus produce of the soil, they would, at the same time, cause the lands which were in cultivation to be better improved and more productive. And while, by their influence, the condition of each individual farmer would be meliorated, the total mass of agricultural production would probably be increased. For this must evidently depend as much upon the degree of improvement, if not more, than upon the number of acres under culture.

It merits particular observation, that the multiplication of manufactories not only furnishes a market for those articles which have been accustomed to be produced in abundance in a country, but it likewise creates a demand for such as were either unknown or produced in inconsiderable quantities. The bowels, as well as the surface of the earth, are ransacked for articles which were before neglected. Animals, plants, and minerals acquire an utility and a value which were before unexplored.

The foregoing considerations seem sufficient to establish, as general propositions, that it is the interest of nations to diversify the industrious pursuits of the individuals who compose them. That the establishment of manufactures is calculated not only to increase the general stock of useful and productive labor, but even to improve the state of agriculture in particular; certainly to advance the interests of those who are engaged in it…

## 2.   "Those Who Labor in the Earth": Jefferson's Opposition to Manufacturing [3]

*Thomas Jefferson led the opposition to the Hamiltonian economic program. Jefferson had long been an advocate of agriculture as the basis for American development. In this passage from his* Notes on the State of Virginia *(1784), Jefferson discussed the deleterious effects of manufacturing and the positive benefits of agriculture. According to his vision, the United States should be a nation of independent farmers who traded their surpluses for goods manufactured in Europe.*

We never had an interior trade of any importance. Our exterior commerce has suffered very much from the beginning of the present contest. During this time we have manufactured within our families the most necessary articles of cloathing. Those of cotton will bear some comparison with the same kinds of manufacture in Europe; but those of wool, flax and hemp are very coarse, unsightly, and unpleasant: and such is our attachment to agriculture, and such our preference for foreign manufactures, that be it wise or unwise, our people will certainly return as soon as they can, to the raising raw materials, and exchanging them for finer manufactures than they are able to execute themselves.

The political œconomists of Europe have established it as a principle that every state should endeavour to manufacture for itself: and this principle, like many others, we transfer to America, without calculating the difference of circumstance which should often produce a difference of result. In Europe the lands are either cultivated, or locked up against the cultivator. Manufacture must therefore be resorted to of necessity not of choice, to support the surplus of their people. But we have an immensity of land courting the industry of the husbandman. Is it best then that all our citizens should be employed in its improvement, or that one half should be called off from that to exercise manufactures and handicraft arts for the other? Those who labour in the earth are the chosen people of God, if ever he had a chosen people, whose breasts he has made his peculiar deposit for substantial and genuine virtue. It is the focus in which he keeps alive that sacred fire, which otherwise might escape from the face of the earth. Corruption of morals in the mass of cultivators is a phænomenon of which no age nor nation has furnished an example. It is the mark set on those, who not looking up to heaven, to their own soil and industry, as does the husbandman, for their subsistance, depend for it on the casualties and caprice of customers. Dependance begets subservience and venality, suffocates the germ of virtue, and prepares fit tools for the designs of ambition. This, the natural progress and consequence of the arts, has sometimes perhaps been retarded by accidental circumstances: but, generally speaking, the proportion which the aggregate of the other classes of citizens bears in any state to that of its husbandmen, is the proportion of its unsound to its healthy parts, and is a good-enough barometer whereby to measure its degree of corruption. While we have land to labour then, let us never wish to see our citizens occupied at a work-bench, or twirling a distaff. Carpenters, masons, smiths, are wanting in husbandry: but, for the general operations of manufacture, let our work-shops remain in Europe. It is better to carry provisions and materials to workmen there, than bring them to the provisions and materials, and with them their manners and principles. The loss by the transportation of commodities across the Atlantic will be made up in happiness and permanence of government. The mobs of great cities add just so much to the support of pure government, as sores do to the strength of the human body. It is the manners and spirit of a people which preserve a republic in vigour. A degeneracy in these is a canker which soon eats to the heart of its laws and constitution.

### 3. Opposition to Hamilton's Program[4]

*There was substantial opposition to Hamilton's program in Congress, particularly among senators and representatives from the south and west. In this newspaper article, Senator William Maclay (1737–1804) of Pennsylvania denounced Hamilton's plan for funding the national debt. Eventually, a compromise was reached whereby the debt was funded, but the nation's capital was moved from New York to Philadelphia and, then, to Washington, DC.*

OBJECTS.
*1st. Extending the powers and influence of the Treasury.*
*2d. Establishing the permanent residence of Court and Congress in New-York*
*3d. Securing the revenues of the Union, to the inhabitants of that city.*

*WAYS AND MEANS.*

ENCREASE the public debt by every possible method—admit all account authorised and unauthorised—blend the state debts with those of the Union, and thus a pretext may be afforded, to seize all the sources of revenue, and depress the state governments; for without reducing them to insignificance, a pompous Court cannot be established; and without such a Court, as a proper machine, not government can be properly managed; or, in other words, the people will be meddling with serious matters, unless you amuse them with trifles. Fund all demands indiscriminately at the highest interest possible; but previous to this communicate the grand secret to all the monied interest of New-York, and to as many influential characters in Congress as may ensure the success of the project; that they may, by an united effort of speculation, secure all the certificates. Thus the whole Union will be subsidized to the city of New-York. The revenues of the United States will flow entire into the hands of her citizens. Thus possessed of the wealth of the Union, she will govern the Councils of the Empire, secure the residence of the Court and Congress, and grow in power, splendor and population, while there is room left on the island to build another house. The idle and affluent will croud to her from all the new world, as well as many adventurers from the old. New loans must be opened on every pretext, in Holland and elsewhere; for the greater the mass of public debt, the greater will be the influence of the Treasury, which has the management of it, and all this will redound to the emolument of the favoured city. Thus shall the capital of the United States in a few years equal London or Paris in population, extent, expence and dissipation, while for the aggrandisement of one spot, and one set of men, the national debt shall tower aloft to hundreds of millions.

### 4. The Whiskey Rebellion[5]

*To fund Hamilton's fiscal program, Congress adopted an excise tax on whiskey. In the summer of 1794 there were widespread protests against the tax along the frontier, particularly in western Pennsylvania where violent protests and attacks on tax collectors led to two deaths. Washington called on the states to provide him with troops and dispatched Alexander Hamilton to suppress the rebellion. By the time the army arrived, the rebellion had subsided. In this letter Washington discusses the rebellion and his fear that mob rule might destroy the American republic.*

In the moment I was leaving the City of Philadelphia for this place, your letter of the 24th Ulto. was put into my hands. Although I regret the occasion which has called you into the field, I rejoice to hear you are there; and because it is probable I may meet you at Fort Cumberland, whither I shall proceed, so soon as I see the Troops at this rendezvous in condition to advance. At that place, or at Bedford, my ulterior resolution must be taken, either to advance with the Troops into the Insurgent Counties of this State, or to return to Philadelphia for the purpose of meeting Congress the 3d. of next month.

Imperious circumstances alone can justify my absence from the Seat of Government whilst Congress are in Session; but if these, from the disposition of the People in the refractory Counties, and the state of the information I expect to receive at the advanced Posts, should appear to exist the lesser must yield to the greater duties of my office and I shall cross the mountains with the Troops; if not, I shall place the command of the combined force under the orders of Governor Lee of Virginia and repair to the Seat of Government.

I am perfectly in sentiment with you, that the business we are drawn out upon, should be effectually executed; and that the daring and factious spirit which has arisen (to overturn the laws, and to subvert the Constitution,) ought to be subdued. If this is not done, there is, an end of and we may bid adieu to all government in this Country, except Mob and Club Govt. from whence nothing but anarchy and confusion can ensue; for if the minority, and a small one too, are suffered to dictate to the majority, after measures have undergone the most solemn discussions by the Representatives of the people, and their Will through this medium is enacted into a law; there can be no security for life, liberty or property; nor if the laws are not to govern, can any man know how to conduct himself with safety for there never was a law *yet made*, I conceive, that hit the taste *exactly* of every man, or every part of the community; of course, if this be a reason for opposition no law can be execd. at all witht. force and every man or set of men will in that case cut and carve for themselves; the consequences of which must be deprecated by all classes of men who are friends to order, and to the peace and happiness of the Country; but how can things be otherwise than they are when clubs and Societies have been instituted for the express purpose though clothed in another garb by their diabolical leader Gt whose object was to sow sedition, to poison the minds of the people of this Country, and to make them discond. with the Government of it, and who have labored indefatigably to effect these purposes.

As Arms &c. have been sent on from Phila. in aid of those from New London, I hope, and trust, your supplies have been ample. I shall add no more at present but my best wishes and sincere regard for you, and that I am &c.

## 5. Washington's Farewell Address[6]

*As Washington prepared to leave office at the conclusion of his second term, he issued a letter to the American people which came to be known as the Farewell Address. Largely written in collaboration with James Madison and Alexander Hamilton, the Farewell Address reflects the trials and tribulations of Washington's presidency. In the address Washington defends the constitution and condemns political parties, sectionalism, and factionalism. The main portion of the address concerns foreign policy. Washington defends his 1793 neutrality proclamation and warns the United States about the dangers of foreign alliances.*

Friends and Fellow Citizens:
The period for a new election of a Citizen, to Administer the Executive government of the United States, being not far distant, and the time actually arrived, when your thoughts must be employed in designating the person, who is to be cloathed with that important trust, it appears to me proper, especially as it may conduce to a more distinct expression of the public voice, that I should now apprise you of the resolution I have formed, to decline being considered among the number of those, out of whom a choice is to be made.

I beg you, at the same time, to do me the justice to be assured, that this resolution has not been taken, without a strict regard to all the considerations appertaining to the relation, which binds a dutiful citizen to his country, and that, in withdrawing the tender of service which silence in my situation might imply, I am influenced by no diminution of zeal for your future interest, no deficiency of grateful respect for your past kindness; but am supported by a full conviction that the step is compatible with both...

The impressions, with which I first undertook the arduous trust, were explained on the proper occasion. In the discharge of this trust, I will only say, that I have, with good intentions, contributed towards the Organization and Administration of the government, the best exertions of which a very fallible judgment was capable. Not unconscious, in the outset, of the inferiority of my qualifications, experience in my own eyes, perhaps still more in the eyes of others, has strengthened the motives to diffidence of myself; and every day the encreasing weight of years admonishes me more, and more that the shade of retirement is as necessary to me as it will be welcome. Satisfied that if any circumstances have given peculiar value to my services, they were temporary, I have the consolation to believe, that while choice and prudence invite me to quit the political scene, patriotism does not forbid it.

In looking forward to the moment, which is intended to terminate the career of my public life, my feelings do not permit me to suspend the deep acknowledgment of that debt of gratitude wch. I owe to my beloved country for the many honors it has conferred upon me; still more for the stedfast confidence with which it has supported me; and for the opportunities I have thence enjoyed of manifesting my inviolable attachment, by services faithful and persevering, though in usefulness unequal to my zeal...

Here, perhaps, I ought to stop. But a solicitude for your welfare, which cannot end but with my life, and the apprehension of danger, natural to that solicitude, urge me, on an occasion like the present, to offer to your solemn contemplation, and to recommend to your frequent review, some sentiments; which are the result of much reflection, of no inconsiderable observation, and which appear to me all-important to the permanency of your felicity as a People. These will be offered to you with the more freedom, as you can only see in them the disinterested warnings of a parting friend, who can possibly have no personal motive to biass his counsel...

The Unity of Government which constitutes you one people is also now dear to you. It is justly so; for it is a main Pillar in the Edifice of your real independence, the support of your tranquility at home; your peace abroad; of your safety; of your prosperity; of that very liberty which you so highly prize. But as it is easy to foresee, that from different causes and from different quarters, much pains will be taken, many artifices employed to weaken in your minds the conviction of this truth; as this is the point in your political fortress against which the batteries of internal and external enemies will be most constantly and actively (though often covertly and insidiously) directed, it is of infinite moment that you should properly estimate the immense value of your national Union to your collective and individual happiness; that you should cherish a cordial, habitual, and immovable attachment to it; accustoming yourselves to think and speak of it as of the Palladium of your political safety and prosperity; watching for its preservation with jealous anxiety; discountenancing whatever may suggest even a suspicion that it can in any event be abandoned, and indignantly frowning upon the first dawning of every attempt to alienate any portion of our Country from the rest, or to enfeeble the sacred ties which now link together the various parts.

For this you have every inducement of sympathy and interest. Citizens, by birth or choice, of a common country, that country has a right to concentrate your affections. The name of American, which belongs to you in your national capacity, must always exalt the just pride of Patriotism, more than any appellation derived from local discriminations. With slight shades of difference, you have the same Religeon, Manners, Habits, and political Principles. You have in a common cause fought and triumphed together. The independence and liberty you possess are the work of joint councils, and joint efforts; of common dangers, sufferings, and successes.

But these considerations, however powerfully they address themselves to your sensibility are greatly outweighed by those which apply more immediately to your Interest. Here every portion of our country finds the most commanding motives for carefully guarding and preserving the Union of the whole.

The *North*, in an unrestrained intercourse with the *South*, protected by the equal Laws of a common government, finds in the productions of the latter, great additional resources of Maratime and commercial enterprise and precious materials of manufacturing industry. The *South*, in the same Intercourse, benefitting by the Agency of the *North*, sees its agriculture grow and its commerce expand. Turning partly into its own channels the seamen of the *North*, it finds its particular navigation envigorated; and, while it contributes, in different ways, to nourish and increase the general mass of the National navigation, it looks forward to the protection of a Maratime strength, to which itself is unequally adapted. The

*East*, in a like intercourse with the *West*, already finds, and in the progressive improvement of interior communications by land and water, will more and more find a valuable vent for the commodities which it brings from abroad, or manufactures at home. The *West* derives from the *East* supplies requisite to its growth and comfort, and what is perhaps of still greater consequence, it must of necessity owe the *secure* enjoyment of indispensable *outlets* for its own productions to the weight, influence, and the future Maritime strength of the Atlantic side of the Union, directed by an indissoluble community of interest as *one Nation*. Any other tenure by which the *West* can hold this essential advantage, whether derived from its own separate strength, or from an apostate and unnatural connection with any foreign Power, must be intrinsically precarious.

While then every part of our country thus feels an immediate and particular Interest in Union, all the parts combined cannot fail to find in the united mass of means and efforts greater strength, greater resource, proportionably greater security from external danger, a less frequent interruption of their Peace by foreign Nations; and, what is of inestimable value, they must derive from Union an exemption from those broils and Wars between themselves, which so frequently afflict neighbouring countries, not tied together by the same government; which their own rivalships alone would be sufficient to produce, but which opposite foreign alliances, attachments, and intriegues would stimulate and imbitter. Hence, likewise they will avoid the necessity of those overgrown Military establishments, which under any form of Government are inauspicious to liberty, and which are to be regarded as particularly hostile to Republican Liberty: In this sense it is, that your Union ought to be considered as a main prop of your liberty, and that the love of the one ought to endear to you the preservation of the other.

These considerations speak a persuasive language to every reflecting and virtuous mind, and exhibit the continuance of the Union as a primary object of Patriotic desire. Is there a doubt, whether a common government can embrace so large a sphere? Let experience solve it. To listen to mere speculation in such a case were criminal. We are authorized to hope that a proper organization of the whole, with the auxiliary agency of governments for the respective Sub divisions, will afford a happy issue to the experiment. 'Tis well worth a fair and full experiment. With such powerful and obvious motives to Union, affecting all parts of our country, while experience shall not have demonstrated its impracticability, there will always be reason, to distrust the patriotism of those, who in any quarter may endeavor to weaken its bands...

To the efficacy and permanency of Your Union, a Government for the whole is indispensable. No Alliances however strict between the parts can be an adequate substitute. They must inevitably experience the infractions and interruptions which all Alliances in all times have experienced. Sensible of this momentous truth, you have improved upon your first essay, by the adoption of a Constitution of Government, better calculated than your former for an intimate Union, and for the efficacious management of your common concerns. This government, the offspring of our own choice uninfluenced and unawed, adopted upon full investigation and mature deliberation, completely free in its principles, in the distribution of its powers, uniting security with energy, and containing within itself a provision for its own amendment, has a just claim to your confidence and your support. Respect for its authority, compliance with its Laws, acquiescence in its measures, are duties enjoined by the fundamental maxims of true Liberty. The basis of our political systems is the right of the people to make and to alter their Constitutions of Government. But the Constitution which at any time exists, 'till changed by an explicit and authentic act of the whole People, is sacredly obligatory upon all. The very idea of the power and the right of the People to establish Government presupposes the duty of every Individual to obey the established Government.

All obstructions to the execution of the Laws, all combinations and Associations, under whatever plausible character, with the real design to direct, control, counteract, or awe the regular deliberation and action of the Constituted authorities are destructive of this fundamental principle and of fatal tendency. They serve to organize faction, to give it an artificial and extraordinary force; to put in the place of the delegated will of the Nation, the will of a party; often a small but artful and enterprising minority of the Community; and, according to the alternate triumphs of different parties, to make the public administration the Mirror of the ill-concerted and incongruous projects of faction, rather than the organ of consistent and wholesome plans digested by common counsils and modified by mutual interests. However combinations or Associations of the above description may now and then answer popular ends, they are likely, in the course of time and things, to become potent engines, by which cunning, ambitious, and unprincipled men will be enabled to subvert the Power of the People, and to usurp for themselves the reins of government, destroying afterwards the very engines which have lifted them to unjust dominion...

I have already intimated to you the danger of Parties in the State, with particular reference to the founding of them on Geographical discriminations. Let me now take a more comprehensive view, and warn you in the most solemn manner against the baneful effects of the Spirit of Party, generally.

This spirit, unfortunately, is inseparable from our nature, having its root in the strongest passions of the human Mind. It exists under different shapes in all Governments, more or less stifled, controuled, or repressed; but, in those of the popular form it is seen in its greatest rankness and is truly their worst enemy.

The alternate domination of one faction over another, sharpened by the spirit of revenge natural to party dissension, which in different ages and countries has perpetrated the most horrid enormities, is itself a frightful despotism. But this leads at length to a more formal and permanent despotism. The disorders and miseries, which result, gradually incline the minds of men to seek security and repose in the absolute power of an Individual: and sooner or later the chief of some prevailing faction more able or more fortunate than his competitors, turns this disposition to the purposes of his own elevation, on the ruins of public liberty.

Without looking forward to an extremity of this kind (which nevertheless ought not to be entirely out of sight) the common and continual mischiefs of the spirit of Party are sufficient to make it the interest and the duty of a wise People to discourage and restrain it.

It serves always to distract the Public Councils and enfeeble the Public administration. It agitates the Community with ill founded jealousies and false alarms, kindles the animosity of one part against another, foments occasionally riot and insurrection. It opens the door to foreign influence and corruption, which find a facilitated access to the government itself through the channels of party passions. Thus the policy and the will of one country, are subjected to the policy and will of another.

There is an opinion that parties in free countries are useful checks upon the Administration of the Government and serve to keep alive the spirit of Liberty. This within certain limits is probably true, and in Governments of a Monarchical cast Patriotism may look with endulgence, if not with favor, upon the spirit of party. But in those of the popular character, in Governments purely elective, it is a spirit not to be encouraged. From their natural tendency, it is certain there will always be enough of that spirit for every salutary purpose. And there being constant danger of excess, the effort ought to be, by force of public opinion, to mitigate and assuage it. A fire not to be quenched; it demands a uniform vigilance to prevent its bursting into a flame, lest instead of warming, it should consume…

## 6.  The Alien and Sedition Acts

*In 1798 the Federalist-dominated Congress passed a series of laws, known collectively as the Alien and Sedition Acts. These were intended to be wartime measures to protect the country from radical foreign influence and seditious publications which might weaken the government. Three of these acts are reproduced here, including two giving the president power to deport immigrants and one which curtails the right of free speech. Although these were adopted in anticipation of a war between France and the United States many Republicans suspected that the laws were intended to weaken their party.*

### 6a.  An Act Concerning Aliens, June 25, 1798[7]

SECTION 1. *Be it enacted by the Senate and the House of Representatives of the United States of America in Congress assembled,* That it shall be lawful for the President of the United States at any time during the continuance of this act, to *order* all such *aliens* as he shall judge dangerous to the peace and safety of the United States, or shall have reasonable grounds to suspect are concerned in any treasonable or secret machinations against the government thereof, to depart out of the territory of the United Slates, within such time as shall be expressed in such order, which order shall be served on such alien by delivering him a copy thereof, or leaving the same at his usual abode, and returned to the office of the Secretary of State, by the marshal or other person to whom the same shall be directed. And in case any alien, so ordered to depart, shall be found at large within the United States after the time limited in such order for his departure, and not having obtained a *license* from the President to reside therein, or having obtained such *license* shall not have conformed thereto, every such alien shall, on conviction thereof, be imprisoned for a term not exceeding three years, and shall never after be admitted to become a citizen of the United States...

SEC. 3. *And be it further enacted,* That every master or commander of any ship or vessel which shall come into any port of the United States after the first day of July next, shall immediately on his arrival make report in writing to the collector or other chief officer of the customs of such port, of all aliens, if any, on board his vessel, specifying their names, age, the place of nativity, the country from which they shall have come, the nation to which they belong and owe allegiance, their occupation and a description of their persons, as far as he shall be informed thereof, and on failure, every such master and commander shall forfeit and pay three hundred dollars, for the payment whereof on default of such master or commander, such vessel shall also be holden, and may by such collector or other officer of the customs be detained. And it shall be the duty of such collector or other officer of the customs, forthwith to transmit to the office of the department of state true copies of all such returns...

### 6b.  An Act Respecting Alien Enemies, July 6, 1798[8]

SECTION 1. *Be it enacted by the Senate and House of Representatives of the United States of America in Congress assembled,* That whenever there shall be a declared war between the United States and any foreign nation or government, or any invasion or predatory incursion shall be perpetrated, attempted, or threatened against the territory of the United States, by any foreign nation or government, and the President of the United States shall make public proclamation of the event, all natives, citizens, denizens, or subjects of the hostile nation or government, being males of the age of fourteen years and upwards, who shall be within the United States, and not actually naturalized, shall be liable to be apprehended, restrained, secured and removed, as alien enemies. And the President of the United States shall be, and he is hereby authorized, in any event, as aforesaid, by his proclamation thereof, or other public act, to direct the conduct to be observed, on the part of the United States, towards the aliens who shall become liable, as aforesaid; the manner and degree of the restraint to which they shall be subject, and in what cases, and upon what security their residence shall be permitted, and to provide for the removal of those, who, not being permitted to reside within the United States, shall refuse or neglect to depart therefrom; and to establish any other regulations which shall be found necessary in the premises and for the public safety...

### 6c. An Act in Addition to the Act, Entitled "An Act for the Punishment of Certain Crimes Against the United States"[9]

SECTION 1. *Be it enacted by the Senate and House of Representatives of the United States of America, in Congress assembled,* That if any persons shall unlawfully combine or conspire together, with intent to oppose any measure or measures of the government of the United States, which are or shall be directed by proper authority, or to impede the operation of any law of the United States, or to intimidate or prevent any person holding a place or office in or under the government of the United States, from undertaking, performing or executing his trust or duty; and if any person or persons, with intent as aforesaid, shall counsel, advise or attempt to procure any insurrection, riot, unlawful assembly, or combination, whether such conspiracy, threatening, counsel, advice, or attempt shall have the proposed effect or not, he or they shall be deemed guilty of a high misdemeanor, and on conviction, before any court of the United States having jurisdiction thereof, shall be punished by a fine not exceeding five thousand dollars, and by imprisonment during a term not less than six months nor exceeding five years; and further, at the discretion of the court may be holden to find sureties for his good behaviour in such sum, and for such time, as the said court may direct.

SEC. 2. *And be it farther enacted,* That if any person shall write, print, utter or publish, or shall cause or procure to be written, printed, uttered or published, or shall knowingly and willingly assist or aid in writing, printing, uttering or publishing any false, scandalous and malicious writing or writings against the government of the United States, or either house of the Congress of the United States, or the President of the United States, with intent to defame the said government, or either house of the said Congress, or the said President, or to bring them, or either of them, into contempt or disrepute; or to excite against them, or either or any of them, the hatred of the good people of the United States, or to stir up sedition within the United States, or to excite any unlawful combinations therein, for opposing or resisting any law of the United States, or any act of the President of the United States, done in pursuance of any such law, or of the powers in him vested by the constitution of the United States, or to resist, oppose, or defeat any such law or act, or to aid, encourage or abet any hostile designs of any foreign nation against United States, their people or government, then such person, being thereof convicted before any court of the United States having jurisdiction thereof, shall be punished by a fine not exceeding two thousand dollars, and by imprisonment not exceeding two years...

## 7. The Virginia and Kentucky Resolutions

*On November 13 and December 24, 1798, the legislatures of Kentucky and Virginia adopted a series of resolutions, drafted by Jefferson (Kentucky) and Madison (Virginia), that condemned the Alien and Sedition Acts and endorsed a strict interpretation of the Constitution asserting the government had no authority to adopt such restrictive measures. The resolutions were premised on the belief that the individual states should determine whether federal legislation was constitutional or not. No other state endorsed the resolutions.*

### 7a.  Virginia Resolutions, December 21, 1798[10]

RESOLVED, That the General Assembly of Virginia, doth unequivocably express a firm resolution to maintain and defend the Constitution of the United States, and the Constitution of this State, against every aggression either foreign or domestic; and that they will support the Government of the United States in all measures warranted by the former.

That this Assembly most solemnly declares, a warm attachment to the Union of the States, to maintain which it pledges its powers; and, that for this end, it is their duty to watch over and *oppose every infraction of those principles which constitute the only basis of that Union*, because a faithful observance of them, can alone secure its existence and the public happiness.

That this Assembly doth explicitly and peremptorily declare, THAT IT VIEWS THE POWERS OF THE FEDERAL GOVERNMENT, AS RESULTING FROM THE COMPACT, TO WHICH THE STATES ARE PARTIES, AS LIMITED BY THE PLAIN SENSE AND INTENTION OF THE INSTRUMENT CONSTITUTING THE COMPACT, AS NO FARTHER VALID THAN THEY ARE AUTHORIZED BY THE GRANTS ENUMERATED IN THAT COMPACT; AND THAT IN CASE OF A DELIBERATE, PALPABLE, AND DANGEROUS EXERCISE OF OTHER POWERS, NOT GRANTED BY THE SAID COMPACT, THE STATES, WHO ARE PARTIES THERETO, HAVE THE RIGHT, AND ARE IN DUTY BOUND, TO INTERPOSE, FOR ARRESTING THE PROGRESS OF THE EVIL, AND FOR MAINTAINING WITHIN THEIR RESPECTIVE LIMITS, THE AUTHORITIES, RIGHTS AND LIBERTIES APPERTAINING TO THEM.

That the General Assembly doth also express its deep regret, that a spirit has, in sundry instances, been manifested by the Federal Government, to enlarge its powers by forced constructions of the constitutional charter which defines them; and, that implications have appeared of a design to expound certain general phrases (which, having been copied from the very limited grant of powers in the former articles of confederation were the less liable to be misconstrued) so as to destroy the meaning and effect, of the particular enumeration which necessarily explains, and limits the general phrases, and so as to *consolidate the states by degrees, into one sovereignty, the obvious tendency and inevitable result of which would be, to transform the present republican system of the United States, into an absolute, or at best, a mixed monarchy.*

That the General Assembly doth particularly protest against the palpable, and alarming infractions of the Constitution, in the two late cases of the "Alien and Sedition Acts" passed at the last session of Congress; the first of which, exercises a power no where delegated to the Federal Government, and which by uniting Legislative and Judicial powers to those of Executive, subverts the general principles of free government, as well as the particular organization and positive provisions of the Federal Constitution; and the other of which acts, exercises in like manner, a power not delegated by the Constitution, but on the contrary, expressly and positively forbidden by one of the amendments thereto; a power, which more than any other, ought to produce universal alarm, because it is levelled against the right of freely examining public characters and measures, and of free communication among the people thereon, which has ever been justly deemed, the only effectual guardian of every other right.

That this state having by its Convention, which ratified the Federal Constitution, expressly declared, that among other essential rights, "the liberty of conscience and of the press cannot be cancelled, abridged, restrained, or modified by any authority of the United States," and from its extreme anxiety to guard these rights from every possible attack of sophistry or ambition, having with other States, recommended an amendment for that purpose, which amendment was, in due time, annexed to the Constitution, it would mark a reproachable inconsistency, and criminal degeneracy, if an indifference were now shewn, to the most palpable violation of one of the rights, thus declared and secured; and to the establishment of a precedent which may be fatal to the other.

That the good people of this Commonwealth, having ever felt, and continuing to feel the most sincere affection for their brethren of the other States; the truest anxiety for establishing and perpetuating the union of all; and the most scrupulous fidelity to that Constitution, which is the pledge of mutual friendship, and the instrument of mutual happiness; the General Assembly doth solemnly appeal to the like dispositions in the other states, in confidence, that they will concur with this Commonwealth, in declaring, as it does hereby declare, that the acts aforesaid, are UNCONSTITUTIONAL; and, that the necessary and proper measures will be taken *by each* for co-operating with this State, in maintaining unrepaired the authorities, rights, and liberties, referred to the States respectively, or to the people.

That the Governor be desired to transmit a copy of the foregoing resolutions to the Executive authority of each of the other States, with a request, that the same may be communicated to the Legislature thereof; and that a copy be furnished to each of the Senators and Representatives representing this State in the Congress of the United States.

### 7b.  *Kentucky Resolutions, December 3, 1799*[11]

The representatives of the good people of this Commonwealth, in General Assembly convened, having maturely considered the answers of sundry States in the Union, to their resolutions passed the last session, respecting certain unconstitutional laws of Congress, commonly called the Alien and Sedition Laws, would be faithless, indeed, to themselves and to those they represent, were they silently to acquiesce in principles and doctrines attempted to be maintained in all those answers, that of Virginia only excepted. To again enter the field of argument, and attempt more fully or forcibly to expose the unconstitutionality of those obnoxious laws, would, it is apprehended be as unnecessary as unavailing. We cannot, however, but lament, that, in the discussion of those interesting subjects, by sundry of the Legislatures of our sister States, unfounded suggestions, and uncandid insinuations, derogatory to the true character and principles of this Commonwealth has been substituted in place of fair reasoning and sound argument. Our opinions of those alarming measures of the General Government, together with our reasons for those opinions, were detailed with decency, and with temper, and submitted to the discussion and judgment of our fellow citizens throughout the Union. Whether the like decency and temper have been observed in the answers of most of those States, who have denied or attempted to obviate the great truths contained in those resolutions, we have now only to submit to a candid world. Faithful to the true principles of the Federal Union, unconscious of any designs to disturb the harmony of that Union, and anxious only to escape the fangs of despotism, the good people of this commonwealth are regardless of censure or calumniation. Least, however, the silence of this commonwealth should be construed into an acquiescence in the doctrines and principles advanced and attempted to be maintained by the said answers, or least those of our fellow-citizens throughout the Union who so widely differ from us on those important subjects, should be deluded by the expectation, that we shall be deterred from what we conceive our duty; or shrink from the principles contained in those resolutions—therefore.

*Resolved.* That this Commonwealth considers the Federal Union, upon the terms and for the purposes specified in the late compact, as conducive to the liberty and happiness of the several States: That it does now unequivocally declare its attachment to the Union, and to that compact, agreeably to its obvious and real intention, and will be among the last to seek its dissolution: That if those who administer the General Government be permitted to transgress the limits fixed by that compact, by a total disregard to the special delegations of power therein contained, an annihilation of the State Governments, and the creation upon their ruins, of a General Consolidated Government, will be the inevitable consequence: *THAT THE PRINCIPLE AND CONSTRUCTION CONTENDED FOR BY SUNDRY OF THE STATE LEGISLATURES, THAT THE GENERAL GOVERNMENT IS THE EXCLUSIVE JUDGE OF THE EXTENT OF THE POWERS DELEGATED TO IT, STOP NOTHING SHORT OF DESPOTISM—SINCE THE DISCRETION OF THOSE WHO ADMINISTER THE GOVERNMENT, AND NOT THE CONSTITUTION, WOULD BE THE MEASURE OF THEIR POWERS:* That the several States who formed that instrument being sovereign and independent, have the unquestionable right to judge of its infraction; and, THAT A NULLIFICATION, BY THOSE SOVEREIGNTIES, OF ALL UNAU-THORIZED ACTS DONE UNDER COLOUR OF THAT INSTRUMENT, IS THE RIGHTFUL REMEDY: That this Commonwealth does, upon the most deliberate reconsideration, declare, that the said Alien and SeditionLaws are, in their opinion, palpable violations of the said Constitution; and, however cheerfully it may be disposed to surrender its opinion to a majority of its sister States, in matters of ordinary or doubtful policy, yet, in momentous regulations like the present, which so vitally wound the best rights of the citizen, it would consider a silent acquiescence as highly criminal: That although this Commonwealth, as a party to the Federal compact, will bow to the laws of the Union, yet, it does, at the same time declare, that it will not now, or ever hereafter, cease to oppose in a constitutional manner, every attempt at what quarter soever offered, to violate that compact.

And, finally, in order that no pretext or arguments may be drawn from a supposed acquiescence on the part of this Commonwealth in the constitutionality of those laws, and be thereby used as precedents for similar future violations of the Federal compacts—this Commonwealth does now enter against them its SOLEMN PROTEST.

## Notes

1. Alexander Hamilton, First Report on Public Credit, January 14, 1790, *American State Papers: Finance,* 1:15–18. This document has been edited for length. The full version can be found at the book's website (http://www.routledge.com/textbooks/revolutionaryamerica/).
2. Alexander Hamilton, Report on Manufactures, December 5, 1791, *American State Papers: Finance,* 1:123, 125–127. This document has been edited for length. The full version can be found at the book's website (http://www.routledge.com/textbooks/revolutionaryamerica/).
3. Thomas Jefferson, *Notes on the State of Virginia* (Philadelphia: Prichard and Hall, 1788), 174–175. This document has been edited for length. The full version can be found at the book's website (http://www.routledge.com/textbooks/revolutionaryamerica/).
4. *Pennsylvania Independent Gazetteer,* February 6, 1790.
5. "George Washington to Daniel Morgan, October 8, 1794," in John C. Fitzpatrick (ed.), *The Writings of George Washington,* 39 vols. (Washington, DC: Government Printing Office, 1931-44), 33:522–524.
6. "George Washington's Farewell Address, September 19, 1796," in Fitzpatrick (ed.), *Writings of George Washington,* 35:214–238. This document has been edited for length. The full version can be found at the book's website (http://www.routledge.com/textbooks/revolutionaryamerica/).
7. *Statutes at Large,* 5th Congress, 2nd Session, 570-72. This document has been edited for length. The full version can be found at the book's website (http://www.routledge.com/textbooks/revolutionaryamerica/).
8. *Statutes at Large,* 5th Congress, 2nd Session, 577. This document has been edited for length. The full version can be found at the book's website (http://www.routledge.com/textbooks/revolutionaryamerica/).
9. *Statutes at Large,* 5th Congress, 2nd Session, 596–597. This document has been edited for length. The full version can be found at the book's website (http://www.routledge.com/textbooks/revolutionaryamerica/).
10. Jonathan Elliot (ed.), *The Virginia and Kentucky Resolutions of 1798 and '99* (Washington, DC: 1832), 5–6.
11. Jonathan Elliot (ed.), *The Virginia and Kentucky Resolutions of 1798 and '99* (Washington, DC: 1832), 19–20.

CHAPTER **11**

# An Empire of Liberty, 1801–1815

## Introduction

Westward expansion and overseas trade were the twin pillars of the Republican Party during the presidential administrations of Thomas Jefferson and James Madison (1801–1817). In the Ordinance of 1784 (document 1), Jefferson outlined a scheme for the orderly western expansion of the United States, under the terms of which new states could be carved out of western territory and would enter the union on equal terms with the original states. This established the pattern for the westward expansion of the United States during the early republic. Jefferson articulated his republican vision in his first inaugural address (document 2). He sought to strike a conciliatory tone in this address. Nonetheless, the Federalist opposition to Jefferson remained potent as evidenced by cartoons such as "Mad Tom in a Rage" (document 3). Despite domestic opposition, Jefferson pursued a policy of westward expansion. Jefferson's instructions to Meriwether Lewis (document 4) reveal the multiple motives—political, diplomatic, economic, and scientific—behind this policy. The great achievement of Jefferson's presidency was the Louisiana Purchase, and Jefferson's letter of September 7, 1803, to Senator Wilson Cary Nicholas (document 5) and his subsequent message to Congress on October 17, 1803 (document 6) consider the reasons for the purchase as well as examine the constitutional issues arising from the transaction.

For Jefferson, land without commerce was useless. During Jefferson's second administration and the first term of his successor, James Madison, the United States was confronted by persistent interference with its overseas trade. While the United States, as a neutral carrier, championed free trade; the warring European powers, particularly France and Britain, sought to restrict American commerce. In an effort to protect its commercial rights, the United States instituted a trade embargo in 1807. The embargo proved to be economically deleterious for the United States and was very unpopular as shown by the anti-embargo "Ograbme" cartoon (document 7). Ultimately, the United State failed to secure its trade, and James Madison asked Congress for a declaration of war against Britain in June of 1812. The war, seen by many Americans as a "second war of independence," prompted an outpouring of nationalism in the new republic as seen in documents 8 and 9, including Francis Scott Key's poem, which became the national anthem of the United States. Notwithstanding the surge in nationalism that accompanied the war, there was substantial domestic opposition to the conflict, particularly in the northeast. In December of 1814 leading New England Federalists gathered in Hartford, Connecticut, and discussed secession as a response to what they perceived as a Republican war intended to benefit the south and west (document 10). The Hartford Convention occurred as the war drew to an end and discredited the Federalists who were tainted with disloyalty. The Federalists' ignominy was sealed several days after the Hartford Convention when Andrew Jackson led American forces to a decisive victory over the British in the final battle of the war (document 11). The Battle of New Orleans was fought several weeks after the Treaty of Ghent, which formally ended the War of 1812—though had the British captured New Orleans in 1815, they may have sought to retain that strategic port.

## 1.  The Ordinance of 1784[1]

*The Ordinance of 1784 was an early effort by the United States government to organize territory north and west of the Ohio River. Thomas Jefferson was the author of the ordinance which called for the division of western land into separate territories to be governed by the United States until they had attained the same population as the least populous state in the United States. At that point, the territories could apply for statehood. The new states would have the same rights as the original thirteen states. The provisions of the Ordinance of 1784 were incorporated into the Northwest Ordinance of 1787. The Ordinance of 1784 was testimony to Jefferson's belief that the future of the American republic lay in western expansion and settlement.*

*By the* UNITED STATES *in* Congress *Assembled,* April 23, 1784

RESOLVED, THAT so much of the territory ceded, or to be ceded by individual states, to the United States, as is already purchased, or shall be purchased, of the Indian inhabitants, and offered for sale by Congress, shall be divided into distinct states in the following manner, as nearly as such cessions will admit; that is to say, by parallels of latitude, so that each state shall comprehend from north to south two degrees of latitude, beginning to count from the completion of forty five degrees north of the equator; and by meridians of longitude, one of which shall pass through the lowest point of the rapids of Ohio, and the other through the western cape of the mouth of the great Kanhaway: but the territory eastward of this last meridian, between the Ohio, Lake Erie, and Pennsylvania, shall be one state, whatsoever may be its comprehension of latitude. That which may lie beyond the completion of the forty-fifth degree between the said meridians shall make part of the state adjoining it on the south: and that part of the Ohio, which is between the same meridians coinciding nearly with the parallel of thirty-nine degrees; shall be substituted so far in lieu of that parallel as a boundary line.

That the settlers on any territory so purchased and offered for sale, shall, either on their own petition or on the order of Congress, receive authority from them, with appointments of time and place, for their free males of full age within the limits of their state to meet together, for the purpose of establishing a temporary government, to adopt the constitution and laws of any one of the original states; so that such laws nevertheless shall be subject to a like alteration, counties, townships, or other divisions, for the election of members for their legislature.

That when any such state shall have acquired twenty thousand free inhabitants, on giving due proof thereof to Congress, they shall receive from them authority with appointments of time and place, to call a convention of representatives, to establish a permanent constitution and government for themselves. Provided that both the temporary and permanent governments be established on these principles as their basis.

FIRST. That they shall for ever remain a part of this confederacy of the United States of America.

SECOND. That they shall be subject to the articles of confederation in all those cases in which the original states shall be subject, and to all the acts and ordinances of the United States in Congress, assembled, conformable thereto.

THIRD. That they in no case shall interfere with the primary disposal of the soil by the United States in Congress assembled; nor with the ordinances and regulations which Congress may find necessary for securing the title in such soil to the bona fide purchasers.

FOURTH. That they shall be subject to pay a part of the federal debts, contracted or to be contracted; to be apportioned on them by Congress, according to the same common rule and measure by which apportionments thereof shall be made on the other states.

FIFTH. That no tax shall be imposed on lands the property of the United States.

SIXTH. That their respective governments shall be republican.

SEVENTH. That the lands of non resident proprietors shall in no case be taxed higher than those of residents within any new state, before the admission thereof to a vote by its delegates in Congress.

That whensoever any of the said states shall have of free inhabitants, as many as shall then be in any one, the least numerous of the thirteen original states, such state shall be admitted by its delegates into the Congress of the United States, on an equal footing with the said original states; provided the consent of so many states in Congress is first obtained as may at the time be competent to such admission. And in order to adapt the said articles of confederation to the state of Congress, when its numbers shall be thus encreased, it shall be proposed to the legislatures of the states, originally parties thereto, to require the assent of two thirds of the United States in Congress assembled, in all those cases wherein by the said articles, the assent of nine states is now required; which being agreed to by them, shall be binding on the new states. Until such admission by their Delegates into Congress, any of the said states after the establishment of their temporary government shall have authority to keep a member in Congress, with a right of debating, but not of voting.

That measures not inconsistent with the principles of the confederation, and necessary for the preservation of peace and good order among the settlers, in any of the said new states, until they shall assume a temporary government as aforesaid, may from time to time be taken by the United States in Congress assembled.

That the preceding articles shall be formed into a charter of compact; shall be duly executed by the President of the United States in Congress assembled, under his hand, and the seal of the United States; shall be promulgated; and shall stand as fundamental constitutions between the thirteen original states, and each of the several states now newly described, unalterable from and after the sale of any part of the territory of such state, pursuant to this resolve, but by the joint consent of the United States in Congress assembled, and of the particular state within such alteration is proposed to be made.

## 2. Thomas Jefferson, First Inaugural Address, March 4, 1801[2]

*Thomas Jefferson took the presidential oath at noon on March 4, 1801, in the Senate chamber in the Capitol. His inauguration was the first peaceful transfer of power between two political parties in the history of the American republic. After the contentious election of 1800, Jefferson sought to strike a conciliatory tone in his address while laying out the fundamental principles which would animate his presidency.*

*Friends and Fellow Citizens,*
Called upon to undertake the duties of the first executive office of our country, I avail myself of the presence of that portion of my fellow-citizens which is here assembled to express my grateful thanks for the favor with which they have been pleased to look toward me, to declare a sincere consciousness that the task is above my talents, and that I approach it with those anxious and awful presentiments which the greatness of the charge and the weakness of my powers so justly inspire. A rising nation, spread over a wide and fruitful land, traversing all the seas with the rich productions of their industry, engaged in commerce with nations who feel power and forget right, advancing rapidly to destinies beyond the reach of mortal eye—when I contemplate these transcendent objects, and see the honor, the happiness, and the hopes of this beloved country committed

to the issue and the auspices of this day, I shrink from the contemplation, and humble myself before the magnitude of the undertaking. Utterly, indeed, should I despair did not the presence of many whom I here see remind me that in the other high authorities provided by our Constitution I shall find resources of wisdom, of virtue, and of zeal on which to rely under all difficulties. To you, then, gentlemen, who are charged with the sovereign functions of legislation, and to those associated with you, I look with encouragement for that guidance and support which may enable us to steer with safety the vessel in which we are all embarked amidst the conflicting elements of a troubled world.

During the contest of opinion through which we have passed the animation of discussions and of exertions has sometimes worn an aspect which might impose on strangers unused to think freely and to speak and to write what they think; but this being now decided by the voice of the nation, announced according to the rules of the Constitution, all will, of course, arrange themselves under the will of the law, and unite in common efforts for the common good. All, too, will bear in mind this sacred principle, that though the will of the majority is in all cases to prevail, that will to be rightful must be reasonable; that the minority possess their equal rights, which equal law must protect, and to violate would be oppression. Let us, then, fellow-citizens, unite with one heart and one mind. Let us restore to social intercourse that harmony and affection without which liberty and even life itself are but dreary things. And let us reflect that, having banished from our land that religious intolerance under which mankind so long bled and suffered, we have yet gained little if we countenance a political intolerance as despotic, as wicked, and capable of as bitter and bloody persecutions. During the throes and convulsions of the ancient world, during the agonizing spasms of infuriated man, seeking through blood and slaughter his long-lost liberty, it was not wonderful that the agitation of the billows should reach even this distant and peaceful shore; that this should be more felt and feared by some and less by others, and should divide opinions as to measures of safety. But every difference of opinion is not a difference of principle. We have called by different names brethren of the same principle. We are all Republicans, we are all Federalists. If there be any among us who would wish to dissolve this Union or to change its republican form, let them stand undisturbed as monuments of the safety with which error of opinion may be tolerated where reason is left free to combat it. I know, indeed, that some honest men fear that a republican government can not be strong, that this Government is not strong enough; but would the honest patriot, in the full tide of successful experiment, abandon a government which has so far kept us free and firm on the theoretic and vision-ary fear that this Government, the world's best hope, may by possibility want energy to preserve itself? I trust not. I believe this, on the contrary, the strongest Government on earth. I believe it the only one where every man, at the call of the law, would fly to the standard of the law, and would meet invasions of the public order as his own personal concern. Sometimes it is said that man can not be trusted with the government of himself. Can he, then, be trusted with the government of others? Or have we found angels in the forms of kings to govern him? Let history answer this question.

Let us, then, with courage and confidence pursue our own Federal and Republican principles, our attachment to union and representative government. Kindly separated by nature and a wide ocean from the exterminating havoc of one quarter of the globe; too high-minded to endure the degradations of the others; possessing a chosen country, with room enough for our descendants to the thousandth and thousandth generation; entertaining a due sense of our equal right to the use of our own faculties, to the acquisitions of our own industry, to honor and confidence from our fellow-citizens, resulting not from birth, but from our actions and their sense of them; enlightened by a benign religion, professed, indeed, and practiced in various forms, yet all of them inculcating honesty, truth, temperance, gratitude, and the love of man; acknowledging and adoring an overruling Providence, which by all its dispensations proves that it delights in the happiness of man here and his greater happiness hereafter—with all these blessings, what more is necessary to make us a happy and a prosperous people? Still one thing more, fellow-citizens—a wise and frugal Government, which shall restrain men from injuring one another, shall leave them otherwise free to regulate their own pursuits of industry and improvement, and shall not take from the mouth of labor the bread it has earned. This is the sum of good government, and this is necessary to close the circle of our felicities.

About to enter, fellow-citizens, on the exercise of duties which comprehend everything dear and valuable to you, it is proper you should understand what I deem the essential principles of our Government, and consequently those which ought to shape its Administration. I will compress them within the narrowest compass they will bear, stating the general principle, but not all its limitations. Equal and exact justice to all men, of whatever state or persuasion, religious or political; peace, commerce, and honest friendship with all nations, entangling alliances with none; the support of the State governments in all their rights, as the most competent administrations for our domestic concerns and the surest bulwarks against antirepublican tendencies; the preservation of the General Government in its whole constitutional vigor, as the sheet anchor of our peace at home and safety abroad; a jealous care of the right of election by the people—a mild and safe corrective of abuses which are lopped by the sword of revolution where peaceable remedies are unprovided; absolute acquiescence in the decisions of the majority, the vital principle of republics, from which is no appeal but to force, the vital principle and immediate parent of despotism; a well-disciplined militia, our best reliance in peace and for the first moments of war till regulars may relieve them; the supremacy of the civil over the military authority; economy in the public expense, that labor may be lightly burthened; the honest payment of our debts and sacred preservation of the public faith; encouragement of agriculture, and of commerce as its handmaid; the diffusion of information and arraignment of all abuses at the bar of the public reason; freedom of religion; freedom of the press, and freedom of person under the protection of the habeas corpus, and trial by juries impartially selected. These principles form the bright constellation which has gone before us and guided our steps through an age of revolution and reformation. The wisdom of our sages and blood of our heroes have been devoted to their attainment. They should be the creed of our political faith, the text of civic instruction, the touchstone by which to try the services of those we trust; and should we wander from them in moments of error or of alarm, let us hasten to retrace our steps and to regain the road which alone leads to peace, liberty, and safety.

I repair, then, fellow-citizens, to the post you have assigned me. With experience enough in subordinate offices to have seen the difficulties of this the greatest of all, I have learnt to expect that it will rarely fall to the lot of imperfect man to retire from this station with the reputation and the favor which bring him into it. Without pretensions to that high confidence you reposed in our first and greatest revolutionary character, whose preeminent services had entitled him to the first place in his country's love and destined for him the fairest page in the volume of faithful history, I ask so much confidence only as may give firmness and effect to the legal administration of your affairs. I shall often go wrong through defect of judgment. When right, I shall often be thought wrong by those whose positions will not command a view of the whole ground. I ask your indulgence for my own errors, which will never be intentional, and your support against the errors of others, who may condemn what they would not if seen in all its parts. The approbation implied by your suffrage is a great consolation to me for the past, and my future solicitude will be to retain the good opinion of those who have bestowed it in advance, to conciliate that of others by doing them all the good in my power, and to be instrumental to the happiness and freedom of all.

Relying, then, on the patronage of your good will, I advance with obedience to the work, ready to retire from it whenever you become sensible how much better choice it is in your power to make. And may that Infinite Power which rules the destinies of the universe lead our councils to what is best, and give them a favorable issue for your peace and prosperity.

### 3.  Mad Tom in a Rage, 1801[3]

*Despite the conciliatory tone of Jefferson's first inaugural address, his administration was characterized by bitter partisanship. This Federalist cartoon depicts Jefferson, assisted by the Devil, attempting to pull down the federal government, represented by the pillar inscribed with the names of his presidential predecessors, George Washington and John Adams.*

**Figure 11.1** Mad Tom in a Rage, 1801. Courtesy of the Granger Collection, New York.

## 4. Instructions to Lewis and Clark[4]

*Jefferson's interest in the west was political, strategic, and scientific. In this letter written to Meriwether Lewis (1774–1809) in anticipation of Lewis's expedition to the Pacific with William Clark (1770–1838), Jefferson emphasizes each of these themes as he instructed Lewis on how he should conduct himself and record his observations during his expedition to the Pacific (1804–1806). Jefferson makes clear that the expedition has strategic as well as diplomatic and scientific objectives.*

Your situation as Secretary of the President of the US. has made you acquainted with the objects of my confidential message of Jan. 18. 1803 to the legislature; you have seen the act they passed, which they expressed in general terms, was meant to sanction these objects, and you are appointed to carry them into execution.

Instruments for ascertaining by celestial observations, the geography of the country through which you will pass, have been already provided. Light articles for barter and presents among the Indians, arms for your attendants, say from 10. to 12. men, boats, tents, & other travelling apparatus with ammunition, medicine, surgical instruments and provisions you will have prepared with such aids as the Secretary at War can yield in his department; & from him also you will recieve authority to engage among our troops, by voluntary agreement, the number of attendants above mentioned, over whom you, as their commanding officer, are invested with all the powers the laws give in such a case.

As your movements while within the limits of the US. will be better directed by occasional communications, adapted to circumstances as they arise, they will not be noticed here. What follows will respect your proceedings after your departure from the United States.

Your mission has been communicated to the ministers here from France, Spain & Great Britain, and through them to their governments; & such assurances given them as to it's objects as we trust will satisfy them. The country of Louisiana having been ceded by Spain to France, the passport you have from the minister of France, the representative of the present sovereign of the country, will be a protection with all its subjects, & that from the minister of England will entitle you to the friendly aid of any traders of that allegiance with whom you may happen to meet.

The object of your mission is to explore the Missouri river, & such principal stream of it as by it's course and communication with the waters of the Pacific ocean whether the Columbia, Oregon, Colorado or any other river may offer the most direct & practicable water communication across this continent for the purposes of commerce.

Beginning at the mouth of the Missouri, you will take observations of latitude & longitude at all remarkable points on the river, & especially at the mouth of rivers, at rapids, at islands, & other places & objects distinguished by such natural marks & characters of a durable kind as that they may with certainty be recognized hereafter. The course of the river between these points of observation may be supplied by the compass, the log-line & by time, corrected by the observations themselves. The variations of the compass too, in different places should be noticed.

The interesting points of the portage between the heads of the Missouri, & of the water offering the best communication with the Pacific ocean, should also be fixed by observation, & the course of that water to the ocean, in the same manner as that of the Missouri.

Your observations are to be taken with great pains & accuracy, to be entered distinctly & intelligibly for others, as well as yourself, to comprehend all the elements necessary, with the aid of the usual tables, to fix the latitude and longitude of the places at which they were taken, and are to be rendered to the war office for the purpose of having the calculations made concurrently by proper persons within the US. several copies of these as well as of your other notes should be made at leisure times, & put into the care of the most trust-worthy of your attendants, to guard by multiplying them against the accidental losses to which they will be exposed. A further guard would be that one these copies be on the paper of the birch, as less liable to injury from damp than common paper.

The commerce which may be carried on with the people inhabiting the line your will pursue, renders a knolege of those people important. You will therefore endeavour to make yourself acquainted, as far as a diligent pursuit of your journey shall admit,

> with the names of the nations & their numbers;
> the extent & limits of their possessions;
> their relations with other tribes of nations;
> their language, traditions, monuments;
> their ordinary occupations in agriculture, fishing, hunting, war, arts & the implements for these;
> their food, clothing, & domestic accomodations;
> the diseases prevalent among them, & the remedies they use;
> moral & physical circumstances which distinguish them from the tribes we know;
> peculiarities in their laws, customs & dispositions;
> and articles of commerce they may need or furnish & to what extent.

And considering the interest which every nation has in extending & strengthening the authority of reason & justice among the people around them, it will be useful to acquire what knolege you can of the state of morality, religion, & information among them; as it may better enable those who may endeavor to civilize & instruct them, to adapt their measures to the existing notions & practices of those on whom they are to operate.

> Other objects worthy of notice will be
> the soil & face of the country it's growth & vegetable productions, especially those not of the US.
> the animals of the country generally, & especially those not known in the US.
> the remains & accounts of any which may be deemed rare or extinct;
> the mineral productions of every kind; but more particularly metals; limestone, pit-coal, & salt-petre; salines & mineral waters, noting the temperature of the last & such circumstances as may indicate their character;
> volcanic appearances;
> climate, as characterized by the thermometer, by the proportion of rainy, cloudy, & clear days, by lightening, hail, snow, ice, by the access & recess of frost, by the winds prevailing at different seasons, the dates at which particular plants put forth or lose their flower, or leaf, times of appearance of particular birds, reptiles or insects.

Altho' your route will be along the channel of the Missouri, yet you will endeavor to inform yourself, by enquiry, of the character & extent of the country watered by it's branches & especially on it's Southern side, the North river or Rio Bravo which runs into the gulph of Mexico, and the North river, or Rio colorado which runs into the gulph of California, are understood to be the principal streams heading opposite to the waters of the Missouri, and running Southwardly. Whether the dividing grounds between the Missouri & them are mountains or flat lands, what are their distance from the Missouri, the character of the intermediate country, & the people inhabiting it, are worthy of particular enquiry. The Northern waters of the Missouri are less to be enquired after, because they have been ascertained to a considerable degree, & are still in a course of ascertainment by English traders, and travellers. But if you can learn any thing certain of the most Northern source of the Missisipi, & of it's position relatively to the lake of the woods, it will be interesting to us. some account too of the path of the Canadian traders from the Missisipi, at the mouth of the Ouisconsing to where it strikes the Missouri, & of the soil and rivers in its course, is desirable.

In all your intercourse with the natives, treat them in the most friendly & conciliatory manner which their own conduct will admit; allay all jealousies as to the object of your journey, satisfy them of it's innocence, make them acquainted with the position, extent character, peaceable & commercial dispositions of the US. of our wish to be neighborly, friendly, & useful to them, & of our dispositions to a commercial intercourse with them; confer with them on the points most convenient as mutual emporiums, and the articles of most desireable interchange for them & us. If a few of their influential chiefs within practicable distance, wish to visit us, arrange such a visit with them, and furnish them with authority to call on our officers, on their entering the US. to have them conveyed to this place at the public expence. If any of them should wish to have some of their young people brought up with us, & taught such arts as may be useful to them, we will recieve, instruct & take care of them. Such a mission whether of influential chiefs or of young people would give some security to your own party. carry with you some matter of the kinepox; inform those of them with whom you may be, of it's efficacy as a preservative from the smallpox; & instruct & encourage them in the use of it. This may be especially done wherever you winter.

As it is impossible for us to foresee in what manner you will be recieved by those people, whether with hospitality or hostility, so is it impossible to prescribe the exact degree of perseverance with which you are to pursue your journey. We value too much the lives of citizens to offer them to probable destruction. Your numbers will be sufficient to secure you against the unauthorised opposition of individuals or of small parties: but if a superior force authorised, or not authorised by a nation, should be arrayed against your further passage, and inflexibly determined to arrest it, you must decline it's farther pursuit, and return. In the loss of yourselves, we should lose also the information you will have acquired. By returning safely with that, you may enable us to renew the essay with better calculated means. To your own discretion therefore must be left the degree of danger you risk, and the point at which you should decline, only saying we wish you to err on the side of your safety, and to bring back your party safe even if it be with less information.

As far up the Missouri as the white settlements extend, an intercourse will probably be found to exist between them & the Spanish posts of St. Louis opposite Cahokia, or Ste. Genevieve opposite Kaskaskia. From still further up the river, the traders may furnish a conveyance for letters. Beyond that, you may perhaps be able to engage Indians to bring letters for the government to Cahokia or Kaskaskia, on promising that they shall there recieve such special compensation as you shall have stipulated with them. Avail yourself of these means to communicate to us, at seasonable intervals, a copy of your journal, notes & observations, of every kind, putting into cypher whatever might do injury if betrayed.

Should you reach the Pacific ocean inform yourself of the circumstances which may decide whether the furs of those parts may not be collected as advantageously at the head of the Missouri (convenient as is supposed to the waters of the Colorado & Oregan or Columbia) as at Nootka sound, or any other point of that coast; and that trade be consequently conducted through the Missouri & U.S. more beneficially than by the circumnavigation now practised.

On your arrival on that coast endeavor to learn if there by any port within your reach frequented by the sea-vessels of any nation, & to send two of your trusty people back by sea, in such way as shall appear practicable, with a copy of your notes: and should you be of opinion that the return of your party by the way they went will be eminently dangerous, then ship the whole, & return by sea, by the way either of cape Horn, or the cape of good Hope, as you shall be able. As you will be without money, clothes or provisions, you must endeavor to use the credit of the U.S. to obtain them, for which purpose open letters of credit shall be furnished you, authorising you to draw upon the Executive of the U.S. or any of it's officers, in any part of the world, on which draughts can be disposed of, & to apply with our recommendations to the Consuls, agents, merchants, or citizens of any nation with which we have intercourse, assuring them, in our name, that any aids they may furnish you, shall be honorably repaid, and on demand. Our consuls Thomas Hewes at Batavia in Java, Wm. Buchanan in the Isles of France & Bourbon & John Elmslie at the Cape of good Hope will be able to supply your necessities by draughts on us.

Should you find it safe to return by the way you go, after sending two of your party round by sea, or with your whole party, if no conveyance by sea can be found, do so; making such observations on your return, as may serve to supply, correct or confirm those made on your outward journey.

On re-entering the U.S. and reaching a place of safety, discharge any of your attendants who may desire & deserve it, procuring for them immediate paiment of all arrears of pay & cloathing which may have incurred since their departure, and assure them that they shall be recommended to the liberality of the legislature for the grant of a souldier's portion of land each, as proposed in my message to Congress; & repair yourself with your papers to the seat of government.

To provide, on the accident of your death, against anarchy, dispersion, & the consequent danger to your party, and total failure of the enterprise, you are hereby authorized, by any instrument signed & written in your own hand, to name the person among them who shall succeed to the command on your decease, and by like instruments to change the nomination from time to time as further experience of the characters accompanying you shall point out superior fitness: and all the powers and authorities given to yourself are, in the event of your death, transferred to, & vested in the successor so named, with further power to him, and his successors in like manner to name each his successor, who, on the death of his predecessor, shall be invested with all the powers & authorities given to yourself.

## 5.   The Constitutional Implications of the Louisiana Purchase[5]

*Soon after dispatching Lewis and Clark to explore the trans-Mississippi West, Jefferson learned that American diplomats in Paris had secured an agreement from Napoleon to sell the Louisiana Territory to the United States. Since the American diplomats, Robert Livingston (1746–1813) and James Monroe (1758–1831), had only been authorized to negotiate a purchase of New Orleans, Jefferson was concerned that they had exceeded their mandate. More generally, he worried about the constitutionality of the Louisiana Purchase. In this letter to Senator Wilson Cary Nicholas (1761–1820) of Virginia, Jefferson discusses the constitutional implications of the Louisiana Treaty upon which the Senate had yet to vote. He also expresses concern that the delay created by a constitutional amendment might cause the French to reconsider the agreement.*

Your favor of the 3d was delivered me at court; but we were much disappointed at not seeing you here, mr Madison & the Govt. being here at the time. I inclose you a letter from Monroe on the subject of the late treaty. you will observe a hint in it to do without delay what we are bound to do. there is reason in the opinion of our ministers, to believe that if the thing were to do over again, it could not be obtained, & that if we give the least opening, they will declare the treaty void. a warning amounting to that has been given to them, & an unusual kind of letter written by their minister to our Secretary of State direct. whatever Congress shall think it necessary to do, should be done with as little debate as possible, & particularly so far as respects the constitutional difficulty. I am aware of the force of the observations you made on the power given by the Constn. to Congress to admit new states into the Union, without restraining the subject to the territory then constituting the US. but when I consider that the limits of the US are precisely fixed by the treaty of 1783, that the constitution expressly declares itself to be made for the US, I cannot help believing the intention was to permit Congress to admit into the union new states which should be formed out of the territory for which & under whose authority alone they were then acting. I do not believe it was meant that they might receive England, Ireland, Holland &c into it, which would be the case on your construction. when an instrument admits two constructions the one safe, the other dangerous, the one precise the other indefinite, I prefer that which is safe & precise. I had rather ask an enlargement of power from the nation where it is found necessary, than to assume it by a construction which would make our power boundless. our peculiar security is in the possession of a written constitution. let us not make it a blank paper by construction. I say the same as to the opinion of those who consider the grant of the treaty making power as boundless. if it is, then we have no constitution. if it has bounds, they can be no others than the definitions of the powers which that instrument gives. it specifies & delineates the operations permitted to the federal government, and gives all the powers necessary to carry these into execution. whatever of these enumerated objects is proper for a law, Congress may make the law, whatever is proper to be executed by way of a treaty, the President & Senate may enter into the treaty; whatever is to be done by a judicial sentence, the judges may pass the sentence. nothing is more likely than that their enumeration of powers is defective. this is the ordinary case of all human works. let us go on then perfecting it, by adding by way of amendment to the constitution, these powers which time & trial show are still wanting, but it has been taken to much for granted that by this rigorous construction the treaty power would be reduced to nothing. I had occasion once to examine it's effect on the French treaty made by the old Congress, & found that out of thirty odd articles which that contained there were one, two, or three only which could not now be stipulated under our present constitution. I confess then I think it important in the present case to set an example against broad construction by appealing for new power to the people. if however our friends shall think differently, certainly I shall acquiesce with satisfaction, confiding that the good sense of our country will correct the evil of construction when it shall produce ill effects…no apologies for writing or speaking to me so freely are necessary. on the contrary nothing my friends can do, is so dear to me & proves to me their friendship so clearly, as the information they give me of their sentiments & those of others on interesting points when I am to act, and where information & warnings are so essential to excite in me that due reflection which ought to precede action…

### 6. Thomas Jefferson, Third Annual Message to Congress, October 17, 1803[6]

*Jefferson called Congress into a special session in October 1803. He wanted the Senate to ratify the treaty as required by the Constitution and both houses of Congress to appropriate the necessary funds to pay for the purchase of Louisiana as well as the cost of taking possession of the province. As such, he outlined the economic, political, and diplomatic justifications for the Louisiana Purchase in this message to Congress. The Senate ratified the Louisiana Treaty on October 20, 1803.*

In calling you together, fellow citizens, at an earlier day than was contemplated by the act of the last session of Congress, I have not been insensible to the personal inconveniences necessarily resulting from an unexpected change in your arrangements. But matters of great public concernment have rendered this call necessary, and the interest you feel in these will supersede in your minds all private considerations.

Congress witnessed, at their last session, the extraordinary agitation produced in the public mind by the suspension of our right of deposit at the port of New Orleans, no assignment of another place having been made according to treaty. They were sensible that the continuance of that privation would be more injurious to our nation than any consequences which could flow from any mode of redress, but reposing just confidence in the good faith of the Government whose officer had committed the wrong, friendly and reasonable representations were resorted to, and the right of deposit was restored.

Previous, however, to this period, we had not been unaware of the danger to which our peace would be perpetually exposed while so important a key to the commerce of the western country remained under foreign Power. Difficulties too were presenting themselves as to the navigation of other streams, which, arising within our territories, pass through those adjacent. Propositions had, therefore, been authorized for obtaining, on fair conditions, the sovereignty of New Orleans, and of other possessions in that quarter interesting to our quiet, to such extent as was deemed practicable; and the provisional appropriation of two millions of dollars, to be applied and accounted for by the President of the United States, intended as part of the price, was considered as conveying the sanction of Congress to the acquisition proposed. The enlightened Government of France saw, with just discernment, the importance to both nations of such liberal arrangements as might best and permanently promote the peace, friendship, and interests of both; and the property and sovereignty of all Louisiana, which had been restored to them, has, on certain conditions been transferred to the United States by instruments bearing date the 30th of April last. When these shall have received the Constitutional sanction of the Senate, they will, without delay be communicated to the Representatives for the exercise of their functions, as to those conditions which are within the powers vested by the Constitution in Congress. Whilst the property and sovereignty of the Mississippi and its waters secure an independent outlet for the produce of the Western States, and an uncontrolled navigation through their whole course, free from collision with other Powers, and the dangers to our peace from that source, the fertility of the country, its climate and extent, promise, in due season important aids to our Treasury, an ample provision for our posterity, and a wide-spread field for the blessings of freedom and equal laws.

With the wisdom of Congress it will rest to take those ulterior measures which may be necessary for the immediate occupation and temporary government of the country; for its incorporation into our Union; for rendering the change of government a blessing to our newly-adopted brethren; for securing to them the rights of conscience and of property: for confirming to the Indian inhabitants their occupancy and self-government, establishing friendly and commercial relations with them, and for ascertaining the geography of the country acquired. Such materials for your information relative to its affairs in general, as the short space of time has permitted me to collect, will be laid before you when the subject shall be in a state for your consideration.

Another important acquisition of territory has also been made since the last session of Congress. The friendly tribe of Kaskaskia Indians, with which we have never had a difference, reduced by the wars and wants of savage life to a few individuals, unable to defend themselves against the neighboring tribes, has transferred its country to the United States, reserving only for its members what is sufficient to maintain them in an agricultural way. The considerations stipulated are, that we shall extend to them our patronage and protection, and give them certain annual aids, in money, in implements of agriculture, and other articles of their choice. This country, among the most fertile within our limits, extending along the Mississippi from the mouth of the Illinois to and up the Ohio, though not so necessary as a barrier since the acquisition of the other bank, may yet be well worthy of being laid open to immediate settlement, as its inhabitants may descend with rapidity in support of the lower country should future circumstances expose that to foreign enterprise. As the stipulations in this treaty also involve matters within the competence of both Houses only, it will be laid before Congress as soon as the senate shall have advised its ratification.

With many other Indian tribes improvements in agriculture and household manufacture are advancing; and, with all our peace and friendship are established on grounds much firmer than heretofore. The measure adopted of establishing trading houses among them, and of furnishing them necessaries in exchange for their commodities, at such moderated prices as leave no gain, but cover us from loss, has the most conciliatory and useful effect upon them, and is that which will best secure their peace and good will.

The small vessels authorized by Congress with a view to the Mediterranean service, have been sent into that sea, and will be able more effectually to confine the Tripoline cruisers within their harbors, and supersede the necessity of convoy to our commerce in that quarter. They will sensibly lessen the expenses of that service the ensuing year.

A further knowledge of the ground in the northeastern and northwestern angles of the United States has evinced that the boundaries established by the treaty of Paris, between the British territories and ours in those parts, were too imperfectly described to be susceptible of execution. It has therefore been thought worthy of attention, for preserving and cherishing the harmony and useful intercourse subsisting between the two nations, to remove, by timely arrangements what unfavorable incidents might otherwise render a ground of future misunderstanding. A convention has therefore been entered into, which provides for a practicable demarkation of those limits to the satisfaction of both parties...

Should the acquisition of Louisiana be Constitutionally confirmed and carried into effect, a sum of nearly thirteen millions of dollars will then be added to our public debt, most of which is payable after fifteen years; before which term, the present existing debts will all be discharged by the established operation of the Sinking Fund. When we contemplate the ordinary annual augmentation of imposts from increasing population and wealth, the augmentation of the same revenue by its extension to the new acquisition, and the economies which may still be introduced into our public expenditures, I cannot but hope that Congress, in reviewing their resources will find means to meet the intermediate interests of this additional debt without recurring to new taxes; and applying to this object only the ordinary progression of our revenue, its extraordinary increase in times of foreign war will be the proper and sufficient fund for any measures of safety or precaution which that state of things may render necessary in our neutral position...

We have seen with sincere concern the flames of war lighted up again in Europe, and nations, with which we have the most friendly and useful relations, engaged in mutual destruction. While we regret the miseries in which we see others involved, let us bow with gratitude to that kind Providence, which, inspiring with wisdom and moderation our late Legislative Councils, while placed under the urgency of the greatest wrongs, guarded us from hastily entering into the sanguinary contest, and left us only to look on and to pity its ravages. These will be heaviest on those immediately engaged. Yet the nations pursuing peace will not be exempt from all evil. In the course of this conflict let it be our endeavor, as it is our interest and desire, to cultivate the friendship of the belligerent nations by every act of justice and of incessant kindness; to receive their armed vessels with hospitality from the distresses of the sea, but to administer the means of annoyance to none; to establish in our harbors such a police as may maintain law and order; to restrain our citizens from embarking individually in a war in which their country takes no part; to punish severely those persons, citizen or alien, who shall usurp the cover of our flag for vessels not entitled to it, infecting thereby with suspicion those of real Americans, and committing us into controversies for the redress of wrongs not our own; to exact from every nation the observance, toward our vessels and citizens, of those principles and practices which all civilized people acknowledge; to merit the character of a just nation, and maintain that of an independent one, preferring every consequence to insult and habitual wrong. Congress will consider whether the existing laws enable us efficaciously to maintain this course with our citizens in all places, and with others while within the limits of our jurisdiction; and will give them the new modifications necessary for these objects. Some contraventions of right have already taken place, both within our jurisdictional limits and on the high seas. The friendly disposition of the Governments from whose agents they have proceeded, as well as their wisdom and regard for justice, leave us in reasonable expectation that they will be rectified and prevented in future; and that no act will be countenanced by them which threatens to disturb our friendly intercourse. Separated by a wide ocean from the nations of Europe, and from the political interests which entangle them together, with productions and wants which render our commerce and friendship useful to them and theirs to us, it cannot be the interest of any to assail us, nor ours to disturb them. We should be most unwise, indeed, were we to cast away the singular blessings of the position in which nature has placed us, the opportunity she has endowed us with, of pursuing, at a distance from foreign contentions, the paths of industry, peace, and happiness; of cultivating general friendship, and of bringing collisions of interest to the umpirage of reason rather than of force. How desirable, then, must it be, in a Government like ours, to see its citizens adopt, individually, the views, the interests, and the conduct which their country should pursue, divesting themselves of those passions and partialities which tend to lessen useful friendships, and to embarrass and embroil us in the calamitous scenes of Europe! Confident, fellow-citizens, that you will duly estimate the importance of neutral dispositions toward the observance of neutral conduct, that you will be sensible how much it is our duty to look on the bloody arena spread before us, with commiseration, indeed, but with no other wish than to see it closed, I am persuaded you will cordially cherish these dispositions in all discussions among yourselves, and in all communications with your constituents; and I anticipate, with satisfaction, the measures of wisdom which the great interests now committed to you will give *you* an opportunity of providing, and *myself* that of approving and carrying into execution with the fidelity I owe to my country.

### 7. "Ograbme" Cartoon, c. 1808[7]

*During his second term as president, Jefferson faced increasing international problems as the United States was caught between France and Britain. In an effort to compel the warring European powers to respect the rights of the United States as a neutral carrier, Jefferson encouraged Congress to adopt the Embargo Act in 1807. Under its terms the United States foreswore almost all international trade. Economically the embargo was disastrous for the United States. Politically it was damaging for the Republicans, especially after Congress provided the government with enhanced police powers to enforce the embargo. This cartoon, critical of the "Ograbme" (embargo spelled backwards), reflected the widespread domestic opposition to the policy.*

**Figure 11.2** Embargo Cartoon, 1811. Courtesy of the Granger Collection, New York.

## 8. A Boxing Match, or Another Bloody Nose for John Bull, 1813[8]

*For many Americans the War of 1812 was the "Second War of Independence." This image reflects widespread assumptions about the superiority of American republicanism to British monarchism. James Madison, dressed as a simple republican, batters King George III.*

**Figure 11.3** A Boxing Match, or Another Bloody Nose for John Bull. War of 1812 Cartoon, 1813. Courtesy of the Granger Collection, New York.

### 9.   Francis Scott Key, "Star-Spangled Banner," September 14, 1814[9]

*Despite the relatively poor performance of American forces during the war, many Americans viewed the War of 1812 as a vindication of American independence and a triumph of American nationhood. The apparent disparity between the results on the battlefield and the American nationalist zeal engendered by the war is reflected in this poem by Francis Scott Key (1779–1843). Key, a Baltimore lawyer and amateur poet, wrote the "Star-Spangled Banner" in September 1814 to commemorate the successful resistance of Fort McHenry in Baltimore against a British bombardment in the wake of the British capture and burning of Washington in August 1814. Key's poem, which captured the national mood despite setbacks on the battlefield, was set to the tune of a popular British drinking song and was made the national anthem of the United States in 1916.*

O! say can you see, by the dawn's early light,
What so proudly we hail'd at the twilight's last gleaming?
Whose broad stripes and bright stars through the perilous fight
O'er the ramparts we watched were so gallantly streaming!
And the rockets' red glare, the Bombs bursting in air,
Gave proof through the night that our flag was still there;
O! say, does that star-spangled Banner yet wave
O'er the Land of the free and the home of the brave?

On the shore, dimly seen through the mists of the deep,
Where the foe's haughty host in dread silence reposes,
What is that, which the breeze o'er the towering steep,
As it fitfully blows, half conceals, half discloses?
Now it catches the gleam of the morning's first beam,
In full glory reflected now shines on the stream;
'Tis the star-spangled banner. O! long may it wave
O'er the land of the free and the home of the brave.

And where is that band who so vauntingly swore
That the havoc of war and the battle's confusion,
A home and a country should leave us no more?
Their blood has wash'd out their foul footsteps' pollution.
No refuge could save the hireling and slave,
From terror of flight or the gloom of the grave:
And the star-spangled banner in triumph doth wave,
O'er the land of the free and the home of the brave.

Oh! thus be it ever, when freemen shall stand
Between their lov'd homes, and the war's desolation
Blest with victory and peace, may the Heaven-rescued land
Praise the Power that made and preserved us a nation!

Then conquer we must, wher our cause it is just,
And this be our motto:—"In God is our trust!"
And the star-spangled banner in triumph shall wave
O'er the land of the free and the home of the brave.

## 10.   The Hartford Convention, 1814[10]

*Despite the surge in nationalism which accompanied the conflict, the War of 1812 was fought in the face of significant domestic opposition. The war was especially unpopular among Federalists, particularly in the northeast. Between December 15, 1814, and January 5, 1815, twenty-six leading Federalists from across New England gathered in Hartford, Connecticut, to discuss and coordinate their opposition to the war. As this record of their deliberations shows, the delegates considered secession, denied the authority of Congress, and proposed various constitutional amendments intended to limit the power of the Republicans. The Federalists, having been out of power for fifteen years, had become a regional party advocating disunion.*

…That acts of Congress in violation of the Constitution are absolutely void, is an undeniable position. It does not, however, consist with the respect and for-bearance due from a confederate State towards the General Government, to fly to open resistance upon every infraction of the Constitution. The mode and the energy of the opposition, should always conform to the nature of the violation, the intention of its authors, the extent of the injury inflicted, the determination manifested to persist in it, and the danger of delay. But in cases of deliberate, dangerous, and palpable infractions of the Constitution, affecting the sovereignty of a State, and liberties of the people; it is not only the right but the duty of such a State to interpose its authority for their protection, in the manner best calculated to secure that end. When emergencies occur which are either beyond the reach of the judicial tribunals, or too pressing to admit of the delay incident to their forms, States, which have no common umpire, must be their own judges, and execute their own decisions. It will thus be proper for the several States to await the ultimate disposal of the obnoxious measures, recommended by the Secretary of War, or pending before Congress, and so to use their power according to the character these measures shall finally assume, as effectually to protect their own sovereignty, and the rights and liberties of their citizens…

If the war be continued, there appears no room for reliance upon the national government for the supply of those means of defence, which must become indispensable to secure these States from desolation and ruin. Nor is it possible that the States can discharge this sacred duty from their own resources, and continue to sustain the burden of the national taxes. The Administration, after a long perseverance in plans to baffle every effort of commercial enterprize, had fatally succeeded in their attempts at the epoch of the war. Commerce, the vital spring of New-England's prosperity, was annihilated. Embargoes, restrictions, and the rapacity of revenue officers, had completed its destruction. The various objects for the employment of productive labour, in the branches of business dependent on commerce, have disappeared. The fisheries have shared its fate. Manufactures, which Government has professed an intention to favour and to cherish, as an indemnity for the failure of these branches of business, are doomed to struggle in their infancy with taxes and obstructions, which cannot fail most seriously to affect their growth. The specie is withdrawn from circulation. The landed interest, the last to feel these burdens, must prepare to become their principal support, as all other sources of revenue must be exhausted. Under these circumstances, taxes, of a description and amount unprecedented in this country, are in a train of imposition, the burden of which must fall with the heaviest pressure upon the States east of the Potowmac...

Negociations for Peace are at this hour supposed to be pending, the issue of which must be deeply interesting to all. No measures should be adopted, which might unfavorably affect that issue; none which should embarrass the Administration, if their professed desire for peace is sincere; and none, which on supposition of their insincerity, should afford them pretexts for prolonging the war, or relieving themselves from the responsibility of a dishonorable peace. It is also devoutly to be wished, that an occasion may be afforded to all friends of the country, of all parties, and in all places, to pause and consider the awful state to which pernicious counsels, and blind passions, have brought this people...Our nation may yet be great, our union durable. But should this prospect be utterly hopeless, the time will not have been lost, which shall have ripened a general sentiment of the necessity of more mighty efforts to rescue from ruin, at least some portion of our beloved Country.

THEREFORE RESOLVED—
THAT it be and hereby is recommended to the Legislatures of the several States represented in this Convention, to adopt all such measures as may be necessary effectually to protect the citizens of said States from the operation and effects of all acts which have been or may be passed by the Congress of the United States, which shall contain provisions, subjecting the militia or other citizens to forcible drafts, conscriptions, or impressments, not authorised by the Constitution of the United States.

*Resolved,* That it be and hereby is recommended to the said Legislatures, to authorize an immediate and earnest application to be made to the Government of the United States, requesting their consent to some arrangement, whereby the said States may, separately or in concert, be empowered to assume upon themselves the defence of their territory against the enemy; and a reasonable portion of the taxes, collected within said States, may be paid into the respective treasuries thereof, and appropriated to the payment of the balance due said States, and to the future defence of the same. The amount so paid into the said treasuries to be credited, and the disbursements made as aforesaid to be charged to the United States.

*Resolved,* That it be, and it hereby is, recommended to the Legislatures of the aforesaid States, to pass laws (where it has not already been done) authorizing the Governours or Commanders in Chief of their militia to make detachments from the same, or to form voluntary corps, as shall be most convenient and conformable to their Constitutions, and to cause the same to be well armed, equipped and disciplined, and held in readiness for service; and upon the request of the Governour of either of the other States to employ the whole of such detachment or corps, as well as the regular forces of the State, or such part thereof as may be required and can be spared consistently with the safety of the State, in assisting the State, making such request to repel any invasion thereof which shall be made or attempted by the public enemy.

*Resolved,* That the following amendments of the Constitution of the United States, be recommended to the States represented as aforesaid, to be proposed by them for adoption by the State Legislatures, and, in such cases as may be deemed expedient, by a Convention chosen by the people of each State.

And it is further recommended, that the said States shall persevere in their efforts to obtain such amendments, until the same shall be effected.

*First.* Representatives and direct taxes shall be apportioned among the several States which may be included within this union, according to their respective numbers of free persons, including those bound to serve for a term of years, and excluding Indians not taxed, and all other persons.

*Second.* No new State shall be admitted into the union by Congress in virtue of the power granted by the Constitution, without the concurrence of two thirds of both Houses.

*Third.* Congress shall not have power to lay any embargo on the ships or vessels of the citizens of the United States, in the ports or harbours thereof, for more than sixty days.

*Fourth.* Congress shall not have power, without the concurrence of two thirds of both Houses, to interdict the commercial intercourse between the United States and any foreign nation or the dependencies thereof.

*Fifth.* Congress shall not make or declare war, or authorize acts of hostility against any foreign nation without the concurrence of two thirds of both Houses, except such acts of hostility be in defence of the territories of the United States when actually invaded.

*Sixth.* No person who shall hereafter be naturalized, shall be eligible as a member of the Senate or House of Representatives of the United States, nor capable of holding any civil office under the authority of the United States.

*Seventh.* The same person shall not be elected President of the United States a second time; nor shall the President be elected from the same State two terms in succession.

*Resolved.* That if the application of these States to the government of the United States, recommended in a foregoing Resolution, should be unsuccessful, and peace should not be concluded, and the defence of these States should be neglected, as it has been since the commencement of the war, it will in the opinion of this Convention be expedient for the Legislatures of the several States to appoint Delegates to another Convention, to meet at Boston, in the State of Massachusetts, on the third Thursday of June next, with such powers and instructions as the exigency of a crisis so momentous may require.

## 11.    The Battle of New Orleans[11]

*Despite American difficulties during the war, the War of 1812 ended on a victorious note for the United States when, in hard-fought battle on January 8, 1815, American forces led by General Andrew Jackson (1767–1845) successfully defended New Orleans against a British expeditionary force. This broadside announced the American victory. It appeared shortly before Americans learned of the Treaty of Ghent, agreed on December 24, 1814, which formally ended the war. News of the peace following closely on that of the victory at New Orleans (which actually occurred* after *the peace treaty was concluded) fostered a sense that the United States had triumphed in the war. Broadsides were an important means by which breaking news circulated in early America.*

The New-York papers by this morning's mail, furnished us with the following most glorious intelligence from New-Orleans. Gen. JACKSON will be immortalized—the bravery of the Kentuckians, the Tennesseans, &c. shall be handed down to the latest posterity.—If there ever was a stain upon "raw militia," it was wiped away on the 8th of January. The result of this day's contest is of more importance in a national point of view, than any occurrence since the war.

*The following is a letter from Mr. Le Blanc, a French merchant at New-Orleans, to a gentleman of New-York.*

New-Orleans, Jan. 9—7 P.M.
The battle of the 8th of January was one of the hottest that we have hitherto had, and has happily terminated in our favour. The enemy at break of day appeared in a body principally upon our left, in order to make a passage and turn our line in that direction; —he had for that purpose prepared sealing ladders and fascines to fill up the ditch. For nearly two hours the battle was contested with the greatest fury. The enemy was for five minutes in possession of one of our batteries. Not one of those who attempted the assault escaped—they all fell under our batteries; the plain was strewn with killed and wounded, heaped upon each other. We made 175 prisoners, among whom are several Majors and officers; more than 500 wounded are in our hospitals, the greater part of whom are mortally wounded; from 8 to 900 were killed on the field of battle. The enemy in their retreat carried off as many wounded as they could, and we believe that that day cost them more than 2000 men killed, wounded & prisoners.

We had opposite to the enemy's camp upon the right bank of the river 3 batteries containing altogether 12 pieces of heavy ordnance, which played upon them in flank; —these batteries were attacked at the same time as our line, by a party which the enemy landed by means of barges and sloops, which were sent from the camp for that purpose. Our batteries being feebly guarded, were obliged to be evacuated after spiking all the guns.—We learn this afternoon that the enemy not being able to hold that position and make use of our guns, had contented himself with burning the carriages, and had crossed the river to return to their camp.

The English General sent yesterday at noon a flag of truce to demand a suspension of arms for 24 hours, to bury the dead and carry away the wounded, which was agreed to by Gen. Jackson.

What will appear to you astonishing and surprising after so hot an affair is, that we have had but 18 or 20 men killed, and from 50 to 60 wounded in that engagement. I hope in my next to inform you of their retreat.

P.S. One of our posts upon Lake Borgne has captured an enemy's brig laden with provisions, which has been burned, and 10 men made prisoners.

## Notes

1. *By the United States in Congress assembled. April 23, 1784* [Ordinance of 1784] (Hartford, CT: Hudson & Goodwin, 1785).
2. James D. Richardson, *A Compilation of the Messages and Papers of the Presidents, 1789–1897*, 10 vols. (Washington DC: Government Printing Office, 1896), 1:321–324.
3. The Granger Collection, New York.
4. Thomas Jefferson Papers. Washington, DC: Library of Congress.
5. Thomas Jefferson Papers. Washington, DC: Library of Congress.
6. *Annals of Congress*, Senate, 8th Congress, 1 Session, 11–15.
7. The Granger Collection, New York.
8. The Granger Collection, New York.
9. *Patriot and Evening Advertiser* (Baltimore), September 20, 1814.
10. *Proceedings of a Convention of Delegates from the States of Massachusetts, Connecticut, and Rhode Island, the Counties of Cheshire and Grafton in the State of New Hampshire and the County of Windham, in the State of Vermont, Convened at Hartford in the State of Connecticut, December 15, 1814* (Boston: Wells and Lilly, 1815), 9–12, 19–21.
11. *Broadside: Glorious News from New Orleans! Splendid Victory over the British Forces* (Salem, MA: Warwick Palfray, 1815).

# Appendix

## 1. The Declaration of Independence

IN CONGRESS, July 4, 1776.

The unanimous Declaration of the thirteen united States of America,

When in the Course of human events, it becomes necessary for one people to dissolve the political bands which have connected them with another, and to assume among the powers of the earth, the separate and equal station to which the Laws of Nature and of Nature's God entitle them, a decent respect to the opinions of mankind requires that they should declare the causes which impel them to the separation.

We hold these truths to be self-evident, that all men are created equal, that they are endowed by their Creator with certain unalienable Rights, that among these are Life, Liberty and the pursuit of Happiness.—That to secure these rights, Governments are instituted among Men, deriving their just powers from the consent of the governed,—That whenever any Form of Government becomes destructive of these ends, it is the Right of the People to alter or to abolish it, and to institute new Government, laying its foundation on such principles and organizing its powers in such form, as to them shall seem most likely to effect their Safety and Happiness. Prudence, indeed, will dictate that Governments long established should not be changed for light and transient causes; and accordingly all experience hath shewn, that mankind are more disposed to suffer, while evils are sufferable, than to right themselves by abolishing the forms to which they are accustomed. But when a long train of abuses and usurpations, pursuing invariably the same Object evinces a design to reduce them under absolute Despotism, it is their right, it is their duty, to throw off such Government, and to provide new Guards for their future security.—Such has been the patient sufferance of these

Colonies; and such is now the necessity which constrains them to alter their former Systems of Government. The history of the present King of Great Britain is a history of repeated injuries and usurpations, all having in direct object the establishment of an absolute Tyranny over these States. To prove this, let Facts be submitted to a candid world.

He has refused his Assent to Laws, the most wholesome and necessary for the public good.

He has forbidden his Governors to pass Laws of immediate and pressing importance, unless suspended in their operation till his Assent should be obtained; and when so suspended, he has utterly neglected to attend to them.

He has refused to pass other Laws for the accommodation of large districts of people, unless those people would relinquish the right of Representation in the Legislature, a right inestimable to them and formidable to tyrants only.

He has called together legislative bodies at places unusual, uncomfortable, and distant from the depository of their public Records, for the sole purpose of fatiguing them into compliance with his measures.

He has dissolved Representative Houses repeatedly, for opposing with manly firmness his invasions on the rights of the people.

He has refused for a long time, after such dissolutions, to cause others to be elected; whereby the Legislative powers, incapable of Annihilation, have returned to the People at large for their exercise; the State remaining in the mean time exposed to all the dangers of invasion from without, and convulsions within.

He has endeavoured to prevent the population of these States; for that purpose obstructing the Laws for Naturalization of Foreigners; refusing to pass others to encourage their migrations hither, and raising the conditions of new Appropriations of Lands.

He has obstructed the Administration of Justice, by refusing his Assent to Laws for establishing Judiciary powers.

He has made Judges dependent on his Will alone, for the tenure of their offices, and the amount and payment of their salaries.

He has erected a multitude of New Offices, and sent hither swarms of Officers to harrass our people, and eat out their substance.

He has kept among us, in times of peace, Standing Armies without the Consent of our legislatures.

He has affected to render the Military independent of and superior to the Civil power.

He has combined with others to subject us to a jurisdiction foreign to our constitution, and unacknowledged by our laws; giving his Assent to their Acts of pretended Legislation:

For Quartering large bodies of armed troops among us:

For protecting them, by a mock Trial, from punishment for any Murders which they should commit on the Inhabitants of these States:

For cutting off our Trade with all parts of the world:

For imposing Taxes on us without our Consent:

For depriving us in many cases, of the benefits of Trial by Jury:

For transporting us beyond Seas to be tried for pretended offences

For abolishing the free System of English Laws in a neighbouring Province, establishing therein an Arbitrary government, and enlarging its Boundaries so as to render it at once an example and fit instrument for introducing the same absolute rule into these Colonies:

For taking away our Charters, abolishing our most valuable Laws, and altering fundamentally the Forms of our Governments:

For suspending our own Legislatures, and declaring themselves invested with power to legislate for us in all cases whatsoever.

He has abdicated Government here, by declaring us out of his Protection and waging War against us.

He has plundered our seas, ravaged our Coasts, burnt our towns, and destroyed the lives of our people.

He is at this time transporting large Armies of foreign Mercenaries to compleat the works of death, desolation and tyranny, already begun with circumstances of Cruelty & perfidy scarcely paralleled in the most barbarous ages, and totally unworthy the Head of a civilized nation.

He has constrained our fellow Citizens taken Captive on the high Seas to bear Arms against their Country, to become the executioners of their friends and Brethren, or to fall themselves by their Hands.

He has excited domestic insurrections amongst us, and has endeavoured to bring on the inhabitants of our frontiers, the merciless Indian Savages, whose known rule of warfare, is an undistinguished destruction of all ages, sexes and conditions.

In every stage of these Oppressions We have Petitioned for Redress in the most humble terms: Our repeated Petitions have been answered only by repeated injury. A Prince whose character is thus marked by every act which may define a Tyrant, is unfit to be the ruler of a free people.

Nor have We been wanting in attentions to our Brittish brethren. We have warned them from time to time of attempts by their legislature to extend an unwarrantable jurisdiction over us. We have reminded them of the circumstances of our emigration and settlement here. We have appealed to their native justice and magnanimity, and we have conjured them by the ties of our common kindred to disavow these usurpations, which, would inevitably interrupt our connections and correspondence. They too have been deaf to the voice of justice and of consanguinity. We must, therefore, acquiesce in the necessity, which denounces our Separation, and hold them, as we hold the rest of mankind, Enemies in War, in Peace Friends.

We, therefore, the Representatives of the united States of America, in General Congress, Assembled, appealing to the Supreme Judge of the world for the rectitude of our intentions, do, in the Name, and by Authority of the good People of these Colonies, solemnly publish and declare, That these United Colonies are, and of Right ought to be Free and Independent States; that they are Absolved from all Allegiance to the British Crown, and that all political connection between them and the State of Great Britain, is and ought to be totally dissolved; and that as Free and Independent States, they have full Power to levy War, conclude Peace, contract Alliances, establish Commerce, and to do all other Acts and Things which Independent States may of right do. And for the support of this Declaration, with a firm reliance on the protection of divine Providence, we mutually pledge to each other our Lives, our Fortunes and our sacred Honor.
[signed by] John Hancock

[Georgia]
Button Gwinnett
Lyman Hall
George Walton

[North Carolina]
William Hooper
Joseph Hewes
John Penn

[South Carolina]
Edward Rutledge
Thomas Heyward, Jr.
Thomas Lynch, Jr
Arthur Middleton

[Delaware]
Caesar Rodney
George Read
Thomas McKean

[New York]
William Floyd
Philip Livingston
Francis Lewis
Lewis Morris

[New Jersey]
Richard Stockton
John Witherspoon
Francis Hopkinson
John Hart

[Maryland]
Samuel Chase
William Paca
Thomas Stone
Charles Carroll of Carrollton

[Virginia]
George Wythe
Richard Henry Lee
Thomas Jefferson
Benjamin Harrison
Thomas Nelson, Jr.
Francis Lightfoot Lee
Carter Braxton

[Pennsylvania]
Robert Morris
Benjamin Rush
Benjamin Franklin
John Morton
George Clymer
James Smith
George Taylor
James Wilson
George Ross

Abraham Clark

[New Hampshire]
Josiah Bartlett
William Whipple

[Massachusetts]
Samuel Adams
John Adams
Robert Treat Paine
Elbridge Gerry

[Rhode Island]
Stephen Hopkins
William Ellery

[Connecticut]
Roger Sherman
Samuel Huntington
William Williams
Oliver Wolcott

[New Hampshire]
Matthew Thornton

## 2. The Constitution of the United States

We the People of the United States, in Order to form a more perfect Union, establish Justice, insure domestic Tranquility, provide for the common defence, promote the general Welfare, and secure the Blessings of Liberty to ourselves and our Posterity, do ordain and establish this Constitution for the United States of America.

Article I

*Section 1*

All legislative Powers herein granted shall be vested in a Congress of the United States, which shall consist of a Senate and House of Representatives.

*Section 2*

The House of Representatives shall be composed of Members chosen every second Year by the People of the several States, and the Electors in each State shall have the Qualifications requisite for Electors of the most numerous Branch of the State Legislature.

No Person shall be a Representative who shall not have attained to the Age of twenty five Years, and been seven Years a Citizen of the United States, and who shall not, when elected, be an Inhabitant of that State in which he shall be chosen.

Representatives and direct Taxes shall be apportioned among the several States which may be included within this Union, according to their respective Numbers, which shall be determined by adding to the whole Number of free Persons, including those bound to Service for a Term of Years, and excluding Indians not taxed, three fifths of all other Persons. The actual Enumeration shall be made within three Years after the first Meeting of the Congress of the United States, and within every subsequent Term of ten Years, in such Manner as they shall by Law direct. The Number of Representatives shall not exceed one for every thirty Thousand, but each State shall have at Least one Representative; and until such enumeration shall be made, the State of New Hampshire shall be entitled to chuse three, Massachusetts eight, Rhode-Island and Providence Plantations one, Connecticut five, New-York six, New Jersey four, Pennsylvania eight, Delaware one, Maryland six, Virginia ten, North Carolina five, South Carolina five, and Georgia three.

When vacancies happen in the Representation from any State, the Executive Authority thereof shall issue Writs of Election to fill such Vacancies.

The House of Representatives shall chuse their Speaker and other Officers; and shall have the sole Power of Impeachment.

*Section 3*
The Senate of the United States shall be composed of two Senators from each State, chosen by the Legislature thereof for six Years; and each Senator shall have one Vote.

Immediately after they shall be assembled in Consequence of the first Election, they shall be divided as equally as may be into three Classes. The Seats of the Senators of the first Class shall be vacated at the Expiration of the second Year, of the second Class at the Expiration of the fourth Year, and of the third Class at the Expiration of the sixth Year, so that one third may be chosen every second Year; and if Vacancies happen by Resignation, or otherwise, during the Recess of the Legislature of any State, the Executive thereof may make temporary Appointments until the next Meeting of the Legislature, which shall then fill such Vacancies.

No Person shall be a Senator who shall not have attained to the Age of thirty Years, and been nine Years a Citizen of the United States, and who shall not, when elected, be an Inhabitant of that State for which he shall be chosen.

The Vice President of the United States shall be President of the Senate, but shall have no Vote, unless they be equally divided.

The Senate shall chuse their other Officers, and also a President pro tempore, in the Absence of the Vice President, or when he shall exercise the Office of President of the United States.

The Senate shall have the sole Power to try all Impeachments. When sitting for that Purpose, they shall be on Oath or Affirmation. When the President of the United States is tried, the Chief Justice shall preside: And no Person shall be convicted without the Concurrence of two thirds of the Members present.

Judgment in Cases of Impeachment shall not extend further than to removal from Office, and disqualification to hold and enjoy any Office of honor, Trust or Profit under the United States: but the Party convicted shall nevertheless be liable and subject to Indictment, Trial, Judgment and Punishment, according to Law.

*Section 4*
The Times, Places and Manner of holding Elections for Senators and Representatives, shall be prescribed in each State by the Legislature thereof; but the Congress may at any time by Law make or alter such Regulations, except as to the Places of chusing Senators.

The Congress shall assemble at least once in every Year, and such Meeting shall be on the first Monday in December, unless they shall by Law appoint a different Day.

*Section 5*
Each House shall be the Judge of the Elections, Returns and Qualifications of its own Members, and a Majority of each shall constitute a Quorum to do Business; but a smaller Number may adjourn from day to day, and may be authorized to compel the Attendance of absent Members, in such Manner, and under such Penalties as each House may provide.

Each House may determine the Rules of its Proceedings, punish its Members for disorderly Behaviour, and, with the Concurrence of two thirds, expel a Member.

Each House shall keep a Journal of its Proceedings, and from time to time publish the same, excepting such Parts as may in their Judgment require Secrecy; and the Yeas and Nays of the Members of either House on any question shall, at the Desire of one fifth of those Present, be entered on the Journal.

Neither House, during the Session of Congress, shall, without the Consent of the other, adjourn for more than three days, nor to any other Place than that in which the two Houses shall be sitting.

*Section 6*
The Senators and Representatives shall receive a Compensation for their Services, to be ascertained by Law, and paid out of the Treasury of the United States. They shall in all Cases, except Treason, Felony and Breach of the Peace, be privileged

from Arrest during their Attendance at the Session of their respective Houses, and in going to and returning from the same; and for any Speech or Debate in either House, they shall not be questioned in any other Place.

No Senator or Representative shall, during the Time for which he was elected, be appointed to any civil Office under the Authority of the United States, which shall have been created, or the Emoluments whereof shall have been encreased during such time; and no Person holding any Office under the United States, shall be a Member of either House during his Continuance in Office.

*Section 7*
All Bills for raising Revenue shall originate in the House of Representatives; but the Senate may propose or concur with Amendments as on other Bills.

Every Bill which shall have passed the House of Representatives and the Senate, shall, before it become a Law, be presented to the President of the United States: If he approve he shall sign it, but if not he shall return it, with his Objections to that House in which it shall have originated, who shall enter the Objections at large on their Journal, and proceed to reconsider it. If after such Reconsideration two thirds of that House shall agree to pass the Bill, it shall be sent, together with the Objections, to the other House, by which it shall likewise be reconsidered, and if approved by two thirds of that House, it shall become a Law. But in all such Cases the Votes of both Houses shall be determined by yeas and Nays, and the Names of the Persons voting for and against the Bill shall be entered on the Journal of each House respectively. If any Bill shall not be returned by the President within ten Days (Sundays excepted) after it shall have been presented to him, the Same shall be a Law, in like Manner as if he had signed it, unless the Congress by their Adjournment prevent its Return, in which Case it shall not be a Law.

Every Order, Resolution, or Vote to which the Concurrence of the Senate and House of Representatives may be necessary (except on a question of Adjournment) shall be presented to the President of the United States; and before the Same shall take Effect, shall be approved by him, or being disapproved by him, shall be repassed by two thirds of the Senate and House of Representatives, according to the Rules and Limitations prescribed in the Case of a Bill.

*Section 8*
The Congress shall have Power To lay and collect Taxes, Duties, Imposts and Excises, to pay the Debts and provide for the common Defence and general Welfare of the United States; but all Duties, Imposts and Excises shall be uniform throughout the United States;

To borrow Money on the credit of the United States;

To regulate Commerce with foreign Nations, and among the several States, and with the Indian Tribes;

To establish an uniform Rule of Naturalization, and uniform Laws on the subject of Bankruptcies throughout the United States;

To coin Money, regulate the Value thereof, and of foreign Coin, and fix the Standard of Weights and Measures;

To provide for the Punishment of counterfeiting the Securities and current Coin of the United States;

To establish Post Offices and post Roads;

To promote the Progress of Science and useful Arts, by securing for limited Times to Authors and Inventors the exclusive Right to their respective Writings and Discoveries;

To constitute Tribunals inferior to the supreme Court;

To define and punish Piracies and Felonies committed on the high Seas, and Offences against the Law of Nations;

To declare War, grant Letters of Marque and Reprisal, and make Rules concerning Captures on Land and Water;

To raise and support Armies, but no Appropriation of Money to that Use shall be for a longer Term than two Years;

To provide and maintain a Navy;

To make Rules for the Government and Regulation of the land and naval Forces;

To provide for calling forth the Militia to execute the Laws of the Union, suppress Insurrections and repel Invasions;

To provide for organizing, arming, and disciplining, the Militia, and for governing such Part of them as may be employed in the Service of the United States, reserving to the States respectively, the Appointment of the Officers, and the Authority of training the Militia according to the discipline prescribed by Congress;

To exercise exclusive Legislation in all Cases whatsoever, over such District (not exceeding ten Miles square) as may, by Cession of particular States, and the Acceptance of Congress, become the Seat of the Government of the United States, and to exercise like Authority over all Places purchased by the Consent of the Legislature of the State in which the Same shall be, for the Erection of Forts, Magazines, Arsenals, dock-Yards, and other needful Buildings;--And

To make all Laws which shall be necessary and proper for carrying into Execution the foregoing Powers, and all other Powers vested by this Constitution in the Government of the United States, or in any Department or Officer thereof.

*Section 9*

The Migration or Importation of such Persons as any of the States now existing shall think proper to admit, shall not be prohibited by the Congress prior to the Year one thousand eight hundred and eight, but a Tax or duty may be imposed on such Importation, not exceeding ten dollars for each Person.

The Privilege of the Writ of Habeas Corpus shall not be suspended, unless when in Cases of Rebellion or Invasion the public Safety may require it.

No Bill of Attainder or ex post facto Law shall be passed.

No Capitation, or other direct, Tax shall be laid, unless in Proportion to the Census or enumeration herein before directed to be taken.

No Tax or Duty shall be laid on Articles exported from any State.

No Preference shall be given by any Regulation of Commerce or Revenue to the Ports of one State over those of another; nor shall Vessels bound to, or from, one State, be obliged to enter, clear, or pay Duties in another.

No Money shall be drawn from the Treasury, but in Consequence of Appropriations made by Law; and a regular Statement and Account of the Receipts and Expenditures of all public Money shall be published from time to time.

No Title of Nobility shall be granted by the United States: And no Person holding any Office of Profit or Trust under them, shall, without the Consent of the Congress, accept of any present, Emolument, Office, or Title, of any kind whatever, from any King, Prince, or foreign State.

*Section 10*

No State shall enter into any Treaty, Alliance, or Confederation; grant Letters of Marque and Reprisal; coin Money; emit Bills of Credit; make any Thing but gold and silver Coin a Tender in Payment of Debts; pass any Bill of Attainder, ex post facto Law, or Law impairing the Obligation of Contracts, or grant any Title of Nobility.

No State shall, without the Consent of the Congress, lay any Imposts or Duties on Imports or Exports, except what may be absolutely necessary for executing it's inspection Laws: and the net Produce of all Duties and Imposts, laid by any State on Imports or Exports, shall be for the Use of the Treasury of the United States; and all such Laws shall be subject to the Revision and Controul of the Congress.

No State shall, without the Consent of Congress, lay any Duty of Tonnage, keep Troops, or Ships of War in time of Peace, enter into any Agreement or Compact with another State, or with a foreign Power, or engage in War, unless actually invaded, or in such imminent Danger as will not admit of delay.

Article II

*Section 1*

The executive Power shall be vested in a President of the United States of America. He shall hold his Office during the Term of four Years, and, together with the Vice President, chosen for the same Term, be elected, as follows:

Each State shall appoint, in such Manner as the Legislature thereof may direct, a Number of Electors, equal to the whole Number of Senators and Representatives to which the State may be entitled in the Congress: but no Senator or Representative, or Person holding an Office of Trust or Profit under the United States, shall be appointed an Elector.

The Electors shall meet in their respective States, and vote by Ballot for two Persons, of whom one at least shall not be an Inhabitant of the same State with themselves. And they shall make a List of all the Persons voted for, and of the Number of Votes for each; which List they shall sign and certify, and transmit sealed to the Seat of the Government of the United States, directed to the President of the Senate. The President of the Senate shall, in the Presence of the Senate and House of Representatives, open all the Certificates, and the Votes shall then be counted. The Person having the greatest Number of Votes shall be the President, if such Number be a Majority of the whole Number of Electors appointed; and if there be more than one who have such Majority, and have an equal Number of Votes, then the House of Representatives shall immediately chuse by Ballot one of them for President; and if no Person have a Majority, then from the five highest on the List the said House shall in like Manner chuse the President. But in chusing the President, the Votes shall be taken by States, the Representation from each State having one Vote; A quorum for this purpose shall consist of a Member or Members from two thirds of the States, and a Majority of all the States shall be necessary to a Choice. In every Case, after the Choice of the President, the Person having the greatest Number of Votes of the Electors shall be the Vice President. But if there should remain two or more who have equal Votes, the Senate shall chuse from them by Ballot the Vice President.

The Congress may determine the Time of chusing the Electors, and the Day on which they shall give their Votes; which Day shall be the same throughout the United States.

No Person except a natural born Citizen, or a Citizen of the United States, at the time of the Adoption of this Constitution, shall be eligible to the Office of President; neither shall any Person be eligible to that Office who shall not have attained to the Age of thirty five Years, and been fourteen Years a Resident within the United States.

In Case of the Removal of the President from Office, or of his Death, Resignation, or Inability to discharge the Powers and Duties of the said Office, the Same shall devolve on the Vice President, and the Congress may by Law provide for the Case of Removal, Death, Resignation or Inability, both of the President and Vice President, declaring what Officer shall then act as President, and such Officer shall act accordingly, until the Disability be removed, or a President shall be elected.

The President shall, at stated Times, receive for his Services, a Compensation, which shall neither be increased nor diminished during the Period for which he shall have been elected, and he shall not receive within that Period any other Emolument from the United States, or any of them.

Before he enter on the Execution of his Office, he shall take the following Oath or Affirmation:—"I do solemnly swear (or affirm) that I will faithfully execute the Office of President of the United States, and will to the best of my Ability, preserve, protect and defend the Constitution of the United States."

*Section 2*
The President shall be Commander in Chief of the Army and Navy of the United States, and of the Militia of the several States, when called into the actual Service of the United States; he may require the Opinion, in writing, of the principal Officer in each of the executive Departments, upon any Subject relating to the Duties of their respective Offices, and he shall have Power to grant Reprieves and Pardons for Offences against the United States, except in Cases of Impeachment.

He shall have Power, by and with the Advice and Consent of the Senate, to make Treaties, provided two thirds of the Senators present concur; and he shall nominate, and by and with the Advice and Consent of the Senate, shall appoint Ambassadors, other public Ministers and Consuls, Judges of the supreme Court, and all other Officers of the United States, whose Appointments are not herein otherwise provided for, and which shall be established by Law: but the Congress may by Law vest the Appointment of such inferior Officers, as they think proper, in the President alone, in the Courts of Law, or in the Heads of Departments.

The President shall have Power to fill up all Vacancies that may happen during the Recess of the Senate, by granting Commissions which shall expire at the End of their next Session.

*Section 3*
He shall from time to time give to the Congress Information of the State of the Union, and recommend to their Consideration such Measures as he shall judge necessary and expedient; he may, on extraordinary Occasions, convene both Houses, or either of them, and in Case of Disagreement between them, with Respect to the Time of Adjournment, he may adjourn them to such Time as he shall think proper; he shall receive Ambassadors and other public Ministers; he shall take Care that the Laws be faithfully executed, and shall Commission all the Officers of the United States.

*Section 4*

The President, Vice President and all civil Officers of the United States, shall be removed from Office on Impeachment for, and Conviction of, Treason, Bribery, or other high Crimes and Misdemeanors.

Article III

*Section 1*

The judicial Power of the United States shall be vested in one supreme Court, and in such inferior Courts as the Congress may from time to time ordain and establish. The Judges, both of the supreme and inferior Courts, shall hold their Offices during good Behaviour, and shall, at stated Times, receive for their Services a Compensation, which shall not be diminished during their Continuance in Office.

*Section 2*

The judicial Power shall extend to all Cases, in Law and Equity, arising under this Constitution, the Laws of the United States, and Treaties made, or which shall be made, under their Authority;—to all Cases affecting Ambassadors, other public Ministers and Consuls;—to all Cases of admiralty and maritime Jurisdiction;—to Controversies to which the United States shall be a Party;—to Controversies between two or more States;—between a State and Citizens of another State,—between Citizens of different States,—between Citizens of the same State claiming Lands under Grants of different States, and between a State, or the Citizens thereof, and foreign States, Citizens or Subjects.

In all Cases affecting Ambassadors, other public Ministers and Consuls, and those in which a State shall be Party, the supreme Court shall have original Jurisdiction. In all the other Cases before mentioned, the supreme Court shall have appellate Jurisdiction, both as to Law and Fact, with such Exceptions, and under such Regulations as the Congress shall make.

The Trial of all Crimes, except in Cases of Impeachment, shall be by Jury; and such Trial shall be held in the State where the said Crimes shall have been committed; but when not committed within any State, the Trial shall be at such Place or Places as the Congress may by Law have directed.

*Section 3*

Treason against the United States, shall consist only in levying War against them, or in adhering to their Enemies, giving them Aid and Comfort. No Person shall be convicted of Treason unless on the Testimony of two Witnesses to the same overt Act, or on Confession in open Court.

The Congress shall have Power to declare the Punishment of Treason, but no Attainder of Treason shall work Corruption of Blood, or Forfeiture except during the Life of the Person attainted.

## Article IV

### Section 1
Full Faith and Credit shall be given in each State to the public Acts, Records, and judicial Proceedings of every other State. And the Congress may by general Laws prescribe the Manner in which such Acts, Records and Proceedings shall be proved, and the Effect thereof.

### Section 2
The Citizens of each State shall be entitled to all Privileges and Immunities of Citizens in the several States.

A Person charged in any State with Treason, Felony, or other Crime, who shall flee from Justice, and be found in another State, shall on Demand of the executive Authority of the State from which he fled, be delivered up, to be removed to the State having Jurisdiction of the Crime.

No Person held to Service or Labour in one State, under the Laws thereof, escaping into another, shall, in Consequence of any Law or Regulation therein, be discharged from such Service or Labour, but shall be delivered up on Claim of the Party to whom such Service or Labour may be due.

### Section 3
New States may be admitted by the Congress into this Union; but no new State shall be formed or erected within the Jurisdiction of any other State; nor any State be formed by the Junction of two or more States, or Parts of States, without the Consent of the Legislatures of the States concerned as well as of the Congress.

The Congress shall have Power to dispose of and make all needful Rules and Regulations respecting the Territory or other Property belonging to the United States; and nothing in this Constitution shall be so construed as to Prejudice any Claims of the United States, or of any particular State.

### Section 4
The United States shall guarantee to every State in this Union a Republican Form of Government, and shall protect each of them against Invasion; and on Application of the Legislature, or of the Executive (when the Legislature cannot be convened), against domestic Violence.

## Article V

The Congress, whenever two thirds of both Houses shall deem it necessary, shall propose Amendments to this Constitution, or, on the Application of the Legislatures of two thirds of the several States, shall call a Convention for proposing Amendments, which, in either Case, shall be valid to all Intents and Purposes, as Part of this Constitution, when ratified by the Legislatures of three fourths of the several States, or by Conventions in three fourths thereof, as the one or the other Mode of Ratification may be proposed by the Congress; Provided that no Amendment which may be made prior to the Year One thousand eight hundred and eight shall in any Manner affect the first and fourth Clauses in the Ninth Section of the first Article; and that no State, without its Consent, shall be deprived of its equal Suffrage in the Senate.

Article VI

All Debts contracted and Engagements entered into, before the Adoption of this Constitution, shall be as valid against the United States under this Constitution, as under the Confederation.

This Constitution, and the Laws of the United States which shall be made in Pursuance thereof; and all Treaties made, or which shall be made, under the Authority of the United States, shall be the supreme Law of the Land; and the Judges in every State shall be bound thereby, any Thing in the Constitution or Laws of any State to the Contrary notwithstanding.

The Senators and Representatives before mentioned, and the Members of the several State Legislatures, and all executive and judicial Officers, both of the United States and of the several States, shall be bound by Oath or Affirmation, to support this Constitution; but no religious Test shall ever be required as a Qualification to any Office or public Trust under the United States.

Article VII

The Ratification of the Conventions of nine States, shall be sufficient for the Establishment of this Constitution between the States so ratifying the Same.

The Word, "the," being interlined between the seventh and eighth Lines of the first Page, the Word "Thirty" being partly written on an Erazure in the fifteenth Line of the first Page, The Words "is tried" being interlined between the thirty second and thirty third Lines of the first Page and the Word "the" being interlined between the forty third and forty fourth Lines of the second Page.

Attest William Jackson Secretary

Done in Convention by the Unanimous Consent of the States present the Seventeenth Day of September in the Year of our Lord one thousand seven hundred and Eighty seven and of the Independence of the United States of America the Twelfth In witness whereof We have hereunto subscribed our Names,

G°. Washington
Presidt and deputy from Virginia

| Delaware | New Hampshire |
|---|---|
| Geo: Read | John Langdon |
| Gunning Bedford jun | Nicholas Gilman |

John Dickinson
Richard Bassett
Jaco: Broom

Maryland
James McHenry
Dan of St Thos. Jenifer
Danl. Carroll

Virginia
John Blair
James Madison Jr.

North Carolina
Wm. Blount
Richd. Dobbs Spaight
Hu Williamson

South Carolina
J. Rutledge
Charles Cotesworth Pinckney
Charles Pinckney
Pierce Butler

Georgia
William Few
Abr Baldwin

Massachusetts
Nathaniel Gorham
Rufus King

Connecticut
Wm. Saml. Johnson
Roger Sherman

New York
Alexander Hamilton

New Jersey
Wil: Livingston
David Brearley
Wm. Paterson
Jona: Dayton

Pennsylvania
B Franklin
Thomas Mifflin
Robt. Morris
Geo. Clymer
Thos. FitzSimons
Jared Ingersoll
James Wilson
Gouv Morris

## 3.  The Bill of Rights

Congress of the United States begun and held at the City of New-York, on Wednesday the fourth of March, one thousand seven hundred and eighty nine.

THE Conventions of a number of the States, having at the time of their adopting the Constitution, expressed a desire, in order to prevent misconstruction or abuse of its powers, that further declaratory and restrictive clauses should be added: And as extending the ground of public confidence in the Government, will best ensure the beneficent ends of its institution.

RESOLVED by the Senate and House of Representatives of the United States of America, in Congress assembled, two thirds of both Houses concurring, that the following Articles be proposed to the Legislatures of the several States, as amendments to the Constitution of the United States, all, or any of which Articles, when ratified by three fourths of the said Legislatures, to be valid to all intents and purposes, as part of the said Constitution; viz.

ARTICLES in addition to, and Amendment of the Constitution of the United States of America, proposed by Congress, and ratified by the Legislatures of the several States, pursuant to the fifth Article of the original Constitution.

### Amendment I
Congress shall make no law respecting an establishment of religion, or prohibiting the free exercise thereof; or abridging the freedom of speech, or of the press; or the right of the people peaceably to assemble, and to petition the Government for a redress of grievances.

### Amendment II
A well regulated Militia, being necessary to the security of a free State, the right of the people to keep and bear Arms, shall not be infringed.

### Amendment III
No Soldier shall, in time of peace be quartered in any house, without the consent of the Owner, nor in time of war, but in a manner to be prescribed by law.

### Amendment IV
The right of the people to be secure in their persons, houses, papers, and effects, against unreasonable searches and seizures, shall not be violated, and no Warrants shall issue, but upon probable cause, supported by Oath or affirmation, and particularly describing the place to be searched, and the persons or things to be seized.

### Amendment V
No person shall be held to answer for a capital, or otherwise infamous crime, unless on a presentment or indictment of a Grand Jury, except in cases arising in the land or naval forces, or in the Militia, when in actual service in time of War or public danger; nor shall any person be subject for the same offence to be twice put in jeopardy of life or limb; nor shall be compelled in any criminal case to be a witness against himself, nor be deprived of life, liberty, or property, without due process of law; nor shall private property be taken for public use, without just compensation.

### Amendment VI
In all criminal prosecutions, the accused shall enjoy the right to a speedy and public trial, by an impartial jury of the State and district wherein the crime shall have been committed, which district shall have been previously ascertained by law, and to be informed of the nature and cause of the accusation; to be confronted with the witnesses against him; to have compulsory process for obtaining witnesses in his favor, and to have the Assistance of Counsel for his defence.

*Amendment VII*

In Suits at common law, where the value in controversy shall exceed twenty dollars, the right of trial by jury shall be preserved, and no fact tried by a jury, shall be otherwise re-examined in any Court of the United States, than according to the rules of the common law.

*Amendment VIII*

Excessive bail shall not be required, nor excessive fines imposed, nor cruel and unusual punishments inflicted.

*Amendment IX*

The enumeration in the Constitution, of certain rights, shall not be construed to deny or disparage others retained by the people.

*Amendment X*

The powers not delegated to the United States by the Constitution, nor prohibited by it to the States, are reserved to the States respectively, or to the people.

# Permissions and Sources

Every effort has been made to cite completely the original source material for each work compiled in this collection. In the event that something has been inadvertently used or cited incorrectly, every effort will be made in subsequent editions to rectify the error. We offer our sincere thanks to all of the sources that were courteous enough to help us reproduce the contents of this volume.

## Chapter 1: Native Americans and the American Revolution

1.  **Southern Indians During the Seven Years' War**
    James Glen, *A Description of South Carolina; Containing Many curious and interesting Particulars relating to the Civil, Natural and Commercial History of that Colony...* (London: R. and J. Dodsley, 1761), 59–65.

2.  **Petition from the Paxton Boys, 1764**
    *A Declaration and Remonstrance Of the distressed and bleeding Frontier Inhabitants Of the Province of Pennsylvania, Presented by them to the Honourable the Governor and Assembly of the Province, Shewing the Causes Of their late Discontent and Uneasiness and the Grievances under which they have laboured, and which they humbly pray to have redress'd* (Philadelphia, 1764), 12–16.

3.  **Logan's Lament, 1775**
    Thomas Jefferson, *Notes on the State of Virginia* (Philadelphia: Prichard and Hall, 1788), 67–68.

4.  **Congress Appeals to the Six Nations, July 13, 1775**
    *Journals of the Continental Congress*, Vol. 2, 177–183.

5.  **Joseph Brant Speaks to Lord George Germain, March 14, 1776**
    "Speech of Captain Brant to Lord George Germain," in E. B. O'Callaghan (ed.), *Documents Relative to the Colonial History of the State of New-York;*

*Procured in Holland, England and France, by John Romeyn Brodhead, Esq.* (Albany, NY: Weed, Parsons and Company, 1857), 670–671.

6. **Joseph Brant, 1786**
   Gilbert Stuart (1775–1828), Joseph Brant, 1786, Oil on canvas. The Northumberland Estates, Alnwick Castle, Collection of the Duke of Northumberland at the Metropolitan Museum of Art, New York.

7. **A Missionary Speaks on Behalf of the Oneidas and Onondagas, 1777**
   *Copy of a Letter from the Rev. Samuel Kirkland, Missionary and Interpreter for the Six Nations: Together with a Message from the Six Nations Chiefs, to Major General Gates, commanding the Army of the United States, in the Northern Department, dated at Oneida, October 31, 1777* (Yorktown, PA: Hall and Sellers, 1777).

8. **Treaty with the Delawares, 1778**
   "Treaty with the Delawares, 1778," in Charles J. Kappler (ed.), *Indian Affairs: Laws and Treaties*, Vol. 2: Treaties (Washington, DC: Government Printing Office, 1904), 3–5.

9. **Chickasaw Chiefs Appeal to Congress, 1783**
   "To His Excellency the President of the Honorable Congress of the United American States," in William P. Palmer (ed.), *Calendar of Virginia State Papers and Other Manuscripts, Preserved in the Capitol at Richmond*, Vol. 3: From January 1, 1782, to December 31, 1784 (Richmond, VA: James E. Goode, 1883), 515–517.

10. **The Eve of War, 1811**
    "William Eustis to the Indians, October 8, 1811," *Michigan Pioneer and Historical Collections*, 8 (1886), 601.

11. **Aftermath of the War of 1812**
    Robert McDonall to Major Foster, October 10, 1815, *Mississippi Pioneer and Historical Collections*, 16 (1890), 325–327.

## Chapter 2: British North America in 1763

1. **Bill of Rights, 1689**
   "William and Mary, 1688: An Act declareing the Rights and Liberties of the Subject and Setleing the Succession of the Crowne. [Chapter II. Rot. Parl. pt. 3. nu. 1.]," Statutes of the Realm: Volume 6: 1685–94 (1819), pp. 142–145.

2. **Benjamin Franklin, Observations Concerning the Increase of Mankind, Peopling of Countries, 1751**
   Benjamin Franklin, *Observations On the late and present Conduct of the French, with Regard to their Encroachments upon the British Colonies in North America.... To which is added, wrote by another Hand; Observations concerning the Increase of Mankind, Peopling of Countries, &c.* (Boston: S. Kneeland, 1755), 2–8, 10–15.

3. **Servants and Slaves in Virginia, 1722**
   Robert Beverley, *The history of Virginia, in four parts...By a native and inhabit-
   ant of the place*, 2nd edition (London: F. Fayram, J. Clarke and T. Bickerton,
   1722), 235–239, originally published by R. Parker in London in 1705.
4. **Advertisements for Runaways, 1752, 1766**
   *Virginia Gazette*, Williamsburg, July 3, 1752; *Virginia Gazette*, Williamsburg,
   April 11, 1766.
5. **Albany Plan of Union, 1754**
   Benjamin Franklin, "Plan of a proposed Union of the several Colonies of
   Massachusetts's Bay, New Hampshire, Connecticut, Rhode Island, New
   York, New Jersey, Pennsylvania, Maryland, Virginia, North Carolina, and
   South Carolina for their mutual Defence and Security, and for extending the
   British Settlements in North America," in Leonard W. Labaree and Whitfield
   J. Bell, Jr. (eds.), *The Papers of Benjamin Franklin*, Vol. 5 (New Haven, CT:
   Yale University Press, 1962), 387–392.
6. **Join, or Die, 1754**
   Benjamin Franklin, "Join or Die," *The Pennsylvania Gazette*, May 9, 1754.
   Available from Library of Congress, Prints and Photographs Division,
   Washington, DC.
7. **Treaty of Paris, 1763**
   *The Definitive Treaty of Peace and Friendship Between His Britannick Maj-
   esty, the Most Christian King, and the King of Spain, Concluded at Paris, the
   10th Day of February, 1763. To Which, the King of Portugal acceded on the
   same Day* (London: E. Owen & T. Harrison; Charlestown, SC: Robert Wells,
   1763), 3–7.
8. **Governing a New World**
   "By the King. A Proclamation, October 7, 1763" in *The Annual Register, or
   a View of the History, Politics and Literature, For the Year 1763* (London: R.
   & J. Dodsley, 1764), 208–213.

## Chapter 3: The Imperial Crisis

1. **The Stamp Act, March 22, 1765**
   *The Statutes at Large, from the fifth year of King George the Third, to the tenth
   year of King George the Third, inclusive. To which is prefixed, a table of the
   titles of all the statutes during that time. With a copious index. Volume the
   eighth* (London, 1771), 17, 22–23.
2. **Virginia Resolves, May 29, 1765**
   *Maryland Gazette* (Annapolis), July 4, 1765.
3. **The Stamp Act Congress Asserts American Rights and Grievances,
   October 19, 1765**
   *Proceedings of the Congress at New York* (Annapolis, MD: Jonas Green,
   1766), 15–16.

4. **The Death of Liberty, October 31, 1765**
   *Pennsylvania Journal* Masthead, October 31, 1765, The Granger Collection, New York.

5. **New York Stamp Act Riot**
   *Pennsylvania Gazette* (Philadelphia), November 7, 1765.

6. **Examination of Benjamin Franklin before the House of Commons, 1766**
   *The Examination of Doctor Benjamin Franklin, before an August Assembly, relating to the Repeal of the Stamp Act, &c.* (Philadelphia: Hall and Sellers, 1766), 1–4, 6, 8–9, 11–13, 16.

7. **Parliament Repeals the Stamp Act, March 18, 1766**
   *The Statutes at Large, from the fifth year of King George the Third, to the tenth year of King George the Third, inclusive. To which is prefixed, a table of the titles of all the statutes during that time. With a copious index. Volume the eighth* (London, 1771), 183.

8. **Parliament Declares Its Authority, March 18, 1766**
   *The Statutes at Large, from the fifth year of King George the Third, to the tenth year of King George the Third, inclusive. To which is prefixed, a table of the titles of all the statutes during that time. With a copious index.* Volume the eighth (London, 1771), 183.

9. **The Boston Massacre**
   *Boston Gazette and Country Journal*, March 12, 1770.

10. **Paul Revere's Engraving of the Boston Massacre**
    Paul Revere, *The Bloody Massacre Perpetrated in King Street Boston on March 5th, 1770* from The Granger Collection, New York.

11. **First Continental Congress, Declaration of Rights and Grievances, October 14, 1774**
    Worthington C. Ford et al. (eds.), *Journals of the Continental Congress, 1774–1789*, 34 vols. (Washington, DC, 1904-37), 1:63–73.

12. **Broadside: New Hampshire Non-Importation Agreement, 1774**
    Library of Congress Printed Ephemera Collection; Portfolio 87, Folder 16, Washington, DC.

## Chapter 4: Revolution, 1775–1776

1. **Patrick Henry, Give Me Liberty or Give Me Death, March 23, 1775**
   William Wirt, *Sketches of the Life and Character of Patrick Henry* (Philadelphia: Desilver Thomas, 1836),138–42.

2. **The Battles of Lexington and Concord, April 19, 1775**
   "Isaac Merrill to John Currier, Essex County, Massachusetts, April 19, 1775," Gilder Lehrman Collection, New-York Historical Society.

3. **Battle of Lexington, 1775**
   Amos Doolittle, Battle of Lexington, 1775, from The Granger Collection, New York.

4. **General Gage's Proclamation, June 12, 1775**
   Hon. Thomas Gage, Esq., *A Proclamation* (New York, 1775, n.p.). Library of Congress Printed Ephemera Collection; Portfolio 38, Folio 17, Washington, DC.

5. **Bunker's Hill or America's Head Dress, 1776**
   The Granger Collection, New York.

6. **Declaration of the Causes and Necessity of Taking Up Arms, July 6, 1775**
   Worthington C. Ford et al. (eds.), *Journals of Continental Congress, 1774–1779*, 34 vols. (Washington DC: Government Printing Office, 1904-37), 2:140–157.

7. **Olive Branch Petition, July 8, 1775**
   Worthington C. Ford et al. (eds.), *Journals of Continental Congress, 1774–1779*, 34 vols. (Washington DC: Government Printing Office, 1904-37), 2:158–161.

8. **George III Proclaims the Americans in a State of Rebellion, August 23, 1775**
   *By the King, A Proclamation, For suppressing Rebellion and Sedition* (London: Charles Eyre and William Straban, 1775).

9. **Thomas Paine, *Common Sense,* 1776**
   Thomas Paine, *Common Sense* (Philadelphia: Robert Bell, 1776), ii, 4–9, 11–15, 17–20.

10. **Jefferson's Original Rough Draft of the Declaration of Independence**
    Thomas Jefferson, June 1776, Rough Draft of the Declaration of Independence, Thomas Jefferson Papers, Series 1: General Correspondence, 1651–1827. Library of Congress, Manuscript Division, Washington, DC.

11. **Statue of George III Demolished, July 9, 1776**
    The Granger Collection, New York.

## Chapter 5: Winning Independence: The Wars of the American Revolution

1. **A British View of the Siege of Boston**
   "Letter from a surgeon to one of His Majesty's ships at Boston, May 26, 1775," in Margaret Wheeler Willard (ed.), *Letters on the American Revolution, 1774–1776* (Boston: Houghton Mifflin, 1925), 120–121.

2. **George Washington Reflects on His Appointment to Command the Continental Army**
   "George Washington to Martha Washington, Philadelphia, June 18, 1775," in John C. Fitzpatrick (ed.), *The Writings of George Washington*, 39 vols. (Washington, DC: United States Government Printing Office, 1931), 3:293–295.

3. **Harassment of Loyalists in South Carolina**
   "Lord William Campbell to Lord Dartmouth, Charlestown, August 19,

1775," in *Manuscripts of the Earl of Dartmouth*, Vol. 2 (London: HMSO, 1887–1896), 354.

4. **Observations of a New Hampshire Loyalist**
   "Observations by Benjamin Thompson (afterwards Count Rumford)," in *Report on The Manuscripts of Mrs. Stopford Sackville of Northamptonshire*, Vol. 2 (Hereford, England: Hereford Times Co. Ltd., 1910), 15–18.

5. **Congress Resolves to Protect Loyalists, June 18, 1776**
   "Continental Congress Resolution on Loyalists," *Pennsylvania Gazette*, June 19, 1776.

6. **Washington Reflects on the Challenges Facing the Continental Army**
   "George Washington to The President of Congress," in John C. Fitzpatrick (ed.), *The Writings of George Washington*, 39 vols. (Washington, DC: United States Government Printing Office, 1931–44), 6:106–114.

7. **Letters From a Rebel Prisoner**
   James Kimball, *A Journal giving an account of the sufferings & privations of the American Prisoners confined in the 'Old Mill Prison' Plymouth, England made prisoners, whilst serving under the American Flat, Written by William Russell of Boston, Clerk to John Manley Esq, Commander of the Continental Ship Jason, Also Appended a list of Prisoners; with the names of vessels in which taken; during the whole period of the American War. With notes and annotations from British and American State Papers.*

8. **Treaty of Paris, 1783**
   *The Definitive Treaty, Between Great-Britain and the United States of America, signed at Paris the 3d day of September, 1783* (Baltimore: M.K. Goddard, 1783).

9. **A Loyalist Returns**
   George Atkinson Ward (ed.), *Journal and Letters of the late Samuel Curwen, Judge of Admiralty, Etc., An American Refugee in England, from 1775 to 1784, Comprising Remarks on the Prominent Men and Measures of that Period To Which Are Added, Biographical Notices of Many American Loyalists and Other Eminent Persons* (New York: C.S. Francis and Co., 1842), 393–394, 415.

## Chapter 6: African Americans in the Age of Revolution

1. **Virginia Revolutionaries Defend Slavery**
   "Proslavery Petition, November 10, 1785," Library of Virginia Taken from transcription at http://www.lva.virginia.gov/lib-edu/education/psd/nation/halifax.htm

2. **Lord Dunmore Promises Freedom to Virginia Slaves**
   *Virginia Gazette* [Purdie], November 24, 1775.

3. **Thomas Jefferson on Slavery and African Americans**
   **3a. Rough Draft of Declaration of Independence, July 1, 1776**
   Thomas Jefferson, June 1776, Rough Draft of the Declaration of Independence, Thomas Jefferson Papers, Series 1: General Correspondence,

1651–1827, Library of Congress, Manuscript Division, Washington, DC.

**3b. *Notes on the State of Virginia*, 1781–1782**
Thomas Jefferson, *Notes on the State of Virginia* (Philadelphia: Prichard and Hall, 1788), 145–154, 172–174.

**3c. Benjamin Banneker to Thomas Jefferson, Baltimore County, August 10, 1791**
*Copy of a letter from Benjamin Banneker to the secretary of state, with his answer* (Philadelphia: Daniel Lawrence, 1792).

**3d. Thomas Jefferson to Benjamin Banneker, August 30, 1791**
Ibid.

4. **Massachusetts Slaves Petition for Freedom**
"Petition for Freedom to the Massachusetts Council and House of Representatives, January 13, 1777," Belknap Papers. Boston: Massachusetts Historical Society.

5. **Rebel Soldiers**
Jean Baptiste Antoine de Verger, *Soldiers in Uniform (1781–1784)*, Anne S.K. Brown Military Collection, Brown University Library, Providence, RI.

6. **Gradual Abolition in Pennsylvania**
"Preamble to An Act for the General Abolition of Slavery, " in James T. Mitchell and Henry Flanders, *The Statutes at Large of Pennsylvania from 1682 to 1801, Vol. 10: 1779 to 1781* (Pennsylvania: Wm. Stanley Ray, 1904), 67–68.

7. **Freedom Certificate, 1783**
Halifax, Canada: Nova Scotia Archives and Records Management.

8. **Pennsylvania Abolitions Petition Congress, 1790**
"The Pennsylvania Abolition Society to the United States Congress, February 3, 1790." Washington, DC: Records of the United States Senate, Center for Legislative Archives, National Archives.

9. **An Account of Toussaint L'Ouverture**
"Tobias Lear to James Madison, Cape Francoise, July 17, 1801," Miscellaneous Letters, General Records of the Department of State, Record Group 59; National Archives, Washington, DC.

10. **Revolution in Haiti**
J. Barlow and Marcus Rainford, *Revenge taken by the Black Army for the Cruelties practiced on them by the French* (London: James Cundee, 1805). JCB Archive of Early American Images, The John Carter Brown Library, Brown University, Providence, RI. Available at http://jcb.lunaimaging.com/luna/servlet/detail/JCB~1~1~576~230088:Revenge-taken-by-the-Black-Army-for

11. **Ben Woolfolk, Testimony in the Trial of Gabriel, October 6, 1800**
Governor's Office, Letters Received, James Monroe, Record Group 3, Library of Virginia. Available from transcription at http://www.lva.virginia.gov/exhibits/DeathLiberty/gabriel/gabtrial17.htm

12. **Rebel's Statement from Gabriel's Conspiracy, September 25, 1804**
Robert Sutcliffe, *Travels in Some Parts of North America in the years 1804, 1805 and 1806* (York, England: C. Peacock, 1811), 50.

## Chapter 7: The Confederation Era

1. **John Adams Calls for New Constitutions, 1775**
John Adams autobiography, part 1, "John Adams," through 1776, sheet 29 of 53 [electronic edition]. *Adams Family Papers: An Electronic Archive.* Boston: Massachusetts Historical Society. http://www.masshist.org/digitaladams/

2. **Pennsylvania's New Constitution—A Critical View**
'Benjamin Rush to Anthony Wayne, April 2, 1777, in L.H. Butterfield (ed.), *Letters of Benjamin Rush*, Vol. 1 (Princeton, NJ: Princeton University Press, 1951) 136-137.

3. **Massachusetts Voters Reject A Constitution**
Return of Brookline (Suffolk County), May 21, 1778 in Robert J. Taylor (ed.), *Massachusetts, Colony to Commonwealth: Documents on the Formation of Its Constitution, 1775–1780* (Chapel Hill: University of North Carolina Press, 1961), 70.

4. **Massachusetts Tries Again, 1780**
*An Address of the Convention, for framing a new constitution of government, for the state of Massachusetts-Bay, to their Constituents* (Boston: White and Adams, 1780).

5. **The Articles of Confederation, 1777**
Engrossed and corrected copy of the Articles of Confederation, showing amendments adopted, November 15, 1777, Papers of the Continental Congress, 1779–1789, Records of the Continental Congresses and the Constitutional Convention 1779–1789, Record Group 360; National Archives, Washington, DC.

6. **Alexander Hamilton Decries the Weakness of Congress**
Sept. 3, 1780. Letter to Duane on Government. Alexander Hamilton, The Works of Alexander Hamilton, ed. Henry Cabot Lodge (Federal Edition) (New York: G.P. Putnam's Sons, 1904). In 12 vols. Vol. 1. Chapter: "The Government and the Constitution." Available from http://oll.libertyfund.org/title/1378/64139/1590430 on 2009-10-09.

7. **Banknotes**
Granger Collection, New York.

8. **Shays's Rebellion**
*By His Excellency James Bowdoin Esquire, A Proclamation. September 2, 1786* (Boston: Adams and Nourse, 1786).

9. **The Shaysites Make Their Case**
George Richard Minot, *The History of the Insurrections, in Massachusetts,*

*In the Year 1786, and the Rebellion Consequent Thereon* (Worcester, MA: Isaiah Thomas, 1788), 85–87.

10. ***The Cumberland Gazette*, January 12, 1787.**

11. **Massachusetts Pursues a Contradictory Strategy in Response to the Rebels**
Declaration of the General Court, February 4, 1787, Massachusetts State Archives.

12. **"A Little Rebellion Now and Then is a Good Thing": Jefferson Reacts to Shays's Rebellion**
Thomas Jefferson to James Madison, January 30, 1787, with List of Decoded Passages, The Thomas Jefferson Papers, Series 1: General Correspondence, 1651–1827, Library of Congress, Manuscript Division, Washington, DC.

## Chapter 8: Creating the Constitution

1. **Madison on the Flaws of the Articles of Confederation**
James Madison, May 7, 1787. Vices of the Political System of the U. States, James Madison Papers, Series 1: General Correspondence, Library of Congress, Manuscript Division, Washington, DC.

2. **The Virginia Plan**
From Virginia (Randolph) Plan as Amended (National Archives Microfilm Publication M866, 1 roll); The Official Records of the Constitutional Convention; Records of the Continental and Confederation Congresses and the Constitutional Convention, 1774–1789, Record Group 360; National Archives, Washington, DC.

3. **The New Jersey Plan**
Max Farrand (ed.), *The Records of the Federal Convention of 1787*, 3 vols. (New Haven, CT: Yale University Press, 1911), 1:242–245.

4. **Franklin Addresses the Constitutional Convention**
Max Farrand (ed.), *The Records of the Federal Convention of 1787*, 3 vols. (New Haven, CT: Yale University Press, 1911), 2:641–643.

5. **Federalist Number 10**
*Daily Advertiser* (New York), November 22, 1787.

6. **Political Creed of Every Federalist**
*The New-York Journal, and Daily Patriotic Register*, Wednesday, December 12, 1787.

7. **Opposition to the Constitution in Pennsylvania**
*Pennsylvania Packet and Daily Advertiser* (Philadelphia), December 18, 1787.

8. **The Grand Federal Edifice**
*Massachusetts Centinel*, (Boston), February 9, 1788. Boston: Massachusetts Historical Society.

9. **Bill of Rights, 1789**
Engrossed Bill of Rights, September 25, 1789; General Records of the United States Government; Record Group 11; National Archives, Washington, DC.

## Chapter 9: American Women in the Age of Revolution

1. **Deborah Franklin Describes the Stamp Act Riots**
"Deborah Franklin to Benjamin Franklin, Philadelphia, September 22, 1765," in Leonard W. Labaree et al. (eds.), *The Papers of Benjamin Franklin*, 39 vols. to date (New Haven, CT: Yale University Press, 1959–), 12:270–274

2. **Benjamin Franklin to Deborah Franklin, London, April 6, 1766**
Leonard W. Labaree et al. (eds.), *The Papers of Benjamin Franklin*, 39 vols. to date (New Haven, CT: Yale University Press, 1959–), 13:233–234

3. **Deborah Franklin: Power of Attorney, October 14, 1768**
William B. Willcox et al. (eds.), *The Papers of Benjamin Franklin*, 39 vols. to date (New Haven, CT: Yale University Press, 1959–), 15:227–228

4. **Boston Women Boycott Tea, 1770**
*Boston Evening Post*, February 12, 1770.

5. **The Edenton Tea Party, 1774**
The Granger Collection, New York.

6. **Abigail Adams to John Adams**
Letter from Abigail Adams to John Adams, March 31–April 5, 1776 [electronic edition]. *Adams Family Papers: An Electronic Archive*. Boston: Massachusetts Historical Society. Available from http://www.masshist.org/digitaladams/

7. *The Sentiments of an American Woman,* **1780**
*Sentiments of An American Woman* (Philadelphia: John Dunlap, 1780).

8. **The Deposition of a Female Spy, 1781**
"Baron Ottendorf to Henry Clinton, August 15, 1781," Sir Henry Clinton Collection, Clements Library, Ann Arbor, MI.

9. **Petition of Rachel Wells to the Continental Congress, 1786**
Petitions Address to Congress, 1775–1789, *Papers of the Continental Congress* (M-247), Roll 56, Vol. 8, Item 42, 354–355.

10. **Benjamin Rush, *Thoughts upon Female Education,* 1787**
Benjamin Rush, *Thoughts Upon Female Education* (Philadelphia: Prichard & Hall, 1787), 5–12, 14, 19–20.

11. **Diary of Hannah Callender, July 4, 1788**
George Vaux Collection, American Philosophical Society, Philadelphia.

12. **Extracts from the New Jersey Constitution, 1776, 1844**
New Jersey State Library, Trenton.

13. **Declaration of Sentiments, 1848**
*First Convention Ever Called to Discuss the Civil and Political Rights of*

*Women, Seneca Falls, New York, July 19, 20, 1848*, Miller NAWSA Suffrage Scrapbooks, 1897–1911, Library of Congress, Rare Book and Special Collections Division, Washington, DC. Available from http://hdl.loc.gov/loc.rbc/rbcmil.scrp4006801

## Chapter 10: The Federalist Era

1. **A Federalist Vision of Economic Development**
   **1a. The Report on Public Credit**
   Alexander Hamilton, First Report on Public Credit, January 14, 1790, *American State Papers: Finance*, 1:15–18.
   **1b. The Report on Manufactures**
   Alexander Hamilton, Report on Manufactures, December 5, 1791, *American State Papers: Finance*, 1:123, 125, 127.
2. **"Those Who Labor in the Earth": Jefferson' Opposition to Manufacturing**
   Thomas Jefferson, *Notes on the State of Virginia* (Philadelphia: Prichard and Hall, 1788), 174–175.
3. **Opposition to Hamilton's Program**
   *Pennsylvania Independent Gazetteer*, February 6, 1790.
4. **The Whiskey Rebellion**
   "George Washington to Daniel Morgan, October 8, 1794" in John C. Fitzpatrick (ed.), *The Writings of George Washington*, 39 vols. (Washington DC: United States Government Printing Office, 1931-44), 33:522–524.
5. **Washington's Farewell Address**
   "George Washington's Farewell Address, September 19, 1796," in John C. Fitzpatrick (ed.), *The Writings of George Washington*, 39 vols. (Washington DC: United States Printing Office, 1931-44), 35:214–238.
6. **The Alien and Sedition Act**
   **6a. An Act Concerning Aliens, June 25, 1798**
   *Statutes at Large*, 5th Congress, 2nd Session, 570–572.
   **6b. An Act Respecting Alien Enemies, July 6, 1798**
   *Statutes at Large*, 5th Congress, 2nd Session, 577.
   **6c. An Act in Addition to the Act, Entitled "An Act for the Punishment of Certain Crimes Against the United States"**
   *Statutes at Large*, 5th Congress, 2nd Session, 596–597.
7. **The Virginia and Kentucky Resolution**
   **7a. Virginia Resolution, December 24, 1798**
   Jonathan Elliot (ed.), *The Virginia and Kentucky Resolutions of 1798 and '99* (Washington, DC: 1832), 5–6.
   **7b. Kentucky Resolve, December 3, 1799**
   Jonathan Elliot (ed.), *The Virginia and Kentucky Resolutions of 1798 and '99* (Washington, DC: 1832), 19–20.

## Chapter 11: An Empire of Liberty, 1801–1815

1. **The Ordinance of 1784**
   *By the United States in Congress assembled. April 23, 1784* [Ordinance of 1784] (Hartford, CT: Hudson & Goodwin, 1785).

2. **Thomas Jefferson, First Inaugural Address, March 4, 1801**
   James D. Richardson, *A Compilation of the Messages and Papers of the Presidents, 1789–1897*, 10 vols. (Washington DC: Government Printing Office, 1896), 1:321–324.

3. **Mad Tom in a Rage, 1801**
   The Granger Collection, New York.

4. **Instructions to Lewis and Clark**
   Thomas Jefferson to Meriwether Lewis, June 20, 1803, Thomas Jefferson Papers, Series 1: General Correspondence. 1651–1827, Library of Congress, Manuscript Division, Washington, DC.

5. **The Constitutional Implications of the Louisiana Purchase**
   Thomas Jefferson to Wilson Cary Nicholas, Monticello, September 7, 1803, Thomas Jefferson Papers, Series 1: General Correspondence. 1651–1827, Library of Congress, Manuscript Division, Washington, DC.

6. **Thomas Jefferson, Third Annual Message to Congress, October 17, 1803**
   *Annals of Congress*, Senate, 8th Congress, 1 Session, 11–15.

7. **"Ograbme" Cartoon, c. 1808**
   The Granger Collection, New York.

8. **A Boxing Match, or Another Bloody Nose for John Bull, 1813**
   The Granger Collection, New York.

9. **Francis Scott Key, "Star-Spangled Banner," September 14, 1814**
   *Patriot and Evening Advertiser* (Baltimore), September 20, 1814.

10. **The Hartford Convention, 1814**
    *Proceedings of a Convention of Delegates from the States of Massachusetts, Connecticut, and Rhode Island, the Counties of Cheshire and Grafton in the State of New Hampshire and the County of Windham, in the State of Vermont, Convened at Hartford in the State of Connecticut, December 15, 1814* (Boston: Wells and Lilly, 1815), 9–12, 19–21.

11. **The Battle of New Orleans**
    *Broadside: Glorious News from New Orleans! Splendid Victory over the British forces!* (Salem, MA: Warwick Palfray, 1815).

# Index